Uncertain Futures

Why is the world not moving fast enough to solve the climate crisis? Politics stand in the way, but experts hope that green investments, compensation, and retraining could unlock the impasse. However, these measures often lack credibility. Not only do communities fear these policies could be reversed, but they have seen promises broken before. *Uncertain Futures* proposes solutions to make more credible promises that build support for the energy transition. It examines the perspectives of workers, communities, and companies, arguing that the climate impasse is best understood by viewing the problem from the ground up. Featuring voices on the front lines such as a commissioner in Carbon County deciding whether to welcome wind, executives at energy companies searching for solutions, mayors and unions in Minnesota battling for local jobs, and fairgoers in coal country navigating their uncertain future, this book contends that making economic transitions work means making promises credible.

ALEXANDER F. GAZMARARIAN is a doctoral candidate in the Department of Politics at Princeton University, where he is researching how to unlock the climate impasse. He is currently writing a book with Helen Milner about how global warming will reshape politics.

DUSTIN TINGLEY is Professor of Government at Harvard University. He is the author of numerous articles on the politics of climate change, international relations, international political economy, and statistical methodology. His book *Sailing the Water's Edge*, with Helen Milner, won the Gladys M. Kammerer Award for the best book on U.S. national policy.

The Politics of Climate Change

Climate change may be the most important political challenge of our time. This new series will address large questions about the politics of climate change and feature scholarship that is problem-driven, crosses traditional subfield boundaries, and meets the discipline's highest standards for innovation, clarity and empirical rigor. Although focused on political science, it will incorporate empirical work on climate politics from across the social sciences.

Series Editor
Michael Ross, UCLA

Editorial Board Members
Thomas Bernauer (ETH, Zurich)
Xun Cao (Penn State)
Navroz K. Dubash (Center for Policy Research, New Delhi)
Kathryn Hochstetler (London School of Economics)
Robert O. Keohane (Princeton University)
Matto Mildenberger (UC Santa Barbara)
Helen Milner (Princeton University)
Megan Mullin (Duke University)
Barry Rabe (University of Michigan)
Kenneth Scheve (Yale University)
Leah Stokes (UC Santa Barbara)
Dustin Tingley (Harvard University)

Books in the Series
Joshua W. Busby, *States and Natures: The Effects of Climate Change on Security*

Uncertain Futures

How to Unlock the Climate Impasse

ALEXANDER F. GAZMARARIAN
Princeton University

DUSTIN TINGLEY
Harvard University

Shaftesbury Road, Cambridge CB2 8EA, United Kingdom

One Liberty Plaza, 20th Floor, New York, NY 10006, USA

477 Williamstown Road, Port Melbourne, VIC 3207, Australia

314–321, 3rd Floor, Plot 3, Splendor Forum, Jasola District Centre, New Delhi – 110025, India

103 Penang Road, #05–06/07, Visioncrest Commercial, Singapore 238467

Cambridge University Press is part of Cambridge University Press & Assessment, a department of the University of Cambridge.

We share the University's mission to contribute to society through the pursuit of education, learning and research at the highest international levels of excellence.

www.cambridge.org
Information on this title: www.cambridge.org/9781009405294

DOI: 10.1017/9781009405331

© Alexander F. Gazmararian and Dustin Tingley 2023

This publication is in copyright. Subject to statutory exception and to the provisions of relevant collective licensing agreements, no reproduction of any part may take place without the written permission of Cambridge University Press & Assessment.

First published 2023

A catalogue record for this publication is available from the British Library

A Cataloging-in-Publication data record for this book is available from the Library of Congress

ISBN 978-1-009-40529-4 Hardback
ISBN 978-1-009-40530-0 Paperback

Cambridge University Press & Assessment has no responsibility for the persistence or accuracy of URLs for external or third-party internet websites referred to in this publication and does not guarantee that any content on such websites is, or will remain, accurate or appropriate.

To the people who welcomed us into their communities and shared their stories, this book would not be possible without you. To our families, whose durable support was without doubt.

Contents

List of Figures		*page* ix
Acknowledgments		xi
1	Introduction	1
2	Problems and Solutions	34
3	Asking People, Communities, and Companies	70
4	Opportunity Knocks?	96
5	Making Government Policy Credible	116
6	Bargaining for the Future	147
7	Making Workforce Programs Work	176
8	Green Jobs under the Spotlight	201
9	Conclusion	233
Bibliography		261
Index		291

Figures

1.1	Map of fossil fuel communities in the United States	*page* 9
3.1	Map of regional survey samples	76
3.2	Photograph of county fairgrounds	78
3.3	Photograph of county fair survey enumeration	79
3.4	Map of local policymaker survey sampling frame	80
3.5	Government credibility beliefs across samples	82
3.6	History of kept promises beliefs across samples	84
3.7	National public expectations of IRA reversal	86
3.8	National public and local policymaker beliefs about business' credibility concerns	90
4.1	National public beliefs about future regional employment growth and local job creation	101
4.2	National public beliefs about future raises and job duration	102
4.3	Comparisons of national and fossil fuel community beliefs about green investments	108
4.4	County fair-goer beliefs about the durability of green jobs	109
4.5	National public and local policymakers expectations of business' green investment concerns	110
5.1	Multi-attribute policy experiment design	120
5.2	Support for green investments with institutional constraints	122
5.3	Effect of policy design choices on credibility and green investment support	123
5.4	Effect of local job creation on green investment support	128
5.5	Effect of laws versus promises on credibility	130
5.6	Effects of bipartisan coalitions and institutional constraints on credibility	132
5.7	Effect of revealed national consensus on credibility	134
5.8	Effect of delegation to communities on credibility	140

x   *List of Figures*

6.1	UMW Journal cartoon	150
7.1	Adult and youth interest in careers	190
7.2	Career pathway preferences of fossil fuel community middle schoolers	192
7.3	Effects of hand-tying and costly signals on local economic opportunity	194
8.1	Photograph of out-of-state license plates at a Minnesota wind farm construction site	203
8.2	Union and national public support for local wind jobs	210
8.3	Effect of transparency on national public perceptions of local benefits from green investments	222
8.4	Effect of transparency on local policymaker perceptions of local benefits from green investments	223
8.5	Local journalism's effect on accountability	225
8.6	Effect of clawback provisions on national public support for green investments	227
8.7	Effect of clawback provisions on local policymaker support for green investments	228

Acknowledgments

This book began with a phone call in June 2021. We were separately conducting surveys and interviews in Southwest Pennsylvania, and Helen Milner, Dustin's former dissertation adviser and Alex's current, thought we needed to connect. On the phone, we quickly realized that what we heard from people on the front lines of the energy transition did not line up with how academics, policymakers, and advocates typically think about the climate policy impasse and potential solutions. We wrote an article that developed these ideas. It was long, too long. Our colleagues told us it should be a book. We listened.

This project would not have been possible without exceptional institutional support. The Niehaus Center for Globalization and Governance and the Survey Research Center, both at Princeton University, backed the local survey work in Appalachia. The Roosevelt Project provided a rich intellectual environment that also helped to lay the groundwork for our study along with its support for some of the national and regional surveys. This initiative was led by the Massachusetts Institute of Technology in a collaboration with Harvard, under the direction of former Energy Secretary Ernie Moniz and Executive Director Michael Kearney, and has been primarily supported by the Emerson Collective, and had the important Southwest Pennsylvania case study directed by Harvard Professor Steve Ansolabehere. Harvard University President Larry Bacow engaged and generously assisted the Roosevelt Project. The Andrew W. Mellon Foundation through the Harvard Fellows at the Forefront program supported some of the national and regional surveys. Robert Keohane's Balzan Award made possible earlier research that laid some

xii   *Acknowledgments*

of the groundwork for this project. Harvard's Weatherhead Center for International Affairs supported some teaching sabbatical.

We also received fantastic research assistance. We particularly thank Shirleen Fang, Alison Hu, Gabriella Kennealy, Erta Kurti, Christina Li, Kyler Legault, Jaya Nayar, Thor Reimann, Alice Zhang, along with Aleksandra Conevska who helped to foster a dynamic experience for our research partners. This assistance was made possible by the Harvard University Center for the Environment, Weatherhead Center for International Affairs, and Harvard Fellows at the Forefront program run by the Center for Public Service and Engaged Scholarship.

Surveys don't run themselves. We appreciate the dedicated work of our survey partners, including Allison Corbett and the Qualtrics team, Nathan Lee and the CivicPulse team, and Dritan Nesho and Jason Sclar at HarrisX in conjunction with the Center for American Political Studies (CAPS) at Harvard University led by Ryan Enos.

We received excellent feedback from audiences at Harvard, Princeton, Stanford, the University of Pittsburgh, the 2022 American Political Science Association meeting, and the 2022 International Political Economy Society meeting. Michael Ross, Leah Stokes, Matto Mildenberger, and Ken Scheve generously took time out of their busy schedules to provide fantastic comments at a book conference as we wrapped up the manuscript. David Victor provided especially insightful feedback on an early draft of the book. We are grateful for the feedback we received along the way from Michaël Aklin, Jim Alt, Michelle Anderson, Stephen Ansolabehere, Inês Azevedo, Parrish Bergquist, Peter Buisseret, Marshall Burke, Bruce Cain, Bill Clark, Jeff Colgan, Jim Engell, Jeff Frieden, Sean Gailmard, Alan Garber, Federica Genovese, Johnathan Guy, Tom Hale, Alice Hsiaw, Alison Hu, Nate Jensen, David Keith, Amanda Kennard, Gabriella Kennealy, Robert Keohane, Margaret Levi, David Lewis, Devin Judge-Lord, Helen Milner, Roz Naylor, Valerie Nelson, Michelle Nicholasen, Krzysztof Pelc, Madeline Ranalli, Dani Reiter, Stephanie Rickard, Peter Rosendorff, Nita Rudra, Michael Sandel, Elizabeth Shwe, Arthur Silve, Robert Stavins, Robert Stowe, and Virginia Tingley. We also thank the reviewers for their insightful comments that helped to advance the project.

Alex and Dustin thank their adviser Helen Milner for training, connecting, and inspiring us. We are two of many.

Alex wishes to thank Dani Reiter, whose unwavering support convinced him to pursue graduate school. He also thanks Dustin, who has served as a constant inspiration and a fantastic colleague. Alex's parents

Acknowledgments   xiii

Julie and Paul, brother Isaac, and grandparents provided invaluable encouragement and good humor along the way.

Dustin wishes to thank his students, colleagues, and most of all his co-author, Alex. Without the support of his family and friends, both those still with us and those who have passed, this project would not mean what it does to him.

I

Introduction

Carbon County in Wyoming has seen better days. Coal mines that provided for generations of local jobs have shuttered. The reasons for the industry's decline are myriad; cheap natural gas prices and the growth of renewable electricity certainly contributed. But this is no consolation for residents who feel that their community's identity and economy are under siege.

Terry Weickum, the county commissioner, had a hard decision to make. Should he allow new wind farms to be built in the heart of coal country? Wyoming, endowed with sweeping vistas and constant gusts of wind, is one of the best places in the nation for wind energy. Wind turbine construction could offer a path to diversify the stagnant local economy with new jobs and tax revenue.

However, the benefits from wind were not self-evident. Outside Carbon County, concern about climate change drives the deployment of renewable energy. Inside Carbon County, Terry warns that people only mention global warming "if they want to be punched in the face."[1] This is coal country, after all. Locals were "horrified that wind would change our way of life." It would take up land for hunting and camping, threaten tourism, and, worst of all, it would compete with coal. Change is hard, Terry declared, and "the fear of the unknown is the scariest thing in the world."

Terry leapt into this uncertain future. He welcomed wind but is clear that "I didn't do it for idealistic reasons." Carbon County needed the jobs and tax revenue. Wind did make a difference. However, Terry is

---

[1] Interview, November 3, 2022. Also see Hu (2021) and Searcey (2021).

clear-eyed about the scale of the benefits. For one, the jobs largely went to outside teams and have proven temporary. "There would be 300–400 people who would come in and do work, and then they are gone," recalled Terry, now the mayor of Rawlins, Wyoming. And while the tax revenue brought in by wind projects "helped our community immensely," it by no means has offset the economic decline in the area. "The last year I was a county commissioner, we collected about $30,000 worth of taxes, and that will fix about 30 feet of road, so grandma at the end of the block on a fixed income would have to pick up a tab." In the same year, Terry lost his re-election to the commissioner's office by 24 votes, a loss he attributes to his support for wind.

Would other communities make this leap into the clean energy future? In Carbon County, "coal is not coming back," according to Terry, so the decision was easier. But in neighboring Campbell County, where coal remains king, as well as oil, there is no question about what industry the community wants to bet on. As Terry puts it, "I'm not going to shoot the horse I'm riding until I have another horse."

Carbon County is not alone in the challenges that it faces. Across the country and around the world, a massive transformation in energy and industrial systems is already underway. New legislation hopes to accelerate that process, and still, more is in store. Communities that rely on fossil fuels and those where clean energy must be built have hard choices to make about their futures.

THE CLIMATE IMPASSE

These transitions will be necessary to tackle the climate crisis. And we cannot afford to wait. Each day we burn fossil fuels adds more greenhouse gases (GHG) to the atmosphere, which further bakes the planet. The consequences of elevated temperatures are dire. The United Nations body that brings together scientists from around the world to assess knowledge about climate change concluded that global warming has already worsened fires that burn through homes, hurricanes that flatten communities, and sea level rise that floods cities (IPCC, 2022). These impacts will only intensify if temperatures climb unchecked.

Contrary to what some might say, the clean energy transition is not just an engineering challenge. It's a political problem. We know what needs to be done to solve the climate crisis. The world must move away from coal, oil, and gas, the primary sources of harmful carbon dioxide emissions and other planet-warming gases, and toward cleaner

Breaking the Impasse? 3

energy sources. While innovation will be crucial, humanity already possesses the technologies needed to start this transition. As early as 2004, studies showed how current technologies could be scaled up to decarbonize the economy (Pacala and Socolow, 2004). More recently, a team of researchers as part of the *Net-Zero America Project* found that the United States could use already existing technologies to reach net-zero emissions, the condition where global emissions plateau because the amount of GHGs that enter the atmosphere is balanced by removal from the atmosphere (Larson et al., 2021). The relevant question is not if it is feasible to start the transition but how governments and stakeholders should proceed.

But governments are not moving fast enough to solve the climate crisis. The world came together in 2015 to ratify the Paris Agreement, which sought to limit global warming to well below 2°C, or better yet, 1.5°C. However, there is no magic threshold at which the planet is safe; every degree matters. Nonetheless, it is worrisome that the latest assessments show that even if all countries kept their pledges, the world would still fall short of that 1.5°C target (Meinshausen et al., 2022).

Some had hoped that as clean energy became cheaper, the problem would resolve itself through market forces. Experts thought that coal use had plateaued in 2021, with renewable energy sources at their lowest prices ever. However, the next year, global demand for coal soared to record highs.[2] Even if coal use flattens out or starts to decline, this still represents substantial emissions that we cannot afford. And outside of coal, so-called natural gas and oil remain ubiquitous sources of emissions. How can we break this climate impasse?

BREAKING THE IMPASSE?

There are two strategies for political reform that could break the climate deadlock: reduce opposition and create allies. Governments could help the people, communities, and companies harmed by the energy transition with compensation for lost jobs, tax revenue, and health impacts. Households will lose income, and workers must retrain. Localities will lose funds to provide public goods like schools. Workers and their families may lose health benefits, even as they carry the health burden from hazards at their old jobs and proximity to pollution. The anticipation of these costs creates opposition, but the government could reduce

---

[2] For energy projections, see International Energy Agency (2022b).

this resistance with transitional support for workers, their families, communities, and maybe even companies.

Reformers could also use the benefits from the new green economy to create allies. They could attempt to reframe the climate issue in a way that makes political action feasible, which political scientist Robert Keohane (2015) argues is a potential strategy to break the impasse. Rather than focus on costs, advocates should emphasize the short-term benefits of the energy transition, such as jobs and tax revenue generated from the construction of solar farms, the assembly of batteries, and the installation of energy-efficient products. It is these benefits that convinced Terry in Carbon County to welcome wind. This is also the logic behind "green industrial" policies that hope to encourage the growth of new industries that create or strengthen constituencies that defend climate policy (e.g., Rodrik, 2014). Look no farther than the 2022 Inflation Reduction Act (IRA) in the United States, which ushered in billions of dollars of green incentives, as well as funds for fenceline communities that have suffered from industrial pollution. Experts are also optimistic that new green industries will be a tremendous source of jobs that could even offset employment losses in carbon-intensive industries.[3] If new allies can be created, then the opponents of the energy transition, such as fossil fuel companies, could be outflanked or even converted into supporters.

Despite the promise of these strategies, attempts to break the climate impasse have struggled. This book diagnoses why and what can be done. Credibility and economic opportunity are the watchwords in our analysis. We have spent time on the front lines of the energy transition, listening and learning. What we hear from workers, communities, and companies are concerns about whether the government will follow through on its promises to provide compensation and make investments. Worse, they've seen these promises made before and broken. And doubts abound about whether clean energy will support livelihoods and uplift communities. This is a book about uncertain futures, but it is also about how these promises could be more credible.

VIEW FROM ON HIGH

Experts typically view strategies to break the climate impasse from the *top down*. From this 30,000-foot perspective, it would be a simple task for the government to reduce costs, create allies, and then break the

---

[3] For example, Sustainable Development Solutions Network (2020).

climate impasse. All the government would have to do is identify the correct level and target of support for dislocated workers and new industries. To this end, political scientists have amassed reams of studies that explore how social programs like unemployment insurance can buffer the public from economic disruption (e.g., Iversen and Soskice, 2006; Ruggie, 1982). Likewise, economists propose – and debate – place-based development programs that aim to promote growth in stagnant regions "left behind" (e.g., Austin, Glaeser, and Summers, 2018). These challenges with economic transitions are familiar. Since the advent of markets, industries and occupations have emerged and disappeared at the hands of policymakers and technological change – carriage-makers obsolesced by the automobile, assembly line workers replaced by robots, and coal miners displaced by new energy sources.

But what stands in the way if we have been here before and have the tools for political reform?

Three Challenges Remain

Why Do Fossil Fuel Communities Resist Compensation?

First, why are the people whom compensation and investments hope to help skeptical of these promises? From the top-down perspective, the inability to reach a compensatory bargain with those who would lose from climate policy is puzzling. Some even set aside oil and gas and ask, shouldn't it be a simple task to "buy out" coal miners who are small in number? Given the political will, a country like the United States could easily provide abundant aid to places impacted by the energy transition. Such a bargain would appear politically shrewd since public opinion polls show how compensation for fossil fuel workers garners support from the national public and residents of coal, oil, and gas communities.[4] Yet, voters in fossil fuel regions overwhelmingly support politicians who block compromise on climate policy. Why have fossil fuel communities resisted the clean energy transition despite the availability of popular compensation and investments?

---

[4] See Bergquist, Mildenberger, and Stokes (2020), Gaikwad, Genovese, and Tingley (2022b), and Gazmararian (2022c). Studies on responses to economic or policy risks find that individuals become more supportive of compensation (e.g., Iversen and Soskice, 2001; Scheve and Serlin, 2023; Walter, 2010). Lawmakers also support costly reforms when there are more generous social welfare policies (e.g., Kono, 2020).

6   *Introduction*

Why Do Reformers Struggle to Find Allies?

Second, why do advocates struggle to find allies despite the prospect of benefits from the clean energy transition? Major renewable energy projects have been canceled due to local opposition.[5] Despite there being solutions to share resources with traditional opponents of solar and offshore wind like farmers and fishers, groups struggle to find these pathways to cooperation. One county official we surveyed in Louisiana said, "[I] don't think renewable energy is a good sector for investment." A politician from a municipality in Kansas implored, "please don't invest my money into the renewable energy currently being offered." Even outside of political officials whose views might be clouded by partisanship, in our interviews, unions engaged in renewable energy projects also raised concerns about local benefits.[6] A report from a network of global investors concluded that the "[l]ack of community support could undermine the rapid deployment of clean energy at precisely the time we need it most" (Ceres, 2020, p. 5). Why do communities not always see the benefits from the clean energy transition?

Why Do Green Workforce Shortages Persist?

Third, why do governments and the private sector struggle to build a green labor force despite the societal demand for clean energy? The *Net-Zero America* team estimates that the energy transition would create 300,000 to 600,000 green jobs by mid-century. A similar expansion around the globe will be needed, which could create up to 11.6 million direct and indirect energy sector jobs (Gielen et al., 2019). Yet, there are already hiring difficulties and warning signs that the clean energy transition will run up against "employment bottlenecks" (Larson et al., 2021, p. 306). Why do workforce issues persist despite the growing demand for green jobs?

* * *

These questions are puzzling from the top-down perspective. People fall back on simple answers. One view is that fossil fuel lobbyists have bought off politicians and misinformed the public's beliefs about climate science. Another explanation is that partisan polarization is so great that meaningful political reforms cannot pass. Money in politics and polarization are undeniable features of the American political landscape. Yet

---

[5] See the abandoned plans for a 400-megawatt solar farm in Williamsport, Ohio (Gearino, 2022).

[6] For a review of the literature on opposition to energy projects, see Carley et al. (2020).

these challenges with the energy transition exist throughout the world, even in countries with less business influence and with low polarization. And from the perspective of what is to be done, the answers these diagnoses afford are unsatisfying. Remove money from politics? Good luck. Change the minds of a climate skeptic with scientific facts? Not in this lifetime. New ideas and solutions are needed.

But what is especially puzzling about these explanations for the climate impasse is that they ignore the complex and sometimes contradictory beliefs that people have about the energy transition. When we listen to residents of Southwest Pennsylvania, local officials in Carbon County, and the leadership at electric power companies, a different picture emerges. In their unique ways, they raise a common concern: credibility. How can one be confident that the government will deliver on promises to support workers, their families, and communities in the transition? How can one be sure that promises of new jobs and tax revenue from green industries will materialize, endure, and provide local benefits? What looks certain from the top down is fraught with ambiguity from the ground up – that is, from the standpoint of workers, communities, and companies.

Many communities already know what's coming because they, like Carbon County, have been living the energy transition. They have been crushed as the nation has begun to move to gas and other rivals for coal. Worse, the policies experts say can help provide a safety net to communities harmed along the way, such as job retraining, have been promised before, and these workers, their families, and communities have seen those promises evaporate.

In places that might benefit from the clean energy transition, including communities that have borne the cost and received none of the gains, there is also an uncertain future. They, too, have seen the pendulum swing of political control and, with it, support for new investments. Local leaders, business people, and workers wonder whether their community would be better off by embracing the green transition.

OUR ARGUMENT

The main argument of this book is that the credibility of the government's promises and the availability of local economic opportunities shape individuals' attitudes, beliefs, and preferences regarding the clean energy transition. Credibility refers to the concern that the government may not deliver on its promises, and local economic opportunity captures the idea that people worry about whether investments will make communities and workers better off than before. Credibility and economic opportunity are essential. The energy transition will require people, communities, and companies to leap into an *uncertain future*. People would be more likely to jump into this green future if they believed in the government's promises of compensation and investments, as well as the economic opportunities provided by new industries and occupations.

Why do these credibility challenges exist? We identify at least three reasons. People worry that economic and political conditions will change and unwind political reforms, that voters are unwilling to pay for the cost of the transition, and that the government cannot be trusted to keep its word.

The origin of this uncertainty becomes apparent when one considers the energy transition from the ground up. Throughout the book, we spotlight stories from people in communities on the front lines of the energy transition to show how these concerns manifest. At a time when social, economic, and political divisions can make us feel so far apart, we often fail to stop, listen, and learn. Our ground-up perspective provides a voice to people often left out of the national dialogue. Their experiences must inform the discussion around decarbonization, associated policy changes, and institutional developments if we are to understand the problem and find lasting solutions.[7]

While we primarily focus on the United States, a major producer and consumer of fossil fuels, credibility challenges confront all countries, levels of government, and even companies. In developing nations like China, India, Indonesia, and South Africa, these challenges might be even greater. In places with established social safety nets and greater trust in government, like some European countries, these issues might be less intense. Despite these differences, credibility remains a fundamental constraint on any long-term political reform.

Problems need solutions. What can make government promises more credible? How can investments deliver local benefits so people think they would be as well or better off by embracing the energy transition? One strategy to create credibility is to delegate to communities to make their voices feel heard. Another solution is to implement reforms with laws that are harder to overturn rather than unilateral actions by presidents that future leaders can reverse. Policies to create transparency around

---

[7] For other efforts to listen, see Ansolabehere et al. (2022), Beckfield et al. (2022), Cha et al. (2021), Cramer (2016), Curtis et al. (2022), Foster et al. (2022), Maxmin and Woodward (2022), Moniz and Kearney (2022), and Wuthnow (2018).

the local benefits of green investments can also ensure that companies do not over-promise and are held accountable if they fail to deliver. These are just some of the tools we develop – grounded in decades of social science scholarship – and examine with evidence. The most important finding is that efforts to make policy credible and deliver local benefits can build support for the clean energy transition, even when these reforms are costly.

CLIMATE TRANSITIONS FROM THE GROUND UP

What do climate transitions look like from the ground up? The rapid rise in GHG emissions affects not only the climate but also communities as they try to adapt to impacts like rising seas, wildfires, and floods. This adaptation represents the first facet of climate transitions. The second facet of climate transitions is the transformation of the basic structure of the economy, which relies on fossil fuels. Our book focuses on this second aspect of climate transitions, the clean energy transition.

This transition will be challenging because carbon-intensive energy permeates all economic activities: fossil fuels power our homes, factories, and cars (Unruh, 2000). As the energy transition unfolds, the impacts will ripple from coal, oil, and gas to broader swaths of the economy. The geographic scope of this transition in the United States is vast. Figure 1.1 shows how much fossil-fuel intensive industries contribute to

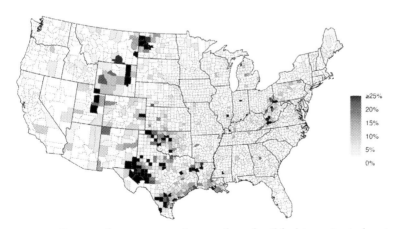

FIGURE 1.1 Percent of county wages in 2020 from fossil fuel-intensive industries, including oil and gas extraction, coal mining, petrochemical manufacturing, electric power generation, internal combustion engine manufacturing, and gasoline stations.

local wages.[8] The map focuses on pay because it represents the extent to which an industry supports livelihoods. We try to capture the vast array of industries and occupations tied to coal, oil, and gas. This includes jobs in oil and gas to drill wells, build pipelines, and manufacture petrochemicals; careers in coal to mine under and above the surface; and people who work to generate electric power from fossil fuels.

The energy transition's effects will be felt in unexpected ways beyond these traditional industries. For example, as consumers shift to electric vehicles (EVs), there will be less demand for internal combustion engines, which impacts automotive workers who assemble these parts. Car mechanics will also see their occupations change since EVs with fewer moving parts require less maintenance. For this reason, the map also includes workers on assembly lines who manufacture traditional car engines, gas station attendants, and auto mechanics.

The places most dependent on fossil fuels for local wages concentrate in the Gulf Coast, Appalachia, New Mexico, and the Rocky Mountains. Employment in gasoline engine manufacturing predominates in the Industrial Midwest, but there are also pockets of activity in the Southeast. These are the communities on the front lines of the energy transition. They have also been on the front lines of exposure to pollution from fossil fuel-powered industries.

This map also highlights the uneven economic effects of the energy transition throughout the country.[9] Carbon-intensive industries concentrate in regions rather than being diffuse, and extractive industries, in particular, are often in rural areas. As the energy transition accelerates, the economic prospects of these communities will increasingly diverge from their less carbon-intensive counterparts. Industrial areas have already seen this divergence before with the impacts of trade, offshoring, and automation (Broz, Frieden, and Weymouth, 2021), and with devastating consequences that have fueled resentment of more economically resilient cities.

This map is also incomplete in three consequential ways.

Wide-Ranging Effects

First, the energy transition will touch many more occupations and industries than the map depicts. For example, agricultural regions will

---

[8] Annual wage data from the 2020 County Business Patterns (CBP) survey.
[9] See Rickard (2020) for a review of the importance of economic geography.

Climate Transitions from the Ground Up

encounter costs because fossil fuels are a major input in fertilizer. Farmers will also face trade-offs between developing solar energy and planting certain crops. Suburban and urban areas already confront land use challenges that will intensify but they will also have opportunities to rethink the design of their communities. The geographic scale of the energy transition is large and diverse.

Local Dependence

Second, the significance of these industries for the local economy varies. In some counties, like Boone in West Virginia, Greene in Pennsylvania, and Schleicher in Texas, fossil fuels provide over 10 percent of local employment. Elsewhere the share is close to zero. The economic development challenges associated with the closure of a coal-fired power plant or an internal combustion engine assembly line may also be more significant in rural areas, which tend to be more heavily dependent on a single industry, whereas urban areas are more economically diverse and resilient to economic shocks. Energy transition experiences will not be uniform but depend on the local context.

It is not just jobs and pay that matter, but also tax revenue. Places like Carbon County rely on fossil fuels for tax revenue that provides public goods like schools and infrastructure. One study estimates that federal, state, and local governments receive an estimated $138 billion per year from the fossil fuel industry (Raimi et al., 2022). The effects of declining fossil fuel use also manifest in diffuse ways. In India, for example, coal shipments on railways subsidize passenger fares (Tongia, Sehgal, and Kamboj, 2020). Natural resources are not the most stable source of tax revenue since demand can fluctuate dramatically, so there could be long-term benefits of reduced dependence, but short-term adjustments have costs for communities.

Skill Differences

Third, energy transitions will look different within the same industry and even within the same firm. In coal mining, the 5 percent of workers in management roles will have an easier time applying their skills elsewhere.[10] However, 60 percent work in construction and extraction. These occupations differ in their transferability; 5 percent are electricians,

[10] See Bisbee and Rosendorff (2022) for the link between occupational specificity and political preferences.

which are in high demand in the clean energy sector, whereas 25 percent are underground mining machine operators who might have more trouble (BLS, 2021). Likewise, for oil and gas, the needs of managers, who comprise 13 percent of the industry, will differ from the 20 percent who work in extraction as rig workers or roustabouts. How these skills match new opportunities already available or yet to be created by the clean energy transition in one's community will be crucial.[11]

Green Energy Expansion

On the flip side, the scope of the green energy expansion will be vast. New jobs will be created in communities throughout the world. Some of these jobs will be created in fossil fuel communities (Tomer, Kane, and George, 2021), but many will not because solar and wind potential does not neatly overlap where coal, oil, and gas are extracted, especially in places outside of the United States (Pai et al., 2020). However, one must be clear-eyed about how disruptive this transition will be. Experts – and advocates – often fail to appreciate and even recognize the concerns that workers, their families, and communities have, which can lead to policies that not only fail politically but could also leave entire regions behind.

WHY EXPERTS CAN GET THIS WRONG

One perspective is that government interventions to solve the climate crisis simply do not work and could even make the problem worse. This argument holds that the government picks more losers than winners, and its programs become opportunities for rent-seeking, potentially even corruption. The solution would be to sit back and let market forces do their work.

It would be marvelous if markets could carry the day. But governments have already picked winners with billions in fossil fuel subsidies doled out each year, which creates a path dependence that makes it harder to shift into cleaner investments (Acemoglu et al., 2016). Free market proponents would agree that these subsidies should be cut. Still, even then, the damage that GHG emissions do to the planet would not be fully captured in economic transactions like when we fill our cars up with gasoline. This is why economists favor a carbon tax that puts a price on pollution, which would drive down fossil fuel consumption and create

---

[11] Alabdulkareem et al. (2018) document polarization of skills that can impair career mobility.

Why Experts Can Get This Wrong 13

incentives to invent solutions. However, countries struggle to implement this market-based approach because of political obstacles.[12] The need for rapid technological deployment and to overcome political opposition has caused reformers to turn to industrial policy and compensation (Meckling et al., 2022a).

Regardless of if it is market forces or government policy that accelerates the clean energy transition, workers, their families, and communities will face severe disruptions. However, not all recognize the need to provide transitional support to smooth these disruptions. One view is that compensation policies are ineffectual, would be too costly, and embolden interest groups to frustrate other reforms. As with the climate crisis, they argue that market forces alone are the best way for those impacted to adjust. This view accepts that economic and technological change is the cost of living in a capitalist society. As the political economist Joseph Schumpeter (1942) described, there is an unavoidable process of creative destruction where new innovations replace the old. The automobile displaced the horse and buggy, and one day cars will be replaced by something newer and better. An extreme laissez-faire position would argue that the government should not interfere with the operation of the market. There would be no role to help workers, their families, and communities adjust. They would be left on their own.

However, there are moral, economic, and political reasons why the government should play a role. And these reasons call into question experts' assumptions about how society responds to disruption. The idea of a smooth, self-adjusting transition is not rooted in reality. The energy transition will not be automatic. It will require governments to curtail carbon pollution and accelerate green energy deployment. Yet these interventions will also disrupt workers, their families, and communities that have based their livelihoods – knowingly or unknowingly – on demand for fossil fuels.

Moral

There is a moral obligation to help workers, their families, and communities adjust to the disruption from the energy transition. The government should not leave people behind when its policies are the cause of their dislocation. From the top down, it is easy to think that workers in the fossil fuel industry should have recognized the risk of dislocation, so the

---

[12] Carbon pricing schemes have a mixed track record (Green, 2021).

government has no responsibility to help. However, as the political sociologist John Gaventa (1982) observed, workers often turn to dangerous jobs like coal mining because of the lack of alternative options. And one should not forget the sacrifices these communities made to power the industrial revolution. Legitimate concern about climate change can easily devolve into moralism about what jobs are ethical, which can come across as condescending to people who have worked these careers for generations. Rusty Justice, a former coal miner from Pikeville, Kentucky, reflected, "if we want a just transition ... we've got to stop this whiplash. They say coal is bad after 100 and something years, and our whole culture is built around that ... everyone has gotten so bifurcated that we can't have dialogues about it ... all of a sudden this is good and this is bad."[13]

The failure to help means that communities will be left behind, which is unacceptable. It's also not just about jobs. The loss of local revenue raised by taxes on extractive industries further compounds the situation. Local governments will increasingly struggle to fund schools, infrastructure, and essential services. When communities get left behind, there are painful consequences. The economists Anne Case and Angus Deaton (2020) document the rise in "deaths of despair" from drug and alcohol poisonings, suicide, and chronic diseases in places where job opportunities have deteriorated for people without college degrees.

Economic

Experts hope these costs can be avoided as people adjust to the energy transition. The idea that people will move and find new jobs elsewhere is baked into models of how society responds to disruptions. This assumption leads to the recommendation that relocation to places where there are better employment prospects should be the solution. Not only is this assumption unrealistic, it's dangerous. These "suitcase solutions," as legal scholar Michelle Anderson (2022) calls them, ignore the deep social and cultural costs that relocation entails. People have strong loyalties to their communities (Wuthnow, 2018). This may be why in response to past economic disruptions like the decline of manufacturing, surprisingly few people moved elsewhere (Autor, Dorn, and Hanson, 2013). Exorbitant moving costs and the lack of resources contribute to this low mobility.[14] Even when governments have sought to overcome resource barriers, outcomes have been dismal. One program in the United States

---

[13] Interview, November 15, 2022.
[14] See Kennan and Walker (2011) who quantify mobility costs.

tried to provide vouchers to impoverished households to cover the cost of moving to a better neighborhood. Still, less than half of the recipients took the opportunity (Katz, Kling, and Liebman, 2001). When relocation does occur, the outflow of residents compounds the problem with a self-fulfilling prophecy where younger, educated individuals leave. This further accelerates the areas' decline. Labor market mobility cannot be relied upon to smooth economic transitions. People are not atomized dots that move frictionlessly. They have intimate connections to place, family, and community. The top-down policy of relocation is a political nonstarter.

Political

Lastly, it is smart politics to reduce the costs of the energy transition. If workers, communities, and companies view themselves as harmed by the green future, they have a powerful motivation to mobilize in opposition to defend their livelihoods and profits.[15] A core insight from the economist and political scientist Mancur Olson (1965) is that when there are concentrated costs from policy, those who expect costs can better engage in collective action such as lobbying to defend their interests. The opposition usually out-maneuvers reformers because they have more at stake, at least in the short term. A public good like a safe climate will benefit all, but people often discount these future gains, especially when the effects of policy will take a while to materialize and the benefits are uncertain.[16]

Company Opposition

The expected costs from the energy transition can lead companies to oppose climate policy. This is related to what the economist Oliver Williamson (1989) calls a "hold-up" problem. Firms anticipate being made worse off, so they refuse to strike a bargain over a political reform. While relatively small in number, fossil fuel companies can wield disproportionate political power. And these companies profit from delay; they hope that by kicking sand in the gears of the energy transition, they can keep their business model afloat as long as possible. Delay they have.

---

[15] Some hope that lawmakers could design climate policy to hide its costs. Even if this could work politically (which is unclear because of the size of the costs and smart interest group lobbyists), it would be economically devastating for communities.

[16] This can lead policymakers to under-invest in preparedness for long-term risks (e.g., Jacobs, 2011).

Political scientist Matto Mildenberger (2020) shows how fossil fuel companies have successfully stalled climate policy worldwide. One reason is that, unlike other interest groups, there is an alliance between industrial unions with ties to the political left and the owners of coal, oil, and gas companies with ties to the political right, which gives disproportionate voice to fossil fuels. Around the world, leaders have struggled to raise taxes on fossil fuels (Martinez-Alvarez et al., 2022). Even when advocates break this impasse, political scientist Leah Stokes (2020) shows how interest groups reinterpret laws, weaponize the party system, and distort public opinion to derail the implementation of green reforms.

Voter Opposition

Voters in communities impacted by the energy transition are also a consequential political constituency. The Electoral College means that fossil fuel-rich swing states like Pennsylvania can determine the fate of presidential candidates. Institutions like the Senate provide disproportionate weight to rural areas where fossil fuels are abundant. Look no further than Senator Joe Manchin from West Virginia. His power to break the filibuster meant that the IRA had to go through a process called reconciliation, which constrained how ambitious lawmakers could be.[17]

Voters in these regions are active and care about climate policy. While only a fraction work in fossil fuels, residents worry about the energy transition's effects on their community.[18] As coal mines closed in the United States, community members mobilized to support anti-climate politicians who promised to save the industry (Gazmararian, 2022c). The political clout of places that produce fossil fuels in some countries means that winning over the voters in these areas could be necessary to build coalitions to enact and sustain climate policy.

Would Communities Accept Government Support?

Some are doubtful that people in fossil fuel communities would accept compensation and transitional support. The typical portrayal of individuals from these places is that they believe the government is broken, cannot solve problems, and should not be trusted. The most recent manifestation of this mistrust is the refusal of people to take vaccines that

---

[17] Canonical models of lawmaking show how one pivotal Senator can have so much power (Krehbiel, 1998).

[18] Bell and York (2010) show how the coal industry has fostered a community economic identity. Gaikwad, Genovese, and Tingley (2022b) find that residents have community-oriented policy preferences.

Why Experts Can Get This Wrong   17

could save their lives. Sociologists like Arlie Hochschild (2016) document a rugged individualist spirit in places along the Gulf Coast home to petrochemical plants, a worldview that places faith in private enterprise and eschews government. In our conversations with local officials, we hear echoes of this attitude in the refrain that people do not want "handouts." And there has been a coordinated effort by individuals and corporate bodies to exacerbate this distrust of the government, that its leaders are "out of touch" and "government is the problem."

But are anti-government attitudes an insurmountable roadblock? One should be careful not to paint with too broad a brush how widespread and immutable anti-government dogma is. People's views are complex. A simple but often disregarded reason for this skepticism is that people are right to doubt promises of compensation and transitional support. There is a history of ineffective or nonexistent policy responses to past dislocations like offshoring, deindustrialization, and automation, which have had devastating consequences for communities (e.g., Broz, Frieden, and Weymouth, 2021). When there are successes, people often fail to recognize the government as the cause, what political scientist Suzanne Mettler (2011) calls the "submerged state" problem. This context elevates the importance of credibility. Reformers must understand how to design policies so that the people they hope to help see these solutions as durable and effective, while at the same time, the government will need to rebuild its reputation.

It is also easy to forget what the energy transition asks workers, their families, and communities to do. They are being asked to give up secure livelihoods for an uncertain future. Reluctance to embrace this transition may not so much reflect anti-government attitudes but more so their economic self-interest. This is why advocates increasingly focus on the idea of a just transition; that is, a transition that uplifts communities that have not benefited from energy production before and also those that stand to lose from the move away from fossil fuels. Business leaders recognize this reality. Bernard Looney, the chief executive officer (CEO) of British Petroleum, one of the world's largest oil companies, put it clearly: "however much people want change, no one truly gets behind the change if it hurts them. It's just simply human nature. *There will not be a transition if it is not just*" (emphasis added, Looney, 2022).

Yet, there is cause for optimism that people are not dogmatically opposed to compensation and transitional support. The surveys that both Alex and Dustin have fielded in fossil fuel regions reveal that people would embrace support for lost income and retraining, especially when it uplifts the community.[19] This last bit is key – community – and the top-down view often misses it. As sociologist Robert Wuthnow (2018, p. 4) found in over a thousand interviews with rural Americans, "[t]hey may be rugged individualists. But they are not fundamentally that. Spend some time in rural America and you realize one thing: people there are community-oriented." People want to be self-sufficient, but at the end of the day, they support policies that would help their community. The key is how to make these policies credible.

The top-down approach risks making people feel like the energy transition is being hoisted upon them by outsiders without listening to what they think. This can flame culture wars that do nobody any favors. Rusty Bell, the commissioner of Campbell County, Wyoming, one of the largest coal producers in the country, said, "the biggest challenge that we face as a community is that we don't get to determine our future."[20] While it has become vogue to have sections of reports about energy transitions that mention fossil fuel communities (e.g., International Energy Agency, 2022a; McKinsey & Company, 2022), without engaging with people in these areas – that is, from the ground up – it is hard to fully appreciate the challenges and opportunities these places face. It is essential to incorporate the voices of people in communities rather than treating them as a token mention.

LEARNING FROM HISTORY

The clean energy transition is not the first time governments have tried to facilitate an economic transition. Logging in the Pacific Northwest and globalization show how economic and political changes have dramatic consequences for communities. Yet even when the government promises transitional support to help, credibility challenges can undermine these efforts.[21]

Logging in the Pacific Northwest

Rural communities in the Pacific Northwest – California, Oregon, and Washington – revolved around timber, much of it harvested from 10 million hectares of public lands managed by the federal government. Not only did workers depend on the industry for their livelihoods, but timber

---

[19] For example, Gaikwad, Genovese, and Tingley (2022b) and Gazmararian (2022a).
[20] Interview, September 22, 2022.
[21] Other examples include military base closures (e.g., Lynch, 1987).

Learning from History

sales also provided revenue for schools and local services (Anderson, 2022, pp. 90–92).

Economic disruption hit these logging communities in 1978. That year, the federal government expanded the Redwood National Park, which impacted swaths of previously harvestable land.[22] Congress knew the park would harm loggers, so they created the Redwood Employee Protection Program to provide generous severance and wage replacement payments for displaced workers.

However, these payments were only a partial solution. They were not tethered to participation in workforce programs that would have helped to transition loggers into new careers. And the training program that the government promised was delayed by over a year due to implementation troubles. Lloyd Shumard, a displaced logger, lamented, "[t]he government, you know, they're supposed to have this rehabilitation program where we can go, but after a year and a half, we're still talking about it" (Berthelsen, 1979). When loggers entered workforce programs, there was no effort to see if the initiatives worked. An audit concluded that a crucial "lesson learned" was there should have been broader investments to create jobs and retraining should have started before dislocation (GAO, 1993a, pp. 3–4). Loggers felt that the government broke its promise of transitional support.

The next disruption involved the spotted owl, an endangered species native to the Pacific Northwest. One year before a judge's ruling about this creature sent shock waves through the region, 145,000 still worked in lumber (Egan, 1993). This changed in 1991. A federal court ruled that the government's plans to protect the endangered owl were insufficient. Until the White House could develop a suitable protection plan, timber sales would have to stop on federal lands. In the interim, rural communities shed jobs. Employment fell to 125,000 by 1992 – that is, 20,000 jobs lost in a blink.

The Clinton administration faced a dilemma. It had to find a way to not only protect the spotted owl but also avoid harm to rural communities reliant on forestry. The White House attempted to strike this balance with its 1993 Northwest Forest Plan, which would permit logging on a reduced scale. The initiative also called for economic development assistance to help logging communities. The support was generous, totaling $1.2 billion over five years. While the administration estimated that the plan would impact 6,000 jobs, they promised that the economic

---

[22] Factors such as mechanization of sawmills also led to employment declines.

20   *Introduction*

initiatives would create 8,000 new jobs and fund 5,400 "retraining" opportunities (Clinton, 1994).

What was the effect of retraining and investments? Job training, despite some successes, did not reach all workers nor match their previous wages. Political uncertainty also plagued the program. More than once, Congress almost failed to fund the program. Even when the initiative was saved, resources declined dramatically (Anderson, 2022, p. 93). Despite the lofty aims, there has not been a long-term transformation of rural timber communities as promised. They have been left behind and, to this day, endure the consequences of rural industrial decline.

Globalization

Globalization marks another economic disruption with profound social consequences. Political scientist John Ruggie (1982) describes how high-income democracies attempted to buffer the consequences of globalization by embedding the market within society through the creation of robust social safety nets – the "embedded liberalism" approach. In the United States, compensation has played an important role in the country's turn to free trade. Labor unions were fierce opponents to trade liberalization, which raised a roadblock when the Kennedy administration sought to further open American markets to the world.[23] Unions, a core bloc of the Democratic Party's base, stood in the way of a trade deal.

Undeterred, the White House created a plan to solve the political impasse by reducing costs to unions. The bargain would work as follows: unions would drop their opposition to the trade bill if the government would assist workers dislocated by trade. Compensation would make up for lost income, and there would be funds to train for new careers. With this Trade Adjustment Assistance (TAA) proposal, Kennedy secured the support of unions (Alden, 2017).[24]

But unions now call TAA, "burial insurance" (Rosen, 2006, p. 103). Once the government kills your job, at least they pay for the funeral. From the start, critics cast the program as woefully narrow in scope and underfunded. In its first seven years, no worker out of the 25 who petitioned received assistance due to narrow eligibility requirements

---

[23] Obviously, trade liberalization was a long-term process with different amounts of attention paid to demands from workers and firms hurt by competition (e.g., Goldstein and Gulotty, 2021).

[24] See Kim and Pelc (2020) for how compensation and protectionism can act as substitutes.

Understanding the Problem

21

(Rosen, 2006, p. 81). Subsequent reforms attempted to reinvigorate the program. One bill in 1974, for instance, expanded eligibility. However, the issue became politicized as more workers began to receive assistance. Ronald Reagan accused President Jimmy Carter of using the program to dole out political favors. Shortly after Reagan's victory, he slashed funding for TAA. This whiplash between administrations created considerable uncertainty, which has not stopped. In 2022, TAA expired, affecting nearly 100,000 workers who depend on the program, only to be saved with a short-term extension at the end of the year.[25] Even good faith efforts to help workers adjust are clouded by political uncertainty.

The consequences have been stark. In the United States, places left behind by globalization have suffered economically, and voters have turned to far-right politicians (e.g., Autor et al., 2020). This backlash has taken place worldwide, even in countries with more established safety nets than the United States.[26] Attempts to diagnose why governments have been unsuccessful in their efforts to buffer the costs of globalization have focused on top-down answers such as the supply and target of assistance. This reasoning would imply that if governments had established well-funded compensatory mechanisms, sustained them despite financial pressures (e.g., Mansfield and Rudra, 2021), and made investments in communities instead of individuals (e.g., Broz, Frieden, and Weymouth, 2021), countries might have smoothed adjustment costs and minimized political backlash to globalization. More and better-targeted resources would undoubtedly have helped. However, our book shows how even when policies are well-funded and designed, they can still fail politically if they are not credible.

UNDERSTANDING THE PROBLEM

Our argument for why economic transitions can fail despite an abundance of resources and the possibility of benefits comes down to one word: credibility. The credibility of the government's promises and local economic opportunities provided by investments influence the beliefs, preferences, and behavior of individuals impacted by economic transitions. If government credibility and local economic opportunity challenges can be reduced, reformers could build support for climate transitions.

---

[25] See DOL (2022) for details on the impact of the expired program.
[26] See Colantone and Stanig (2018), Milner (2021), Rickard (2023), and Walter (2021).

Government Credibility

The concept of credibility provides enormous explanatory power. Political scientists and economists have used it to understand an array of issues, such as the outbreak of war, democratization, the structure of governments, and economic growth.[27] We make use of two notions of credibility. The first is a commitment problem, which refers to the idea that policies made today could be reversed in the future. A government could promise generous compensation and investments, but these programs could be reversed. The second manifestation of credibility is uncertainty about whether the government represents the best interests of its constituents or has the ability to do so. Leaders do not always act in the public's interest, and even the best-intentioned politicians might be unable to fulfill their promises.

When voters and companies are uncertain about the government's credibility, it undermines the reformer's ability to reduce costs and create allies. The anticipation of costs leads fossil fuel companies to oppose reforms with lobbying, political contributions, and public relations campaigns. This organized effort to sow doubt about established climate science distorts the public's beliefs and undermines political support (Brulle, 2014; Oreskes and Conway, 2011). Even if this disinformation did not exist, underlying credibility challenges would remain, so our book focuses on how to create credibility which could generate support that counterbalances efforts to delay the transition.

We diagnose three sources of these credibility challenges: political and economic volatility, tax burden, and low trust in government. First, the pendulum swing of political control means there's always the chance that new leaders and parties will come to power and undo the work of the last leader. This injects considerable uncertainty into promises to compensate communities or invest in new industries. Economic conditions can also change, such as a recession or energy crisis, and cause political reforms to unwind.

Second, the cost of compensation and investments could undermine long-term support for the energy transition. Someone has to pick up the bill. Usually, that means voters, who generally do not like higher taxes. Even if voters say they support compensation and investments, there

---

[27] For example, Acemoglu and Robinson (2006), Fearon (1995), Moravcsik (1998), North and Weingast (1989), Powell (2006), Rodrik (1989), Tomz (2012), and Walter (2002).

Understanding the Problem

could be uncertainty about their true level of support, especially when voters feel the effects of tax increases on their pocketbooks.[28]

Third, low government trustworthiness can create skepticism about promises of compensation and investment. As scholars like Margaret Levi (1998) point out, trust matters for our ability to work together to solve problems (e.g., Hetherington, 1998). Even in a high-trust society like Denmark, the fundamental credibility problems described above can slow transitions. In the United States, there is the perfect storm of credibility challenges plus distrust of the government.

These insights about credibility extend beyond the federal government. They are relevant for states and localities that are active participants in energy transitions. They speak to the challenges faced by governmental organizations like the Appalachian Regional Commission (ARC) and nongovernmental organizations like the Just Transition Fund that have long worked on local economic development. And they are significant for companies in search of solutions for how to help transition their workers and communities where they operate.

Local Economic Opportunity

The second challenge for economic transitions is what we call local economic opportunity. This concept draws upon a colloquial understanding of credibility. When people consider an investment in their community or a move to a new job, they think about whether they will be as well or better off than they were before. We focus on four aspects of an industry that underlie these assessments: employment growth, temporariness of careers, quality of pay, and the share of jobs going to the local workforce. Though it is not our primary focus, people might also consider the health risks of an occupation.

A cloud of uncertainty hangs over the economic benefits promised by the clean energy transition. Will new jobs be temporary, well-paid, and local? With the threat of automation, people increasingly second-guess the longevity of even well-worn career paths. Workers, who may already have secure livelihoods, must also decide whether to incur the cost of training for a new occupation without a guarantee of employment. Communities must determine whether to encourage investments in unfamiliar industries. These choices are consequential. The economic

---

[28] Regarding the impact of cost on public support, see, for example, Ansolabehere and Konisky (2014) and Bechtel and Scheve (2013).

and social fabric of towns, regions, and countries are at stake. Whether to embrace this green future is the hard choice that Terry Weickum of Carbon County had to make. These are also considerations that communities have about any potential investment, but they are especially acute when secure livelihoods from old industries are on the line.

Support for the energy transition could hinge on whether new green industries create local economic opportunities. Jobs and tax revenue are the most immediate benefits of climate legislation, in addition to cleaner air and water. However, despite these benefits, local support for renewable energy is not guaranteed, especially given the land-use challenges that wind and solar run up against.

A variety of factors influence how people think about the benefits and costs of investments. The surveys, interviews, and fieldwork we conducted show that perceptions of local economic opportunities are multifaceted and cannot be reduced to a single cause. There are also consistent partisan differences in beliefs when it comes to clean energy jobs, which is likely the consequence of partisan messages and interest groups (e.g., Skocpol and Hertel-Fernandez, 2016; Zaller, 1992). Rhetoric skeptical of green energy can become unmoored from reality and instill community opposition. Yet even if some concerns about green jobs are not grounded in truth, one must take them seriously if the goal is to devise more credible policies that create allies and facilitate the energy transition.

FIXING THE PROBLEM WITH CREDIBLE POLICIES

If reformers had the tools to make government promises credible and the economic opportunities from investments apparent, they could build support for the energy transition. As political scientist Erik Patashnik (2014, p. 5) argues, when reforms garner more political support, these positive changes can endure and make society better off. Advocates need to be strategic and think about how to leverage policy design choices to usher in transitions that are more credible and difficult to unwind.

What solutions could make policies more credible? We draw on theoretical ideas from economics and political science to develop seven strategies to create credibility. For each strategy, we come up with concrete recommendations.

First, institutional constraints can shape the incentives and ability of governments to reverse political reforms (e.g., Shepsle, 1991). There are at least three ways to leverage institutions to make the energy transition more durable. Reformers should pursue laws that require more steps to overturn, as opposed to executive orders that could be reversed with the stroke of the president's pen; take control out of the hands of the federal government and delegate to communities impacted by transitions (e.g., North and Weingast, 1989); and, insulate programs from reversals by minimizing how often funds must be renewed (e.g., Patashnik, 2000). These proposals are tactical ways to create institutions that are harder to reverse.

A second solution is to design reforms that tie the hands of future leaders. This strategy eliminates the option of reversal, or at the very least raises the costs of doing so (Fearon, 1997; Spence, 1976). One such approach is to use fixed decision rules that hold a government to a course of action (Kydland and Prescott, 1977). Another tactic is to strategically accumulate debt to tie the hands of subsequent administrations (Alesina and Tabellini, 1990). Governments could also link compensation and green investments with unrelated issues, which would create incentives to support climate transitions unless one is willing to sacrifice the tied issue (e.g., Axelrod and Keohane, 1985).

The third tool to enhance credibility is to build broad coalitions. In particular, bipartisanship represents a promising route to durable political reforms (e.g., Patashnik, 2014). However, bipartisan consensus is difficult in polarized countries like the United States. To overcome this challenge, efforts to build bipartisan coalitions could highlight the benefits that accrue to broad constituencies, which would contribute to the perception that both parties, or at least a simple majority, will defend compensation and green investments in the future. Reformers could also reveal what common ground already exists. There is evidence that the public supports compensation for fossil fuel workers, but these communities might not know this. Reformers could reveal this information and shift expectations about the size of the coalition that supports compensation and investments (e.g., Kuran, 1991).

Fourth, governments could design policies to create lock-in effects. The idea is that reformers could use the benefits from the energy transition, like jobs and tax revenue, to create new allies and convert opponents (e.g., Colgan, Green, and Hale, 2021; Patashnik, 2014). These benefits could inspire technological innovation that has increasing returns, which reduce the costs of future energy transition policies (e.g., Pierson, 2000). One way to create benefits that lock-in support is to make investments in communities impacted by the energy transition. These investments would reduce economic dependence on fossil fuels and provide a financial stake in the continuance of the transition. Another strategy is to encourage companies to invest in assets whose profitability depends on the durability of the energy transition. For instance, incentives for power companies to invest in renewable energy and phase-out coal could lead these firms to defend green subsidies.

Fifth, political scientist Elinor Ostrom (1990, p. 12) describes how governments could foster credibility and trust by developing reputations for keeping their promises. Reputation is critical when people are uncertain about the motives or ability of the government. One way to do this is to provide opportunities for local input about green projects or retraining, which would demonstrate that the government is not acting unilaterally but cares about the views of the people impacted by the transition (Levi, 1998). Another approach is to provide accurate and helpful information, which over time would demonstrate that leaders are reliable (Sobel, 1985). Since climate change and the energy transition will have complicated and uncertain effects, information takes on an essential role. Workers, communities, and companies will face difficult decisions that high-quality data about their potential consequences would help.

Sixth, leaders could send costly signals to demonstrate that they share their constituents' interests and can fulfill their promises. A costly signal refers to an action that incurs a cost the sender would not have paid if she were unwilling to fulfill the promise. A classic example from the economist Michael Spence (1973) is about job markets. To demonstrate that one is a quality candidate for a job, a student goes through four grueling years of college. For governments, one costly signal is to assume risks others would not be willing to take. A concrete solution is to help cover the cost of training programs for green jobs, especially if they fail to materialize. Another tactic is to make unexpected investments. While previous work has argued that climate policy is more popular when coupled with broader social programs (e.g., Bergquist, Mildenberger, and Stokes, 2020; Gaikwad, Genovese, and Tingley, 2022b), these extra investments could instead be thought of as signaling devices that enhance the government's credibility.

Lastly, the government could take steps to enhance the transparency of its reforms and investments. A challenge that confronts even well-intentioned policies is that governments and firms cannot be held accountable for broken promises that people are unaware of. Transparency could remedy this shortfall by providing information that enables accountability (Holmström, 1979). Think of a company that promises to create local jobs. Shining a spotlight on its track record would create powerful incentives to deliver real, local benefits to workers and communities. However, in Chapter 8, we demonstrate how accountability is not automatic.

While we propose solutions, we also recognize the enormity of the challenge. Unfortunately, there are groups of individuals and corporate bodies that want to stop or slow this transition, not because they personally will be thrown out of work or because they even have sympathy for those who will lose their jobs, but because they want to continue business and profits as usual. At every step, they have tried to create uncertainty and derail progress. Yet, in our interviews, surveys, archival research, and experiments, we also find cause for hope. Credible policies that recognize the resilience and ingenuity of communities can unlock the climate impasse.

EVIDENCE FROM THE GROUND UP

We seek to understand the perspective of communities on the front lines of the energy transition, the entire nation, and companies. We explore a diverse range of voices such as policymakers, union organizers, and youths, with a particular focus on people in fossil fuel communities who have been left out of the national conversation. We deploy multiple genres of evidence, including interviews, fieldwork, public opinion surveys, messaging experiments, and archival records. In total, we surveyed over 22,000 people and interviewed 84 individuals across multiple geographies, industries, and roles.

Communities on the front lines of energy transitions are crucial to understand because these are the places with the most at stake. These areas are often understudied due to the challenge of reaching residents.[29] National surveys that are the go-to tool to measure public opinion disproportionately reflect the attitudes of people in urban areas. In contrast, individuals who face dislocation from the energy transition often reside in rural regions. It is common to see nationally representative surveys of 1,000 respondents with only one or two from states like West Virginia.

Many in these communities feel left out of and disparaged by conversations around the energy transition. Kris Mitchell, who directs the Boone County Development Authority in West Virginia, told us how the top-down approach could inflict real harm.

---

[29] For exceptions, see Carley, Evans, and Konisky (2018), Cha (2020), Cha et al. (2022), Roemer and Haggerty (2021), and Mayer (2018).

From the outside, it's difficult because other people want to tell our story ... [we're] portrayed as ignorant hillbillies who are holding on to a dying industry. It's the way we are constantly portrayed in the media ... We're not uneducated. I have all my natural teeth. My husband is not related to me. If you name a stereotype, we've heard it. And that doesn't help when you're trying to sell a state or an area because people believe that ... We're not who people portray us to be.[30]

To let people tell their own stories, we go directly to these areas to hear from people in their own words. As social scientists, we listen with a critical ear since we recognize the broader context within which people's preferences, attitudes, and beliefs form. Our ground-up approach stemmed from our desire to better understand the perspective of workers and individuals in fossil fuel communities. We began working on the topics in this book years ago, well before the most recent climate policymaking efforts during the Biden administration. Alex was conducting surveys at county fairs and carrying out fieldwork in Southwest Pennsylvania, while Dustin was running surveys and working on a transition strategy for the region.

Building on our previous research, we conducted interviews with residents and local officials in fossil fuel communities across the country, as well as instructors at workforce programs in regions with and without fossil fuels. Our questions focus on the challenges and opportunities they saw in the clean energy transition and what they thought was being left out of the national dialogue. Alex also returned to Southwest Pennsylvania to field new questions at county fairs. Then to capture the attitudes of residents in communities crucial to the energy transition, we brought to bear considerable resources to field surveys in the Industrial Midwest, Gulf Coast, Southwest Pennsylvania area, and New Mexico.

We also made a deliberate effort to reach people who are not typically surveyed but are nonetheless vital for the energy transition. Youths are significant because they are making important decisions about their future careers. In one national survey, we recruited youth participants to understand their views better. We also collaborated with a vocational training center in Southwest Pennsylvania to analyze a survey they did of middle schoolers in coal, oil, and gas country.

Unions also play a central role. Union leaders influence the attitudes, preferences, and beliefs of their members, which could help or slow support for climate policy (e.g., Ahlquist and Levi, 2013). However, the views of union members in fossil fuel industries are difficult to collect.

---

[30] Interview, November 10, 2022.

We overcome this barrier by gaining access to an internal survey conducted by unions around the Great Lakes region. Union leaders designed these surveys to understand how to navigate the energy transition, which provides unparalleled insight into their perspective.

The views of local policymakers matter because they serve as opinion leaders in their communities and help to implement energy transition policies like compensation and investments.[31] To learn about their perspective, we conducted surveys of local officials such as mayors and county executives. To do this, we partnered with an organization called CivicPulse.

We recognize that no one individual can speak for the entire community and that interest groups often work to cultivate a narrative about what communities believe. For this reason, we talk to a diversity of actors – residents, workers, nonprofits, unions, and local officials – who hold a complex set of views. While it is impossible to capture every perspective, the common responses we hear make us more confident in our conclusions.

We also listen to voices from across the United States using nationally representative samples. This is because the clean energy expansion must occur across the entire United States and worldwide. In some of these surveys, we embedded messaging experiments, a strategy used by scholars, political campaigns, and consumer marketing agencies. These experiments expose people to different information about a political reform, such as whether there is a bipartisan coalition, and then measure the survey-taker's attitudes, preferences, and beliefs. By comparing how people respond, we can test whether our proposed solutions to create credibility increase willingness to support the energy transition.

Our surveys focus on people's beliefs because these perceptions can be consequential for the efficacy of policies. If a potential wind turbine mechanic perceives the industry as relying on outside labor or a program as ineffective, she may decide not to enter a training program. Local leaders may also decide not to approve permits or provide tax credits for a new, unfamiliar industry if they are uncertain about the benefits and fear the potential electoral consequences of squandering community resources.[32]

Lastly, we turn our lens to the perspective of companies involved in the energy transition. We conducted semistructured interviews with senior

---

[31] See Rabe (2004) for the importance of state climate policy, and Bulkeley (2010) for cities.

[32] But see Jensen and Malesky (2018) on the incentives politicians have to pander.

officials at electric power utilities, an oil major, and renewable energy developers. These are stakeholders that will be at the forefront of the green energy expansion, so it is valuable to learn from their point of view. However, we listen with a critical ear since some of these organizations have historically opposed action on climate change. Yet the energy transition will require cooperation by all, so a crucial step is to understand the barriers that firms face so that these concerns can be addressed when they are legitimate.

BOOK STRUCTURE

The plan of the book is as follows. The first half of Chapter 2 explains the source of the problem: why credibility challenges exist. We draw on stories recounted to us in our interviews and those recorded by the local and national press to make concrete what might otherwise feel like an abstract academic concern. The second half of the chapter turns to solutions: how the government can enhance credibility. We synthesize insights from a rich body of political science and economics research on bargaining and institutions to generate solutions to make political reforms last. We also use ideas developed in sociology and other disciplines to highlight the social context that reform efforts must navigate.

Chapter 3 explores how the public, elected leaders, and firms think about credibility. Across the national public, local policymakers, and fossil fuel community residents, there is a common thread: credibility is top of mind. Over 70 percent of the national public think government investments in their community won't last; local officials, youths, and fossil fuel communities are even more pessimistic. We then turn the lens to companies and find that the government's inability to commit can undermine the predictability needed to make significant capital investments in clean energy.

Chapter 4 analyzes beliefs about the local economic opportunities from investments. We develop novel question batteries to capture perceptions of the quality of jobs across industries and the local benefits from investments. We find that nationally, there are optimistic evaluations of renewable energy jobs with respect to industry growth and potential for raises, but the public thinks these industries employ fewer local workers and provide more temporary careers than established industries like healthcare. Relative to the national public, fossil fuel communities are more pessimistic about the local benefits from green jobs, but they are nonetheless open to investments. Local policymakers share these views.

Book Structure

Chapter 5 provides the first empirical tests of our solutions. We devise a multi-attribute policy experiment that allows us to simultaneously manipulate several policy design choices to assess which ones enhance credibility. We also develop messaging experiments to test the political efficacy of delegation to communities, lock-in effects, bipartisan consensus, shifting expectations by revealing common ground, and deep laws versus shallow promises. Then to generate ground-up solutions, we ask local leaders what strategies they think would create local benefits. We ask similar questions in our interviews with firms. We find that our solutions to create credibility can build support for the energy transition among the public, local policymakers, and companies, even when these reforms are costly.

Then Chapter 6 explores what can be learned from history. We focus on the Clean Air Act (CAA) Amendments of 1990, the last major environmental statute in the United States.[33] Efforts to amend the CAA to deal with acid rain sparked a showdown between high-sulfur coal users and producers that the law would hurt, and the lawmakers and White House that refused to share the costs of the reform. We draw on Congressional debates, memoirs, interviews, and archives of the *United Mine Workers Journal* (UMWJ) to show how credibility challenges constrained the bargain reformers could reach. We uncover the aftereffects of economic dislocation in coal communities that followed these top-down attempts to transition and the lasting impact on the trustworthiness of the government. To put the American experience in context, we contrast the CAA Amendments with Germany's coal phase-out. This comparison underscores the importance of credibility challenges, even in places with institutions that make commitments more durable.

In Chapter 7, we shift attention to workforce development. Credibility challenges abound when it comes to (re)training. There is uncertainty about continued government support for green industries alongside concerns about whether one will find a job. We build on our conversations and contacts with vocational schools to analyze a survey of what careers middle schoolers in a fossil fuel community prioritize. We find that solutions to create credibility, like the strategic use of debt, can enhance willingness to train for green jobs. We also discuss how credibility is significant for groups traditionally underrepresented in green industries such as women and people of color. Making climate transitions credible goes hand-in-hand with making them inclusive.

---

[33] The IRA passed in 2022 provides supply-side incentives for renewable energy, but the law does not directly limit fossil fuel production or consumption.

32

Introduction

Chapter 8 explores a prominent dimension of local economic opportunity: whether green investments generate local jobs. We examine how transparency policies to shine a light on local hiring practices could create credible local benefits and foster support for green energy projects. We also delve into a conflict between energy developers and unions in Minnesota. Developers had begun to sidestep unions by bringing in outside teams of laborers. The unions fought back and lobbied the state to require that developers report on the share of jobs going to local labor. Comparing local hiring in Minnesota and neighboring North Dakota, we find promising signs that transparency helped to increase the share of Minnesotan workers at wind projects. These local benefits matter for the energy transition. We unearth findings from internal union surveys that show how fossil fuel workers are more willing to support wind energy when the industry provides local jobs. National survey results paint a similar picture. However, we highlight the limits of transparency. Accountability may not be forthcoming if there are not robust institutions like local journalism. Policymakers should proceed with caution. Alluring solutions like provisions to clawback tax credits as part of an enforcement mechanism might decrease support for green investments. This points to a potential dark side of efforts to enhance credibility.

This book synthesizes and extends a range of academic literatures from American politics on institutions, interest groups, and political reforms;[34] from public opinion on energy and climate change;[35] from political economy on the consequences of places "left behind" by economic changes[36] and theories of strategic interaction;[37] and, from comparative politics studies of institutions in the clean energy transition.[38]

The conclusion provides a synopsis of our argument and findings, discusses enduring challenges and future research, and considers how our framework applies to recent events like the 2022 IRA that passed as we finalized this book. Enduring challenges include the politics of

---

[34] For example, Berry, Burden, and Howell (2010), Patashnik (2014), and Stokes (2020).

[35] For example, Ansolabehere and Konisky (2014), Bechtel and Scheve (2013), Bergquist, Mildenberger, and Stokes (2020), Egan and Mullin (2017), Gaikwad, Genovese, and Tingley (2022b), and Tingley and Tomz (2014).

[36] For example, Anderson (2022), Austin, Glaeser, and Summers (2018), Baccini and Weymouth (2021), Broz, Frieden, and Weymouth (2021), Rickard (2023), and Shambaugh and Nunn (2018).

[37] For example, Alesina and Tabellini (1990), Fearon (1997), Kydland and Prescott (1977), Persson and Tabellini (2012), and Spence (1973).

[38] For example, Aklin (2021), Meckling et al. (2022b), and Mildenberger (2020).

place-based policies, the tensions between green industrial policy and the international trade regime, credibility problems around climate finance commitments, and other issues that do not neatly fit into our credibility framework.

We also set an agenda for future research. Adaptation to adjust to the impacts of global warming is a critical topic that could be fruitfully explored through the lens of credibility (e.g., Javeline, 2014). Our framework also invites cross-national comparisons, especially since credibility challenges might be even more severe in developing countries with weaker institutions and fewer resources. Further research on how to make the clean energy transition equitable and inclusive will be vital. Lastly, our discussion of the IRA considers the challenges of partisan legislation, the importance of renewable energy siting and transmission, and the trade-offs of green industrial policy. Even the IRA confronts credibility challenges that will be essential to understand as the landmark law is implemented.

By better understanding credibility challenges in climate transitions, we hope to not only provide a voice to often unheard individuals and their communities but also to lay the groundwork for the design of more effective and durable policies in the climate context and beyond. We see our main contribution as a sober, clear-eyed perspective on the incredible challenge and opportunity of climate transitions that is informed by listening and engaging with a range of communities that will – and have already been – directly impacted.

2

Problems and Solutions

When asked, "if you could have a hotline to Senator Manchin and say, 'this is what we need'" Tracy Bertram, the Mayor of Becker, Minnesota, did not hesitate: "a crystal ball."[1]

Tracy's city is home to the Sherco coal-fired power plant, the largest power plant in the state. But this generator's days are numbered. In 2016, Xcel revealed plans to decommission Sherco and more recently announced a solar farm in its place. The new federal climate law, the Inflation Reduction Act (IRA), may lower the cost for Xcel to build solar, but this change is part of an energy transition that began years before.

Becker faces two fundamental challenges when it comes to this transition. The first challenge is whether the city can secure durable transitional support. Compensation, retraining, and investments cannot be taken for granted. "For us to sit here and say, 'well, okay, we're going to get some transition aid as the power plant phases out, and transitional aid will ramp up, so we're not just hammering the taxpayers, it'll ease it in.' I don't know. We're going to have to fight for that. That's not just going to get handed to us," emphasized Greg Lerud, the city administrator.[2]

With no crystal ball, city officials, workers, and residents face profound uncertainty. "Let me see what the city of Becker looks like in 15 years. And then let me come back to today, and I'll know what to do," Tracy said. From the perspective of Becker, support from the state and federal government cannot be relied upon. "If there's one thing I've learned as the mayor is that local government is the only thing that I can change, the only thing that I can *really have faith in*."

[1] Interview, August 30, 2022.
[2] Interview, August 30, 2022.

Becker will also have to figure out how to make investments that offset the loss of the coal plant. This is easier said than done. Tracy is solemn as she describes what will happen to her community, "when you take one of the biggest businesses from a city you're almost rewriting history, you're rewriting a whole city ... the legislature and also our governor don't realize what happens to a city that has been a host to an industry like this, but they think it's a great and grand thing that we have this huge solar project. But they're forgetting about ... the hole that is left for the community to back-fill." You can hear in Tracy's voice the frustration that Becker has had this change hoisted upon them with little consultation.

Becker is not alone in the energy transition. Within Minnesota, there is a coalition of cities home to coal-fired power plants that may be next in line to be decommissioned. Across the nation and worldwide, there are communities in a similar predicament. Even places without ties to the fossil fuel industry have decisions to make about whether to invest in green energy, a choice that raises questions about the durability of investments and new economic opportunities.

These challenges exemplify the issues our book argues are at the heart of the clean energy transition: government credibility and local economic opportunity. In the first half of this chapter, we explain what these problems are and why they exist.

Then, the second half of this chapter proposes solutions to create credibility and local economic opportunities. We provide a framework grounded in decades of social science research to understand how to make economic transitions work. Examples of our solutions include institutional constraints to impede policy reversal; tools to tie the hands of future decision-makers; ways to build broader coalitions; mechanisms to lock in benefits from reforms; steps to foster a reputation of promise-keeping; and transparency initiatives to hold leaders and companies accountable. All of these solutions serve to create credibility and deliver local economic benefits.

WHAT IS ALL THE FUSS ABOUT?

Government Credibility

One must first understand the problem to find solutions. Otherwise, any potential remedy might address the wrong cause and could even exacerbate the problem. We focus on two credibility challenges that not only governments face but also individuals, companies, and nongovernmental organizations.

First, governments may struggle to convince the public and companies that they would fulfill a commitment when the future is uncertain and there could be incentives to abandon the reform later. Credible commitment problems are ubiquitous in politics and economics (e.g., Acemoglu, 2003; Alesina and Tabellini, 1988; Kydland and Prescott, 1977; Persson and Tabellini, 1994). What someone says she will do in the future might be different when the time comes. For instance, the government could promise policies to accelerate the energy transition, such as tax subsidies for renewable energy. However, the economic or political context might change. There could be a recession that makes the subsidies too expensive or an energy crisis that increases demand for fossil fuels. New political parties that oppose green energy or have different priorities could gain power. Individuals and companies know the future is uncertain, so they hesitate to invest in renewable energy for fear that subsidies will be reduced. This is the credible commitment problem.[3]

The second credibility challenge stems from uncertainty about whether the government represents the interests of its constituents and has the ability to fulfill its promises (e.g., Rodrik, 1989; Sobel, 1985; Spence, 1973).[4] It is easy for a leader to say she has the public's interest at heart, but politicians can also be inept, biased, and corrupt. As noted political economist Bruce Springsteen penned in the song *Badlands*, "poor man wanna be rich, rich man wanna be king, And a king ain't satisfied till he rules everything." For instance, the government could promise compensation to fossil fuel workers, but people might think that leaders will abuse these funds and little would go to workers. Even if a politician faithfully represents her constituents, there could be doubts about whether compensation policies are effective or if there are enough resources to sustain them.

These two government credibility problems have at least three sources: economic and political volatility, the tax burden on voters, and trust in government.

As the World Goes Round: Economic and Political Volatility

Economic and political volatility is a common source of commitment problems, the first credibility challenge (e.g., Persson and Tabellini,

---

[3] Individuals face a related problem with intertemporal choice. Alex and Dustin should go to the gym more next week, but when next week arrives and they want to work on their new book, which is more fun than the gym, will they?

[4] Rodrik (1989) discusses how these two credibility challenges differ and arise in policy reforms.

2012). Promises of compensation and investment may not be sustainable if the broader economic context changes due to an unforeseen shock (Rochet, 2004). Rising energy prices could create pressure to roll back climate policy (Furman et al., 2008). A recession could force the government to tighten its belt, including compensation programs or green investments (Victor and Yanosek, 2011). Technological change could undermine tax revenue for policies necessary to buffer the effects of economic changes (e.g., Mansfield and Rudra, 2021). These problems also impact promises of investments by companies. Unanticipated inflation and supply chain bottlenecks, for instance, have thrown offshore wind projects into limbo over cost concerns (Storrow and Richards, 2022).

Political circumstances can also evolve and lead reforms to be reversed (e.g., Moe, 1990; Shepsle, 1991). Little is sure in politics save for one regularity: leaders will eventually be replaced by others with different views. This pendulum swing creates the risk that a new coalition will win and overturn the prior's policies.[5] For example, when President Reagan entered office, he cut aid promised by the previous administration to workers impacted by foreign trade (Alden, 2017, p. 113). Politicians may also adopt a popular platform to win an election but then deviate once in office to pursue the policy they truly prefer (e.g., Alesina, 1988). Even the very same party that enacted a policy could reverse its reform if priorities evolve.

With the mosaic of federal, regional, and local actors involved in the energy transition, there are multiple points where changes in political control could generate uncertainty. For example, consider the Regional Greenhouse Gas Initiative (RGGI), a group of states in the Northeast that banded together to usher in a cap-and-trade program. Participation has fluctuated in this initiative to limit power sector emissions. When Republican Chris Christie became governor of New Jersey, he quit RGGI (Navarro, 2011). Eight years later, political control changed, and Democratic Governor Phil Murphy rejoined.

These credible commitment challenges are global. The Czech Republic, for instance, introduced a coal phase-out plan in the 1990s, but since the restrictions were enacted through a government resolution that a simple majority could overturn, this exposed the effort to future political changes that made it easier for coal interests to unwind the plan

---

[5] Game theoretic models of credible commitment problems often treat the actor with a time inconsistency problem as unitary. While we discuss different political leaders, from the perspective of individuals and firms, the actor is just the "government."

(Lehotský and Černík, 2019). Every country faces the problem that political and economic circumstances can change, which can derail political reforms.

The pendulum swing complicates climate transitions which will require sustained policy implementation over the long run (e.g., Bernauer, 2013; Hovi, Sprinz, and Underdal, 2009). Fossil fuel communities may doubt whether compensation and investments would last if priorities and leaders change. Workers could be less willing to train for jobs in uncertain industries (see Chapter 7). One solar energy instructor recounted how political changes in her state meant "there was a time when we could not even write the word solar or wind in our reports."[6] Local officials fear their economic development efforts could stall if federal support subsides or rules for funding change.

Once enacted, one would hope that government programs are hard to unwind, but this claim does not stand up to history. One study examined the lifespan of every federal domestic program between 1971 and 2003 and found that partisan changes undermine program durability and size (Berry, Burden, and Howell, 2010). More than half of federal tax credit programs in the United States were eliminated between 1975 and 2001 (Corder, 2004). Political volatility has wide-ranging effects that occur across countries and levels of government, especially given the growth in polarization (e.g., Baker et al., 2014; Canes-Wrone and Park, 2012).

Economic and political volatility has real consequences for the energy transition. Consider companies that must make large investments in new clean technologies. Firms might hesitate to do so if future demand for green energy or products is uncertain. For this reason, a National Academies report (2010), a group that brings together leading academics to study solutions to societal problems, highlights the lack of sustained policy due to political changes as one of the top three barriers to renewable energy development. Likewise, the economist Nicholas Stern (2022) identifies "lack of confidence in the future of government policy" as a "major deterrent to investment." Representative Garret Graves (2022), a Republican who was part of the House Select Committee on the Climate Crisis, describes the challenge, "you're an investor; you're looking for predictability and certainty … and you've got all of this crazy pendulum swinging or uncertainty … we've got to look at devising strategies that are going to have the durability of different administrations or political winds." Unsurprisingly, studies that quantify the economic effect

---

[6] Interview, August 16, 2022.

of policy uncertainty find that it undermines investments in low-carbon technologies (see Chapter 3).

Changes in political control also exacerbate hold-up problems, another form of time inconsistency. The idea of a hold-up problem comes from economics to explain why firms fail to cooperate despite the possibility that everyone could be made better off. Cooperation breaks down because of the fear that one's rival could gain bargaining power and renege on an earlier agreement. There are two ways to think about the hold-up problem in the context of economic transitions.

The first is from the perspective of individuals and their communities. If fossil fuel communities were to accept compensation in exchange for climate policy support, the industry and unions that advocate for the community would lose political influence that might be necessary to protect the bargain. As a senior official at an electric power company put it, "in certain areas when a coal plant goes down, that community is gone."[7] The community, unions, and companies are a source of political power to hold the government accountable for continued compensation (e.g., Dixit and Londregan, 1995).[8] With population outflow as people search for new jobs, one local official from coal country in Illinois said, "[the] loss of voter base would create less of a chance for continued support."

This is one reason why unions have worked to make new green industries unionized. Liz Shuler (2021), the president of the AFL-CIO, said unequivocally, "Offshore wind, solar, electric vehicles and more – no exceptions – every clean energy sector [should be unionized]." The anticipation that communities will be made worse off by climate policy and the inability of the government to credibly commit to providing compensation because communities will lose their leverage to hold the government accountable causes compensatory bargains to get "held up."

The second hold-up problem confronts companies. Businesses face a dilemma. The government could promise them tax credits if they invest in green technologies, but once they have sunk money in investments, the government could renegotiate for a lower credit (Williamson, 1989). This hold-up problem is acute for regulated industries like electric utilities. The anticipation that companies might be taken advantage of in the future creates a deterrent to making highly specific investments that can be used for only one purpose as opposed to those that can be redeployed for other purposes. Green energy production is an example of a specific investment. Solar panels have one purpose. In countries with strong rule

---

[7] Interview, November 8, 2022.
[8] Also see Davis (2019).

of law, this type of hold-up problem can be reduced with contracts, but it is no guarantee.

Asset specificity could also create hold-up problems for individuals. If workforce programs emphasize occupations with a highly specific skill set, people might hesitate to train for those careers since they fear they might be more vulnerable to economic, technological, or political changes. However, suppose training emphasized a more general set of skills or those with clear linkages to several industries. In that case, participants might be more confident that even if they do not find a solar job, for instance, they could apply their skills to another career.

These hold-up problems speak to how the benefits and costs of the energy transition for individuals, communities, and companies shape the contours of climate policy debates and the coalitions that form. Unlike other issue areas, "[t]he very nature of environmental policymaking makes crafting durable policy commitments challenging. While the benefits of environmental policies are often long-term and diffused, the costs may be immediate and concentrated on influential interests" (Patashnik, 2000, p. 8). Yet, environmental policy can provide immediate economic benefits in the form of jobs and investments, but these should be most persuasive when they appear durable.

Tax Bills

Compensation and investments are not free. They come with a cost that falls on the taxpayers in one way or another. Is the public willing to pay? Do the recipients of compensation and investments think the public would be willing to incur these costs? These considerations relate to uncertainty about what governments and the taxpayers that fund them actually want or can do, the second credibility problem. Even if these costs are spread out, voter support is a general constraint. It especially contributes to credibility challenges when people are uncertain about the size of the costs and the shape of voter preferences.

One may not want to bet on the altruism of voters to bear these costs. Chapter 7 discusses how cost concerns led to drastically less comprehensive and effective aid for coal miners dislocated by the 1990 CAA Amendments. Tracy Bertram and Greg Lerud, the city officials in Becker, did not think they could count on assistance, but that they are "gonna have to fight."

However, there is evidence that the public might support compensatory programs. For example, public opinion polls show that most

Democrats, Republicans, and Independents would back training programs for people employed in the coal, oil, and gas industries (Gaikwad, Genovese, and Tingley, 2022b). This support may be because of the belief that individuals dislocated by policy deserve assistance. It could also be because the public recognizes the political strategy behind compensation. Yet compensation recipients might not be aware of this consensus or doubt that the public would put their money where their mouth is.[9]

The cost to voters can also influence the durability of other policies necessary for the energy transition. Firms or communities that receive green investments could anticipate that public support for these projects might sour. Budgetary pressures have undermined the administrative capacity needed to implement climate policies in places like New York (Times Union, 2022), which illustrates how cost concerns could slow the energy transition even if policies are not reversed outright.

Can I Trust the Government?

Low trust in government exacerbates credibility challenges. Governments can be inept, biased, and even corrupt, which instills doubts about whether the government represents the public's interests. Distrust in government is endemic in the United States, as political scientists Jack Citrin and Laura Stoker (2018) document in a review of academic studies.[10] National surveys since 1958 that track how much the public trusts the federal government to do the right thing show that trust is at an all-time low. Only two in ten Americans trust DC to do what is right just about always or most of the time (Pew Research Center, 2022). There is also relatively little trust in governmental organizations that implement energy transition policies like the Environmental Protection Agency (EPA) (Brewer and Ley, 2013).

Mistrust may be acute in communities that have experienced economic disruptions. The lack of trust may be warranted given the government's anemic response to regional decline like deindustrialization (Broz, Frieden, and Weymouth, 2021), which contributes to the perception of broken promises.

---

[9] However, maybe these concerns are warranted. There is evidence that 43 percent of the American public would approve of leaders reneging on a deal to compensate the coal industry once the power plants have been shut down (Arel-Bundock and Pelc, 2023).

[10] Declines in trust in national government may have been more extreme than in local government (Jennings, 1998).

Low trust has consequences. Political scientist Marc Hetherington (2006) shows how the decline of trust coincides with greater opposition to government programs like food stamps.[11] Citrin and Stoker (2018, p. 61) conclude that the "core claim" from studies of trust "is that people will not be willing to support policies that entail personal risk or sacrifice if they do not trust the government." When the costs and benefits of policies are uncertain, as is the case for the energy transition, trust in government serves "as a heuristic to decide whether positive outcomes will materialize," which influences policy preferences and political behavior.

As Margaret Levi (1998) points out, not only does trust matter but so does trustworthiness. To say that an institution is trustworthy implies that its procedures and constraints lead agents within the institution to act in the public's interest on average.[12] If individuals do not trust the government nor perceive institutions as trustworthy, they will see the government as less credible (Levi, 1998, p. 86).

Sources of distrust include a history of broken promises, incompetent governance, and antagonism of the government toward its constituents (Levi, 1998, p. 88). Political scientist Katherine Cramer (2016), through her conversations with rural Wisconsinites, shows how resentment is a powerful political force. Identity and the lack of recognition are also salient for individuals in fossil fuel communities who believe that outsiders look down on them. Many scholars and political commentators have observed that coal, oil, and gas communities are proud of their history and work. Kris Mitchell from Boone County, West Virginia, expressed frustration with how outsiders did not understand why "we have a coal heritage festival. It doesn't matter what your opinion is on coal. It's the heritage of this area. It built a nation. It was the building of the Industrial Revolution."[13] A common refrain we hear from people in coal country is the feeling that outsiders are hypocrites who criticize coal communities for a fuel that pollutes, yet at the same time, outside elites are the ones who have benefited most from coal.

---

[11] Distrust reduces willingness to raise taxes to reduce pollution when the government isn't credible (Fairbrother, 2019).

[12] "Institutional trustworthiness implies procedures for selecting and constraining the agents of institutions so that they are competent, credible, and likely to act in the interests of those being asked to trust the institution. Thus, it is not actually the institution or government that is being trusted or is acting in a trustworthy manner. Rather, when citizens and clients say they trust an institution, they are declaring a belief that, on average, its agents will prove to be trustworthy" (Levi, 1998, p. 80).

[13] Interview, November 10, 2022.

What Is All the Fuss About? 43

There can be spirals of distrust when people think that the government and elites do not trust them (Levi, 1998, p. 93). Distrust is a reasonable response by those who have faced systematic disadvantages (Peel, 1998, p. 316). A coal miner in Australia voiced frustration that outsiders thought they knew what was best for their area and concealed their true intentions.

They seem to think they can just add this "just transition" stuff to their rhetoric and suddenly it'll be okay for them to come up here and shut down the mines ... If you want to shut us down, just say so, and we can have that fight. But do not pretend like you're Santa Claus coming to bring us gifts and save us from ourselves. (MacNeil and Beauman, 2022, p. 121)

When Ireland moved away from peat farming, a high-carbon energy source, "the sense that the government only pretended to implement social policies [like retraining] to enhance their reputation at the expense of the peat workers was widespread" (Banerjee and Schuitema, 2022, p. 8).

Even if there is complete trust, credible commitment problems can emerge because the future is uncertain. Yet to understand how people think about government promises, the more social concepts of trust and trustworthiness are crucial.[14] Both self-interest and incentives alongside trust and trustworthiness will shape when people believe the government's promises to support political reform.

How the Sausage Gets Made: Institutional Context
The institutional context – that is, rules for how decisions are made – also shapes government credibility and the durability of political reforms (e.g., Patashnik, 2000, 2014).[15] A deep body of research considers how institutional arrangements, like the rule of law, property rights, and transparency, influence the ability and incentives of government actors to renege on promises (e.g., North and Weingast, 1989; Shepsle, 1991).[16] These institutional features become most relevant when interest groups or voters disagree about political reforms or there is uncertainty generated by political and economic volatility.

---

[14] Political philosopher Jon Elster (1989, pp. 274–275) argues that the credible commitment concept "captures most of the arguments about the causes and consequences of trust." See also Levi and Stoker (2000, p. 494).

[15] Institutions are rules, procedures, and norms that constrain human interactions, what North (1990) calls "rules of the game." A second view of institutions sees them as focal points that may induce coordination (Shepsle, 2006).

[16] See Aklin (2021) on regime type and renewable energy development.

Institutions such as veto points where political actors can block policy changes can also reinforce the status quo. While veto points can make political reforms harder to enact in the first place, they can also facilitate their durability when reformers clear these hurdles. One study of 125 countries over four decades finds that countries with fewer political constraints enact faster clean energy reforms (Bayulgen and Ladewig, 2017). For example, one explanation for the divergence of American and Germany renewable energy trajectories is that the fragmentation and interbranch conflict from Madisonian institutions in the United States have slowed the growth of green industries (e.g., Laird and Stefes, 2009).[17]

The shape of state-business relations could also influence the government's ability to make credible commitments. For example, corporatist systems, which involve ongoing relationships between the government, companies, and unions, may facilitate credibility through opportunities for repeated interactions that develop reputations and foster trust (e.g., Meckling and Nahm, 2022; Mildenberger, 2020). Relatedly, differences in electoral systems might explain when governments can make credible commitments. For example, proportional representation systems where multiple parties form coalition governments could make promises to groups represented by a party in the coalition more credible (e.g., Iversen and Soskice, 2006).[18]

Beyond Credibility

While we orient our argument around credibility, it is not the only barrier to economic transitions. There are two additional explanations for why stakeholders might fail to reach bargains despite their potential to make everyone better off: information and issue indivisibility.

An information-based explanation for the inability to pass and sustain climate policy is that there is so much uncertainty about the effects of global warming, the costs of climate policy, and the efficacy of compensation that stakeholders are unable to reach an agreement. When citizens have little information about the future, politicians will prioritize short-term issues, which leads to the neglect of long-term challenges like climate change (Jacobs, 2016). When the benefits are uncertain, even those who could gain from a reform might not back it. This weakens support for a policy and creates a bias toward the status quo (Fernandez and Rodrik, 1991).

---

[17] See also Busby (2008). However, other institutions like federalism may spark innovation (e.g., Fiorino, 2018; Vogel, 1993, ch. 7).

[18] For climate examples, see Finnegan (2022) and Lockwood (2021).

What Is All the Fuss About? 45

Yet, credible commitment challenges would remain even if informational problems could be solved. Moreover, uncertainty should decline over time as the costs of climate change and climate policy become clearer, whereas credible commitment problems will not recede on their own.[19] Ultimately, information-based explanations complement our argument. Uncertainty about the government's ability is part of the credibility challenge (e.g., Rodrik, 1989; Sobel, 1985). Further, our next concept of local economic opportunity captures the uncertainty that one might have about the effectiveness of an investment, which stems partly from a lack of information. However, uncertainty also emerges because investments depend on sustained government support, which could change because of political or economic volatility. Sources of bargaining failure can reinforce each other.

Another explanation for bargaining failure is issue indivisibility. Think of a bargain as an attempt to split a pizza among friends. It is straightforward (usually) to allocate slices. But sometimes, the issues at stake cannot be divided like a pizza. A common example is when two countries dispute who can control a religious holy site, which cannot be cut in half. Scholars contest the degree to which indivisibility is a real concern since it is almost always possible to come up with a creative deal. However, in coal communities, for example, residents care about not only money but also their way of life and collective history (e.g., Bell and York, 2010), which would be hard to replace as part of a climate bargain.

While the importance of identity arises in our interviews, what we hear is a call for *recognition* rather than an immutable barrier to reform. People believe that outsiders do not appreciate their hard work and sacrifice and that alternatives to fossil fuel jobs would not support good livelihoods. If one spends time in places like Southwest Pennsylvania, it quickly becomes apparent that residents' views of the coal, oil, and gas industries are more complex than commonly portrayed. Yes, the industry is historically significant. But people are also aware of the health consequences of these jobs and local pollution, which makes them open to other opportunities (e.g., Gazmararian, 2022b; Jerolmack, 2021). The problem is that nothing credible seems to be on offer. Group attachment and nonmaterial values do not render the issue indivisible. They only heighten the importance of credibility.

---

[19] For evidence of declining uncertainty, see Egan and Mullin (2012), Gazmararian and Milner (2022b), Hoffmann et al. (2022), and Marlon et al. (2021).

Local Economic Opportunity

The next challenge for economic transitions is a concept we call local economic opportunity. This refers to expectations about whether the transition would make one's community better or worse off than before. This concept raises questions like, will new jobs from an investment be well-paying, long-lasting, and served by locals? How do these new opportunities compare to what came before? The concept captures the idea that when the government promises to foster new industries or businesses pledge to create jobs and local benefits, recipients of these investments must believe that the benefits will last and accrue to the community. Otherwise, there will be strong incentives to defend the status quo, or the level of investment might be lower than necessary. These considerations are distinct from the definition of credibility above in terms of preferences, incentives, and ability but relate to a more colloquial understanding.

Efforts to build political support for the clean energy transition must convince communities – not only those that produce fossil fuels but also those with no ties to coal, oil, and gas, where clean energy projects will also be built – that the transition will make them as well or better off than before. Otherwise, opposition will emerge. As a senior official at an electric power company described,

> when communities don't understand the value of a project being located in its community ... you will get a lot of pushback. We are starting to see in some communities the pushback for wind, and that's concerning because *we're just at the beginning* of [the transition]![20]

A team of sociologists studying the oil-rich Gulf Coast of the United States as part of the Roosevelt Project summarized the clear concerns about green jobs that emerged in interviews concerning their pay, longevity, and location – all themes we develop. As one Gulf Coast resident put it, "[p]eople would be a lot more receptive if the energy transition was here now with jobs here now to support their livelihood" (Beckfield et al., 2022, p. 49).

These concerns are global. In Germany, unions call attention to the lower wages of wind and solar compared to manufacturing (see Chapter 6). In South Africa, only a small fraction of renewable energy jobs have been long-lasting maintenance careers, which has compromised

---

[20] Interview, November 8, 2022.

What Is All the Fuss About? 47

union support for climate policy (IPPP, 2021; Kalt, 2022, p. 515). In India, opposition to wind projects has also emerged (Lakhanpal, 2019).

Creating compelling benefits from clean energy sector jobs will be essential for places where these facilities must be built. But when it comes to the phase-out of fossil fuels, the goal should not be a one-to-one transition from fossil fuel to green jobs. This might even be counter-productive. It would be most efficient to boost employment in industries with comparable skills to fossil fuel workers, irrespective of whether they are in new clean sectors. The goal should be to create alternative options outside of fossil fuels. However, the political debates around the energy transition often emphasize the substitutability of these careers, regardless of economic or political efficacy.

These concerns about whether the transition would make one's community better off and support good livelihoods can stem from government credibility challenges. Varied perceptions of economic opportunity can also emerge from the economics of an industry, regional endowments, and personal abilities. The origin of these beliefs is likely the product of objective economic assessments, interest group messages, elite cues, the media, and personal experience. In some settings, an investment might have such favorable prospects that concerns about government credibility evaporate. At the other extreme, worries about the local benefits from investments could be so great that even the most iron-clad guarantees from the government are ineffectual.

We break economic opportunity into constituent parts: industry growth, local jobs, pay, and temporariness. Of course, these are not the only aspects of a career that matter. Health risks are another. However, these dimensions largely capture the overall picture.[21] We study individual beliefs about these components in Chapter 4.

Future Jobs

It may seem obvious, but people should prefer jobs in industries that are on their way up rather than down. The term "future jobs" refers to beliefs about employment growth (or decline) in an industry. These beliefs could depend on factors like economic conditions, foreign competition, or technological change, which could render an industry or occupation obsolete (Wike and Stokes, 2018). Perceptions of the future growth of an industry

---

[21] People might be uncertain about these dimensions of jobs, which could contribute to aversion. They could also be certain about their beliefs about an industry but hold them in low regard, which would have an equivalent effect.

48 *Problems and Solutions*

may be crucial to encourage communities to support investments and workers to train for new careers.

Concerns about future jobs are impactful. Outside the entrance to a coal mine in a white trailer that had been converted into an office, Alex had a conversation with a coal miner and another resident from Southwest Pennsylvania that illustrates the impact of uncertainty.

AFG: You said that some of the people who are young, the way they think about coal has changed because of what's happened to the industry. Has that affected your ability to recruit people?

Miner: Yes. Some people are hesitant to come to work for a coal mine that they're not sure how long it will be here or operating. And a lot of people left the industry because just coming to work not knowing day to day if things are going to be good.

Resident: And I think of the stress it would have on you and your family.

Miner: Yeah. I've went through it, honestly. When I first started in the coal industry, you know, I grew up with coal. My dad was a coal miner. We had a good life, made good money. I started out when I got out of college. If you could get in coal mining you were like set. You know you were going to be taken care of. You have a good job. You can retire there. And then in the last six to eight years when...the down spiral started, it started to get really concerning...and then it's like, every couple of years, you're wondering...

Resident: ...what's next.

Miner: Yes, what's next.[22]

The ups and downs of coal have impacted miners, their families, and their communities. The uncertainty also dampened recruitment, which could help the energy transition if people increasingly doubt the security of fossil fuel jobs.

Concerns about growth may be especially salient for new industries. This matters for the energy transition, which will require the widespread adoption of new technologies. Take electric cars. Lordstown Motors, an EV upstart, took over an old General Motors plant and promised to revitalize the Ohio community. However, a series of delays, scandals, and market changes left production in limbo (Domonoske, 2021). Rivian has struggled to convince communities that the jobs will last since few electric car companies have successfully brought vehicles to market (Scheiber, 2021b).

New industries may also rely on government support, which raises concerns about credibility that we unpacked above. Renewable energy has undergone a series of booms and busts driven partly by policy pendulum swings and design flaws. To name a few examples, inflated solar

[22] Interview, August 9, 2021.

tax credits in New Jersey caused a flood of projects that led to a subsequent price collapse (Walton, 2018). Illinois' solar incentive programs spurred over-expansion beyond the program's resources, which resulted in layoffs once funds ran dry (SEIA, 2020). Nevada faced a self-imposed collapse of solar energy after the public utility commission allowed for an increase in fees imposed on residential solar (Hernandez, 2016; Stokes, 2020). At the federal level in the United States, there is a patchwork of programs that "are poorly optimized, characterized by a boom and bust cycle of aid and withdrawal" (Jenkins et al., 2012, p. 5). The wind production tax credit (PTC), for instance, has expired three times since the 1990s (Barradale, 2010).[23]

Local Jobs

Investments must deliver local benefits if they are to earn the support of communities and make sure none are left behind. However, just because an investment attracts a business to a location does not guarantee that the jobs will go to community members. We refer to this dimension of economic opportunity as local jobs.

There are several reasons why jobs might not go to community members. An occupation could require technical skills that the local workforce does not possess. Expectations that there will not be future jobs in the area might undermine incentives to invest in skills. An industry could be transitory, as is common with construction projects, where firms prefer to use the same traveling team because of the transaction costs of hiring afresh in each community. Local workers could also be unionized and demand higher wages that companies do not want to pay.

In our conversations with local officials and energy developers, the lack of a trained local workforce often constrained their ability to hire from the area. Terry from Carbon County described how the wind industry provided "a lot of jobs" such as "restaurant, motel, and gas station workers, but most of these people who work on the wind farms are very specially trained people, and we didn't have that pool."[24] A National Laboratory study of the Rush Creek Wind Farm in Colorado found that there was an "influx of temporary workers" due in part to the shallow local talent pool (Stefek et al., 2019, p. ix). Other analyses of challenges to renewable energy development have identified the need to create local jobs (e.g., Ceres, 2020).

---

[23] The IRA hopes to solve some of these issues.
[24] Interview, November 3, 2022.

50   *Problems and Solutions*

The lack of local jobs could threaten the ability of reformers to create allies in the energy transition.[25] In North Dakota, only 14 percent of wind construction jobs at some projects have gone to locals (Franco, 2019a). Unions in Minnesota have fought political battles with multinational developers who hire crews that travel from Texas, Utah, and California to take jobs created by new wind projects (see Chapter 8). A Republican official we surveyed from Ohio expressed pessimism, "we have had approximately 4,000 solar panels added to our community in 4 separate projects. All jobs were from outside companies that added no new jobs to our area or community." A Democrat from Wisconsin said, "the more local support, the better it will be accepted by the community."

The fear of outside labor can also impact other aspects of the transition, such as workforce development. For example, one concern raised by automobile workers about the EV transition is that outside specialists would replace them. One worker said, "I think that if they have to hire new people to retool it...They'll try to bring in people from the outside" (Foster et al., 2022, p. 13). This expectation could discourage people from training for jobs in new green industries, which would exacerbate the local jobs problem by suppressing the pool of local talent.

Pay

The next dimension of local economic opportunity is pay, which is the belief about whether salaries in an industry will rise or fall. People do not want any job. They would like a career that offers a good livelihood. This is especially true when one's current occupation provides secure pay and benefits.

Clean energy jobs may not be seen as an economic opportunity that makes workers and communities better off than fossil fuel industries due to their relatively lower pay. A snapshot from the Bureau of Labor Statistics (2021) estimates that solar panel installers earn a median hourly wage of $22.55, wind service technicians bring in $29.19, and electricians receive $28.87. These are clean energy jobs that will be created by the green transition. By contrast, the median hourly wage for construction and extraction occupations in coal mining is $29.54, while oil and gas make $36.47, while mechanics at fossil fuel electric power plans bring in $46.86. Pay within and across industries can also differ with

---

[25] These concerns are not unique to green jobs. When the gas boom took off in Pennsylvania, many of the early jobs went to outside teams from Oklahoma and Texas (Interview with Southwest Pennsylvania County Official, May 27, 2021).

unionization rates.[26] Even when the government invests in green jobs, wages often remain stagnant. For every $1 million of green stimulus after the 2008 financial crisis, 15 new jobs emerged, nearly all in manual labor, which did not see wage gains (Popp et al., 2020).

Pay is a meaningful feature of jobs that could impact the speed of the energy transition. Workers in an oil-rich part of Wyoming "expressed concern over what [wind] jobs would pay, saying the salaries paled in comparison to what they could earn on an oil rig" (Cardwell, 2017). Local officials we surveyed stressed the importance of good pay and benefits to make green jobs succeed. One Democrat from a township in Pennsylvania said, "[to] make jobs that pay enough to support families not $10.00 to $15.00 per hour, more like $21.00 to $31.00 per hour to start, with healthcare benefits." A Republican from a county in South Dakota remarked, "jobs that pay well, with benefits." People must believe that the career to which they transition will provide an income and benefits that sustain good livelihoods. Otherwise, they might not leap into an uncertain future.

Temporariness

The final but not exhaustive component of local economic opportunity is temporariness. Temporariness is the perception that careers in an industry are short-lived because of the nature of the task. Temporariness presents a challenge for renewable energy, which tends to be capital intensive since much of the investment goes to purchasing large assets like solar panels or wind turbines. Although the initial construction of solar arrays and wind farms generates employment, those jobs disappear upon project completion, and it takes only a handful of people to operate facilities once online. Greg Lerud, the city administrator of Becker said that the solar plant jobs "will be temporary during the construction of the farm, but then it was like a dozen employees or something like that long-term to maintain it..."[27]

In a Southwest Pennsylvania community where there are plans to build a solar farm, one resident remarked, "realistically, solar jobs, and I don't mean to sound that this is a negative, but solar jobs are not going to take the manpower of a mine. It will never truly be a replacement. I mean, obviously, any job is going to be a good thing. But realistically,

---

[26] While there is regional variation, fossil fuel jobs are relatively more unionized, which can contribute to their higher pay (Scheiber, 2021a).

[27] Interview, August 30, 2022.

that's not going to be a replacement for a mine worker."[28] In another coal community, a developer noted that "[a]ll but a dozen of the solar jobs will be temporary, lasting between 12 to 18 months..." (Buckley, 2022).

Concerns about temporariness also arose in our survey of local officials. A Republican from Oregon said, "We have many solar arrays in our county, none of which supply power locally. They provide 'temporary' work at best for our local community." One Republican from a municipality in Washington state said, "locally, we have some large renewable energy projects, both solar and wind. There are very few permanent jobs that come along with them." But this same official proposed solutions to create long-lasting jobs, solutions that we reveal in this chapter.

Comparing Futures

While we have discussed future jobs, local jobs, pay, and temporariness in absolute terms, relative assessments that compare a new industry to incumbent employers may matter most. For example, if residents of West Virginia viewed coal as on the decline due to market forces, they might be more inclined to try new opportunities despite uncertainty. However, if fossil fuel energy communities view their jobs as secure, they might resist change. There is a psychological bias to avoid losses and overvalue what one presently has, which could make people hesitant to embrace change (e.g., Kahneman and Tversky, 1979).

Social identity plays a role in these relative assessments. In fossil fuel communities, sociologists and political scientists document a strong affinity to extractive industries. The strength of this identity is partially the consequence of a political project of elites who try to shape residents' views with the memory of previous generations that have made sacrifices (Bell and York, 2010; Gaventa, 1982), but these appeals are also effective because of their emotional resonance. Lewin (2019) records how community members view coal mining as a "way of life." Coal miners are proud of how their jobs power the country, which echoes Lamont (2000) description of how working men value the dignity and respect that their jobs confer. The strength of this social identity influences the policy preferences of individuals from fossil fuel communities (Gaikwad, Genovese, and Tingley, 2022b). If a new career does not afford the same feeling of dignity, workers might resist the transition.

---

[28] Interview, August 9, 2021.

Stop Complaining and Start Solving 53

The racial and gender composition of industries can also shape evaluations of economic opportunities. Women and people of color may not see industries that lack diversity as viable paths to make themselves and their communities better off. Green industries tend to be older, male-dominated, and lack racial diversity (e.g., E2, 2021). This can make it harder for individuals from marginalized groups to find careers since they may be outside social networks or fear they would not have the same professional opportunities. A solar instructor in North Carolina explained,

these communities maybe don't know about the industry as much because traditionally they don't have friends or families who are in it. Just to get people to know that this industry exists and that it's here to stay would help. There's a feeling that it might be another boom-bust cycle that it could be done.[29]

In Chapter 7, we unpack these issues to learn how to make workforce development equitable, inclusive, and just.

STOP COMPLAINING AND START SOLVING

The energy transition must solve a two-part problem. First, the government must convince workers, their families, and communities that it will deliver on its promises of compensation and investment. Nongovernmental organizations that work on the transition also face these issues in their engagements. Firms, too, confront credibility challenges as they transition their workforces for the future. Second, the places impacted by the clean energy transition must believe that they would be better off with the compensation and investments offered. The previous section explained why government promises can lack credibility and why the economic opportunities in new industries might not be self-evident.

We now turn to solutions to create credibility and local economic opportunity. For each idea, we provide specific recommendations that we evaluate in subsequent chapters. The aim is to better understand the constraints and opportunities that governments face when they make political reforms. This knowledge should help to inform policies that will be durable and effective. Of course, the appropriate policy will depend on the local context. Our framework should be interpreted not solely as a menu of interventions ready to be taken off the shelf but as a set of design constraints that stakeholders should consider when they craft policies.

These policies might not be efficient in the conventional economic sense. However, do not conflate efficiency with feasibility. Political

[29] Interview, August 16, 2022.

Problems and Solutions

constraints like credibility mean that the most efficient policy might not garner political support. "[E]ven a durable 'bad' policy is better than a fragile 'good' one" (Patashnik, 2014, p. 6). Once passed, reformers can build upon these policies to improve their efficiency.[30] The critical challenge is to make the initial, durable reform.

Institutional Constraints

Institutional constraints are a powerful tool to make commitments credible (e.g., Weingast and Marshall, 1988). Our focus departs from large, hard-to-change institutions like the rules for how elections work. Instead, we examine specific policies that could alleviate credibility concerns. The main idea is that the ease of policy reversal differs according to the rules, procedures, and norms for lawmaking (e.g., Shepsle, 1991). Reformers can leverage these tools to decrease the likelihood that opponents overturn compensation and investments. We propose three specific institutional strategies that could enhance durability: pass laws rather than executive orders, delegate to independent groups like communities, and insulate funding from pendulum swings.

Lead with Laws

Legislation represents an especially credible policy instrument compared with other vehicles, such as executive action. For example, in the United States, executive orders by presidents can be overturned with the stroke of a pen, whereas it takes a majority in both the House and the Senate to rewrite a law. It also requires a highly visible action to overturn a law, which raises barriers to reversal (Brunner, Flachsland, and Marschinski, 2012; Lazarus, 2009).

Laws can be difficult to pass, so the remainder of this chapter introduces strategies to build credibility when the legislative option is not available. But as a starting point, laws are worth the struggle. Even controversial legislation like the Superfund program for toxic waste sites and the Affordable Care Act (ACA) for health coverage have proven resistant to major changes despite strident criticism. Some of the endurance is due to the benefits of these programs, which we discuss later. Durability can also stem from the challenges to pass legislation in the first place, which also confront any subsequent attempts to amend or repeal a law (e.g., Posner, 2014). Of course, laws are not immune to reversal,

---

[30] This is the idea of policy sequencing (e.g., Pahle et al., 2018).

Stop Complaining and Start Solving 55

and their durability varies with political context (Maltzman and Shipan, 2008). The way that a law delegates authority and structures funding also influences its staying power, which we examine next.

Stop Hogging the Ball: Delegate to Communities

Who gets to make decisions can shape the government's credibility. The classic illustration comes from the economists Douglass North and Barry Weingast (1989), who argue that institutional changes in who had the power to levy taxes explain the success of Great Britain's industrialization.[31] Before the Glorious Revolution of 1688, the monarch could spend lavishly at the cost of the British public, which hindered economic development. The revolution redistributed political power from the monarchy to the parliament, which helped the government make its commitments not indiscriminately to tax credible.

Luckily, there are ways to alter who makes decisions that do not require a revolution. Delegation is one approach that policymakers frequently employ (e.g., Miller and Whitford, 2016; Rogoff, 1985). Delegation is where a principal, such as a president, confers decision-making authority to an agent, such as a bureaucrat. If the agent has distinct preferences, she can carry out actions that the principal would have otherwise reneged on if the principal were in charge. One can think of the Glorious Revolution of 1688 as an instance where a predatory state, the monarch, was forced to delegate expropriation power to an agent with different preferences, a Parliament of property owners.[32] Of course, the principal has to have the incentive to delegate power in the first place.

For the energy transition, the government could delegate authority over policy implementation to an independent agency (e.g., Brunner, Flachsland, and Marschinski, 2012; Lazarus, 2009), or to the communities that will be impacted by compensation or investments. The independent agency or communities could have the ability to decide what investments to make. One could also set up an insulated revenue stream to further protect the organization from outside influences.[33]

Delegation to communities could be a powerful tool to create credibility. With greater local input, people may perceive the process as more inclusive, which enhances the legitimacy and effectiveness of the political

---

[31] But see Stasavage (2002), who argues that partisan interests and cross-issue coalitions also matter, an issue we take up when we discuss coalition building as a strategy.

[32] Central banks are another example (Rogoff, 1985).

[33] The Federal Reserve Board, for example, can raise revenue from its operations.

56   *Problems and Solutions*

reforms (e.g., Fishkin, 2011). Community members could also participate in the design of projects, which helps them understand and see the benefits (e.g., Ferry and Monoian, 2023). However, community involvement is not a panacea. Representatives from an area may not reflect the views of the entire community, and local input could be subverted to veto meaningful policies as seen with the growth of "not in my backyard" (NIMBY) opposition to renewable energy (e.g., Carley et al., 2020). Delegation must strike a balance.[34]

Protect the Purse and Insulate Funding

Clever reformers can design policies to insulate funding from reversals. One way to do this is to minimize how often funds must be renewed, which reduces opportunities for opponents to kill a reform. For example, the Farm Bill in the United States is renewed every five years. This avoids a problem that used to plague wind energy investors, where tax credits had to be re-authorized every year and sometimes fell through the cracks (Barradale, 2010). Reformers could also raise revenue with popular policies, such as closing tax loopholes, which might decrease public pressure for reversal.

Another approach is to create trust funds that solve credible commitment problems by insulating access to resources (Patashnik, 2000). Trust funds are restricted for specific purposes and differ from general revenues. They can even be self-sustaining. For example, Chapter 6 discusses the Black Lung Disability Trust Fund, a health program for coal workers. While trust funds are not always immune to tampering, a problem the black lung fund has faced, this approach helps to insulate funding and can even tie the hands of future leaders.

Hand-tying

Hand-tying eliminates or raises the cost of alternative options that might be desirable in the future (e.g., Fearon, 1997; Spence, 1976). The classic example is Ulysses in the Odyssey, who longs to hear the song of the

---

[34] Another challenge is that the agent is often not set up to succeed. Interest groups can influence the design of agencies (e.g., Moe, 1990). However, lawmakers can counterbalance this bias with tools like fixed term limits of agency appointees (e.g., Lewis, 2004). Despite the inevitable bias, delegation may be better for credibility than leaving matters in the hands of politicians with short-term reelection incentives that could exacerbate policy uncertainty. For a review, see Gailmard and Patty (2012a,b).

Stop Complaining and Start Solving

Sirens but fears he will not be able to prevent himself from jumping overboard. Ulysses has his sailors tie him to the mast and plug their ears with wax, eliminating the option of heeding the Sirens' song. What Ulysses did can be thought of as an individual commitment device. When it comes to the government and relationships between individuals or groups, there are also strategies to tie the hands of leaders – present and future.

Of course, there is an inherent tension where tying hands can limit desirable future responsiveness (Rodrik and Zeckhauser, 1988). The value of responsiveness will depend on the particular issue but is a valid consideration that must be weighed. Sometimes hand-tying could even enhance responsiveness, if policies lock in dynamic responsiveness through fixed decision rules or create incentives for leaders to act in the public's best interest when they otherwise would not have.

Autopilot: Devise Fixed Decision Rules

One hand-tying strategy is to require that the government follows a fixed decision rule (e.g., Kydland and Prescott, 1977; Rodrik and Zeckhauser, 1988).[35] An example of a fixed decision rule is how Congress indexes the size of Social Security payments to the cost of living. This automatic procedure eliminates the discretion of lawmakers to cut benefits and fosters confidence in the program's durability. While the government could disregard the rule, the procedure forces politicians to take visible action to contravene the institution.

For climate policy, fixed rules could serve as a hand-tying device for emissions mitigation targets.[36] One could also imagine various ways to create fixed rules for compensation and investments. For example, payments for lost income could be indexed to cost of living changes. Funding for training programs could be required to increase as the number of communities in need expands.

Constrain with (Future) Costs

Another hand-tying strategy is to change future leaders' incentives to maintain a reform. One such example developed by the economists Alberto Alesina and Guido Tabellini (1990) is for the government to accumulate debt that constrains the policy choices of a successor. The

---

[35] This is also an institutional constraint.

[36] However, these proposals have fallen by the wayside due to enforcement concerns (Hovi, Sprinz, and Underdal, 2009, pp. 23–24).

next leader would be forced to pay the bills or spend less on other priorities.

Inspired by this logic, in Chapter 7, we develop a related hand-tying mechanism. We show how the government could take on debt to finance workforce training loans that would not have to be paid back if there are no future green job opportunities. This policy would incentivize a future government to continue supporting green investments that help workers find jobs, so the government gets paid back. Otherwise, there would be a budget shortfall that forces a trade-off with other political priorities.

Of course, the strategy to use costs to constrain future leaders must strike a careful balance. For example, the tax burden of policies can serve as a motivation for reversal, which could create a political barrier to tying hands in the first place. But if hands can be tied, the incentives become self-reinforcing and could deter reversal by even those dissatisfied with the price of a program.

Together Is Better? Link Issues

Another strategy to constrain future leaders is issue linkage. This is when two groups connect agreement on one issue with cooperation on another (e.g., Axelrod and Keohane, 1985; Davis, 2004). Issue linkage could provide an avenue to create durable bargains, especially when the issues are complementary (Currarini and Marchiori, 2022). For example, the IRA coupled inflation reduction measures with green investments. Strategic policymakers could link support for the energy transition to issues that have bipartisan support, such as infrastructure spending, which could make opponents think twice before pursuing reversal.[37] Governments might also tie promises for compensation and green investments to broader international climate commitments to create diplomatic costs if they fail to follow through (e.g., Fearon, 1994; Lazarus, 2009; Tingley and Tomz, 2021).[38]

Coalition Building

Not only do institutions matter, but so too do the preferences of the public, parties, and interest groups (e.g., Stasavage, 2002). These political

---

[37] Of course, reformers must be able to credibly threaten not to cooperate on the issue to which they seek to link the energy transition.

[38] However, the Trump administration was happy to withdraw from the Paris Agreement, so it is not clear that such costs would be a sufficient constraint given the distributive stakes.

Stop Complaining and Start Solving 59

actors form the basis of coalitions that could support or oppose a reform. One cause of policy reversal identified above is that political parties have different preferences.[39] One party might oppose any action on climate change, whereas another would immediately ban fossil fuel extraction, while others fall in between these extremes. When a party inevitably loses power, the winner could roll back any progress that has been made on the energy transition.

Red and Blue Glue: Build Bipartisan Support

However, this political pendulum need not swing drastically if compensation and investment policies have bipartisan support. Political parties and the national public do not have to be dogmatic opponents of climate policy. Advocates could build coalitions that appeal to bipartisanship and foster national consensus. The fact of bipartisanship and the existence of a national consensus, in turn, should enhance the credibility of the government's promises (which we show in Chapter 5). Bipartisanship can insulate a policy from reversal since neither party could muster the votes to overturn or significantly amend the status quo. While bipartisanship does not eliminate the possibility of reversal, since coalitions can fall apart, the strategy should provide short-term credibility that enables the implementation of additional commitment devices for the long term.[40]

It is not a simple task to build bipartisan coalitions, especially in countries like the United States where there is a high level of partisan polarization (e.g., McCarty, Poole, and Rosenthal, 2006). While it is beyond the scope of this book to solve polarization, there are reasons for why it is still a fruitful task to contemplate the possibility of a bipartisan climate coalition. Consider the United States. First, green jobs hold the potential to deliver tangible economic benefits in both Democratic and Republican areas (e.g., Tomer, Kane, and George, 2021). Job creation is a bread-and-butter issue for which election-motivated politicians love to claim credit, so politicians from both parties could gain if they back the green transition.[41] While the opposition has disproportionately come

---

[39] See Gard-Murray and Henderson (n.d.) for additional perspectives on uncertainty and coalition building in climate transitions.

[40] See Arnold (1990) and Niskanen (2003), but also Maltzman and Shipan (2008), on bipartisanship and divided government.

[41] Stokes and Warshaw (2017) find that Republicans become more supportive of renewable energy when the issue is framed in terms of economic benefits. Conservative clean energy advocates also appeal to how renewable energy can help property owners reclaim freedom from power companies (interview with clean energy trade group member, September 21, 2022).

from Republican lawmakers at the federal level, it is also in Republican-controlled states like Texas and Iowa where renewable energy sources like wind have grown considerably, but not without a fight (Stokes, 2020). Taken together, it is plausible that members of both parties could align on the energy transition if there are credible benefits. That is not to say this is easy to do.

Second, there is evidence that divided government does not impede the passage of significant reforms (Mayhew, 2005, but see Binder, 2003). For example, the last major environmental statute, the 1990 acid rain law we discuss in Chapter 6, passed with a Republican-controlled White House and Democrat-controlled Congress. While bipartisanship may seem elusive, the possibility of electoral benefits from green jobs and the history of major legislation despite divisions suggests that the energy transition could garner support across the aisle.

Reveal Common Ground and Shift Expectations

One barrier to bipartisan consensus is a self-fulfilling prophecy where the *expectation* of opposition leads people to not try to forge consensus. This paradoxically reinforces the belief that bipartisanship is not possible.

However, there is evidence that the public supports compensation and investment for fossil fuel communities, at least in the United States and Germany (e.g., Gaikwad, Genovese, and Tingley, 2022b; Mares, Scheve, and Toenshoff, 2022). Yet, people may not be aware that others share these beliefs. One example is that the public often underestimates the extent to which others believe climate change is happening and merits action. These erroneous "second-order beliefs" may inhibit broader support for climate policies (Mildenberger and Tingley, 2019). The logic of this argument mirrors the explanation that Timur Kuran (1991) gives for why revolutions can be so unexpected. People do not know how many other people share their views, but once they see other people in the street protesting, they learn that they are not alone and become willing to engage in collective action.[42] Political reformers could shift expectations about the size of the coalition that supports compensation and investments by revealing information about the true level of support (see Chapter 5).

There is no single route to build societal consensus. One insight from studies of public opinion about welfare is that support for targeted

---

[42] Economists study similar situations, such as those around reporting sexual misconduct (Cheng and Hsiaw, 2022).

Stop Complaining and Start Solving

programs often depends on whether the public perceives the recipients as deserving (e.g., Gilens, 2000). Views about who deserves to receive help from the government are complex and often colored by race, class, and gender. One must also convince residents in these communities that the government would follow through with its promises. The solutions in this chapter, such as giving communities a seat at the table and building bipartisan consensus, could help. Messages from trusted leaders at local and national levels could also build confidence in the national consensus behind the energy transition.

Lock-in Effects

The next way to reduce the threat of policy reversal is to generate lock-in effects. Here's how it works. Individuals, communities, and firms that oppose economic transitions can be converted to supporters by providing them benefits from political reform. There are two ways that these benefits can enhance policy durability.

First, as voters, communities, and companies reap the gains of a political reform, they become a new political constituency that will mobilize to defend their benefits (e.g., Meckling et al., 2015). This is most effective when people expect a future stream of benefits that depends on the sustained implementation of the political reform and when the benefits go to former opponents, in effect buying them off so these groups would have little to gain from reversal (Patashnik, 2014).

The second way that lock-in effects manifest is through increasing returns. This is the logic of path dependence (e.g., Pierson, 2000). A policy made today alters subsequent policies and investments, which influence the costs and benefits of future attempts at reversal. If people, communities, and companies expect a political reform to set the country down a path that will be hard to turn back because each subsequent step becomes easier as clean technology costs decline, the fear of policy reversal should fall.

Create New Constituencies

One way to generate lock-in effects is to make place-based investments in communities. These investments can create targeted benefits, such as new green jobs and tax revenue, which empower new constituencies that will now have a stake in the energy transition and also weaken ties to incumbent fossil fuel industries (e.g., Aklin and Urpelainen, 2013; Meckling et al., 2015; Pahle et al., 2018). As these green constituencies gain political power, there is a feedback effect where pro-climate groups can push to expand and defend initial reforms.[43] Even if the benefits accrue to opponents of the initial policy, these economic rewards could help the reform endure (Aldy, 2019, p. 162). This is the approach that reformers have taken with recent laws like the IRA. The wave of clean energy investment to red states has started to make some skeptics warm to green jobs (e.g., Eckhouse, 2022), but whether this sticks remains to be seen.

One concept that is useful for thinking about when the benefits of reform can lock in support is asset specificity (e.g., Williamson, 1989). A highly specific asset is one that can be used for only one purpose, like a solar panel, as opposed to an asset that can be used for many purposes, like a warehouse. If reforms encourage investments in specific assets, the profitability of their investments will depend on the reform staying in place, so they become strong defenders. Once power companies build solar farms, for instance, they will want the flow of green subsidies to continue. Asset specificity can be both a source of credible commitment problems because firms fear being taken advantage of, as described above, but it can also contribute to the durability of a reform once businesses make investments.

Provide Incentives to Stay

Investments could also encourage lock-in effects at the individual level. For example, place-based investments could incentivize people to stay in the community. A training program could encourage skills specific to a new industry with a comparative advantage in a location. This encouragement might be needed because, as discussed above, individuals might be reluctant to build highly specific skills, but once such skill sets are in place, the knowledge that fellow community members will not leave because their new training creates an incentive to stay. This should reduce the race to the bottom dynamics where communities are hollowed out by population loss as people leave for opportunities elsewhere.

Invest in Communities

One benefit that the energy transition could offer communities is new sources of tax revenue. As we highlight in Chapter 1, the tax revenue generated by fossil fuels is valuable. Localities use these funds to provide public goods like social services, infrastructure, and schools. The

---

[43] Part of the political logic of cap-and-trade programs is that the tradable emissions permits would create a political constituency to defend the program (Lazarus, 2009).

Stop Complaining and Start Solving 63

energy transition could threaten this source of revenue for communities. However, reformers could also turn this liability into an advantage by structuring renewable and energy infrastructure investments in ways that provide tax revenue to localities.[44] Yet, green projects do not always take advantage of these potential local benefits. In California, clean energy projects are exempt from property tax. While that encourages the deployment of renewables, it also decreases their ability to generate lock-in effects via revenue (Plumer, 2022). If taxes increased, the projects could move to other areas, given state-level disparities in renewable energy tax rates, or not be deployed in the first place (Cook and Godby, 2019).

Provide Private Benefits

Renewable energy projects are not the only contentious development that must be built. Transmission lines are needed in vast numbers but are in short supply because of permit difficulties and community opposition. Yet when a transmission line goes through one's property, the landowner receives little to no benefit. But it need not be that way. The property owner could get a cut of the profit. Perhaps people who once opposed transmission lines would welcome them with open arms. Fossil fuel industries have learned this lesson. People with oil and gas wells on their land often receive royalties and even free gas for their homes. Some have already applied this lesson to renewable energy and transmission, and it could be leveraged more ambitiously.

Reputation

The second credibility challenge discussed above concerns whether the government truly represents the interests of the public and has the ability to do so (e.g., Spence, 1973). The trustworthiness of the government is crucial here. A powerful way to solve this problem is for the government to build a reputation for keeping promises and performing costly actions (Keohane, 1984; Milgrom, North, and Weingast, 1990; Ostrom, 1998). Of the many ways to build a reputation, we propose two concrete steps: governments should provide opportunities for public input, and supply accurate and useful information.

---

[44] One study on wind energy found that it increased county revenue by 22 percent through an expansion of the property tax base (Brunner and Schwegman, 2022). Yet this is context-specific because not all green energy projects raise revenue.

Care to Listen: Provide Opportunities for Public Input

The government can build a reputation for fairness with process-oriented steps that allow communities to participate in decision-making. A government that does not seek local input risks developing a reputation that it does not care about the interests of citizens. When local stakeholders have a voice and feel included, political scientist Margaret Levi (1998, p. 92) shows how this can help the community understand the issues at stake, which fosters trust.[45] The perception that a procedure is fair increases the acceptability of even unfavorable decisions, including compliance with costly measures (Grimes, 2017, p. 261). When local governments have open meetings, this helps to "shore up the perception of access, accountability, and responsiveness" (Jennings, 1998, p. 240).

What this could look like for the energy transition is community input about what investments to make, where to develop renewable energy, and how to help workers transition to new careers. There is some evidence that the process matters for renewable energy projects. For example, one study surveyed residents before and after a wind project's construction to see how residents' perceptions of benefits and negative impacts changed. They found that although direct financial compensation to landowners had a short-term effect on attitudes, perceptions about whether the process was fair had a strong relationship with perceived benefits and costs (Mills, Bessette, and Smith, 2019).

Local input already exists to some extent in the United States, which reflects a recognition of its importance by citizens, leaders, and businesses. However, in Chapter 5, we find that local officials believe more community participation is needed to deliver benefits from green investments. Economic transitions in American fossil fuel communities have not always taken the consultative path, whereas relatively more successful countries like Germany and Canada have included stakeholders as a central part of their approach.

As with all solutions, one must be clear-eyed about their limitations. More opportunities for consultation and input could slow the green energy build-out, which could be inconsistent with the need to construct as much renewable energy as possible. However, community input might ultimately be necessary to make the energy transition durable (e.g., Chase

---

[45] There is evidence that partnerships with local organizations can improve faith in government (Metcalf et al., 2015).

and Gearino, 2022). Some governments want to provide genuine opportunities for community input. But doing this right takes time. Yet, efforts to lock in benefits require getting money out the door as quickly as possible. One credibility solution can run into another. Reformers must be mindful of these trade-offs.

Hit the Bull's Eye: Supply Accurate and Useful Information

Another way to improve reputation is to consistently supply accurate and useful information (e.g., Sobel, 1985). There are opportunities to do so when it comes to climate transitions where uncertainty abounds. The physical causes and effects of global warming are complex, and so are the political and economic transformations required to reduce fossil fuel use and adapt to climate change. Navigating these transitions requires tremendous amounts of information. This could include information about how localities could adapt to higher temperatures, the efficacy of new technologies, the availability of jobs in green industries, the impacts of offshore wind on local fisheries, and updates about permit applications for energy and transmission. One local official we surveyed in California described how a barrier to the energy transition is that "it's challenging to measure the data." This official is not alone. The National Research Council (2009) issued a report entitled, *Informing Decisions in a Changing Climate*, which documents a range of knowledge needed to respond to global warming. While less focused on the political dimensions of the transition, one helpful observation from the report is that opportunities for local input can facilitate information provision.

However, information must be believed. Even when information is accurate, individuals, communities, and local leaders may not trust or be persuaded by it. COVID-19 is just one instance where some members of the public and elected leaders dismissed information from federal and state health officials. Interestingly, one line of research considers how bias could aid with persuasion. When one conveys information contrary to her interests, this can be particularly persuasive (Calvert, 1985). For example, when a Republican from a fossil fuel state, such as Congressman Graves of Louisiana, says "we've got to reduce our emissions," this is seen as an unusually credible piece of information because it runs against expectations (Wallace-Wells, 2019).

Another challenge is that it is costly to generate and disseminate knowledge. However, this barrier could be turned into a strength. The cost to provide information could serve as a signal about the government's commitment. One has to collect data, verify it, and aggregate it in helpful ways. Each step requires the expenditure of resources by governments (or companies). This is related to an additional route to generate credibility that we explore next.

Costly Signals

Governments can take costly actions to create credibility; that is, send a costly signal. The idea is that only those who are committed would incur such a cost, whereas the noncommitted would not. A costly signal helps to reveal information about a government's (or business') true interests and abilities to fulfill its promises. Do they care about a community? Are they willing and able to work hard to defend their interests?

One illustration of this idea is job markets. A problem employers face is how to determine if a candidate is productive. An applicant can signal that she is productive with costly actions such as earning a college degree (Spence, 1973). Another example from politics is when leaders mobilize troops to convince their adversaries that their threats are not just cheap talk (Fearon, 1997). We propose two costly signals the government could send in the context of economic transitions.

We'll Help: Assume Risks Others Wouldn't

Governments could assume some of the economic risks from transitions. The public may think that an uncommitted government would not be willing to incur this cost, so the action to absorb the transition risk would reveal the government's true interests and ability to fulfill its promises. A concrete example is conditional loan repayment for training programs (which we explore in Chapter 7). The government could provide student loans for people to train for green jobs. If not enough green jobs are created, the trainees would not have to pay back their loans – that is, repayment is conditional and the government absorbs the risk. Such a program would show that leaders are genuinely committed to creating new green jobs and will pay the price if they fail to do so (it would also tie the hands of future leaders).

Another strategy is for the federal or state government to fill the gap for lost tax revenue in places where fossil fuel production declines. Of course, an empty promise to do this would not be seen as credible. However, upfront payments would be seen as costly and also provide a cushion for localities to invest in economic diversification.

Conclusion 67

Be Bold: Make Unexpected Investments
Governments could make investments that an uncommitted administration would not have, such as visible investments in schools, infrastructure, and public services beyond what is anticipated. Expenditures should be guaranteed rather than contingent and immediate rather than delayed to increase the perceived costliness. Since governments face budget trade-offs, the amount a politician spends is informative about her priorities. Previous work has argued that climate policy should be coupled with broader social programs (e.g., Bergquist, Mildenberger, and Stokes, 2020). Our argument suggests that these extra investments also serve as signaling devices that enhance the government's credibility.

Transparency

There are a variety of tools that have been proposed to create local economic opportunities from green jobs. For instance, there are active efforts to enact policies that encourage the use of union labor to build renewable energy. The IRA, for example, allows companies to receive higher tax credits if they pay prevailing wages and employ registered apprentices. Washington state linked labor standards with its clean energy tax incentives (Cliffton et al., 2021, p. 8). Another idea is to establish tax credits with provisions that allow local governments to "clawback" the credits if companies failed to create local jobs or deliver community benefits.

However, these well-intentioned policies confront an overarching challenge. Governments and firms cannot be held accountable for promises if nobody knows they are broken. For this reason, transparency is crucial. One way to provide transparency is to create institutions that supply information that enables accountability. The content of information could range from the actions of politicians to the outcomes of investment. The supply of information should help the public better hold politicians accountable for their promises (e.g., Holmström, 1979). The logic could also apply to firms that make promises of economic benefits from renewable energy projects. Chapter 8 shows how and when transparency can enhance local economic opportunity.

CONCLUSION

This chapter diagnoses why the energy transition has been so slow despite the possibility of compensation and the promise of green investments. The answer becomes clear when one considers the challenge from the ground up – that is, from the perspective of individuals, communities, and firms. The first source of the problem is the lack of government credibility. Even if a government brought to bear all of its resources to compensate workers and communities impacted by the energy transition or to invest in clean energy, there is a fundamental strategic challenge. These promises might not be believed. People might rightly think that in the future, economic or political conditions can change, the government does not truly have the public's interests at heart, or leaders lack the ability to fulfill their promises. This is crucial because the energy transition will require sustained, long-term support.

The second dimension of the problem is local economic opportunity. New green industries might not be seen as pathways to make workers and communities better off than they were before. This can lead workers to defend their existing jobs, and communities to obstruct green energy projects. In the following two chapters, we draw on a range of data, including surveys, interviews, and local media, to systematically document how the public, local policymakers, and youths think about government credibility (Chapter 3) and local economic opportunity (Chapter 4).

Reformers are not helpless in the face of these challenges. This chapter shows how governments, and even companies, could create credibility and enhance local economic opportunity. We identify solutions that can improve credibility and trust in government: institutional constraints, hand-tying, coalition building, lock-in effects, reputation, costly signals, and transparency. Our framework adds clarity for academics, policymakers, businesses, and communities about the challenges of economic transitions and how they could be solved. For each tool, we propose specific policies such as delegation to communities, place-based investments, and building bipartisan coalitions. We hope our framework helps to better understand the problem and inspires further creative solutions.

In the second half of the book, we evaluate the effectiveness of many of these solutions. In Chapter 5, we test the effect of these solutions on credibility, trust, and support for costly reforms. Specifically, we examine when the government pursues laws, delegates to communities, and insulates funding (institutional constraints); builds bipartisan consensus, and shifts expectations by revealing common ground (coalition building); makes place-based investments and creates public and private benefits (lock-in effects); provides opportunities for public input (reputation); and makes unexpected investments (costly signals). In Chapter 7, we focus on workforce development and how using costs to constrain future leaders

Conclusion 69

(hand-tying) and assuming risks that others would not (costly signals) could encourage people to train for green jobs. Lastly, in Chapter 8, we investigate the power and limits of institutional tools to provide transparency. In doing so, we connect political economy theories with rich behavioral evidence from the ground up.

3

Asking People, Communities, and Companies

On August 3, 2015, President Barack Obama had an announcement he wished he did not have to make. With the Senate's failure to pass a cap and trade bill six years earlier, a law that would have limited carbon emissions, the White House had few options left to tackle the climate crisis. With the legislative option off the table, Obama turned to executive action that Congress could not easily obstruct. On that summer day, Obama stood in the East Room of the White House. In the front row sat Gina McCarthy, the head of the EPA. Obama had an ambitious plan to share, one that took advantage of a Supreme Court ruling that said planet-warming emissions could be regulated as a pollutant. From the podium flanked by civil society leaders, Obama heralded that "the EPA is setting the first-ever nationwide standards to end the limitless dumping of carbon pollution from power plants."

While Obama was optimistic about what his plan could do for the climate, he was sober about the politics of the issue. "Long before the details of this Clean Power Plan (CPP) were even decided, the special interests and their allies in Congress were already mobilizing to oppose it with everything they've got," he warned from the stage. Obama (2020, p. 483) recognized that executive action, especially regulations, would be threatened by the political pendulum: "GOP leaders considered the rollback of federal regulations a tier-one priority, right up there with lowering taxes on the rich."[1] It was this fear that led him to first pursue a binding law. "[T]he ultimate pathway to lasting change, we knew, lay in getting comprehensive climate legislation through Congress...Perhaps

---

[1] Perhaps this is with the benefit of hindsight.

Asking People, Communities, and Companies

most important, federal legislation would have genuine staying power, unlike regulations, which could be reversed unilaterally by a future Republican administration" (Obama, 2020, pp. 486–487).

Two years later, President Donald Trump stood before a crowd at the EPA headquarters. Surrounded by his cabinet members and basking in the applause, Trump appeared giddy. "I guess they like what we're about to sign, huh," he said as he turned to shake the hand of an ecstatic Scott Pruitt, a former fossil fuel lobbyist who now led the nation's environmental watchdog. Trump was there to announce that his administration would begin the process of scrapping Obama's climate rule. "Perhaps no single regulation threatens our miners, energy workers, and companies more than this crushing attack on American industry." Trump turned to his left, where a row of coal miners and industry executives stood. "I want to acknowledge the truly amazing people behind me on this stage: our incredible coal miners. We love our coal miners." The President went and shook the hands of each. "These people haven't had enough thanks. They've had a hard time for a long time," he continued. Trump picked up a sharpie and inked his name on the order. He held the pen above his head. "How about a miner? One of the miners. Who's the miner back there? Only the miner," searched Trump as he extended the trinket. Executive orders are fragile vessels. Obama was right.

The whiplash did not end there. While political commentary usually describes the Trump administration as eliminating Obama's climate rule, the reality is more complex. The administration, a friend of the coal industry, would have undoubtedly repealed the rule in a blink if they could. However, they were constrained by the law. Remember the Supreme Court's ruling from earlier? That decision meant the executive branch had to have a regulation in place that adhered to the letter of the law, which meant a rule that covered carbon emissions. So Trump's team ginned up the cleverly named Affordable Clean Energy (ACE) rule. The administration's lawyers devised a way to effectively eliminate Obama's earlier rule by claiming the replacement would be cheaper. Trump's EPA issued this rule in June 2019. However, the political pendulum swung back with a vengeance when a federal court struck down the replacement rule. As recently as 2022, the Supreme Court threw an additional curve ball with the *West Virginia vs. EPA* case, which limits the agency's discretion to regulate pollution – back and forth, and back again.

This political pendulum swing, among other factors, undermines the government's credibility. The consequences of this uncertainty are tangible for individuals, communities, and companies. In this chapter, we show how concerns about the government's credibility manifest in the minds of the public, elected leaders, and firms. What we find is startling. Seventy-one percent of the national public is uncertain that the government would remain committed to an investment in their community; the outlook is worse for local officials and residents of fossil fuel regions, who are even more convinced that investments will be reduced in the future. Credibility concerns are acute and must be taken seriously if the energy transition is to succeed.

PERCEPTIONS OF GOVERNMENT CREDIBILITY

For the energy transition to succeed, individuals and their communities must believe the government will not renege on promises of assistance to dislocated workers and investments in new industries. Otherwise, people who incur costs may mobilize to obstruct climate policy. Perceptions of the government's credibility may not be objective assessments, but they nonetheless could influence political behavior, which makes them consequential to understand.

In this chapter, we measure perceptions of government commitment with a diverse set of surveys fielded in samples of the national public, youths, fossil fuel community county fairs, and local policymakers. Our questions investigate whether people find government commitments to be credible. Is the government likely to honor or break its commitments? Will the government support workers who need to transition into new careers? Are local government officials concerned about government commitment?

We also extend our analysis to companies and economic decision makers. We pull together studies from different disciplines on how firms respond to changes in government policy, which highlights the presence of commitment problems between governments and companies. We review recent empirical work assessing political uncertainty's impact on renewable energy development. Then we provide the ground-up perspective on green investments with surveys of local policymakers.

The conclusion to this chapter takes up issues that exacerbate credibility concerns like government trustworthiness; the consequences of the low visibility of government programs, what political scientist Suzanne Mettler (2011) calls the "submerged state"; and the ways that social identity shapes state-society relations.

All Ears: Reaching Individuals and Leaders

ALL EARS: REACHING INDIVIDUALS AND LEADERS

In this chapter and throughout the book, we use surveys to reach individuals and leaders on the front lines of the energy transition. Surveys allow us to systematically compare attitudes, preferences, and beliefs across different groups to understand how people see the world. Here, we discuss the process to collect samples of the national public, youths, regions on the front lines of the energy transition, fossil fuel community fair-goers, and local policymakers. For those interested in why and how we reach these populations, read on; otherwise, feel free to skip straight to the results midway through this chapter.

Nation-wide

What the mass public thinks matters. Politicians, companies, and investors pay considerable sums to consultants who run polls and track social media to have a clearer picture of what people think. There is also historical and contemporary evidence that when leaders vote and formulate policy, they take the temperature of the public by reading the latest public opinion surveys (e.g., Page and Shapiro, 1983).

To capture the public's views, we take nationally representative samples of the American population. In total, we fielded eight national surveys with nonprobability quota samples that ranged from around 1,000 to 3,000 respondents. We worked with reputable survey providers to collect this data and implemented rigorous quality controls.[2]

Youths

Teenagers and young adults will play a crucial role in the energy transition. The next generation faces tough choices about their future occupations. At a personal level, these choices will influence lifelong career trajectories. At a planetary level, whether the next generation is inspired to work green jobs will influence the pace and success of the energy transition. As the environmentalist Bill McKibben articulated, "If you know a young person who wants to do something that's going to

---

[2] We contracted with the survey firm Qualtrics, and partnered with CAPS/Harris. There are slight differences in these survey providers' populations. Qualtrics includes all adults. CAPS/Harris includes registered voters. The online appendix provides further details and is available at the author's website (bit.ly/climate_appendix).

74   *Asking People, Communities, and Companies*

help the world and wants to make a good living at the same time, tell them to go become an electrician" (McKibben and Klein, 2022).

To reach youths, we collected a sample of the American public that we calibrated to have half of the respondents between 16 and 24 years of age. These respondents, especially those under 18 years, are often left out of national surveys. We reached 573 teenagers and young adults.[3]

Energy Transition Front Line Regions

National surveys have their value, but often they leave out the voices of people in places hit hardest by economic transitions. These areas tend to be rural, while national samples reflect the views of people in more populous locales. The reasons for this underrepresentation are myriad and will be familiar to those who have paid attention to debates over why polls have performed poorly in forecasting recent American elections. One challenge is survey nonresponse, where a particular segment of the population is unlikely to respond to pollsters. But the other challenge is mechanical; there are fewer people in rural areas, so any national survey by design will only include a handful of respondents from these regions. With so few respondents, it is hard to know if one's measurements are close to the truth or random noise.

We solve this challenge with targeted regional surveys that ensure adequate representation from the Gulf Coast, the Industrial Midwest, New Mexico, and the Southwest Pennsylvania area.[4] These four regions are the target of the Roosevelt Project, which aims to develop effective transition plans for these communities and with whom we fielded the surveys (Ansolabehere et al., 2022).[5] The regions capture differences in geography, exposure to climate change, and challenges as well as opportunities in the energy transition (Moniz and Kearney, 2020).

GULF COAST.   The Gulf Coast spans from Houston to New Orleans and is home to considerable oil and gas production and associated petrochemical industries. The Gulf Coast's reliance on fossil fuels makes the area economically vulnerable to the energy transition. One policymaker we surveyed from Louisiana said, "I fear [climate policy] is completely politically driven and the cost to communities that depend on gas and oil

---

[3] In subsequent survey experiments with this sample, we block randomize treatment conditions by youth and adult status.

[4] Various studies provide evidence of the value of targeted samples (Gaikwad, Genovese, and Tingley, 2022a,b; Gazmararian, 2022a,b,c; Olson-Hazboun, 2018).

[5] See https://ceepr.mit.edu/roosevelt-project/.

exploration, processing, and delivering, will be completely overlooked and forgotten," while another worried about how to "address [the] negative effects to investment with respect to lost jobs and economic value of existing industry." However, the Gulf Coast cannot afford inaction on climate change because of its vulnerability to sea level rise and intensified hurricanes.

INDUSTRIAL MIDWEST. The Industrial Midwest contains Michigan, Ohio, and Indiana. These states are the historical home to American steel and automotives. However, this area has undergone severe deindustrialization. Since 1980, 187 motor vehicle plants have closed in these three states, with painful consequences (Foster et al., 2022). The economists Anne Case and Angus Deaton (2020) document how the deterioration of job opportunities for people without college degrees in places like the Industrial Midwest has given rise to "deaths of despair" from drug and alcohol poisonings, suicide, and chronic diseases. When asked about the energy transition, one local policymaker from Ohio replied, "many other more pressing issues are affecting people. For example, opioids, homelessness, lack of mental health treatment, crime, drug dealing, etc. All of those are higher immediate priority." Green jobs have been hailed as opportunities to revitalize this region (e.g., Economist, 2009). The Industrial Heartland also has automotive manufacturing that will be impacted by the shift to EVs as part of the energy transition. Residents express in interviews a mix of fear of the unknown but also hopefulness about the potential benefits from this transition (Foster et al., 2022).

NEW MEXICO. Over 1,500 miles away from the Industrial Midwest is New Mexico. This arid and mountainous state sits at the intersection of the old fossil fuel economy and the green future. There is a legacy fossil fuel industry alongside a solar industry that continues to expand. The dual presence of these industries creates opportunities and challenges for decarbonization. New Mexico's comparative advantage in solar distinguishes the state from the other regions.

SOUTHWEST PENNSYLVANIA AREA. The Appalachian mountains cut through this region, which includes Southwest Pennsylvania and parts of Ohio and West Virginia. This is fossil fuel country. Coal was once king, but now gas – unlocked by hydraulic fracturing – takes the throne. Petrochemical industries are also taking hold, with multibillion dollar developments like the ethane cracker plant in Beaver County, Pennsylvania, that will break down gas into the building blocks for plastics. This region has also felt the effects of coal's decline and saw the meager

76 Asking People, Communities, and Companies

FIGURE 3.1 Location of survey respondents in the Gulf Coast, Industrial Midwest, New Mexico, and Southwest Pennsylvania area regional samples.

support offered by the federal and state governments. One local official from West Virginia we surveyed said, "my concern is that if we do not do anything, our economy will continue to perform poorly, and employment and population will continue to decline, as it has done for 70 years."

We successfully recruited over 1,000 individuals from each region, except for New Mexico, where we targeted 300 respondents.[6] We deliberately recruited people who live outside of core urban counties.[7] This required substantial resources and dramatically helped to reach rural respondents who are often underrepresented. Figure 3.1 uses the ZIP codes of the respondents in our regional samples to show where they reside.

Let's Go to the Fair

We also fielded highly local surveys to reach the voices of individuals in rural fossil fuel communities that can be difficult to capture. These

---

[6] Surveys fielded with Qualtrics in December 2021–April 2022.
[7] We set a quota for two-thirds of respondents to come from rural areas. This required relaxing some quotas, such as Hispanic because these regions have different racial demographics.

All Ears: Reaching Individuals and Leaders

surveys took place in the Southwest Pennsylvania area, which is home to multiple types of fossil fuel extraction such as coal, oil, and gas.[8]

To reach people who might not traditionally answer surveys, Alex set up booths at county fairs (see Figures 3.2 and 3.3). This builds on Alex's earlier work that used surveys at fairs in the region.[9] County fairs are significant cultural events that attract a broad cross-section of the community. While it is undoubtedly a peculiar sight for residents to see a graduate student from Princeton University at their fair, the community welcomed Alex, even if they were somewhat baffled at times.[10] Although this is a convenience sample, the respondents generally match local demographics in terms of gender, age, and party affiliation. The results we present also weight the respondents, so they are representative of the county in terms of age, gender, race, income, and education.[11] The first survey took place in the summer of 2021 and recruited 249 participants across two fairs. Alex returned the following summer with a new survey and collected 358 responses. Residents were surprised to see him return since their typical experience is that their area is ignored or people fly through for a one-off project. Sustained engagement is vital to build trust and foster mutual understanding.

Local Leaders and Credibility

The success of the energy transition will be in the hands of thousands of local leaders in communities around the world. These individuals on the ground will have crucial decisions, such as whether to support new renewable energy projects or direct workforce programs to emphasize green jobs. Local officials will also be critical conduits linking compensation and investments from the federal government to tangible community projects.

We surveyed elected officials in American counties, municipalities, and townships to understand the perspective of local policymakers. We partnered with CivicPulse, a nonprofit, to field the survey of local political

---

[8] We do not identify the particular county to maintain the confidentiality of the respondents.

[9] See Gazmararian (2022a,b,c).

[10] Participants received $5 for a five to ten-minute survey.

[11] We use data from the five year American Community Survey on the joint distribution of age, gender, race; the joint distribution of age, gender, and education; and the distribution of income to construct weights with raking.

FIGURE 3.2 County fairgrounds in Southwest Pennsylvania. August 2021. Source: Alexander F. Gazmararian.

leaders across the United States.[12] We focus on local officials in charge of policy. These individuals are the top elected officials or governing board

---

[12] CivicPulse handles recruitment, survey administration, and respondent de-identification. Visit www.civicpulse.org for additional background. We worked with this organization because they have rigorous protocols to respect the limited time of

FIGURE 3.3 Southwest Pennsylvania county fair survey enumeration. August 2022. Source: Colleen R. Nelson.

members of their locality. They set their communities' agendas and are accountable to voters in elections.

Localities will differ in how they feel the effects of the energy transition. For some counties, the decision is whether to permit a solar farm. For others, the question is how to manage the closure of a coal mine. We expend considerable resources to capture the voices of policymakers from a multitude of communities. Our first sample includes 405 elected leaders who are representative of all communities across the United States.

Our second sample targets fossil fuel communities, though the energy transition will have effects that extend beyond these industries.[13] Since economic shocks reverberate beyond county borders, our geographic scope is states with coal, oil, and gas employment. The sampling frame includes only rural counties. Rural areas tend to have the highest reliance on extractive industries, such as Carbon County in Wyoming, whereas cities and suburbs have more diversified economies, such as Harris County in Texas, home to Houston. This undoubtedly includes and

policymakers, transmit knowledge from scholarship back to communities, and foster productive relations between elected leaders and researchers.

[13] There is debate over what constitutes an energy community (e.g., Raimi and Pesek, 2022).

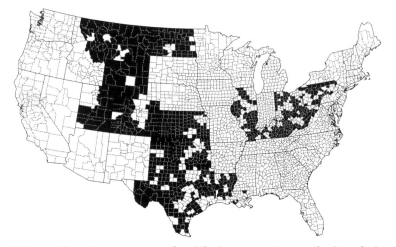

FIGURE 3.4 Counties in grey are fossil fuel communities on the list of places where we contacted local officials to participate in the survey. Alaska is included but not shown.

excludes some localities that are distant and near fossil fuel production. However, practical and budgetary constraints necessitate a balance between a narrow and broad sampling frame. Figure 3.4 shows the locations of these fossil fuel counties where we contacted local policymakers to take the survey.[14] We reached 205 local officials from these communities.[15]

HOW PEOPLE THINK ABOUT CREDIBILITY

How do the public and local leaders think about credibility? Descriptive questions like this are fundamental yet often understudied. We present the results from various questions and samples that help to make sense of how credibility concerns manifest, if at all.

---

[14] CivicPulse protects the identity of the counties surveyed.
[15] We fielded the survey in 2022, the year the IRA passed. Part of the national sample took place before the IRA's passage, while much of the fossil fuel community sample was collected after the bill became law. If anything, the law's passage might make the government's credibility appear more solid than earlier promises of action, which would introduce bias against detecting evidence of credibility challenges.

How People Think about Credibility 81

Commitment to Local Investments

Place-based investments are at the center of economic transitions, whether the investment is part of a plan to support a fossil fuel community or is to develop green energy in a place previously distant from the energy sector. What does the public think about the credibility of government promises to invest in local economic development? Do people think these promises are iron-clad guarantees, or are they worried about reversal?

Across the populations we surveyed, we asked the following question to measure beliefs about government credibility:

Consider a promise by the federal government to make a 10-year investment for economic development in your area. Over the next 10 years, do you think the government would be likely to: *Reduce the investment; Keep the investment at the same level; Expand the investment*

The question focuses on the long-term, a ten-year investment. This reflects how the energy transition will required sustained support. The answer options include the possibility that the government could expand its commitment, which avoids bias that would exaggerate credibility concerns. We also ask the respondent to rate her confidence in her answer.[16]

The results in Figure 3.5 are striking. Over 70 percent of the national public is uncertain whether the government would keep an investment in their community at the same level or think that reversal is likely.[17] Local policymakers, youths, and county fairgoers are the most certain that investments would be reduced compared to the national public. These differences across the samples appear on the right-hand side of the figure, which shows the average response across the groups. Local officials are apprehensive about commitments, which may be due to their greater political awareness.

Since Alex fielded these surveys at county fairs, he could witness contemporaneous reactions to the questions. These responses, while anecdotal, are informative of the considerations top of mind as respondents reason through the question. One person said, "it's hard to answer if you trust the government to do anything they promise. I think they're

---

[16] The follow-up asks the respondent to rate whether they were "very" or "somewhat sure" about their answer. We did not include "not sure" to keep the scale manageable.

[17] Fielded August 2022 with CAPS/Harris ($N = 3,018$).

82   *Asking People, Communities, and Companies*

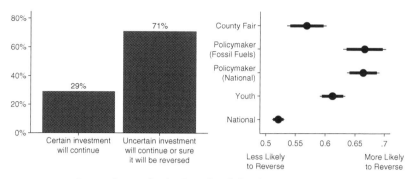

FIGURE 3.5 Perceptions of whether the federal government would keep its promise to make community investments. The left plot shows the percentage of the national public that is certain an investment would continue, or is uncertain or sure it would be reversed. The right plot shows the average response in each sample where 0 represents that one is very sure an investment would be expanded and 1 denotes that one is very sure an investment would be reduced.

just going to lie to us."[18] Another said, "I put reduce because they [the government] always say they'll do more in the beginning."[19]

These answers reflect a recognition of the inability of the government to make credible promises. No matter how one slices the data, there is always a segment of each sociodemographic or political group that thinks the investment is likely to be reduced in the future or is uncertain that it would stay the same. When we use a linear regression model to tease out patterns in the data, the expected correlations appear. Republicans and Independents, for example, are more skeptical of the federal government's promises than Democrats.[20] Key stakeholders in the energy transition are doubtful of long-term support from the government.

Trust and Credibility

Next, we explore how much trust matters for credibility. The vast literature described in Chapter 2 would indicate that the answer is a great deal. To rigorously assess this question, we analyze a survey where we simultaneously had a question about trust in the federal government

---

[18] August 11, 2022.
[19] August 12, 2022.
[20] Linear regression model with controls ($p < 0.001$). See the online appendix for information on control variables. This could be an artifact of the Democrat-controlled White House at the time of our project.

How People Think about Credibility

and beliefs about the government's commitment.[21] Specifically, the commitment question asked how likely the federal government would be to follow through on a promise to send resources to state and local governments to combat climate change.

Only 17 percent of the national public thought the government would keep its promise to help states and localities tackle global warming! How does trust relate to these perceptions? To separate the effect of trust while keeping other factors constant that could also explain this belief, such as partisanship or gender, we estimate a linear regression model. This allows us to include control variables that account for other respondent characteristics that might influence their attitudes, such as income or race. We find that trust has the strongest correlation with beliefs about government credibility.[22] The correlation of trust with beliefs about credibility is even stronger than that of identification with the Republican party or the belief that global warming warrants strong action. Since our analysis accounts for other characteristics of the respondent, we can be more confident that trust has a unique correlation with perceptions of credibility.

The Weight of History

Promises Kept

A promise by the government does not take place in a vacuum. There is a historical context. There might be a reputation of kept or broken promises that could serve as the foundation to make credible commitments or weaken them. To understand how history weighs on the present, one must know how people view the government's track record of keeping promises. If there is a trail of broken promises, distrust of the government begins to make more sense.

Questions that probe an individual's trust in the government often focus on the present. We wind back the clock to focus on perceptions of previous actions. People likely do not have a precise tally in their minds of the promises kept and broken. However, there should be a general impression. To assess this impression, we ask the national public and local officials, "As far back as you can remember when it comes to economic policies that impact your area, has the federal government: Always kept its promises; Sometimes kept its promise; [or] Rarely kept its promises."[23] Since beliefs about kept promises might be colored by

---

[21] Fielded August 2022 with Qualtrics ($N = 2,015$).
[22] Linear regression model with controls ($p < 0.001$).
[23] National survey fielded September 2022 with CAPS/Harris ($N = 2,001$).

84   *Asking People, Communities, and Companies*

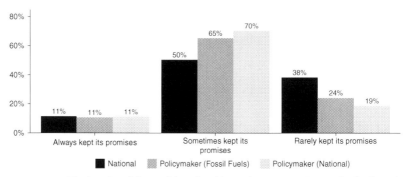

FIGURE 3.6 National public and local policymaker perceptions of whether the federal government has always, sometimes, or rarely kept its promises about economic policies that impact one's community.

partisanship, we ask the respondent to consider a long swath of time that covers multiple political administrations so the question captures the weight of history as opposed to being a referendum on the party in office.

The national public and local officials think the federal government has broken many of its promises to help their communities. Figure 3.6 shows how only a fraction, about 11 percent, believe the government has always kept its promises. The most common answer is that the government sometimes keeps its promises. When we examine the correlations between the perception of kept promises and the respondent's background characteristics in the national sample, we see that Republicans, Independents, and rural residents think the government has broken more promises compared with Democrats and urban residents.[24] Overall, these responses provide evidence of how worries about the government's credibility might arise given its history of past promises.

Past Transitions

While the previous question asked for reflection on the government's history of promises, of relevance are perceptions of how past transitions went. Do people believe the government supported workers and communities impacted by past dislocations? Do people think these communities are better or worse off today?

The local officials we surveyed expressed doubts about the level and effectiveness of transitional support. A Democrat from Arizona said,

---

[24] Linear regression model with controls ($p < 0.05$).

How People Think about Credibility

"[our] a coal-fired plant, was shut down three years ago. Very little assistance was given for retraining and transition support for the citizens and [our city]." A Republican from a part of Utah that produces fossil fuels said, "environmental legislation has not had a great track record of offering employment or job creation to communities and areas impacted by such change." A Democrat from West Virginia coal country lamented, "the past efforts to retrain miners for other industries have been a miserable failure. More talk than action with positive measurable outcomes." The national public may also share these beliefs.

In a national sample, we ask how much support was given in past transitions and whether the community is better or worse off today.[25] We focus on five past and ongoing transitions: coal in Appalachia, lumber in the Pacific Northwest, automobiles in the Industrial Midwest, tobacco in the South, and textile manufacturing in the South. Of those who had heard of these transitions, the most common answer across all industries was that there was "a little" or "a moderate amount" of compensation and investment.[26] This subset of the public perceived tobacco and coal as receiving the least support, whereas steel and auto manufacturing received more compensation. Democrats were more likely to say that there was assistance compared to Republicans.[27] In terms of whether the transitions succeeded, the average response was that communities are no better off today than before. However, people ranked coal as being worse off today than before. Partisan differences emerged again. Democrats held a more optimistic view of the track record of past economic transitions.

These results show that people believe the government has not done much in the past to help places that have undergone economic transitions. The public also sees places impacted by energy transitions, like coal country, as a cautionary tale. These historical perceptions may shape current assessments about whether the government would follow through on its promises of compensation and investments and whether these tools would be effective. For example, in a survey of the American public, including youths, we found that around 70 percent anticipated workers would receive no to little government support to help them if an economic transition impacted them. These expectations did not differ regardless of whether the cause of dislocation was technological change

---

[25] Fielded October 2022 with CAPS/Harris ($N = 2,006$).
[26] Around 20–25 percent had never heard of these transitions.
[27] Linear regression model with controls ($p < 0.05$).

or government policy. These beliefs are background factors that shape current assessments of government credibility.[28]

U-Turn or Green-Turn?

At the tail end of the summer of 2022, the United States passed a sweeping climate law, the Inflation Reduction Act (IRA), which contained ambitious investments in green energy. The legislation eked through along partisan lines; no Republican in the Senate voted for it, a rebuke to those who had hoped and advised to pass bipartisan legislation that might be more durable. While our conclusion analyzes the IRA in greater detail, here we assess how the public perceives the durability of the IRA. Do people anticipate that different groups will attempt to reverse the legislation in the future?

The month right after the climate law passed, we asked the national public about its future.[29] Over the next ten years, would Republicans, Democrats, fossil fuel companies, and renewable energy companies be likely to try to reverse the law, remain neutral, or support it?[30]

Figure 3.7 presents the results. About half of the respondents think fossil fuel companies and the Republican Party would try to reverse the law. By contrast, the public thinks the Democratic Party and renewable energy firms would continue to support it. When we explore the answers

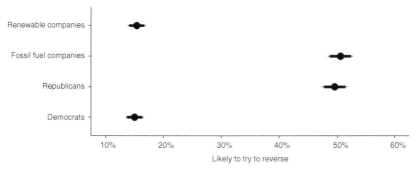

FIGURE 3.7 Share of the national public who think that renewable companies, fossil fuel companies, Republicans, and Democrats are likely to try to reverse the IRA.

---

[28] Fielded spring 2022 with Qualtrics ($N = 1,136$).
[29] Fielded September 2022 with CAPS/Harris ($N = 2,001$).
[30] We also included independents but omit them for exposition. We randomized the order the groups are presented to avoid bias from ordering effects.

Lessons from Listening to Local Leaders 87

broken-down by the party affiliation of the respondent, partisan differences emerge. Interestingly, Democrats think the Republican Party is more likely to reverse the legislation than Republicans think of their own party.[31] In other words, Republicans, on average, think that their party will support or remain neutral, but Democrats are more skeptical.[32] This could be a sign of lock-in effects as discussed in Chapter 2. Republicans may anticipate some benefits from the law, even though Democrats are currently skeptical of the Republican Party's support because of the law's partisan passage. We found evidence that Republicans in fossil fuel areas see some benefits from the law, even if they have reservations. Rusty Bell, the Republican commissioner of Campbell County, Wyoming, criticized the partisan passage of the law, the lack of permitting reform, and focus on green energy, but said, "there's some carbon capture dollars in there, and I know that that's going to help us."[33]

LESSONS FROM LISTENING TO LOCAL LEADERS

Surveys are a valuable tool because they provide a standardized measure of beliefs. However, in some cases, added context is needed to make sense of opinions. To better understand how credibility challenges manifest, we asked an open-ended question of local policymakers. We wanted to know if government credibility impacted their day-to-day activities. Our question asked, "[w]hat effect would uncertainty over possible reductions or changes to federal government investment programs have on economic development in your area?" The results are fascinating and illustrate the sources and impacts of credibility challenges.

Pendulum Swing

One theme that repeatedly emerged was the recognition that changes in political control inject uncertainty into the government's commitments. A Democrat from Hawaii provided what would be a textbook claim in the political science literature on institutions: "inherent in our lengths of office, there is a pendulum swing of political leanings. New administrations and congressional bodies change their minds." A Republican from part of Arkansas with oil and gas named elections as a source of

---

[31] Linear regression model with controls ($p < 0.001$).

[32] Republicans are also slightly more likely than Democrats to think that fossil fuel companies would support the IRA or remain neutral ($p < 0.1$).

[33] Interview, September 22, 2022.

uncertainty, "there is always uncertainty with federal regulations and investments with each election cycle." An independent from Wisconsin warned, "with partisan politics as they are today, every time the pendulum swings, the party in power wants to tear down what the previous party in power started."

Even though the prompt did not mention climate policy, one Democrat in a part of Colorado that produces fossil fuels described how these credibility concerns would impact investments made as part of the IRA:

Polarization along party lines creates uncertainty for all federal programs, which are apparently open game when administrations change from one party to another. We cannot expect the next administration to continue a program, regardless of its individual merits...With IRA funds coming to our state (Colorado), our county will be looking to address the need for low to net zero carbon affordable housing, scale-up of the grid infrastructure by 4x to accommodate electrification, electrified public transportation and charging networks, etc. Our priority is meeting our aggressive climate action goals. A change in Fed administration to [a] climate change denying, fossil fuel centric position will dramatically impact our goals and development of these solutions.

Another local official, a Democrat from an oil-rich part of Texas, said that the impact of uncertainty would be "minimal overall, but it would definitely affect green areas such as solar and wind." This perception is bipartisan. A Republican also from a fossil fuel region in Colorado acknowledged how his county could not count on the continuance of federal investment. "The current level of help does not seem sustainable; infrastructure, stimulus money, Debt relief. I want no more Trump, but I expect the majority party to change at least once in the next ten years. Then promises change too."

Promises and Trust

Some local policymakers expressed skepticism that investments would materialize. An Illinois Republican in the fossil fuel community sample said, "our county is a very rural area, and consequently, we receive little in the way of federal grants. Like counting on rain for the crops, local folks don't count on anything until it's in hand." A Republican official from neighboring Indiana echoed this sentiment, "we would not count our chickens until they were hatched. Promises mean nothing. Decisions shouldn't be made based on promises." Credibility is salient for these local officials.

Impact of Uncertainty

The impact of uncertainty is profound. Local governments often operate on limited resources, which makes durable and predictable federal support essential for their operations and plans. One Democratic official in Kentucky coal country said,

[m]y county is already a small, rural county with limited resources and a shrinking population. The tax base is aging, and wages still lag behind neighboring areas. Any reductions or negative impacts to federal government investment programs would have an equally detrimental effect on economic development ... Several recent projects ... and local industries rely on federal tax dollars to be fulfilled over the next 5–10 years.

Uncertainty at the federal level can also chill investments by private firms. One local policymaker, a Democrat from Illinois, answered that "the private sector often makes investments in anticipation of federal investments, so big changes in the federal timeline hurts area investors and municipalities that plan on the federal role."

Weight of History

One theme that emerged, especially among local officials in rural areas, was that the federal government had overlooked their communities. While uncertainty was significant, they have not received investments in the first place. The tenor and content of these grievances echos what political scientist Katherine Cramer (2016) calls "rural resentment"; that is, the feeling that rural areas don't get their fair share of resources and are looked down upon by outsiders. One Republican in Kentucky coal country had a strong reaction: "what economic investments? The federal government has invested about $500k in our county in the last 20 years from grant awards only. They do not care about small rural counties. Larger populated counties receive all the funding." A Republican in Illinois expressed frustration at the inattention his community has received but was optimistic about what the effects of an investment would be if it were made, "[Our city] seems to have long been forgotten regarding federal investment ... We need the government to believe in the area as strongly as our area leaders do."

This sentiment overlaps with the concerns raised earlier about the government not keeping its promises. One local official, a Republican in a part of Pennsylvania that produces coal, oil, and gas, said, "...we are only acknowledged by the politicians when they want something in our area.

Our concerns are often ignored, or we are told they will be addressed only to never be talked about again."

These responses from local officials highlight how concerns about government commitment are salient and have tangible impacts on economic development. Uncertainty stems both from political institutions and electoral incentives but also from low trust in the government. Local policymakers recognize the benefits of investments but are also clear-eyed about how the tide could shift with the next swing of the pendulum.

COMPANIES, CAPITAL, AND GREEN INVESTMENTS

Credibility challenges also arise in firm investment decisions. Across all industries and sectors, firms might worry about the effect of future government regulations or economic conditions on their investments. To assess the magnitude of uncertainty for firms, we asked local policymakers to rank how sure they are that local business owners would raise concerns about a decrease in federal support for local investment. Elected officials are an important intermediary between businesses and the federal government, so these individuals should have a good barometer of the uncertainty that firms face. We also posed the question in a national survey to provide a benchmark.[34]

Figure 3.8 shows that most local policymakers are very or somewhat sure that business leaders would raise concerns about a reduction of support in investments by the federal government – that is, credibility.

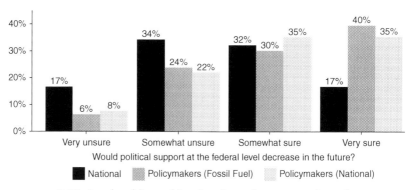

FIGURE 3.8 National public and local policymaker expectations that community business leaders would raise concerns about the credibility of a federal government investment to create renewable energy jobs in the area.

[34] Fielded August 2022 with CAPS/Harris ($N = 3,108$).

Companies, Capital, and Green Investments

The national public is more unsure, which likely reflects a lack of knowledge of business leader concerns, whereas elected officials serve as intermediaries.

Effects of Uncertainty on Firm Investment

Companies and investors with access to substantial resources play a crucial role in the energy transition. They can leverage their capital to foster the development of new clean energy technologies and usher them through the innovation "valley of death" to broad deployment. However, political and economic uncertainty can hold back this vast potential. This uncertainty has real consequences for firm investment decisions, as economists and other scholars document (e.g., Bernanke, 1983; Dixit and Pindyck, 1994; Helm, Hepburn, and Mash, 2003; Pindyck, 1988).[35]

Renewable energy is no stranger to these challenges, especially in its earlier years. One theoretical model shows how companies would have an incentive to make investments in clean energy technologies if they believed there would be a market for their inventions. However, firms fear their innovation will be displaced because the government will encourage the development of newer, cheaper technologies. The result is that companies do not invest in the first place (e.g., Laffont and Tirole, 1996). Governments can only solve this problem with a credible commitment that the firm would be able to benefit from its technological investments.[36]

These concerns are not hypothetical. A range of studies find that political uncertainty has wide-ranging effects. For example, Sendstad et al. (2022) analyzed the impact of green subsidies in Europe by comparing investment levels in countries where a policy change occurred unexpectedly after it was enacted, to those where there were no sudden changes. They estimate that a retroactive subsidy change decreased solar and wind energy investments by 45 and 16 percent, respectively. They conclude that credible policy commitments are essential to encourage private firms to make green investments.[37] While some

---

[35] To manage uncertainty and the effects of policy, firms regularly lobby even after the passage of legislation to shape its implementation (e.g., Stokes, 2020; You, 2017).

[36] Another theoretical paper by Blyth et al. (2007) investigates a model where there is uncertainty about future carbon prices due to policy changes, which creates a risk premium for green investments. Dalby et al. (2018) and others consider models where subsidies might change, highlighting the impacts of policy uncertainty on investment decisions.

[37] Likewise, García-Álvarez, Cabeza-García, and Soares (2018, pp. 872–873) study policy efforts to promote solar energy in the European Union, and conclude that durable and stable policy is "the most relevant issue for policymakers..." This echoes the types of

92   *Asking People, Communities, and Companies*

reformers hope that cost reductions in renewable energy will shield the industry from the effects of uncertainty, it may be too soon to tell. There is initial evidence from Europe that when policymakers remove subsidies for solar once it becomes cost competitive, investment in the technology falls, which suggests that cost competitiveness alone is not yet sufficient (Karneyeva and Wüstenhagen, 2017).

Uncertainty also impacts the pace of the fossil fuel phase-out. One study of the closure of coal-fired power plants used a research design that took advantage of differences in the geographic roll-out of air pollution regulations and found that coal power plants in states where legal challenges injected uncertainty were less likely to receive investments in capital-intensive scrubber technologies (Dorsey, 2019). Fabrizio (2013) documents similar underinvestment when there are legal challenges to state climate policies, such as mandates that a certain share of electricity come from renewable generation. These findings echo the insight from the economist Oliver Williamson (1991), who argues firms will underinvest in large assets that are hard to repurpose if they fear the value of the investment in the future will decrease.[38]

The effects of uncertainty also influence which companies financial markets bet on. One study shows how venture capital funds are less likely to invest in clean-tech start-ups when there are high levels of environmental policy uncertainty (Noailly, Nowzohour, and Heuvel, 2022). Other researchers have fielded surveys of individuals at large energy sector firms and venture capital funds and find that economic uncertainty and regulatory exposure influence investment decisions (Botta, 2019; Chassot, Hampl, and Wüstenhagen, 2014). In Germany, oscillation in the ambition of the *energiewende* undermined perceptions of policy credibility among renewable energy manufacturers (Rogge and Dütschke, 2018). These findings underscore the need for predictable policies that minimize risk from commitment challenges that arise as technology and regulatory environments evolve.

The political sources of this uncertainty are not lost on the business community. For example, the Roosevelt Project team developing a transition plan for the Gulf Coast described how "[u]ncertainty about policy is a major barrier to business investment. We think proposals that can

---

"salami tactics" discussed in the bargaining literature where slow changes in power do not lead to bargaining breakdown (Fearon, 1996; Schelling, 1966). For more on the impact of policy uncertainty, see Liang et al. (2022) and Walls, Rusco, and Ludwigson (2007).

[38] See also, Ulph and Ulph (2013).

outlive one or two election cycles and have bipartisan support are the most likely to provide the sort of certainty investors would want to see" (emphasis added, Beckfield et al., 2022, p. 70).

In Chapter 5, we report findings from interviews with officials at electric utilities, oil majors, and renewable energy developers who emphasized the impact of uncertainty on their planning for the energy transition. There was constant concern about the pendulum swings of policy and how this impacts transition plans. One senior official at an electric power company who works in federal and state policy-making said, "I've been in this industry a long time, and federal funding [for clean energy transitions] comes and goes."[39] As a consequence, firms develop playbooks to hedge against political risk. "The swings are becoming more dramatic and more frequent. We have to have strategies that mitigate and hedge those political risks," another electric power company official told us.[40] This uncertainty can forestall investments and lead to an otherwise higher share of fossil fuels in a company's portfolio.

CONCLUSION

This chapter shows how credibility concerns are salient in the minds of the public, local policymakers, and business leaders. Individuals from all walks of life, including those in communities on the front lines of the energy transition, think that the government might not keep its promises to support workers and localities in transition or investments in new industries. While some are more skeptical of the government than others, especially individuals who believe the government has broken its promises before, what is most striking is the uniformity of reversibility concerns.

These beliefs are consequential for economic transitions. People do not uncritically accept the government's promises of compensation and investments. Companies also slow or avoid investments in uncertain technologies when there is economic and political volatility. Low government trustworthiness exacerbates these credibility challenges (e.g., Levi, 1998).

Economic transitions also take place against a backdrop where the American public, as well as others around the world, struggles to understand how they benefit from government programs. Suzanne Mettler (2011) calls this phenomenon the "submerged state," where

[39] Interview, August 31, 2022.
[40] Interview, October 11, 2022.

the government's role is invisible to citizens. This opacity could be the consequence of the complexity of modern governance but also the product of deliberate efforts by opponents of particular programs. If the public cannot understand, let alone see, the benefits from a government policy, that heightens the challenge of building societal consensus and earning the trust of impacted communities and could even contribute to the view that government is broken and cannot solve problems (e.g., Hochschild, 2016).

For example, the submerged state problem has plagued political strategies to price carbon emissions. Advocates of carbon taxes have hoped that the revenue raised could be distributed back to voters and serve as a carrot that wins support for the policy. Yet in Canada and Switzerland, countries with carbon taxes that provide rebates to the general public, large swaths of citizens are unaware of the programs (Mildenberger et al., 2022). The same study found that efforts to improve citizen information had a limited impact on public support for carbon pricing.

Even when the benefits from a policy are visible, mistrust can impede broader public support. One study in India argued that tepid support for citizen rebates from a carbon tax is likely related to low trust in government, especially in marginalized communities (Gaikwad, Genovese, and Tingley, 2022b). In Washington state's 2016 carbon tax referendum (Washington Initiative 732), a common criticism was that interest groups would gain access to the revenue raised by the tax. Low trust can influence the public's perception that they would benefit from political reform.

Social identity also plays a role. Communities that extract fossil fuels have formed distinct attachments with the industry that may amplify mistrust of government promises. Take coal mining in Appalachia, where shared immigrant ancestry, unionization, and the social status afforded by the jobs have united workers and their communities around a common identity and social structure (Bell, 2009; Bell and Braun, 2010; Douglas and Walker, 2017). The coal industry has taken advantage of this collective identity to frame environmental protections as an attack on their way of life by outsiders (Bell and York, 2010; Lewin, 2019). Some residents feel that the rest of the country subordinates Appalachia, which has led to a sense of abandonment and devaluation by the federal government (Lewin, 2019). These conditions contribute to a mosaic of mistrust that is also visible in the growing urban–rural divide in the United States (Cramer, 2016).

Rather than a cause for despair, our results show that people and companies are clear-eyed about politics, which suggests that they should

Conclusion

respond to strategically designed policy (which we test in Chapter 5). Not only must reformers solve credibility challenges, but they must also address problems of local economic opportunity. The public must believe the investments on offer represent viable opportunities that support good livelihoods. The next chapter turns to this question and reports results from new surveys that measure economic opportunity beliefs across various industries, especially green jobs that are essential for the energy transition.

4

Opportunity Knocks?

"I would rather be a diesel mechanic or a CDL truck driver than a doctor or a lawyer," mused Dale Parsons, a long-time resident of Fayette County, Pennsylvania.[1] Terms like CDL, which stands for commercial driver's license, have become commonplace in Southwest Pennsylvania where water tanker trucks, referred to as "water bottles" by their drivers, dominate the winding roads as they transfer millions of gallons of water to well pads where it is injected deep into the shale beneath the ground to unlock a wealth of methane gas. Hydraulic fracturing has arrived in Pennsylvania.

The bevy of new job opportunities has had a profound effect on what jobs people like Dale see as desirable. Yet despite these new oil and gas jobs, there remains considerable poverty; 20 percent of households lack broadband internet, and 16 percent live below the poverty line. And if the energy transition accelerates, there will be an even more urgent need to create new job opportunities in regions like Southwest Pennsylvania. So we were curious what Dale would think about the prospect of careers in different industries. "There's been a lot of talk about different ways you can create new economic opportunities in places like Fayette," Alex began to ask.

"A lot of the local politicians are trying to attract some high-tech jobs more in the computer and chip type industries, but they've not been very successful, I would say. It's still just a very rural economy, farming, timbering, healthcare," Dale interjected. When people think about jobs, they are concerned with fundamental questions like, would this

---

[1] Interview, April 27, 2021. This is a pseudonym to maintain requested confidentiality.

Opportunity Knocks? 97

support my family? And the most credible career in Dale's mind is not a close contest. "Diesel mechanic is probably the most sought after job in this area right now because everything on a well site, everything underground [in the coal mines], works on a diesel engine...They can't hire a diesel mechanic. They're just none to be had. And if they are, they're getting six figures. Same with CDL driver, the water and stone trucks pay good money."

The energy transition raises questions about local economic opportunity that are salient in the minds of people like Dale, who wonder whether new careers would offer similar pay to existing oil, gas, and coal opportunities. Not only does pay matter, but so too do perceptions of how long new careers would last, whether the industry would grow, and if opportunities would go to locals as opposed to outsiders. These are all dimensions of local economic opportunity.

In this chapter, we systematically measure what people believe about the economic opportunities different industries have to offer. We develop novel question batteries that capture beliefs about the quality of jobs and the effects of government investment. The questions explore a range of industries but focus on green jobs, given their centrality to the energy transition. While previous research on renewable energy has focused on consumers (e.g., Ansolabehere and Konisky, 2014), we turn the focus to green employment. How people perceive the local benefits of green energy is crucial since benefits such as job creation are a potent argument to encourage acceptance of new clean energy projects.

We ask these questions in samples of the national public, regions in transition, and Appalachian county fairs. We also ask related questions in our survey of local policymakers. Together, our new survey data provide a comprehensive picture of how communities throughout the United States understand the economic opportunities different industries offer.

We find meaningful variation in what people believe about clean energy investments. For example, only about 40 percent of the national public thinks that solar and wind energy investments would create jobs that go to local workers. In rural Southwest Pennsylvania and the Gulf Coast, that falls to 33 percent. By contrast, the public sees healthcare as the most reliable source of economic opportunity; 55 percent of the national public and 59 percent of the same fossil fuel regions think that healthcare jobs would go to locals. These regional differences in beliefs about the opportunities of green industries extend beyond local job creation to perceptions of employment growth, pay, and durability. When it comes to local officials, around 70 percent are sure that business leaders would raise questions about the pay, local employment, and duration of investments in renewable energy jobs.

Others also document the challenges fossil fuel workers face in the transition to green energy. One coal miner whom MacNeil and Beauman (2022, p. 121) interviewed in Australia remarked,

[a]sking me to trade my job as an engineer in the coal industry, where I make $110,000 a year, for a gig as a solar panel installer where I'd make half that, do you understand how insulting that is? Do you understand what would happen to my family in that case? I'd need to pick up two full-time jobs just to keep the roof over our heads. Most of these guys would probably have to do the same.

Olson-Hazboun, Howe, and Leiserowitz (2018) find that individuals in fossil fuel regions are more opposed to policies that encourage green energy. A handful of studies strike a more optimistic tone about opportunities in the green economy. Curtis and Marinescu (2022) claim that renewable jobs would provide well-paid opportunities in traditional oil and gas areas such as Texas. However, the higher paying jobs tend to be in management and sales, which are not the occupations with the greatest skills transferability for most fossil fuel workers. Tomer, Kane, and George (2021) also highlight the potential for clean sector jobs in fossil fuel regions of the United States. Yet again, whether green jobs will be well-paid, durable, and served by locals is less clear. And from the political perspective, a crucial question is whether people *perceive* these industries to create local economic opportunities.

MEASURING LOCAL ECONOMIC OPPORTUNITY

Since there is no systematic measurement of local economic opportunity perceptions, we developed a novel question battery to capture beliefs about the local benefits and effects of investment across industries. Each question corresponds with a dimension of local economic opportunity: future jobs, local jobs, pay, and temporariness. We fielded our local economic opportunity questions on two nationally representative samples.[2]

We asked respondents about ten industries. The first three – solar energy, wind energy, and energy efficiency – represent some of the fastest-growing clean economy jobs in the United States. We separate these industries rather than ask a blanket question about green jobs because people may hold different beliefs. Since energy efficiency might be vague

---

[2] Sample 1 fielded 12/2021–2/2022 with Qualtrics ($N = 1,203$). Sample 2 fielded 12/2021–3/2022 with Qualtrics ($N = 1,159$).

Measuring Local Economic Opportunity

in respondents' minds, we provided examples of what energy efficiency jobs would look like, such as "building insulation" and "electrical equipment." This includes jobs like electricians. The green economy is fast evolving, and there will undoubtedly be other occupations and opportunities that emerge that are not captured by these three industries. For example, battery manufacturing is an exciting growth prospect.[3]

Next is automobile manufacturing, a more traditional industry. The auto industry has experienced considerable economic stress, such as the 2007–2008 financial crisis. Automotives will also play a role in the energy transition via EVs.

Then, environmental cleanup refers to environmental remediation and brownfield development. Reports on economic transitions often propose environmental cleanup as a mechanism to help fossil fuel communities transition (e.g., Ansolabehere et al., 2022; Hu and Tingley, 2022; Raimi, 2020). Remediation jobs would be located in the same areas as displaced fossil fuel workers. Often the skills for these jobs are similar to the ones workers used to hold.[4] Remediation would also increase local property values and allow new industries to enter. The potential downside of these jobs is that people might view them as temporary. However, there is a dearth of public opinion data on this question.

The carbon-intensive industries – coal mining, oil, and gas – provide the natural benchmark against which to judge perceptions of green jobs. It is workers in fossil fuel industries who must transition to new lines of work if the country decarbonizes. We group oil and gas together, as the two are often extracted in tandem.

Trucking has partial ties to fossil fuels. In places like Southwest Pennsylvania, demand for trucking comes from the gas industry. However, nationally, trucking is a growing profession with a shortage of drivers. The industry also faces the prospect of change as tractor-trailers electrify and companies consider self-driving vehicles. The job is transitory; it requires movement from place to place. Trucking is also an accessible career for people without a college education. All one needs is a CDL, as Dale Parsons says.

---

[3] See successful examples in Eckhouse (2022). But there is also local opposition to battery assembly plants (AP, 2022).

[4] For example, some techniques used to drill oil wells resemble those for the practice of "plug and abandonment." That is, the process of sealing off an old well, which is necessary so methane and other substances do not leak out and harm the climate and local environment.

Opportunity Knocks?

We include healthcare because it is an industry with a shortage of workers, especially nurses. It is also in high demand in fossil fuel communities with aging populations. This combination should make it a ripe source of employment. However, there might be barriers to transitioning fossil fuel workers to healthcare. The skill set of coal miners differs considerably from nurses, which may influence perceptions of healthcare as a viable career. Coal miners are also disproportionately male, and there might be gendered beliefs that make jobs in the "care economy" less attractive.[5]

The last industry is computer programming, a high-tech job that is well-paid, in high demand and requires specialized training. There have also been initiatives to transition coal miners to programmers with mixed success (see Chapter 7).

Taking the National Pulse

To measure perceptions of regional job growth across industries, we asked, "Over the next 10 years, how likely do you think it is that businesses in your region will hire more than they fire or fire more than they hire in each of these industries."[6] Figure 4.1 shows the distribution of beliefs about future job growth across the ten industries. We provide simple descriptive results here, then turn to multivariate analyses in the subsequent section. People perceive the most employment growth in healthcare and the least in coal mining, oil and gas, and auto manufacturing. Renewable energy jobs are in the middle of the road. More than a quarter of respondents see energy efficiency, environmental cleanup, wind energy, and solar energy as very likely to hire more workers in the future, which is about equivalent to perceptions of the trucking industry. However, these perceptions are relatively worse than healthcare or computer programming, yet better than fossil fuel industries.

The next question explores local job creation beliefs. We ask if the federal government invested in the respondent's region, "how many of the jobs do you think would go to local workers from the area versus workers from outside the area?"[7] The bottom panel in Figure 4.1 shows beliefs about the share of jobs that would go to local workers if there

---

[5] Anecdotally, Alex did meet one former coal miner turned nurse in Southwest Pennsylvania, but the miner acknowledged that he is an outlier.

[6] Answers include, "very likely to hire more; somewhat likely to hire more; somewhat likely to fire more; very likely to fire more; no jobs in this industry."

[7] Answers include, "almost all local workers; mostly local workers; equally local and outside workers; mostly outside workers; almost all outside workers."

Measuring Local Economic Opportunity

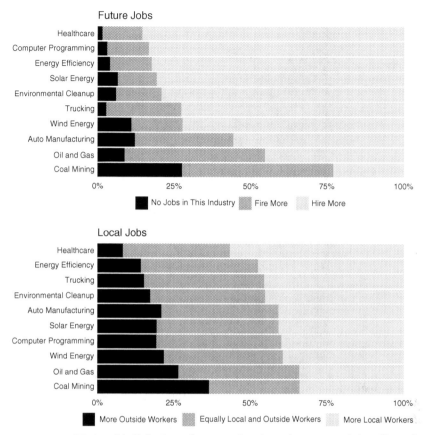

FIGURE 4.1 National beliefs about future regional employment and the effect of federal investment on local job creation across industries. Darker colors represent more pessimism.

was an investment in the respondent's region. Few citizens think that all jobs would go to only outside or local workers. The most common response across industries is that jobs would go equally to outside and local workers. The national public is skeptical that investments in any industry would accrue primarily to local workers.

Nonetheless, there are some noticeable differences. The public sees healthcare as providing more local jobs, whereas they see coal mining and oil and gas as providing more outside jobs. Renewable energy industries fair as well or worse than trucking; less than half of respondents believe that green jobs would go to mostly or all local workers.

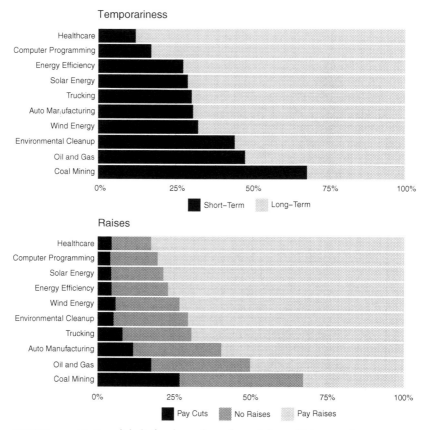

FIGURE 4.2 National beliefs about how long jobs will last and pay across industries. Darker colors represent more pessimism.

Now we turn to perceptions of temporariness and pay.[8] The question about temporariness asks, "if someone took a job in one of the industries below, how short- or long-term do you think the job would be?"[9] Of course, people switch careers. However, many prioritize stability and seek industries where they can work until retirement. Figure 4.2 shows considerable variation in the perceived durability of jobs. As before, about half of the national public sees healthcare jobs as very long-term. By contrast, only about 10 percent see coal mining as a very long-term career. Among green sector jobs, the public sees environmental cleanup as the least long-term, whereas solar energy is relatively more long-term. About

[8] We asked these questions in only the first national sample.
[9] Answers include, "very short-term; somewhat short-term; somewhat long-term; very long-term."

Measuring Local Economic Opportunity

18 to 28 percent of the national public see these four green industries as very long-term sources of employment.

Then, the question about pay asks whether people in a regional industry "will receive large pay raises, small pay raises, no raises, small pay cuts, or large pay cuts" over the next ten years. People often think of the quality of jobs in terms of pay raises, which eases the cognitive burden on the respondent and improves answer quality. Figure 4.2 reveals that about half of respondents think that all industries, save for coal mining, will offer pay raises in the future. The main source of variation comes from whether people think these pay raises will be large or small. Over one-third of the national public think that healthcare and computer programming jobs will provide large pay raises. This share falls to 31 percent for solar energy, 28 percent for wind, 27 percent for energy efficiency, and 25 percent for environmental cleanup. Fossil fuel jobs and auto manufacturing, receive the worst marks. Only 15 percent believe that these industries will experience pay growth.

Regional Differences

Beliefs about local economic opportunity should also vary across regions. Due to natural resource endowments, certain locations may have a comparative advantage in an industry. For example, Wyomingites may be more optimistic about the future of coal given its local abundance. In contrast, New Mexicans may think solar energy jobs are promising, given the state's plentiful sunlight. Regions may also have different experiences with industries and government investment. Rural versus urban differences might arise for similar reasons.

To explore regional differences in local economic opportunity beliefs, we asked our future and local jobs questions in the regional samples of the Gulf Coast, the Industrial Midwest, New Mexico, and the Southwest Pennsylvania area. Since individuals across and within regions have different backgrounds, such as education or income, we conduct an analysis that holds these factors constant while isolating the unique relationship between a region and beliefs.[10] We also separate the regional responses

---

[10] We estimate a linear regression model that controls for age, gender, education, employment, income, party identification, climate change beliefs, and optimism about economic opportunities. For all of the results presented in this section, $p < 0.1$, most $p < 0.05$, and some $p < 0.001$. The online appendix contains details.

based on whether people are in rural or urban areas, because we calibrated our sample to reach these rural areas where the economic effects of the energy transition are acute.

We find regional differences in beliefs about future jobs and the share of local labor created by investments. For clean energy industries, rural residents from Southwest Pennsylvania and the Gulf Coast are more pessimistic than the rest of the country when it comes to the future of wind energy. Views of solar are about the same as the nation in rural parts of the Gulf Coast, but people in the Southwest Pennsylvania area remain much more negative than the national average. A ray of optimism is that people from New Mexico express greater optimism about solar and wind jobs, which could reflect the area's history with these industries and comparative advantage.

When it comes to fossil fuel industries, views of the future of jobs also track with regional comparative advantage. For example, rural and urban residents from the Southwest Pennsylvania area, a place rich in coal, are more optimistic about coal jobs than the rest of the nation. Likewise, for the rural Gulf Coast, where the oil industry dominates, these residents also hold more positive views of their local industry than the average citizen.

Geographic differences also emerge when it comes to beliefs about local job creation. For example, rural residents from the Southwest Pennsylvania area and the Industrial Midwest are more likely to think that an investment in solar and wind would benefit outside workers. In terms of expectations about local jobs provided by fossil fuels, while the nation is relatively pessimistic, Gulf Coast and New Mexico residents are more optimistic about local oil and gas jobs, while Southwest Pennsylvania area locales are more optimistic about the local employment benefits from coal.

We also analyze beliefs about local economic opportunities from environmental cleanup and energy efficiency jobs with the same statistical models. In general, there are more muted geographic differences. One exception is that respondents in the rural Southwest Pennsylvania area are relatively more pessimistic about future and local environmental cleanup jobs. These attitudes are consistent with views uncovered in an interview Dustin conducted with the owner of a local well-capping company.[11] When asked about the impact of a large investment to cap abandoned, leaking gas wells, the owner expressed excitement but

---

[11] Interview, March 9, 2021.

Measuring Local Economic Opportunity

also reservations about the many nonlocal, "fly-by-night" operators that would come to try and capture the investments (and do very bad jobs to boot).

These findings show how beliefs about local economic opportunity vary across regions. In places with ties to fossil fuels, there are relatively more pessimistic perceptions of new clean energy industries and more optimistic perceptions about the jobs they currently have.[12] This matters for the energy transition because communities must believe they would be made as well or better off by leaping into this uncertain future.

Comparisons Made by Individuals

Now we move from regions to individuals. The backgrounds of our survey respondents have interesting relationships with their beliefs.[13] Republicans express more skepticism of future green energy employment growth than Democrats; individuals most concerned about climate change are much more optimistic about regional employment growth in wind and solar. There are also racial and ethnic differences that might reflect the long history of marginalized groups being left out of the benefits from green energy (e.g., Sunter, Castellanos, and Kammen, 2019). Black respondents are more pessimistic about the future of solar and wind energy jobs. However, Latino survey-takers are more optimistic about the future of wind.[14] Occupation also matters. People who work in fossil fuels are more pessimistic about the future of renewable energy jobs in their region. However, their expectations of local green job creation do not differ.

Also crucial are *relative* evaluations of local economic opportunity. Here's what that means. It is not enough to know that someone is pessimistic about coal without also knowing what they think about solar. Beliefs about what industries will make one's community better off do not take place in the abstract but are a comparison against existing and other industries.

---

[12] In models with data on energy production, there is little systematic relationship with beliefs. However, this may be because the economic effects of energy production spill across ZIP codes, and these measures are correlated with sample indicators. For the presence of coal, there is a strong, positive correlation with future and local job expectations (linear regression with controls, $p < 0.001$).

[13] Linear regression model with controls ($p < 0.05$).

[14] Interestingly, there are no racial or ethnic differences in beliefs about local jobs.

Since each individual rates all industries, we have the statistical tools to assess these relative perceptions. We call this a within-subject analysis. What this looks like mechanically is that the outcome variable in our linear regression model is the difference between the respondent's evaluation of industry A and her evaluation of industry B. When that difference is positive, she views industry A as providing more local benefits than B, and vice versa for when it is negative.[15]

Our primary comparison is between how the same respondent rates wind and solar, independently, and oil and gas. Do people think that wind or solar jobs will grow more in the future relative to employment in the oil and gas industry? The answer is yes for people who are most concerned about climate change; these individuals are more optimistic about both the future and local potential of renewable energy jobs relative to oil and gas. However, people who live in the rural Gulf Coast, rural New Mexico, and both rural and urban Southwest Pennsylvania area think that the oil and gas industry is more likely to create jobs for locals than investments in wind and solar. In other words, residents in places that the energy transition will impact are relatively more skeptical about whether clean energy industries would make them better off.

Other consistent correlations emerge. Republicans, and often Independents, are more pessimistic about the local economic opportunities provided by renewable energy relative to fossil fuels. So too are women, Blacks, and low-income individuals, but not always. We also examine a side-by-side comparison of wind and solar versus coal, another fossil fuel, and find similar results. Here, the Southwest Pennsylvania area stands out in its relative assessment that coal jobs provide more local benefits than renewable energy. We also compare solar and wind to the healthcare industry, which received the highest evaluations across samples and find more muted regional and racial differences in perceptions.

LISTENING TO FAIRGOERS

We now turn to our surveys at Southwest Pennsylvania county fairs. This sample, introduced in the last chapter, provides unique access to people on the ground in a major coal, oil, and gas-producing area. Some call it coal country, but one could easily call it gas country, as hydraulic fracturing rigs dot the landscape.

---

[15] Linear regression model with controls ($p < 0.05$).

Unpacking Renewable Energy Beliefs

In this sample, we ask additional questions about local economic opportunity to better understand beliefs about renewable energy. We focus on five aspects of renewable energy – aesthetics, climate change, pay, fossil fuel competition, and land use – though there are certainly more considerations. First, the visual impact of solar and wind energy has been a flash-point when it comes to renewables siting. People who see renewable energy as less attractive might be less willing to support renewable energy investments. Second, people may disagree about renewable energy's importance in fighting global warming. Remember Terry Weickum from Chapter 1? He laughed at the idea that global warming would motivate people in Carbon County to support wind. Third, people may hold different beliefs about how well renewable energy jobs would pay. Fourth, places with fossil fuels might view renewable energy as a threat to existing jobs. This zero-sum lens could motivate individuals to view green industries negatively. The local policymakers whom we surveyed also raised zero-sum competition concerns. One official from Montana said, "in our area, renewable energy may be opposed if it threatens to replace fossil fuel jobs." Fifth, people may differ in their beliefs about the land use challenges posed by renewables.

We asked questions that capture these beliefs at county fairs, as well as a national sample to provide a benchmark.[16] The prompt said, "How much do you agree or disagree with the following statements about a potential investment in renewable energy, such as wind or solar energy, in your area?" There were six statements about whether renewable energy would have a positive aesthetic, be important to fight global warming, provide well-paid jobs, threaten fossil fuel workers, and take up productive land. The sixth question asked if the respondent would support a green investment in her community.

Across all questions, people from the fossil fuel community hold more negative views of renewable energy (Figure 4.3). While Terry Weickum is right that people in coal country are less likely to care about the climate benefits of renewables, a sign of optimism is that a majority of the county fair sample would support a local green investment. The national public tends to have a more positive outlook on the pay of green jobs than fairgoers, likewise for views about land use challenges. Overall, the national public is more supportive of renewable energy investment. However, the

---

[16] National sample fielded August 2022 with Qualtrics ($N = 2,019$).

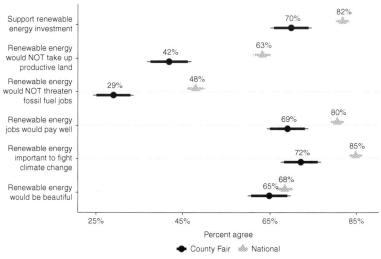

FIGURE 4.3 Comparisons of national and fossil fuel community beliefs about renewable energy investments in their community.

results do indicate an openness to investments in solar and wind, while at the same time, the data highlight reservations.

Will Jobs Last?

The durability of renewable energy jobs relative to fossil fuel occupations repeatedly emerged in our interviews and literature review. To further unpack this dimension, a survey fielded at two county fairs in 2021 asked how long renewable energy jobs would last if they came to the Southwest Pennsylvania area.[17]

We are also interested in whether the messenger mattered. That is, would it make a difference if the promise came from the mouth of a politician or a business leader? Since Alex enumerated the surveys on electronic tablets, we could embed an experiment that randomized whether a politician or a power company is the messenger of benefits from jobs. Surprisingly, there is little difference in how people respond based on the messenger. There is a hint of evidence that people are less trusting of politicians. However, we are not confident in this result because it weakens when probed with additional statistical tests.

[17] The question evaluated only renewable energy jobs, rather than the whole list of industries, due to their salience and space constraints.

Listening to Local Leaders

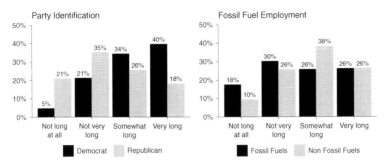

FIGURE 4.4 Fossil fuel community county fair beliefs about how long green jobs would last. The left plot breaks out respondents by party identification, and the right plot breaks out respondents by fossil fuel employment status.

The answers people give are informative. Figure 4.4 shows the responses broken out by the respondent's party and if a member of one's household works in the fossil fuel industry. Democrats are more likely than Republicans to perceive renewable energy jobs as durable,[18] but a bipartisan share of fair-goers think green jobs would not endure. Look at individuals by fossil fuel employment. Those who work outside of fossil fuels may be more optimistic about green jobs.[19] In all, these results corroborate the findings in the national and regional samples; there are doubts about the durability of green jobs, which cuts across both parties but is strongest among Republicans and those with a household member who works in fossil fuels.

LISTENING TO LOCAL LEADERS

Up to this point, our surveys have captured beliefs about local economic opportunity in diverse samples of the public. Local officials' views are also consequential since these leaders can often alter policy to incentivize particular industries. Local policymakers also work daily with community business leaders, so they have a unique perspective on the experiences and views of firms. We took advantage of our policymaker survey to ask whether they thought community business leaders would raise concerns about the temporariness, local jobs, and pay of

---

[18] Linear regression model with controls ($p < 0.1$).
[19] However, this difference weakens when estimated with a linear regression model with controls.

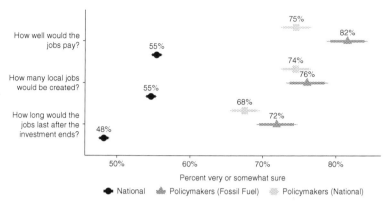

FIGURE 4.5 Percent of the national public and local policymakers who are very or somewhat sure that community business leaders would raise the following concerns about a green investment in the community. Policymakers, especially those in fossil fuel regions, expect business leaders to raise concerns about job pay, local jobs, and duration.

jobs created by a green investment. For a benchmark, we ask the same questions on a nationally representative sample of Americans.[20]

Figure 4.5 plots the responses. In the local policymaker sample, across all three questions, the most frequent answer is "very sure" followed by "somewhat sure." We do not observe any differences among Democrats, Republicans, and Independents, which is notable given the sway of partisanship. The national and fossil fuel community samples also diverge, with local officials in coal, oil, and gas counties being more likely to raise concerns about temporariness and pay.[21] Members of the national public also think that business leaders would raise these concerns, but they are less sure. This might reflect a genuine lack of knowledge on the part of the public, whereas local policymakers have greater awareness.

We asked a follow-up question to investigate whether these concerns are unique to green energy.[22] The most frequent response is that these concerns would apply to *any* potential investment (47 percent), while 25 percent think that the concerns are more likely to apply to renewable energy, and 28 percent think they are less applicable to green investments. Republican policymakers, compared to Democrats, are more likely to

---

[20] Fielded in August 2022 with CAPS/Harris ($N = 3{,}018$).
[21] Linear regression model with controls ($p < 0.05$).
[22] "Do you think that the community business concerns from the previous questions would be greater, the same, or lesser for the healthcare industry than for the renewable energy industry?" The answer options are, "greater," "the same," and "lesser."

Filling the Government Coffers

believe that these concerns are unique to green investments, while Independent are less likely to think so.[23] Overall, this suggests that for some local officials, local economic opportunity concerns are more pertinent to green jobs, even if they would be raised for most investments.

FILLING THE GOVERNMENT COFFERS

A common concern local officials raised in interviews is that a transition from fossil fuels would deplete government coffers. Surprisingly, taxes on fossil fuels provide a sizable revenue stream for state and local governments. This revenue goes to essential government services like roads, libraries, ambulances, and even high school football teams.

With the decline of coal already underway and the prospect of the energy transition on the horizon, local officials have had to have some tough conversations with their constituents. One county commissioner in Southwest Pennsylvania told Alex that "at one time 50 percent of [the] County's taxable assets were under the ground. Now it's about 30 percent. But nothing's picked up that 20 percent deficit."[24] This has created a ticking time bomb for schools, some of which have over 60 percent of their funding come from taxes on coal. The commissioner has traveled to the school districts to warn of the impending crisis. "I don't have a solution. You know, we can talk about consolidating school districts to reduce the administrative overhead. That doesn't get us where we need to be as far as tax revenue." And consolidation is by no means popular; people are loathe to let go of their cherished high school football teams.[25]

The counties Alex visited in Southwest Pennsylvania are not alone in their budgetary struggles. One study from the nonprofit research institute, Resources for the Future, estimates that between 2015 and 2020, federal, state, local, and tribal governments received $138 billion on average each year from taxes on fossil fuels (Raimi et al., 2022). Much of this money comes from gasoline taxes, but substantial sums also come from fees paid for fossil fuel extraction. The federal government even passes on some of the revenue from fossil fuels extracted on federal lands. While these outlays can be erratic, they are still important parts of state budgets; in 2020, New Mexico received $702 million, which amounts to 3 percent

---

[23] Linear regression model with controls ($p < 0.1$).

[24] Interview, August 8, 2022.

[25] Interview with Southwest Pennsylvania resident, June 11, 2021.

of the state's budget, and Wyoming got $438 million which comprises 9 percent of the state's spending (Smith, Haggerty, and Rose, 2021). The reliance on these revenue streams decreases the resiliency of local governments to economic shocks (Roemer and Haggerty, 2022), a phenomenon seen in the literature on the resource curse (e.g., Ross, 1999). The impacts on government finances will become substantial with a shift away from fossil fuels.

Can clean energy fill the gap? This is a difficult question to answer because there is systematic evaluation of the total contributions from renewable energy sources to government tax revenue. It was already an arduous task to compile these data for fossil fuels (e.g., Raimi et al., 2022). Undoubtedly renewable energy will contribute to local coffers. We saw in Carbon County how tax revenue from wind helped smooth the fall of coal, but this tax revenue was variable and declined with time. Given the size of fossil fuel economy, there is no overnight substitution, and there may even be a role for federal and state governments to step.

Efforts to accelerate the energy transition will also face trade-offs when it comes to local finances. Policies that encourage the deployment of green energy sometimes exempt it from taxes, which means there is no revenue to be found. Fights are brewing in places like Kern County, California, where oil and gas wells sit alongside wind and solar resources. Since California exempts solar from property taxes, these renewable energy resources do not fill the local coffers, but oil and gas do (Plumer, 2022).

One hope is that renewable resources like wind or solar might provide more reliable revenue streams than oil, gas, and coal, which can fluctuate widely. There is merit to this argument, but renewable sources also face unforeseen policy changes that can create volatility in their ability to bring in revenue. In Michigan, a change in the tax code accelerated the depreciation of wind turbines. This led electric utilities like Consumer Energy and DTE to try to claw back tax payments they made to municipalities. John Freeman, the director of a renewable energy trade group, lamented to a local reporter that,

[w]ord gets around...The perception is that they are going back on their commitments to the local community when they try to claw back tax revenue... We need them to succeed in getting more solar and wind, but to do that, they've got to treat local people with respect. When they make a commitment, they've got to keep it. (Ellison, 2022)

This blow to local coffers occurs in a context where communities have voted to defeat plans for new wind energy projects.

Conclusion

Whether investments can create tax revenue is a crucial component of local economic opportunity. It is hard to make communities better off if they lack the funds for essential services and public goods like roads, schools, and libraries. In the conclusion, we discuss how these public finance challenges might be addressed. However, the size of the local revenue gap exacerbated by the energy transition is substantial and will require protracted support over the long run. This is the context where credibility matters most.

SIGNS OF GREEN OPTIMISM

Although there are mixed assessments about the future of green energy, we also uncover signs of optimism. In one experiment we embed in a nationally representative survey, we find that the industry has built up a modicum of reputational credibility compared to other sectors.[26] Specifically, we asked whether people think companies would be transparent about the economic benefits or costs of an investment in the respondent's community. Crucially, the experiment randomized whether it is a generic company that makes the investment or a renewable energy company. This allows us to see if there are differences in how people think about a generic company versus a green energy company. The results show that the public sees green companies as 6 percent more likely to be transparent compared to other industries.[27]

In the book's conclusion, we also provide examples of optimism from people in coal country who have cautiously embraced renewable energy projects. In Chapter 8, we explore the importance of transparency, with a focus on clean energy development.

CONCLUSION

Our novel question batteries capture beliefs about local economic opportunity across various industries. Without doubt, the clean energy sector will experience remarkable growth if the energy transition continues and accelerates. But are these jobs seen as good ones? Will they last? Will they go to local workers? And will they pay well? If the public holds negative evaluations of green jobs along these dimensions, there could be resistance from communities where projects will be located.

---

[26] Fielded August 2022 with CAPS/Harris ($N = 1,002$).
[27] Linear regression model with controls $p < 0.05$.

Departing from the standard focus on the national public, we leverage a diverse array of samples to provide a ground-up view from communities with ties to fossil fuels. We also examine the opinions of local officials both across the country and in coal, oil, and gas regions. The results highlight regional differences that are consequential yet masked in national surveys. Nationally, the public sees solar and wind as relatively viable industries, especially compared to coal mining. However, the regions with the most fossil fuel dependence are more skeptical of opportunities in renewable energy. Salient partisan divides also emerge, with Republicans expressing greater skepticism than Democrats.

Our large-N survey results are consistent with our own interviews and those of others. For example, a team of sociologists studying the Gulf Coast referenced in Chapter 1, report that

> [r]esidents are unsure whether the renewables industry could provide the same kind of wages and benefits that they currently enjoy. Moreover, there is also serious concern amongst residents regarding the longevity of jobs in the renewables sector. It is simply unfair and unreasonable to ask oil and gas workers to abandon their jobs and to pursue retraining if new employment opportunities will be of relatively short duration. (Beckfield et al., 2022, p. 49)

This perspective may be challenging for the national public to understand, yet it is consequential if we are to create compelling benefits from the energy transition.

The sources of these beliefs are complex. One hypothesis consistent with our results is economic self-interest. People in places with fossil fuels are worried about the effect of renewable jobs on their employment, so durability, pay, and local job creation are top-of-mind considerations. Another explanation for different beliefs is messaging from partisan elites (e.g., Zaller, 1992). Concerns about local economic opportunities from clean energy emerge in our interviews with local officials, which suggests that messages from these local elites could be shaping the public's attitudes. However, the views of local officials may also be a product of the lobbying efforts by interest groups that see themselves threatened by the energy transition (e.g., Hertel-Fernandez, Mildenberger, and Stokes, 2019).

What will ultimately matter for the energy transition is local economic opportunity. Turning skepticism into optimism – or at least willingness to explore new opportunities – will be key. Skepticism may fade as the abstract benefits of green jobs become more concrete as communities experience them first-hand. However, localities must take the first step to accept these new opportunities, which will depend on their beliefs. The

Conclusion

intensity of local economic opportunity concerns may differ across green industries. Renewable energy may be more likely to be seen as temporary than EVs or battery manufacturing. Whether communities explore these new opportunities will depend, in part, on tools to enhance the credibility of investment in new industries. That is the task we take up in the rest of the book: how to create credibility and local economic opportunities.

5

Making Government Policy Credible

In August 2022, the United States broke through years of climate gridlock and passed the Inflation Reduction Act (IRA), a sweeping bill that commits billions to investments that combat global warming. The climate provisions immediately built a buzz among activists, scholars, and the media, but the IRA is one of *two* recent climate investments. One year earlier, a less trumpeted bevy of green investments within an infrastructure bill became law. While both policies seek to accelerate the energy transition, their differences in political coalitions contain important lessons for political reformers.

The infrastructure bill, formally named the Infrastructure Investment and Jobs Act (IIJA), sailed through the Senate with 69 votes. Nineteen of which came from Republicans, including the minority leader, Mitch McConnell of Kentucky. On the White House lawn, President Biden lauded the bipartisan effort, "the bill I'm about to sign into law is proof that despite the cynics, Democrats and Republicans can come together and deliver results." By contrast, the IRA faced months of nail-biting negotiations that winnowed the scope of the bill to appease centrist Democrats like Joe Manchin of West Virginia, and eked through the Senate with no Republican votes. Vice President Harris stepped in to break the tie.

The different coalitions that formed around the two climate laws may foreshadow the political fights to come that determine the durability and effectiveness of the green investments these bills seek to manifest. Neil Chatterjee, the former conservative chair of the federal agency that regulates electricity markets, said,

[I'm] worried that [with] the partisan nature of how the IRA got done that you might have policymakers around the country at all levels, who might otherwise

Making Government Policy Credible 117

support it, oppose it...for these investments to fully be utilized, realized and gain their benefits...you've got to have some long term bipartisan durability...durable policy, I think it helps...in sending those long term signals to the world that we're not going to have wild pendulum swings back and forth.[1]

For their part, reformers paid attention to credibility with their attempt to focus on benefits to lock in support and protect the purse by raising funds with the elimination of unpopular tax loopholes. This concern about policy durability, by both reformers and skeptics, reflects the gravity of credibility challenges.

The two paths to clean energy investments taken by the same Congress and President show how there are multiple dimensions at play when it comes to policymaking. Should lawmakers reach across the aisle to build bipartisan coalitions? How long should the policy last? How generous should investments be? Should there be additional funds for communities?

In this chapter, we empirically assess the effects of these design choices, which correspond with solutions developed in Chapter 2, on government credibility and support for green investments. We test these solutions with an experimental design that captures these complex trade-offs. Three notable findings flow from this experiment: first, institutional constraints can increase policy support since they reduce the perceived reversal risk from electoral swings; second, bipartisan coalitions can enhance policy support by making compensation and investments appear more durable; and third, costly signals sent through community-wide investment may ameliorate commitment problems among Republicans and Independents who are more skeptical of the government's promises.

This chapter also investigates additional solutions to create credibility. One messaging experiment evaluates the political efficacy of lock-in effects, targeted local benefits from political reform to flip opponents to supporters. The results demonstrate the promise of lock-in effects to change the preferences, attitudes, and intended behavior of the national public when it comes to green investments.

We also assess whether political reforms enacted through laws are seen as more credible than promises of assistance. We find that legislation does make a difference in the minds of elected officials and the public. Talk is cheap, but laws are seen as more durable.

Next, we explore if people would accept costly environmental regulations if there was more credible transitional support for impacted

---

[1] Interview, November 23, 2022.

workers and communities. While scholars have begun to study public opinion about compensation and investments around the energy transition (e.g., Gaikwad, Genovese, and Tingley, 2022b; Gazmararian, 2022a), this work does not consider whether the government would follow through on its promises. We find that when reformers use institutional constraints and build bipartisan coalitions, willingness to support costly regulations increases because promises become more credible.

Then, we study how shifting expectations about the size of the coalition behind the green transition could change beliefs about government credibility. We find in an experiment that revealing the true bipartisan consensus behind compensation and investments alleviates concerns about reversibility.

Subsequently, we pivot from government commitment to local economic opportunity. Rather than presuppose solutions, we ask local policymakers throughout the United States what ideas they have to deliver local benefits from clean energy jobs. This crowd-sourcing exercise yields suggestions that reflect an appreciation of the credibility challenges inherent in the energy transition. One such solution we test in this chapter is delegation to communities. Then in Chapter 8, we explore the power and limits of investment transparency.

Lastly, we report the findings from interviews with electric power companies, oil majors, and clean energy developers. We sought to understand the scope and magnitude of credibility problems for how these firms approach the energy transition. The themes that emerge highlight the salience of the political pendulum swing, which leads companies to hedge their investments. The consequence is that firms retain a higher share of fossil fuel-intensive capital than might otherwise be the case. The interviews underscore the need for policy stability that could be achieved through legislation, especially when it has bipartisan support.

HOW TO BUILD A CREDIBLE POLICY

We first examine how to build a credible policy and whether that credibility translates into support for green investments. The aim is to assess how different solutions shape the public's preferences for investments that would accelerate the energy transition.

Since reformers can assemble policy in different ways with various political coalitions, we need a tool that can measure preferences when multiple factors are at play. We employ a special version of a survey experiment called a multi-attribute experiment that is designed for this task. This technique, also known as a "conjoint" experiment, is

How to Build a Credible Policy

widely used in marketing, psychology, public opinion research, and more recently in political science to learn what people think about choices that involve multiple considerations (e.g., Hainmueller, Hopkins, and Yamamoto, 2014)

Here's how it works. Embedded within a survey, we present a table where each of the two columns represents a policy, and each row contains information about a particular dimension of the policy. We call each way that a policy can differ an "attribute" of that policy. The side-by-side display allows the survey-taker to quickly discern how the policies differ along attributes such as how long an investment would last or how generous it is (Hainmueller, Hangartner, and Yamamoto, 2015). While voters do not often learn about policy this way, the table provides a richer description of the situation. At the bottom of the table, the respondent picks which policy she prefers.[2] She repeats this task several times. Crucially, the values of the attributes (e.g., large or small tax credit) are randomized. Randomization allows us to uncover cause and effect relationships with the guarantee that the attribute level an individual sees is unrelated to factors that could bias her answers. We can then analyze a respondent's choices across multiple comparisons and estimate the effect of a change in an attribute's value on the probability that she selects a policy. These are the tools that political consultants and marketing agencies use to hone their messages.

Our survey experiment presents a choice between two government investment policies to create renewable energy jobs. We frame the scenario as an investment in a county in economic decline. This setup mirrors the context of investments in economically distressed regions. We embed the experiment on a nationally representative survey of 1,203 Americans. Since not all live in a county that has been "left behind," the instructions ask the respondent to adopt the perspective of a resident of such a community.[3] The investment takes the form of targeted tax credits, which are one of the most popular local development policy instruments (Bartik, 2003).[4]

Each policy differs along five attributes: reversibility, bipartisan support, tax credit amount, tax credit duration, and additional community investment.[5] Figure 5.1 provides an overview of the attributes and the values they take. The first attribute, *reversible*, evaluates the effect of

---

[2] We also ask the respondent to rate her level of support for each policy.
[3] People not from places in transition may have different preferences over investment.
[4] Tax credits have potential limitations that we discuss in Chapter 8.
[5] The online appendix describes five steps we implemented to ensure respondent comprehension.

Attribute	Levels
Reversible	Tax credits reversible by Lawmakers Tax credits reversible by President/Governor Tax credits not reversible
Bipartisan Support	High Medium Low
Tax Credit Amount	$10 million per year $15 million per year $20 million per year
Tax Credit Duration	5 years 10 years 15 years
Additional Investment in County Schools	Guaranteed $15 million Ability to apply for $20 million (75% receive funds)

FIGURE 5.1 Multi-attribute policy experiment design

institutional constraints, such as laws, on credibility. The levels of this attribute include whether the tax credits are reversible by the president, reversible by lawmakers, or not reversible at all.[6] These levels go from easiest to hardest to reverse. Actions taken by the president unilaterally can be undone with the stroke of a pen. Reforms made by lawmakers require a majority to reverse. Then the final level, not reversible, can be thought of as a policy that combines all of the tools we described in Chapter 2. This captures what the maximal effect of strategies to enhance credibility could be. Of course, no policy is truly irreversible, so we expect that people might still be doubtful about credibility, which would underestimate the potential impact of these solutions. Our main expectation is that policies that are harder to reverse should increase support for green investments.

Next, the *bipartisan support* attribute varies the extent to which both Democrats and Republicans support the investment. Credibility should increase with greater bipartisan consensus since the public would think that partisan reversals do not threaten support for the tax credits. Since bipartisanship also confers other benefits, below we describe and report results from a follow-up experiment to understand what people think when they see bipartisan policy.

---

[6] We randomize whether the actor is the state or federal government.

How to Build a Credible Policy

To test the effect of costly signals and protecting the purse, we vary the *amount* and *duration* of the tax credits. Long-term and generous tax credits should demonstrate the government's commitment to the investment. Long-term credits should also help to insulate funding since they reduce opportunities for opponents to let an investment expire.[7] In general, we expect respondents to favor larger, longer-term investments.

Then, to evaluate the effect of bold, unexpected, place-based investments as a costly signal, the last attribute is *additional community investments*. The investments in county schools are either a guaranteed, small grant or uncertain, large grant. We specify the probability of receiving a grant in the uncertain scenario. The expected value of both grants is the same, so the only difference is whether the government guarantees funds, which should be seen as more costly. We hypothesize that support should increase for policies when the government sends this costly signal. However, the size of this effect may be mild because of how subtle the costly signal is. In practice, we would anticipate a more considerable impact of large, visible, and unexpected investments.

The main outcome measure is which policy the respondent selected with a given attribute value. From the respondent's choices, we can estimate the average effect of a change in an attribute's value, such as the move from tax credits being reversible by lawmakers to not reversible, on the probability that one supports the investment proposal.[8]

The results from the experiment show that the solutions we proposed to create credibility can lead to greater support for clean energy investments. Look first at the difference institutional constraints make. Figure 5.2 shows that the probability of support for green investments is only 46 percent if the leader can reverse the policy. When the policy is a law that only Congress can overturn, the probability of support rises to 49 percent. When a policy combines all of the tools to create credibility to make it as difficult as possible to reverse, the probability of support is 55 percent.

Figure 5.3 shows the effect of a change from the baseline of an attribute on the probability of support. The circle without confidence intervals denotes the baseline category. See how these estimates match the gaps between the bars in the proceeding Figure 5.2. For example, the

---

[7] These attributes also serve a methodological goal by holding constant features of a policy that could otherwise confound inference.

[8] This is called the average marginal component effect (AMCE), which we estimate with a linear regression model. Since there are multiple observations from the same individual who makes repeated comparisons, we cluster standard errors by respondent.

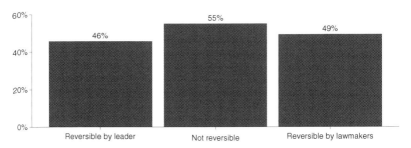

FIGURE 5.2 Probability of support for green investments that are reversible by the leader, not reversible, or reversible by lawmakers. Support is highest when not reversible and lowest when reversible by a leader.

difference between "reversible by leader" (46 percent) and "reversible by lawmakers" (49 percent) is 3 percent, which matches the 3 percent decrease in support depicted in Figure 5.3 for "reversible by leader." How a policy is passed makes a difference in the public's support.

To see if these institutional differences altered policy durability assessments, we designed a follow-on experiment within the same survey. After the respondent finished with the policy comparisons, we asked how many years they think the tax credits would last if they were meant to last for 15 years. However, there was a catch. Unbeknown to the survey-taker, we randomized whether the tax credits were not reversible, could be reversed by lawmakers, or by leaders. This allows us to see what difference this aspect of the policy made on perceptions of reversibility. We find solid evidence that when a policy combines all of the tools that we proposed to make it exceptionally difficult to reverse, the public thinks that tax credits will last three years longer, compared with when the credits could be reversed by lawmakers or the president.[9]

What difference did building bipartisan coalitions make? A great deal. Without bipartisanship, support for green investments falls by 13 percent. Members of all parties prefer green investments with broader political consensus.[10] The magnitude of this effect is notable because it is in comparison to a policy with only medium bipartisan support.

What about bipartisanship makes people more supportive of policies? While bipartisanship conveys a multitude of information about a policy, we argue that an important consequence of bipartisan policy is that

[9] Linear regression with controls ($p < 0.001$).
[10] Linear regression model ($p < 0.001$).

How to Build a Credible Policy

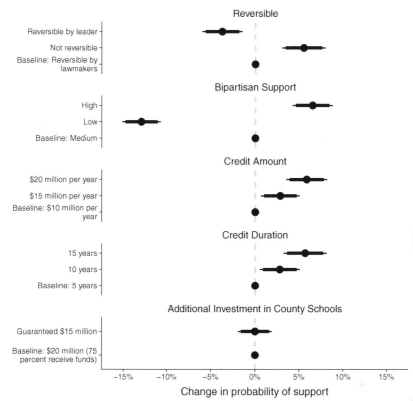

FIGURE 5.3 Effect of policy design choices to create credibility on the national public's support for green energy investments. The baseline category for each attribute is the circle without bars. The effect of each category is calculated relative to this baseline.

people think the reform is less likely to be reversed.[11] To test whether bipartisanship enhances credibility, we fielded a follow-up experiment within the same survey. We asked the respondent how likely they thought a policy would be reversed and randomized whether there is high or low bipartisan support. If we are correct, people should expect policies with high bipartisan support to last longer. Indeed, when there is low bipartisanship, expectations of policy reversal are 40 percent greater than when there is bipartisan consensus. The strength of this effect suggests that

---
[11] For example, people may like bipartisanship because they oppose ideological extremism (Westwood, 2022). However, the conjoint's design counterbalances against the informational equivalence of bipartisanship since the other attributes specify relevant policy components.

Making Government Policy Credible

bipartisanship has an especially large impact on credibility, even if it signals other qualities of the investment.

What effect does the size of the tax credit have on policy support? More generous tax credits should signal greater government commitment, which is precisely what we find. Support for green investments increases when tax credits are more generous. Of course, credibility is not the only factor at play. People might also like larger tax credits because they think they are more effective.

In terms of solutions to protect the purse, does insulating funding have an impact? Yes, it does. Support increases when credits are long-lasting, so there are fewer opportunities to reverse them. We also find evidence in a follow-on experiment that this result is not only because people think longer-lasting tax credits are more effective. A shift to the longest tax credit increases policy support but not beliefs about efficacy relative to the second longest tax credit.

Lastly, what effect do costly signals have on support for green investments? If costly signals matter, support should increase when the government makes a guaranteed investment in community schools. On average, people respond no differently to guaranteed versus uncertain school funding. However, this masks partisan differences. Republicans and Independents are more likely than Democrats to prefer green investments when the government sends a costly signal.[12] This might be because Democrats are more confident that the government, controlled by Democrats at the time of the survey, would be to deliver on an investment in schools.[13]

Maybe people just like schools and this isn't really a costly signal. However, in our follow-up experiment, we found evidence that guaranteed funding influences perceptions of reversibility. We asked respondents how committed they thought the government is to creating jobs in their area. We randomized whether the question said that the government also made a guaranteed or an uncertain investment in their schools, with language that matches the multi-attribute policy experiment. As before, we find in the aggregate there is no effect of the treatment on perceptions of government commitment, but this masks partisan differences. Among Republicans and Independents, there is suggestive evidence that the costly signal reduces concerns about reversibility.[14] When we dig into the data,

[12] Linear regression model ($p < 0.05$). However, they are not likely to increase their rating evaluation of the policy.
[13] The subtleties of the attribute might also have been lost on the respondent.
[14] Linear regression model with controls ($p < 0.1$).

How to Build a Credible Policy

this result is likely driven by a "ceiling effect" among Democrats, who likely have higher baseline levels of trust in the government's commitment compared to Republicans and Independents. The differential effects of costly signals by partisanship are, in part, a result of Republicans and Independents having more room to move up – toward the ceiling. Yet the fact that people who began with skepticism about the government's commitment change their view in response to a costly signal is encouraging. These partisan patterns in the follow-up experiment also mirror the partisan responses to the corresponding attribute in the conjoint, which suggests that the change in perceived government credibility underlies the increase in support for green investments.

We also assess the probability of support for the most credible policy with bipartisan coalitions, institutional constraints on reversibility, costly signaling, long-term and large tax credits versus the least credible policy that lacks these features. The overall impact of credibility is large. The probability of support for the most credible policy bundle is 67 percent, compared to 31 percent for the least credible package.[15] Whether policymakers could craft the most credible policy bundle is not guaranteed because success on one dimension, like bipartisanship, might also trade off on another dimension like cost. Nonetheless, the contrast provides a useful approximation of the level of support in the best and worst-case scenarios.

To summarize, there are five findings. First, institutional constraints like laws, as opposed to presidential actions, increase policy support since they reduce the reversal risk from electoral swings. Second, building bipartisanship enhances support due to the belief that these coalitions are more durable. Third, efforts to protect the purse and insulate funding with long-term policies increase support, potentially because they provide for greater stability. Fourth, community-wide investments that send costly signals may ameliorate credibility problems, especially among Republicans and Independents. These solutions proposed to create credibility work and translate into support for clean energy investments.

---

[15] We estimate the model-based predicted values for an observation with the most and least credible attribute configurations. We construct 95 percent bootstrapped confidence intervals with 1,000 samples with replacement. The confidence intervals for the estimates do not overlap. We caution against over-extrapolating the results because there is no guarantee of sufficient sample support for attribute level configurations.

CAN BENEFITS LOCK IN SUPPORT?

Another solution to make political reforms last is to use policy benefits to lock in support. Opponents of the reform would transform into defenders as they appreciate their newfound benefits. We already see early signs that this might be at work with the IRA, which has brought large EV investments to Republican states that are traditional opponents of climate policy (e.g., Brown and Gluck, 2022).

We evaluate the potential of lock-in effects with a messaging experiment in a nationally representative survey of Americans.[16] The experiment tests whether a message that describes the economic benefits of the energy transition for communities changes the public's preferences, attitudes, and behavior about transition policies. The survey vignette tells each respondent that the "federal government has created incentives for consumers to buy electric vehicles to help fight climate change." Here's where the experiment starts. We next randomly presented the respondent with one of three messages: no local benefits, general local benefits, or specific local benefits. The no local benefits condition is straightforward. This is a control condition where the message does not praise the economic opportunities of EVs.

We evaluate two types of benefits – general and specific – to capture an idea called asset specificity. An asset is highly specific if it can only be used for one thing, but it is general if it has many uses. Think of the difference between a diamond cutter, which has one task, and a Swiss army knife, which unlocks many doors. Asset specificity matters because it can be a source of hold-up problems (Williamson, 1983). Our general and specific treatment conditions show why. In the general benefits treatment condition, the respondent learns that there will be a new EV manufacturing plant in her area that creates well-paid jobs. Importantly, if the government's EV tax credits expire, the plant would have the ability to manufacture different products – the manufacturing plant is a general asset. By contrast, the specific benefits scenario tells respondents that there will be a new EV manufacturing plant in their area, but if the government's tax incentive goes away, the plant will likely have to shut down. This captures the idea that a very specific asset might create worries about demand for that asset.[17]

---

[16] Fielded November/December 2022 with Qualtrics ($N = 1,535$).

[17] We also include a general benefits scenario where we do not include the end of the sentence that says the plant would have the ability to manufacture other products, out of the concern that those words might prime people to be worried about job losses. However, we detect no difference in responses, so we pool these conditions.

As an initial check to see if the message of benefits leaves an impression, we asked an open-ended question about what came to the top of the respondent's mind immediately after they read the scenario. We analyze these answers with a structural topic model (STM), a machine learning method for studying differences in the topics contained within text (Roberts, Stewart, and Tingley, 2019; Roberts et al., 2014). The most frequent topics are: jobs created, issues with purchasing an EV, and the importance of EVs for fighting climate change. Participants are much more likely to mention job creation when they are in the treatment groups, which indicates that the message of benefits successfully made local economic opportunities from green energy salient.

Next, we evaluate a range of outcomes: intent to purchase an EV, support for the federal EV tax credits, support for climate policy, and vote choice for a pro-EV politician. To examine the effects of asset specificity, we asked how worried one would be about the credits being reversed, with the expectation that worry should be greater for tax credits with specific benefits.[18] We also construct an index of the five outcomes to reduce measurement error and capture the overall effect of local benefits on support for green policies and actions.[19]

Did benefits lock-in support? Figure 5.4 presents the effects of the general and specific benefit treatment conditions compared to the control condition where there are no benefits.[20] Overall, the index that captures all outcomes provides strong evidence that when people see a message of general benefits, they are more likely to support green policies. Yet there is only suggestive evidence that specific benefits have the same positive outcomes.

The effect of benefits is pronounced for the intention to purchase an EV. When people expect that an investment will create jobs in their area, they are willing to change their spending patterns to help that industry. This indicates that efforts to lock in support with benefits could have broader effects that change consumer behavior.

There is mixed evidence as to whether local benefits create support for the EV tax credits. When there are general benefits, there is a weak increase in support. However, there is no effect of specific benefits. This is likely because a complex set of factors influence support for policies like tax credits, which we find evidence of in an analysis of open-ended

---

[18] All outcomes are on four-point scales; positive values indicate positive valence.
[19] The index is an equally weighted average of the standardized outcomes, which itself is then standardized.
[20] Linear regression model with controls.

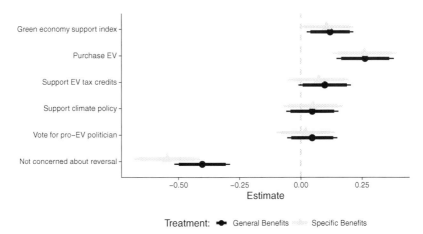

FIGURE 5.4 Effect of a message about the benefits of local EV manufacturing jobs, compared to the control message of no local jobs, on support for the green economy.

responses. People are more likely to discuss issues about how expensive EVs are or their importance in fighting climate change. Job creation is near the top of the list but is not high; it is the seventh most frequent topic.[21]

There is no effect in the aggregate for climate policy support and the likelihood of voting for a pro-EV politician. However, when we examine results by party identification, local benefits may increase Republican support for a climate policy.[22] Despite the increase in support, concerns about reversal remain. It is hard to get away from credibility challenges. People may be more worried about policy reversal when benefits are specific rather than general. However, the absolute level of reversal concern is still high.

Overall, these results demonstrate how a messaging strategy that highlights the local benefits from the green economy could build support for the clean energy transition. The national public becomes more likely to make behavioral changes like purchasing an EV and policy preference changes like supporting green tax credits when they see their

[21] Encouragingly, when respondents see a message of local benefits, they are more likely to mention local job creation when they reflect on their support for (or opposition to) EV tax credits ($p < 0.05$).
[22] Linear regression model with controls ($p < 0.11$). There is evidence of a ceiling effect among Democrats. In the control condition, 93 percent of Democrats support climate policy, 71 percent of Independents, and 45 percent of Republicans.

Shallow Promises or Deep Laws   129

community as beneficiaries. Encouragingly, these effects are generally strong among Republicans, who are otherwise the largest opponents to action on climate change.[23] However, credibility concerns remain, since the public worries about highly specific investments that depend on the government's support, a manifestation of hold-up problems.

Our experiment likely underestimates the potential power of lock-in effects for two reasons. First, policies in practice bundle together multiple instruments, which could further enhance the benefits of green investments beyond what our experiment considers (e.g., Bergquist, Mildenberger, and Stokes, 2020). Second, our experiment manipulated the message respondents saw, which mirrors how political campaigns sell policies to voters. However, when one sees with her own eyes factories opening next door, the magnitude of lock-in effects could be even larger.

SHALLOW PROMISES OR DEEP LAWS

Politicians love to make promises, but talk is cheap. In Chapter 3, we showed how the public and local officials believe that the federal government has not kept all of its commitments to their communities. Given this history, are there steps leaders can take to create credibility?

The solutions developed in Chapter 2 indicate institutions that are harder to reverse, such as laws, should enhance the credibility of the government's commitments. We now test this idea with a survey experiment that compares promises and laws. The contrast between promises and laws is large by design to capture the salience of credibility concerns and also mirror the reality where promises are common and laws are rare.

We embed this experiment in our survey of local policymakers throughout the United States, in addition to a nationally representative survey of Americans.[24] The survey begins by telling the respondent about "a climate policy that would transition the country away from coal, oil, and gas and toward clean energy sources." To help communities impacted by the transition, the federal government will provide compensation and investments. Half of the respondents saw a scenario where the government only promises assistance, which is easily reversible. In contrast, the other half of the survey takers received a scenario where the government passes a law, which is more durable. Our main question is whether this affects how long the support for impacted communities will last. Specifically, we asked if the federal government would be likely to

---

[23] See online appendix for heterogeneous effects by party.
[24] Fielded November/December 2022 with Qualtrics ($N = 1,535$).

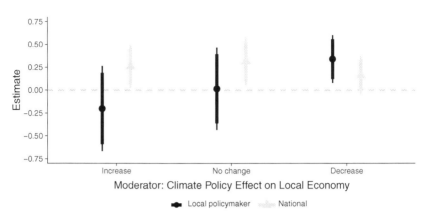

Notes: Thin and thick bars denote 95 and 90 percent confidence intervals.

FIGURE 5.5 Effect of laws versus promises on the credibility of compensation and investments, broken down by the respondent's expectations of climate policy's economic effects.

reduce, expand, or keep the investment at the same level over the next ten years.[25]

What difference do laws make for credibility? Figure 5.5 presents the effect of the law treatment on beliefs about the durability of support for communities impacted by climate policy.[26] Positive values indicate greater durability. We break down the responses by the survey-taker's level of worry about the effects of climate policy on the local economy. Concern about the economic impacts of climate policy should suggest that they are more worried about the credibility of the government's commitment, given the stakes. This variable should "moderate" the effect of the treatment; the law that enhances credibility should make a bigger difference for those most worried about reversal.

Among local policymakers, officials who begin with the greatest concern about credibility – they think that a climate policy would harm their community – laws make them much more confident about the durability of the government's support as compared to promises. The muted response among people who are less worried about the effects of a climate policy might be because these local officials have less at stake, so credibility is not as great of a concern. But for the people with the most at stake, laws make a difference.

---

[25] A follow-up question captures the respondent's uncertainty, which we use to create a scale from certain reversal to certain expansion.
[26] Linear regression model with controls.

Among the national public, there is a uniformly positive response to laws. Americans across the country think that when support for communities is backed by laws, not just words, it is likely to last longer.

These results highlight that local officials and the national public know how institutions shape the durability of the government's commitments. Laws are seen as more credible than promises, and these credibility concerns are greatest in the places with the most uncertainty and exposure to the economic effects of the energy transition. Talk is cheap, but laws are durable.

DON'T LEAVE ME IN THE WIND: COMMUNITY SACRIFICE FOR CREDIBLE COMPENSATION

The energy transition will impose costs on communities. Would people accept those costs if they were provided with credible compensation? That is, does credibility make a difference when it matters most? To answer this question, we employ a survey experiment embedded in a nationally representative sample of Americans.[27] The survey presents the participant with a situation that reflects the trade-offs that workers, their families, and communities face in the energy transition. The vignette says that the government will implement an environmental regulation that will guarantee job losses in the respondent's community. However, the government will also establish a program to retrain impacted workers and provide local economic development grants.

The costs in this experiment are important. Many studies have found that publics worldwide are vocal supporters of climate action. Yet when one asks if someone supports doing something about global warming, it is costless to say yes. However, if one is asked to pay to solve the problem, support drops considerably (e.g., Bechtel and Scheve, 2013). In our experiment, we put costs front and center by making it unambiguous that there will be job losses in the respondent's community.

We explore two solutions to create credibility: bipartisan coalitions and institutional constraints. The bipartisanship treatment randomizes whether there is high or low bipartisan support for the compensation program. High bipartisanship should indicate a larger coalition exists to defend the program. For the reversibility treatment, we randomize whether a policy is reversible or not. The not reversible condition can be thought of as a policy that combines all the institutional solutions

---

[27] Fielded December 2021/January 2022 with Qualtrics ($N = 1,203$).

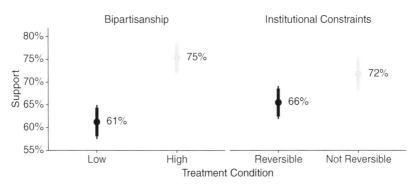

FIGURE 5.6 Effects of bipartisan coalitions for and institutional constraints on the reversibility of compensation for workers on support for a costly environmental regulation.

described in Chapter 2, which captures the total effect of strategies to enhance credibility.

After the respondent sees the scenario and treatments, we asked how likely or unlikely she would be to support the costly regulation.[28] In the control condition of low bipartisanship and a reversible policy, 57 percent of respondents say they support the regulation. This is lower for Republicans; only 42 percent support the regulation, compared to 68 percent of Democrats.

Would people support the costly regulation if it was backed by a bipartisan coalition and had institutional constraints? Yes. When there is high bipartisanship and a policy is not reversible, 77 percent support the environmental and health protections – a 20 percent increase.[29] This includes 58 percent of Republicans and 89 percent of Democrats. Figure 5.6 plots the average level of support in each treatment condition. We see that people respond more strongly to bipartisanship than the reversibility treatment. Perhaps this is because of the lack of specificity about what makes compensation irreversible. Maybe there would have been an even greater effect if we had space to detail each of our solutions to create credibility.

To make sure that bipartisanship and reversibility exert their effects through perceptions of credibility, we devise a follow-on experiment in the same survey. In this test, we asked whether compensation will likely be cut. If the solutions to create credibility work as expected, people should become less worried about future reversal. We find that when

[28] The scale has four points, which we dichotomize at the midpoint.
[29] Linear regression model with controls ($p < 0.001$).

there is low bipartisanship and policy is reversible, 79 percent believe that compensation to communities and workers will be reversed. However, our solutions make a difference. When compensation has a bipartisan coalition and institutional tools to make reversal difficult, only 43 percent of respondents think reversal is likely – a 36 percent drop. When looking at the effects of bipartisan coalitions alone, there is an 11 percent decrease in concern, while institutional constraints bring down reversal concerns by 24 percent.[30] Together, the results show that the public would incur the costs of environmental regulations if there is credible compensation.

MORE US, LESS THEM: SHIFT EXPECTATIONS AND BUILD SUPPORT

A national consensus around compensation and investments for workers, their families, and communities impacted by a political reform could help to enhance the government's credibility. The precise way that national consensus influences credibility is by changing assessments about the government's and voters' preferences. If one thinks there is no national consensus, it would be reasonable to expect lawmakers not to support compensation. However, if there is a broad base of public support, uncertainty about what the government will do in the future reduces. Uncertainty does not vanish since the public could change its mind. Yet, the reduction in uncertainty should be detectable.

We craft a survey experiment to see how revealing the national consensus behind compensation could shift perceptions of the government's credibility. The survey first informed the respondent about a compensation program that will "provide education assistance and training to workers who lost their jobs due to policies to move away from fossil fuels and toward renewable energy." Half of the respondents received information about the true level of support, which is 65 percent of Republicans, 78 percent of Independents, and 94 percent of Democrats. The control group received no such information. The information about the bipartisan national consensus is based on our earlier polling.[31] Our outcome measures capture expectations that funding for compensation and training would be reduced in the future.

---

[30] Linear regression model with controls ($p < 0.001$).

[31] See Gaikwad, Genovese, and Tingley (2022b, Appendix A). Other surveys show similar levels of support (e.g., Leiserowitz et al., 2021).

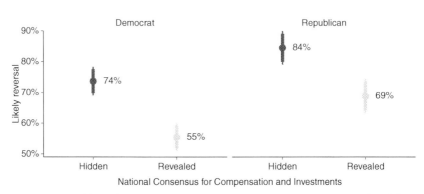

FIGURE 5.7 Effect of revealing the national consensus to compensate fossil fuel workers impacted by climate policy on the national public's beliefs that compensation would be reversed in the future. Results broken down by the partisanship of the respondent.

There are strong results. The revelation that there is a national consensus for compensation and investments increases expectations of durability by 16 percent.[32] Figure 5.7 shows the percentage of Democrats and Republicans who think that compensation will likely be reduced in the future. The dark grey bar on the left shows expectations for people in the control condition, where the national consensus is not revealed. The light grey bar on the right shows the beliefs of those who learn national consensus.[33]

This finding confirms the importance of building a national consensus around political reforms. It also highlights that not only must a consensus exist, but it must be communicated, so people are aware of it (e.g., Kuran, 1991). Since the information we provide is based on actual public opinion, these findings are an optimistic sign for the possibility of enhancing credibility. However, we caution that credibility challenges loom large, as a majority still believe that reversal is likely.

HEADS UP MEANS LISTEN FROM THE GROUND UP: SOLUTIONS FROM LOCAL OFFICIALS

We now pivot explicitly to local economic opportunity. How can the local benefits from green investments be made credible? Rather than presuppose solutions, we ask local policymakers what ideas they have to

---

[32] Linear regression model with controls ($p < 0.001$).
[33] These results mirror findings about second-order beliefs and support for climate cooperation (Mildenberger and Tingley, 2019).

Heads Up Means Listen from the Ground Up   135

deliver community benefits from clean energy investments. Our open-ended question inquired, "what suggestions would you have for the federal government about how to make sure that investments in your area for renewable energy jobs provide local benefits?" To encourage detailed responses, we told officials to feel free to answer with short bullet points. We read through the answers and organized them into the following themes: local input, unequal opportunities, transparency, local ownership, requirements for local benefits, and workforce development. These are not exhaustive but represent important topics that emerge.

Local Input

One solution that repeatedly surfaces is the desire for local input in the investment process. A Democrat from Maryland said, "Local benefits have to be decided by the local community." A Democrat from Minnesota said this process entails "listening to residents and keeping people informed every step of the way."

One benefit of local input is that it increases community buy-in for green energy. A Democrat from Washington said that policies should "help the local citizens and jurisdictions to implement renewable resources themselves. Individuals and governments are more likely to push for implementing programs they understand due to their own positive experiences." Another reason for local input is the sense that communities better understand their own needs. A Republican official in a Wyoming fossil fuel community said that solutions should "provide assistance with MINIMAL oversight. Locals are apprehensive about federal meddling and restrictions." A Republican from Illinois expressed a similar sentiment, "give local government more leeway as to how the money is spent." A Democrat in Kentucky put it simply, "let local governments make decisions."

Unequal Opportunities

One set of responses expresses a strong feeling that their communities have been left out of green investment opportunities. One Democratic official in a Pennsylvania fossil fuel community said, "Give the opportunity to rural communities. Stop overloading already advantaged communities. Spread the growth across the map instead of the same old favorites." A Republican also from Pennsylvania coal country said his county "is currently suffering from depletion of coal reserves and no one

(Federal) has come to help. We have undrinkable water in water authority distribution systems, and no one has come to help. Rural communities get a lot of talk and little action because we do not have the voter base (numbers) that matters in the next election."

One reason for these unequal opportunities is local government capacity. Remember Kris Mitchell of Boone County, West Virginia? She is the only person who works on economic development in her county. A single person tasked with applying for federal grants and attracting new businesses. Other places with more resources have entire grant-writing teams. And that is not to mention how requirements that localities match a certain percentage of a grant lock communities out of applying in the first place. One Democratic official from California emphasized this challenge and suggested that the federal government

provide upfront flexible planning funds prior to competitive grants. Ensure that a fair amount is given for administration in rural areas that actually covers the staffing costs to run and manage (around 10 percent). Change requirements (which may prevent us from access if we simply can't meet it) to incentives such as for local employment, materials, recycled materials, etc. Create a set-aside for rural, low population areas. Our needs and capabilities are different, and competing with Los Angeles is not equitable.

A Democrat from Minnesota echoed this sentiment, "reduce administrative burden and program complexity so that small cities can apply or assist applicants with minimal capacity."

These concerns about unequal opportunities extend beyond the rural-urban divide. For example, a local official in Maryland said that green investments would deliver more local benefits if "Black and Brown older communities are afforded a seat at the table at the outset...People assume that our communities aren't concerned about climate and renewable energy and careers because they don't ask us." These differences across communities also highlight the importance of local input, as discussed above. The official from Maryland continued, "The government should work directly with local governments to tailor an outreach strategy. All Black communities aren't the same."

Transparency

Another collection of responses highlights the need for transparency around local benefits, a topic we take up in Chapter 8. One Democrat from Ohio said, "make sure benefits are documented by a local organization." An independent from Illinois suggested that there should

Heads Up Means Listen from the Ground Up

be "meaningful definitions of local benefits and meaningful reporting/accounting." A Democrat from Michigan said, "please make sure there is transparency."[34]

Local Ownership

A handful of officials suggested that renewable energy projects should be locally owned. This would help to alleviate credibility problems because the people who run the projects would be directly accountable to the community. A Democrat from West Virginia said to make sure that "the renewable installations are locally-owned...not owned by out-of-state electric utilities." A Democrat in a Pennsylvania fossil fuel community also emphasized

...ONLY locally-owned/locally used solar projects retain and re-circulate wealth within a community via lower energy costs and expand wealth via expanded local jobs and new businesses designed to design, install and maintain renewable energy projects. Utility-scale solar is a massive land use change that disrupts local economies, transfers land use decisions to outside investors, and provides the most minimal number of local jobs (temporary construction and long-term maintenance.) To pretend otherwise is a dangerous farce.

There is a potential trade-off here. The energy transition will require the widespread deployment of renewables, which may be most cost-effective if done at scales possible only with large, well-capitalized firms. However, starting with community solar programs may open up subsequent opportunities.

Require Local Benefits

One solution that emerges is to place conditions on green investments to deliver local benefits. For example, a Democrat from Wisconsin said, "require that a certain percentage of the jobs go to local workers." Another Democrat from Massachusetts said to mandate that a minimum "percent of total jobs created are held by residents of a state or set of ZIP codes." Others supported conditions but asked for flexibility. "Make (local benefits) a condition of funding but allow it if it can be proven the local workforce isn't capable or available, perhaps at a lower rate. More

---

[34] One potential concern is that early questions about transparency would prime these considerations. Somewhat alleviating this worry, there are questions in between that question and the open-ended question, which comes at the end to distract the respondent.

local jobs, more money," a Democrat from Indiana suggested. We explore the potential and limits of investment conditions in Chapter 8.

Workforce Development

Some officials emphasized the need for training programs to build a workforce to enable the community to benefit from green investments (see Chapter 7). For example, a Republican from Georgia asked, "will job training be provided to county residents for required trades? Will the best-qualified hires be paid during training if they commit to serving at least two years on the job?" One official in part of Pennsylvania that produces fossil fuels asked for help to create a vocational trade school. "[Then we] can make sure these schools train people to run their own businesses. We are a rural community, with low wages, and desperately in need of plumbers, electricians, contractors, etc." A Democrat from Connecticut emphasized how training programs would help to develop local businesses that insulate green investments from federal uncertainty: "[devise] training programs, for more senior and technical as well as entry-level jobs, so that local workers will qualify, can get promoted, and can develop the skills to establish private businesses once the federal funding runs out."

***

In all, these responses highlight the creativity of ground-up solutions. They also show that policymakers from both parties are not outright opposed to green investments. Policies that provide for more local input, transparency, or workforce development, to name a few, could create local economic opportunities. These insights apply not just to green energy but to any local development project.

CAN DELEGATION DO IT?

Policymakers repeatedly said that more community input would enhance the local benefits from investments. This type of local control over the implementation of energy transition policies is a form of delegation, one of the solutions Chapter 2 proposes. Would willingness to support costly transition policies increase if they were made more credible by delegation to impacted communities?

We use survey experiments of the national public to evaluate the effect of community input on credibility.[35] The survey vignette says that the government is considering a policy that would cause substantial economic harm to the survey-taker's community. This setup mirrors the credible compensation for costly regulation experiment from before. While the government will implement an environmental regulation that causes layoffs at the main job provider in the area, there will also be a program to retrain workers and make investments for local economic development.

To learn what difference delegation makes, half of the respondents saw that an "independent committee that includes community members, workers, and business owners" runs the program to retrain workers and make investments. In contrast, the other half saw that the "federal government" runs the program. When the community has control over implementation, there should be greater credibility.

We also examine the effect of public input. Half of the survey-takers learned that "there would be regular meetings to hear what the public thinks should be done," while the other half are informed that there would be no opportunities for local input. More opportunities for input should enhance credibility and trust in the people running the program.

Lastly, we explore whether a strategy to insulate funding could enhance credibility. The protect the purse tactic that we examine has Congress set aside ten years of funding, which we compare to the control condition where funding must be reauthorized each year. Annual reauthorization should increase concerns about reversibility, whereas a long-term set aside should alleviate fears.[36]

We assess a variety of outcomes. The main focus is whether more credible compensation and local investments increase support for a costly environmental regulation. We also asked about the trustworthiness of the people who administer the program, expectations of input in the process, and funding durability.[37]

Before the respondent answered the main questions, we asked what thoughts came to the top of her mind when she read about the regulation and the transition program. We analyze these open-ended responses

---

[35] Fielded November/December 2022 with Qualtrics ($N = 1,535$).

[36] We present these three attributes in a table, with the rows randomized to avoid ordering effects. Each dimension of the policy is randomized independently.

[37] We also asked how many workers who retrained would find jobs and how many local jobs would be created.

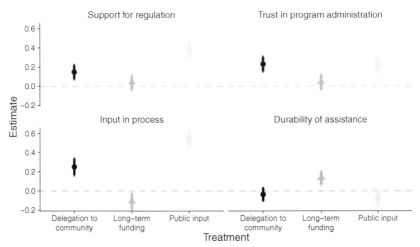

FIGURE 5.8 Effects of public input, delegation to the community, and long-term funding on support for costly environmental regulations, trust in the people who administer compensation and investment programs, perception of meaningful input in the policy process, and expectations of durable support from the federal government.

with machine learning methods (Roberts, Stewart, and Tingley, 2019). The most frequently mentioned topic is mistrust of the government's promises. A typical answer is that the regulation "would devastate our area. I wouldn't count on the federal government to keep its promises." However, survey-takers are less likely to mention this topic when there is community delegation.

Can delegation do it? Figure 5.8 reports the average effect of each treatment condition on the four outcomes.[38] Positive values indicate that the treatment improves support, trust in the program, input in the process, or expectations of durable assistance. When there is delegation to the community and public input, support for the costly regulation increases. What is behind this increase? We analyze open-ended responses and find that people are less likely to mention concerns about the federal government's involvement when the community has control over implementation.

Did community input make a difference in government trustworthiness? Yes. When the community has control over policy implementation and the public has a voice in the process, there is greater trust that the

---

[38] Estimated with a linear regression model with controls.

Listening to Energy Companies

people who administer the program will act in the community's best interest. Policy design has ramifications for government trustworthiness.

When do people think they have meaningful input in the energy transition policies that impact their community? With delegation to the community and the opportunity for public input, perceptions of genuine input in the process improve. Surprisingly, the strategy to protect the purse with long-term funding undermines expectations of community input. Perhaps this is because the annual reauthorization process is a time when such input occurs via Congressional representatives. Another possibility is the public thinks the long-term funding set aside comes with more strings attached, which would undermine input.

Yet, as seen in the bottom right of Figure 5.8, only the long-term funding treatment condition creates the expectation that the program is durable, whereas community delegation has no effect and incorporation of public input has a negative impact. These countervailing effects of delegation and public input could arise if citizens feel their input and preferences are in tension with those of the federal government, which leads to expectations that the program will end. However, the combination of long-term funding with public input reduces the detrimental effects on perceived community input, which shows how these design features could partially offset each other's disadvantages.[39] One solution to create credibility could have countervailing effects for other solutions.

LISTENING TO ENERGY COMPANIES

We conducted interviews with five leading firms in the energy sector. These companies include electric utilities, oil majors, and renewable energy developers, and have a combined annual revenue of $195 billion. Four conduct business domestically within the United States, while one operates internationally. Many of these businesses have significant investments in fossil fuels, but all are actively navigating how to best diversify and bring more clean energy on board. Across these firms, we interviewed ten senior officials who are either at the executive level or involved in federal and state policymaking. After the IRA passed, we conducted follow-up interviews with some individuals. To encourage candid responses, we keep the names of these companies and officials confidential. We recorded the interviews when the participant consented and otherwise took detailed notes to reconstruct the conversation.

[39] This is the average marginal effect of public input and long-term funding (not depicted in Figure 5.8).

142 *Making Government Policy Credible*

While we tailor our questions for each company, our interview guide addresses similar topics including: What effect has the changing political environment had on your ability to plan for the clean energy transition? What are the largest challenges and opportunities your company sees in decarbonization? What federal or state policies would help your company successfully transition its employees and communities where facilities are located? What impact will the IRA have on your energy transition plans? Throughout the book, we bring in the perspective of these firms. Here, we highlight how they experience credibility challenges and how they think they could be reduced.

As discussed in Chapter 3, firms see the political pendulum swing as a significant source of uncertainty. Interviewees emphasized the need for bipartisan and durable political reforms to ease political volatility. One senior official at an electric power company said, "we always look for durable federal climate policies...bipartisan policy is what will last, what will be durable, whereas any agency action is where the pendulum will sometimes swing."[40] Like we saw with the national public's preferences in the multi-attribute policy experiment, companies see bipartisanship as a route to produce more durable policy reforms.

While the recently passed IRA lacked bipartisan support, a topic we take up in the conclusion of our book, senior company officials expressed cautious optimism about some of the bill's provisions. In particular, interviewees identified the long-term extensions of the tax credits as an important source of certainty. A senior official at an electric power company said,

The IRA, I think will help us because it does provide some certainty for some of the tax credits for new clean energy sources. It raises the tax credits for carbon capture and underground storage, makes the wind and solar tax credits longer-term, and allows the production tax credit optionality for solar which is important for us, and it also allows transferability of tax credits.[41]

This mirrors the finding from our multi-attribute policy experiment, where the national public prefers longer-duration tax credits.

Another advantage of the IRA in the eyes of these companies is that it is actual legislation as opposed to an executive action. As our shallow promises experiment above showed, laws make a difference. Our interviewees said that with over a decade of rotating executive actions and

---

[40] Interview, August 31, 2022.
[41] Interview, August 31, 2022.

Listening to Energy Companies 143

false starts, this uncertainty had frustrated energy transition efforts. One electric power company official remarked,

> If we can get something in legislation, durable, cost-effective, climate policy that will stay around...that is definitely preferable to going from one administration saying here's the Clean Power Plan, developed and adopted by the Obama administration, stayed by the Supreme Court, then the Trump administration came up with the Affordable Clean Energy rule.[42]

However, the new climate investments in the IRA did not remove uncertainty around power plant regulations. "Here we are going on close to 10 years later, and we still don't have a rule related to power plant emissions. Legislation is definitely preferable like we had with the 1990 CAA Amendments," the power company lobbyist lamented.

These interviews also stress how the implementation of the new climate law is crucial. While the IRA provides for some legislative stability, agencies now have the football and will determine the fate of key provisions. One lobbyist at an electric power company expressed hope that the Treasury Department would move quickly. "We consider it a positive that it passed, but Treasury needs to move very quickly on guidance."[43] Large wind energy developers raised similar frustration around previous "rollercoasters" of tax credits and hoped that IRA would prove durable.[44] Another critical issue with implementation involves permitting reform, which Chapter 9 discusses.

The need for certainty means that once electric power companies start to make investments, there will be appreciable lock-in effects. A company lobbyist told us, "I think that industry loves certainty, and most of us in industry will say please don't change this. We're trying to make capital decisions, resource decisions, and we can't make it if it's going to swing back and forth." Asset specificity can help with lock-in effects because power companies will want to defend the profitability of their new investments, so they have strong incentives to mobilize to support parts of the law.[45]

A top executive at an electric power company raised broader concerns about the social and economic impacts of the energy transition: "when you shut a coal plant down, it's not a theoretical social policy that's being executed. It's real. It has real impacts on the community from an

[42] Interview, August 31, 2022.
[43] Interview, October 11, 2022.
[44] Interview, August 30, 2022.
[45] Interview, October 11, 2022.

income perspective, from a family perspective."[46] Over the last decade, electric utilities have grappled with the impacts of the energy transition as coal-fired power plants have been replaced by gas and renewable alternatives. Most power companies now have sustainability or climate goals, some of which emphasize just transition issues. To name a few examples, Pacific Gas & Electric, a power company that serves California, lists "[s]upport disadvantaged and vulnerable communities and the workforce in an equitable and just transition to a carbon neutral future" as one of its commitments (PG&E, 2022, p. 32). Duke Energy, one of the largest electric utilities in the country, recently launched a "cross-functional" unit to develop a just transition strategy that builds on experiences from "previous coal facility retirements" (Duke Energy, 2022, p. 38). Other companies (to date) have less clearly publicized policies.

Outside of electricity markets, oil and gas companies have increasingly committed to just transition issues. For example, BP's CEO Bernard Looney (2022) said,

we have to be conscious of workers of communities as we go through this...We've been in oil and gas in Aberdeen (Scotland) for 50 years. I started my career there. We're going to put our global offshore wind center in Aberdeen. So people that worked in our oil and gas facilities will transition into that global offshore wind center. Why wouldn't we do that? They are clever people, they've got great experience, we can give them a bit of retraining them, and transition them into a new economy.

It is heartening to see engagement with long-standing just transition frameworks. How these principles play out in practice will be the true test (e.g., Hale et al., 2022). With the incentive to maximize profits, there are some indications that oil majors may reduce their renewable energy initiatives if they do not turn into revenue generators.

While these firms have their own internal transition efforts, some expressed frustration with the lack of coordinated federal and state policy. When a power plant closes, the impact on the community is tremendous. Even good faith efforts by a company may not be sufficient. Economic transitions require long-term policy plans with cooperation across multiple stakeholders. One top executive at a power company put it bluntly,

...utilities are asked to figure out what to do. This is a societal, state-wide, [and] national change that is happening, and there has to be another industry that's coming in that can help the labor force continue to have jobs and income. We're

[46] Interview, November 8, 2022.

Listening to Energy Companies

able to do it up to a point, but every alternative energy resource isn't going to create the same labor needs as a coal plant ... We can always have a short-term transitional responsibility, but [investments in other industries] are policies that states and the federal government should really be thinking about because they are so impactful.[47]

Another senior official at an electric power company echoed the need for government involvement, "communities need support, and there's a role for the government to help communities more directly, at least just be able to access to know what assistance is possible out there."[48] An executive at an oil company positively referred to government requirements for up-skilling and community development plants in renewable energy project bids.[49]

As companies navigate their own transitions, they, too, are in search of solutions for how they can best serve their workers and communities. One official at a power company described how the firm's community relations managers "have been asked some pretty tough questions about livelihoods, the plant sites ... we have a responsibility and want to be held accountable ... that's what a community expects of us."[50] Some solutions can come from learning between firms. For example, one leader of a just transition unit in a large company said,

we've been trying to learn and understand from peers and stakeholders what are the expectations and real opportunities for strengthening relationships with communities ... what's happening in terms of just transition is [that it is] encouraging companies to do community engagement really well. That's informed our thinking.[51]

However, learning can sometimes be reactive. As the energy transition accelerates, companies will need to be proactive to understand what challenges will emerge and how they can be solved. Our ground-up approach provides one angle to appreciate these challenges from the perspective of workers and communities, which could inform productive and durable solutions.

Our interviews also highlight how the energy transition will require firms to coordinate across multiple levels of government and with civil society organizations. Just as the government faces credibility challenges, firms must overcome these barriers when working with communities.

---

[47] Interview, November 8, 2022.
[48] Interview, July 28, 2022.
[49] Interview, November 29, 2022.
[50] Interview, August 31, 2022.
[51] Interview, November 29, 2022.

Our framework in Chapter 2 speaks to similar issues that firms face. In the book's conclusion, we highlight opportunities for coordination on the clean energy transition.

CONCLUSION

Strategies that create credibility increase support for policies that could accelerate the clean energy transition. This chapter provides a range of evidence, from messaging experiments to interviews with energy stakeholders. Our multi-attribute policy experiment demonstrates how efforts to build bipartisan consensus, design long-term policies, and send costly signals improve public support for green investments; further, this increase is due to enhanced credibility. We also show that local benefits can lock in support and change preferences over incentives for EVs and climate policy, potentially even behavior such as purchasing an electric car. In addition, revealing the hidden bipartisan consensus behind compensation and transitional support for fossil fuel workers can enhance credibility. In our regulation and delegation experiments, we demonstrate how more credible compensation can lead people to embrace costly environmental regulations. Lastly, we find that legislation shapes perceptions of policy durability among local policymakers and the national public.

Every experiment confronts the question of external validity, whether and how the interventions translate into practice. The treatment conditions we manipulate, such as the extent of bipartisan consensus or the duration of the policy, are actual variables that stakeholders can change. These considerations also resonate with the experiences of both the energy firms and local policymakers we interview. If anything, our experiments might underestimate the impact of these interventions. The prospect of economic dislocation should heighten credibility concerns and increase the influence of the solutions explored here. We show this in the next chapter, where we pull back the curtain on the high-stakes political bargains over the future of livelihoods, industries, and communities in American coal country.

6

Bargaining for the Future

It's uncommon to fear being thrown out of an airplane. Even less common is that the 1990 Clean Air Act (CAA) Amendments are the reason for one's fear of defenestration at 30,000 feet. But that's the situation Michael Oppenheimer found himself in seven years later on his flight home from the Kyoto Protocol climate negotiations in Japan.

The source of Oppenheimer's anxiety, Richard Trumka, the barrel-chested president of the United Mine Workers (UMW) of America. The two men were on their way back from an international effort to negotiate an agreement to limit emissions that cause climate change. Trumka came to represent the interest of coal miners who would be impacted by any effort to move away from fossil fuels. Michael was there as an observer for the Environmental Defense Fund, a leading voice for action to mitigate global warming.

As Michael and Richard chatted in the airplane aisle, Michael asked what he thought was an innocuous question, "why couldn't the federal government simply compensate those coal miners who might lose their jobs?" It would be a win–win for the climate and the miners, and it would cost much less than the future damage from global warming and the health effects of air pollution from burning coal to produce electricity.

Trumka grew angry and pointed his finger at Michael's chest. "We will never trust another promise after what happened with the Byrd Amendment," he bellowed. At that point, Michael feared that Trumka would have picked him up and thrown him out without regret if the window had been open.

What was the Byrd Amendment, the cause of Trumka's ire? In 1990, the United States enacted sweeping amendments to the CAA. These

148 *Bargaining for the Future*

amendments aimed to tackle the problem of acid rain caused by the combustion of high-sulfur coal. The clear economic losers of this policy were coal miners in places that extracted coal with high sulfur content. Senator Robert Byrd, a Democrat from West Virginia, introduced an infamous amendment that would have provided substantial support to dislocated coal miners, but opponents killed the proposal in a harrowing, high stakes vote. The death of the Byrd Amendment marked a betrayal that seared itself into Trumka's memory.

Only the late Trumka knows whether he would have accepted compensation in exchange for the union's support of the international climate agreement if the Byrd Amendment had succeeded. There are genuine doubts about Trumka's sincerity, given his coordination with climate deniers and coal-state politicians to defeat the climate agreement in Kyoto, and his career-long endeavor to protect industrial interests from environmental reforms. While part of his reaction to Michael may have been posturing, his response also reflected a genuine distrust. Lawmakers who advocate for environmental reforms have undermined their reputation when it comes to support for fossil fuel communities as part of the energy transition. This meant that Trumka was not interested in coming to the table to discuss the next environmental bargain.

This chapter tells the story of the last time the United States passed legislation to bring about an energy transition. We pull back the curtain on the fight between the high-sulfur coal regions and the rest of the country. Why was it so hard to agree to share the costs of this reform? What are the consequences of the failure to help workers, their families, and communities harmed by this transition? And what might we learn from places that have had relatively greater success with energy transitions?

To answer these questions, we draw on a wealth of archival evidence that captures the perceptions of communities, interest groups, and lawmakers. We read through transcripts of Congressional debates, testimony, and government reports to uncover the issues raised by leaders and interest groups. We gained access to documents from a staffer on Capitol Hill and reviewed memoirs of key players to provide insight into the calculations of lawmakers. We tracked down all issues of the *United Mine Workers Journal* from before and after the amendments to learn how union leaders and their members thought about the bargain as it took place and when it fell apart. We collected local and national media reports to uncover what information the public, especially fossil fuel communities, had at its fingertips. We move beyond the earlier focus on technical aspects of the acid rain program to emphasize the political

Bargaining for the Future

bargains that preceded its enactment and the legacy for the energy transition.[1] Some details from smoke-filled rooms may never see the light of day. However, the resources we draw on point in a consistent direction and provide a reasonably complete picture.

While experts often say that it would be a simple task to "buy off" fossil fuel workers like coal miners, we find that this failed the one time it was seriously tried because of the costs involved and coalitions that formed. The White House and lawmakers from outside of high-sulfur coal regions were unwilling to pay the price of compensation and retraining, and proponents could not credibly commit to keep costs under control. These concerns about expense illustrate how credibility challenges make bargains over economic transitions so fraught.

One might think because the acid rain law succeeded without the Byrd Amendment that communities impacted by the energy transition need not be a focal point for climate policy. That is the wrong lesson. The coalitional politics of acid rain were unique given how they fractured fossil fuel interests along the high- and low-sulfur lines, so they were not a united oppositional block. Unless future attempts to push environmental reforms can achieve such a coalitional sweet spot, compensation may be necessary.

More importantly, we find that the failure to provide meaningful support for workers, their families, and communities has had three repercussions: legislative sabotage, hallowed-out communities, and historical memory. First, unions and power companies that were denied transitional support resisted implementation of the acid rain law by pushing state-level policies that tried to keep high-sulfur coal alive. While many of these efforts ultimately failed, they illustrate how incomplete bargains could give rise to resistance that undermines the energy transition's speed, efficacy, and durability. Second, the transition plowed ahead while workers, their families, and communities were left behind. The available economic evidence indicates that some places never fully recovered, which is morally unacceptable. Third, the memory of the failed Byrd Amendment persists to this day and joins a running list of promises made to coal country, like black lung assistance, that has been mired in uncertainty from political whiplash. This history hangs over present attempts to bargain over the energy transition (Figure 6.1).

---

[1] For important work on the acid rain provisions, see Chan et al. (2012) and Sabel and Victor (2022).

FIGURE 6.1 Cartoon from the October 1993 UMW Journal in the period after the 1990 CAA Amendments.

Lastly, what might be learned from places with relatively successful energy transitions? We look across the ocean to Germany, a historical and contemporary producer and consumer of coal. The United States has provided limited support accompanying its efforts to move away from coal, whereas Germany has pursued a more ambitious coal phase-out plan along with support for coal miners and their communities. However, there are a host of differences between these cases. Germany has a "coordinated" market economy with an established vocational skills training system and safety net, whereas the United States is a "liberal" market economy with less organized workforce programs and a patchwork safety net (e.g., Hall and Soskice, 2001; Thelen, 2004). Nonetheless, we can identify commonalities and differences that illuminate the role credibility plays. Many of the German tactics discussed in this chapter align with our book's proposed solutions: stakeholder engagement, advanced

Credibility and Clean Air

notice and planning, continuity for displaced workers, and place-based investments. However, Germany is by no means a paragon of success. For much of its recent history, the country has moved slowly in the coal phase-out, faced booms and busts in green energy, and the prospect of reversal still looms large.

CREDIBILITY AND CLEAN AIR

Today many take clean air and water for granted in the United States, but it was not always this way. One study in 1990 found that pollution blown from far away power plants rendered one-quarter of the lakes and streams in the Adirondack mountains too acidic to support fish life (New York Times, 2010). Stories about how "acid rain is slowly poising the lakes, estuaries, and forests of the Eastern Seaboard" blanketed newspapers in the 1970s and 1980s (New York Times, 1988). This was the era of acid rain. Any action to address the problem had to go through the coal miners of Appalachia and Midwest power plants that extracted and combusted high-sulfur coal at the root of the problem.[2]

Debate on how to deal with acid rain and air pollution began earlier with the passage of the original CAA and international breakthroughs like the Montreal Protocol, which phased out chemicals that deplete the ozone. Also in the backdrop were ongoing economic transitions spurred by protections for endangered species that impacted logging communities in the Pacific Northwest (e.g., Anderson, 2022) and public health policies to decrease cigarette use that had ramifications in tobacco regions (e.g., Hull, 2002).

The run-up to the 1990 CAA Amendments surfaced deep economic and political challenges. The economy as a whole was shaky. In places that mined coal, there had already been a slow but painful economic contraction due to mechanization and international competition.[3]

Despite the earlier decline, coal regions faced different costs from any attempt to address acid rain. This regional variation stemmed from sulfur intensity and previous adjustments. First, Appalachia and parts of the Midwest had coal with greater sulfur content than other regions. Much of the coal trade was local, so the costs of any restriction would fall

---

[2] Nitrogen dioxide also contributed to acid rain and was a target of the 1990 CAA Amendments.

[3] Mechanization in smelting and steel production also had second-order disruptions for coal.

Bargaining for the Future

on utilities and companies in the high-sulfur coal regions.[4] Second, there were regional differences in previous investments to tackle acid rain. This meant that areas faced varied costs of compliance with a new regulation. These differences in coal geology and previous investments are important because they determined who would be made better or worse off by the legislation, which shaped the coalitions that formed. Instead of unified coal and power company opposition, reformers split these interest groups in half.

In the late 1980s, lawmakers and environmental advocates began to work on what would become the 1990 CAA Amendments. This caught the eye of coal miners, who immediately geared up for a fight. As early as 1988, the UMW Journal, a widely read periodical of the main coal mining union, urged members to write to their legislators to oppose the bill said to cause "the loss of almost 40,000 coal jobs" (UMW Journal, 1988a, p. 16).[5] The UMW Journal would regularly feature the voices of its members in a section entitled, "Rank and File Speaks."[6] Jody Dalton, a miner from Kentucky, warned that "the sulfur dioxide bills now being considered in Congress would virtually wipe out the coal industry as we know it...our schools and local businesses and many entire communities would suffer" (UMW Journal, 1988b, p. 9).

There was an initial effort in 1988 to tackle acid rain that could have saved coal mining jobs (UMW Journal, 1988c, p. 13). Senator George Mitchell, a Democrat from Maine, proposed a compromise where electric utilities would keep burning high-sulfur coal, but would install machines called "scrubbers" that remove the harmful particles from emissions that cause acid rain. While power companies were initially supportive, they balked at having the responsibility placed on them, even with a subsidy to install scrubbers. The utilities won this round. The compromise collapsed.

Trumka sensed that the next pass at legislation would shift the costs from the utilities back to coal miners. If power companies did not install scrubbers, they would switch to different fuels such as low-sulfur coal from the West, or even gas or nuclear. Fuel-switching would be the death

---

[4] Low-sulfur coal regions anticipated benefits from the law. Virginia Congressman Rick Boucher, whose office had been heavily involved in the negotiations, sent a press release about how the bill would increase coal sales in his district (Broadwater, 1990).

[5] Miners in the high-sulfur regions had higher unionization rates than those in the West.

[6] These letters capture the perspective of workers. Of course, what the journal publishes may align with what the union leadership believes, but that is valuable information since it provides insight into the union's viewpoint.

Credibility and Clean Air

knell for high-sulfur coal regions. Trumka knew the opposition hoped to fracture coal country, so he sought to rally unity. "We simply won't accept huge job losses, whether they are in high, low, or medium sulfur coal, in exchange for a wink and a promise of a pie in the sky for a few of us" (UMW Journal, 1989, p. 10). Trumka warned that reformers could not commit to stopping with the high-sulfur regions. "[C]ontrary to the hopes of many low-sulfur operators who see a windfall in acid-rain legislation that promotes fuel switching, this is just the first step in a larger assault on all of coal" (UMW Journal, 1990a, p. 14). The failed compromise legislation to share costs with utilities set the stage for the George H.W. Bush administration's proposal that would define the contours of the ultimate reform.

President Bush's Proposal

President Bush campaigned on the acid rain issue and wanted to deliver. Shortly after entering office in July 1989, the administration proposed legislation to amend the CAA. The proposal drew on the work of legislators known as the "group of nine" led by Democratic Representative Al Swift of Washington.

Their opening salvo contained no provisions to reduce economic dislocation, despite the knowledge that coal mining, coal-fired power plants, and steel manufacturers were at risk. The lack of compensation and investments stemmed, in part, from uncertainty about the extent of the disruption. Reformers argued that these industries had already declined, the scope of the amendments was not as broad as opponents feared, and businesses could adapt with new technologies. Aside from these arguments, the Bush administration and other lawmakers fiercely opposed cost-sharing as a matter of principle.

In testimony to Congress, opponents raised concerns about the economic and social costs for workers, their families, and communities. Unions, firms, and lawmakers with ties to the coal industry led the charge. Trumka warned that direct job losses could be as high as 30,000 and up to 100,000, accounting for the adjacent jobs that coal mining supports. The knock-on effects also would impact public goods and essential services. Gerald Hawkins, a former coal miner turned representative of the UMW, cautioned that the tax base would erode. This would affect "the schools, the roads, and the bridges, and the infrastructure" of coal communities (U.S. Congress, 1989c, p. 5). Keith Ward, a miner from Southern Illinois reiterated these concerns:

154 *Bargaining for the Future*

The money that I make stays here in the community, and it supports my friend who runs the auto parts store. It helps the grocery store owner employ the local kids who need a part-time job and contributes to the sales and property tax base that keeps the Courts open and the fire trucks running ... If we go, we take an awful lot of good people with us....it will be a hollow victory for a man without a job to fill his lungs with the clean air that cost him his piece of the American dream, and that does not have to happen. (U.S. Congress, 1989c, pp. 25–26)

Senators from across Appalachia and the Midwest raised bipartisan objections.[7] A common refrain was that the costs should not fall just on mine workers but should be shared. Senator Coats warned that for the thousands of coal miners in Southern Indiana, the bill "will cost a fifth of those miners their job." Lawmakers could not understand why coal miners had to bear all the costs when in other instances costs were shared. For example, Indiana had stepped up to help others states when they have been hurt in the savings and loans crisis, despite having "contributed little to the problem ... [and] when Hurricane Hugo hit the Carolina coast, we in Indiana don't sit there and say, 'Well that's a problem for South Carolina...'" (U.S. Congress, 1989b, p. 4). These lawmakers tried to build a case for compensation, justified with the language of an appeal to fairness.

Downstream industries that used high-sulfur coal also mobilized. For example, Walter Williams, the Chairman of the iconic Bethlehem Steel Corporation testified that the iron and steel industry could experience job losses because of their interconnections with Appalachian coal. Williams also raised alarm about far-reaching impacts that include "stress-related health problems, alcoholism, spouse and child abuse, and other mental health consequences" (U.S. Congress, 1989a, p. 226). These harms increasingly describe regions of the United States where job opportunities have deteriorated, what economists Anne Case and Angus Deaton (2020) call "deaths of despair."

Some worried the efforts would not stop with the current proposal, which also served as an attempt to unify the opposition. For example, George Sinner, the Democratic governor of North Dakota, said that his state, despite the potential to benefit due to its low-sulfur coal, "is concerned about any attempts future limit growth prevent the development of our vast resources" (U.S. Congress, 1989b, p. 455). In a floor debate, Senator Byrd cautioned that "what hurts the low sulfur regions is going

---

[7] Those voicing concerns include Republican John Heinz of Pennsylvania, Democrat John Glenn of Ohio, Democrat Paul Simon of Illinois, and Republican Dan Coats of Indiana.

Credibility and Clean Air

to hurt the high-sulfur regions ... They will be back after you next" (U.S. Congress, 1990a, p. 3964).

The primary demand of opponents was "cost-sharing." This jargon simply meant that the areas hurt most by the policy should not bear all of the costs. Instead, the costs should be spread evenly. Unsurprisingly, there was fierce opposition. Regional business organizations in the West and Northeast argued that they had already incurred costs with investments to reduce emissions (U.S. Congress, 1989b, pp. 376, 382). The Northern States Power Company testified that any cost-sharing proposal would be "subsidization and, in effect, double taxation of our customers" (U.S. Congress, 1989b, p. 512). Further, cost-sharing would break with the traditional way to pay for environmental clean-up, where the polluter is the one that pays. State governors, such as Roy Romer, a Democrat from Colorado, echoed these points. Simply put, opponents to cost-sharing felt they had already paid to clean up their pollution, so why should they be responsible for others who lagged behind? In response, cost-sharing proponents drew attention to how the country comes together to share costs in response to disasters and economic crises, some of which are also highly regional. And even if utilities had lagged, workers, their families, and communities should not suffer for their lack of investment.[8]

Lawmakers stood at an impasse. Reform advocates, including the Bush administration, sought to push forward without cost-sharing or with a more limited alternative. But high-sulfur coal regions saw a bill without transition assistance as an existential threat. To avert this disaster, Senator Byrd proposed an amendment that kicked off a high-stakes negotiation that would determine what assistance, if any, those harmed by the acid rain law would receive. At stake were funds for compensation, local investment, and workforce development. It is little surprise that Senator Byrd hailed from West Virginia – coal country.

The Byrd Amendment

Byrd, born in North Carolina, and raised in the coal mining region of southern West Virginia, is considered one of the most influential American politicians.[9] Byrd spent 51 years in the Senate, making him one of the longest-serving Senators. His reputation for protecting his constituency

---

[8] In broad strokes, the end deal gave more leeway to Midwestern utilities, while workers and communities got less support.

[9] Byrd also has a complicated legacy. He was a member of the Ku Klux Klan, a decision he later regretted.

earned him the title, "the king of pork." This made him the natural and formidable champion for coal miners.

Yet, Byrd had so far failed to work transition assistance into the legislation, even as many other aspects of the bill had been ironed out by March 1990. George Mitchell (2015, p. 184), the Senate Majority Leader at the time, recalled how negotiators "struggled for years to find the right balance." Byrd participated in a few of these sessions but was "unsatisfied by what was on offer" and withdrew to draft his own proposal. The West Virginian Senator wielded immense power over his colleagues as the Chairman of the Appropriations Committee, which controlled discretionary spending. This elevated the significance of the Byrd Amendment, which became a focal point for negotiations. The political challenge the Byrd Amendment introduced was so notable that Senator Mitchell devoted a large section of his memoir to the episode (Mitchell, 2015, pp. 166–193).

What was in this controversial amendment? Coal miners put out of work would receive income support that amounted to 70 percent of their total compensation for the first year, 60 percent in the second year, and 50 percent in the final year. Byrd and his cosponsors argued that coal miners should be targeted for special help. The acid rain bill would disproportionately impact Appalachia, which mined high-sulfur coal. Byrd doubted that workers would relocate, and there would likely not be demand for new jobs in low-sulfur coal fields due to mechanization (U.S. Congress, 1990a, p. 3962). They also argued that if legislation uniquely impacts a sector, the government has an obligation to provide assistance beyond what is already available from universal programs like unemployment insurance.

Proponents of the amendment, including Senators in and outside of coal country, warned of the existential impacts on workers, their families, and communities. Wendell Ford, the Democratic Senator from Kentucky, cited a Congressional Research Service report that warned "it is unclear whether the communities within these counties would exist without coal," so what was at stake is not just mining jobs, but "the economic viability of selected communities" (U.S. Congress, 1990b, p. 5835). Senator Terry Sanford, a Democrat from North Carolina, contrasted the predicament of West Virginia with the more diversified North Carolina economy. "We expect to take care of [job losses] by bringing in new industry... because of the diversity of our economic base ... But in the Virginia-West Virginia coal mine region you do not have that diversity ... The challenge of rebuilding and expanding the West Virginia economy in those areas is

Credibility and Clean Air

very, very doubtful ... They need some special immediate help, unlike any other industry..." (U.S. Congress, 1990b, p. 5834).

Unions, including the AFL-CIO, voiced their support. Even environmental groups, such as the National Clean Air Coalition, penned a letter to endorse the amendment. These groups believed that transitional support would remove economic costs as a "rhetorical weapon" to not act on acid rain (U.S. Congress, 1990b, p. 5844).

Coal miners paid attention to the negotiations. Dominic Ferri, a miner from Ohio, wrote to the UMW Journal's "Rank and File" section about the importance of both retraining and compensation. If there was retraining but no compensation, "miners would not be able to get the education they need because they'd immediately have to go after other jobs to provide for their families. And in our area, that would probably mean flipping hamburgers" (UMW Journal, 1990b, p. 11). Ferri was willing to train for a new career, but there would have to be policies that support workers and their families.

Opposition

The Byrd Amendment faced stiff pushback from lawmakers and the White House. The program's exclusive coverage for coal workers, as opposed to individuals in other sectors that would also be impacted, drew strident objections. Republican Senator Bob Dole exhorted, "[i]n my State of Kansas, 7,500 transportation equipment workers would be at risk, 2,900 electric goods, and sanitary service jobs, 1,700 rubber and miscellaneous product jobs, and 1,100 petroleum jobs and refinery jobs and related jobs. They do not get assistance under this amendment" (U.S. Congress, 1990b, p. 5950).

Others protested that workers in their states did not receive help for other economic changes, so coal miners should not receive special treatment. For example, Senator William Gramm, a Republican from Texas, bemoaned how gas workers did not receive compensation when there was an earlier law that forced utilities to burn coal rather than gas (U.S. Congress, 1990b, p. 5953). Likewise, Senator Alan Simpson, a Republican from Wyoming, criticized how uranium workers did not receive help when that industry faced turmoil (U.S. Congress, 1990b, p. 5958).

While Byrd insisted that coal workers would be particularly impacted and their relatively high wages should be protected because of their dangerous work, others did not buy the argument. Republican Senator John Chafee of Rhode Island said, "that, to me, is a very, very strange way of proceeding in this Nation that, in effect, the wealthy get treated better than the poor." (U.S. Congress, 1990b, p. 5853).

Another objection was that it would be hard to determine why a miner lost his job. "How are we going to tell out of that 28 percent who lost jobs due to mechanization or changes that might normally come from high-sulfur coal to low-sulfur coal?" asked Senator Chafee (U.S. Congress, 1990a, p. 3952). This attribution challenge confronts other programs that deal with job loss, such as TAA. The lack of a clear mechanism to identify eligible participants led some Senators to question the efficacy of Byrd's amendment. Too narrow the criteria, and not enough would receive help; too broad, and the cost of the program would balloon.

The cost of the amendment presented another sticking point. Senator Mitchell recalls how the White House made clear that President Bush would veto the bill. This meant that the "fate of the clean air bill in the Senate thus would turn on the Byrd Amendment" (Mitchell, 2015, p. 184). Before the floor vote on the amendment, Mitchell warned that each senator should ask "about the consequences of a program like this on the budget deficit. This creates an entire system of benefits without any knowledge of what the ultimate cost will be. It creates a level of benefits that, to my knowledge, is without precedent in our law." (U.S. Congress, 1990b, p. 5855). Even Senator John Kerry, who ultimately voted for the amendment, shared these reservations (U.S. Congress, 1990b, p. 5860).

Opponents worried that costs would balloon over time if more workers lost jobs than expected. For example, Senator Dole fretted that in the second phase of the program, "somebody is going to think you are taking care of them," so more people will take advantage of the benefits, and "that would add another $1.8 billion" (U.S. Congress, 1990a, p. 3957).

Several Senators worried about the precedent the amendment would set. Senator Max Baucus, a Democrat from Montana, asked if the next time there is a cut to a program, "are we then going to add another appropriations bill to give compensation to those people" (U.S. Congress, 1990b, p. 5847)?

These reservations were not entirely unreasonable and represented the interests of the constituents of Byrd Amendment detractors. It is true that the program's costs were uncertain and could grow, that too narrow a set of workers were covered and that as a principle of lawmaking, the need for compensation might lead to legislative stalemate. However, these concerns have to be weighed against political considerations, such

Credibility and Clean Air 159

as obstructionism from the potential losers, and moral questions, such as whether it is just for communities to be intentionally left behind by government actions. This is no easy task.

With vocal cost concerns, the benefits in the amendment shrank, both in terms of the percentage of salary that would be supplemented and the duration of the program. However, the benefits remained larger than what workers displaced by foreign trade received. Yet, as Byrd and others would remind, the amendment offered less generous assistance than the program for workers displaced by the expansion of the Redwood National Park. The original estimate of the Byrd Amendment's total cost ranged between $825 million to $1.375 billion, based on the assumption that 3,000 to 5,000 coal workers would lose their jobs (U.S. Congress, 1990a, p. 3900). Negotiations winnowed the benefits to a maximum of $700 million over four years (U.S. Congress, 1990a, p. 3949).

Credibility Challenges
Even if the Byrd Amendment passed, it would by no means guarantee a smooth transition. Challenges with government credibility and local economic opportunity can undermine even well-funded programs. The discourse around the Byrd Amendment also raised these concerns about retraining. National news stories reported how miners were too old to shift careers and that there were no viable alternative jobs (Ayres, 1990). Ron Phares, a husky 33-year-old Illinois coal miner who first went underground when he was 21, felt that "we're pawns in a big political game." When asked about retraining, "What are they going to retrain you for around here? This is a farming area ... I'd have to relocate. You're not going to make $15 [35 in 2022 dollars] an hour and have good insurance" (Cohen, 1990).

And workforce programs were not guaranteed to work. Republican Senator John Heinz, originally from Pittsburgh, connected retraining to previous attempts to help workers displaced by trade. The government set up TAA, but did not keep its commitment "because people axed the [TAA] Program and rendered it either broke or inoperative" (U.S. Congress, 1990b, p. 5837).

Even if the Byrd Amendment passed, there would be the specter that training and compensation could be cut just as it had for workers dislocated by globalization. This is especially so given the concerns raised about cost by opponents. And if reformers were to take steps that would make commitments to keep costs under control more credible for deficit hawks, that would undermine credibility for the people these policies

160   *Bargaining for the Future*

intended to help. In Chapter 9, we provide examples of the unintended effects of commitment devices.

Down to the Wire

It all came down to March 29, 1990. That's when the Senate would vote on the Byrd Amendment. While nobody knew what would happen, one thing was sure: the vote would come down to the wire. Majority Leader Mitchell (2015, p. 169) recounted,

> I woke up with a throbbing headache, a sore throat, and a very runny nose. On any other day I would have stayed in bed, but March 29, 1990, was not any other day ... adopting the Byrd Amendment could mean the end of our effort. The outcome was uncertain; the vote would be very close. I had to be there to speak and to vote against the amendment, no matter how bad I felt.

The White House, through letters from Chief of Staff John Sununu read on the Senate floor, threatened that the president would veto the entire bill if it included Byrd's provision. Cost-sharing was a nonstarter, and the amendment would bust Bush's budget.

The day before, as it became clear that the vote would be extremely close, Sununu dialed up his lobbying. He phoned then-Senator Joe Biden, who left the Senate floor to take the call. Sununu reinforced to Biden that the bill would be vetoed if it included the Byrd Amendment. Biden was torn. While the future president, who later passed a landmark climate law in 2022, supported Byrd's proposal, he decided that the bill as a whole was too important to risk a veto (Coal Week, 1990; Mitchell, 2015). Biden voted no.

The nays won, 49–50. Tom Korologos, an influential Republican lobbyist, recalled, "it was one of the classic struggles of the Senate. There was more high drama in that thing than I've seen in a long time" (Kuntz and Hager, 1990). It would have been 50–50 if Democratic Senator Bennett Johnston of Louisiana, whom Byrd marked as a supporter, had not missed the vote (he was delayed by weather upon return from a funeral). Even if the Senator had made it to the floor, Vice President Dan Quayle would have broken the tie and killed the amendment.

The vote had a lasting impact on Byrd. Mitchell (2015, p. 188) recalls how Byrd took the roll call vote from that day and "had it framed, and hung it next to the door leading into his Appropriations Committee office" so that "anyone who entered his office was reminded of that vote." As we saw from Trumka's reaction to Michael on the plane back from Kyoto, unions remember this day, too.

The mining community bemoaned the defeat. Danny James, a miner from Indiana, said, "what really gripes me is that Senator Byrd came up with a deal that would put $500 million toward helping to retrain coal miners but the Senate threw it out. But they approved spending billions of dollars helping bail out savings and loans banks" (UMW Journal, 1990b, p. 11).

While scholars are often skeptical of how much attention the public pays to politics (e.g., Stokes and Miller, 1962), miners who were directly impacted, in large part, paid attention and understood what happened. Unions also helped to facilitate this understanding and shape the preferences of its members (e.g., Ahlquist and Levi, 2013). The UMW Journal was one such vehicle.

On April 3, 1990, the Senate passed its version of the bill with 89 ayes and 11 nays. This kicked the legislation to the House, where there would be a last-ditch effort to soften the law's economic impact.

Wise Amendment

When the House took up the legislation, Representative Bob Wise, a Democrat from West Virginia, introduced an amendment to cushion the cost of the acid rain bill for workers. Wise's amendment paid attention to lessons from Byrd's defeat. To mollify objections of special treatment, the proposal covered workers from any impacted industry, not just coal. To address cost concerns, spending could not exceed $250 million over five years, and no more than $50 million could be spent each year. Finally, to quell fears that workers would become dependent, recipients must begin retraining almost immediately. Proponents in the House drew on the same arguments made in the Senate (U.S. Congress, 1990c).

The feeble condition of job training programs that workers would have to fall back upon made the additional support from the Wise Amendment crucial. The primary federal job training program had been chronically underfunded (U.S. Congress, 1990c, p. 11944). Representative James Scheuer, a New York Democrat, emphasized that workers needed more than promises, but long-term support: "Too often we have made a commitment to the people who are the backbone of our society and then pulled the rug from under their feet by reducing or eliminating [funds for retraining]" (U.S. Congress, 1990c, p. 11957).

Even with the dramatically pared-back program, lawmakers reiterated cost concerns. Congressmen Norman Lent and others argued that the funding cap was not credible, so costs could balloon (U.S. Congress,

162   *Bargaining for the Future*

1990c, p. 11942). Representative Jim Cooper, a Democrat from Tennessee, speculated, "...a multi-billion dollar liability that could be a permanent one ...Wait until conference and Senator Byrd gets another crack" (U.S. Congress, 1990c, p. 11953). Bush's Chief of Staff Sununu dusted off the playbook for the Byrd Amendment and opposed the amendment (U.S. Congress, 1990c, p. 11947).

The Wise Amendment avoided Byrd's fate, or so it appeared, clearing the House in a 274 to 146 vote. The assistance package was a shadow of the initial Byrd Amendment, with less funding for more workers. There was less than a quarter of Byrd's original request. Scholars of the period characterize the provisions as "relatively small" (Ellerman et al., 2000, p. 30). Even with this haircut, the House "Whip card," handed out by Majority Whip William Gray to tell members how and why to vote – and provided to us by a staff member involved in the negotiations – still mentioned the funds as a positive feature of the bill. However, the legislative debate reveals reluctance to support the amendment, even in its slimmed-down form.

The House voted on May 23, 1990, to pass its version of the acid rain law. The vote on this sweeping environmental reform was bipartisan: 420 in favor, 21 opposed. But the political saga was not over. The House and the Senate now had two distinct versions of the law that would have to be reconciled. Would the Wise Amendment survive?

Across the Finish-Line

Compensation advocates had a problem. The House version of the bill had the Wise Amendment. The Senate version did not. Something had to give. "The House yielded to the Senate's stronger acid rain provisions, but on almost all other issues the Senate yielded, and the stronger provisions of the House bill prevailed," recalled Majority Leader Mitchell (2015, p. 192).

The Wise amendment was not so lucky. In closed-door negotiations, White House officials demanded that the already slimmed-down amendment be scaled back even further. If not, Bush would veto the law. Wise amendment defenders "virtually conceded the issue" (Cohen, 1992, p. 163). Funds for job displacement were revised to be a shallow promise to encourage technical assistance for job searches. The income allowance for workers fell to less than 1 percent of the total amount promised by Byrd. The workforce provisions went from a mandatory unemployment benefits program to being shoehorned into a larger job training program that relied on yearly appropriations, which undermined its sense of durability (Mills, 1990).[10] "Even its supporters agree that the compromise was a pale shadow of the Wise Amendment" (Cohen, 1992, p. 163).

Despite bruises left by debates, Congress reached a bipartisan consensus. The reconciled bill passed both chambers in October 1990 by wide margins: 401-25 in the House and 89-10 in the Senate. On November 15, 1990, President Bush signed the 1990 CAA Amendments into law.

Union Response

The passage of legislation did not mean it was game over (e.g., Stokes, 2020; You, 2017). The UMW swung into action to try to influence state policies to alleviate the impacts of the law by pushing for requirements to install scrubbers. The miners focused on the Midwest because power plants in this region relied most on high-sulfur coal.

These efforts bore temporary fruit. Despite opposition from utilities, in April 1991, Indiana passed a law that required power companies to consider the social costs of sulfur reduction efforts and authorized regulators to reject moves that would decrease the use of Indiana coal (UMW Journal, 1991a, p. 15). Illinois passed a law in 1991 to require scrubbers (UMW Journal, 1991b, p. 9). A May 1993 article entitled, "Scrub, Don't Switch: A Fight to Save Jobs," detailed campaigns in other Midwestern states (UMW Journal, 1993, pp. 12–13). However, union efforts failed elsewhere. Matt Lucas, a coal miner, bemoaned, "right here in Ohio with the new Clean Air Act, some of the politicians are writing off the Mine Workers just because we are few in number in relation to the population" (UMW Journal, 1991c).

The union also aimed its lobbying activity at the federal level. After an intense campaign in 1991, the House introduced a bill that would provide tax credits to power companies to install scrubbers. Cosponsors for the proposal came from the predictable set of Midwestern states. Trumka and others argued (again) that without passage, coal workers would lose their jobs. The legislation died in committee, an indication that lawmakers lacked political will.

Surviving Assistance Provisions

The main surviving assistance provision was the Clean Air Employment Transition Assistance Program (CAETAP), which aimed to help workers

[10] The larger job training program was the Economically Dislocated Workers Assistance Act as part of the Job Training Partnership Act.

find new careers. This program ran from 1992 to 1994, when its life was abruptly cut short by Congress, which denied its renewal.[11] Between 1992 and 1996, the effort distributed $82 million and supported 6,366 workers, predominantly in West Virginia and Illinois (EPA, 2001, p. 16). This was a fraction of the initial proposal by Byrd, and a far reach from what was needed to smooth the costs of transition.[12]

The program was also poorly managed. CAETAP, along with other worker training programs of the era, faced challenges that sparked a series of reports by government auditors. One report entitled, "Most Federal Agencies Do Not Know If Their Programs Are Working Effectively," uncovered how programs did not collect information on whether participants found jobs or any other metric of effectiveness (GAO, 1994b). Successful transition of workers and communities was not the focus.

The challenges ran deep and extended to the approach to helping displaced workers. A committee created to review federal job training programs concluded, "[t]he fragmented, uncoordinated approach to the delivery of human services should no longer be accepted. It is inefficient, wasteful, and frustrates the consumers of these services" (GAO, 1994a, p. 31). A review of the program to help workers impacted by trade, TAA, revealed similar issues. A federal audit found that TAA "...is often slow in reaching workers as a result of the complex certification process. TAA participants may receive services that are not tailored to their needs ... TAA lacks the ongoing counseling and support often cited as necessary to ensure the completion of training" (GAO, 1993b, p. 3). A watchdog organization within the Department of Labor (1993), which administers TAA, reached similar conclusions. Secretary of Labor Robert Reich described how this process looks like a "maze" to participants (U.S. Congress, 1994, p. 18).

Yet, many reports and policies take a top-down perspective that does not appreciate the challenges workers face. For example, a 2001 report that examined the CAA's training program did not "consider whether any difficulties might arise for displaced workers in finding new employment opportunities" (EPA, 2001, p. 17). Workers received little to no income assistance while retraining, despite needing to support themselves

---

[11] Some support continued as part of the discretionary fund by the Department of Labor under Part B of Title III of the JTPA.

[12] A working paper version of Walker (2013, p. 30) indicated that CAETAP "was severely underfunded in terms of compensating workers for any earnings losses pertaining to regulatory induced reallocation." With this dramatic shortfall, there were persistent calls to expand the program (U.S. Congress, 2013).

Credibility and Clean Air

and their families. "Presently, the workers attending school are living at below poverty level and have to apply for welfare assistance," explained Rebecca Barna, the Director of the UMW's Unemployment Assistance Fund (U.S. Congress, 1991, p. 118). The abrupt closure of many mines exacerbates these challenges by providing little time to plan. A ground-up approach might have appreciated that moving to a new career is not seamless.

Black Lung Disease

Coal country was not surprised by the broken and failed promises of assistance. For decades, coal country has been on a similar political roller-coaster when it came to black lung disease. Formally known as coal workers' pneumoconiosis, the non-curable respiratory ailment is caused by inhaling coal dust.

However, companies nor the government did not always recognize the existence of black lung. There was a long conflict between workers and companies that arose in the 1960s and 1970s with a union-led movement for a federal dust-control standard and compensation for black lung victims (Smith, 2020). It was one of the most common issues discussed in the UMW Journal publications we reviewed, and it remains salient to this day (Blackley et al., 2018).[13] Black lung represents a reminder of broken promises and a source of distrust.

Why did this distrust emerge? After concerted organizing, the federal government acted in 1969 and established the Black Lung Program that would help provide benefits for afflicted workers if their company ceased to exist or could no longer pay benefits (Szymendera and Sherlock, 2019, p. 4). Such a fund was necessary because mine owners that should assume the liability would often declare bankruptcy and reorganize, leaving workers in the dust. But just as with the Byrd and Wise Amendments, the program faced opposition because of its cost. Opponents of the compensation in the 1990 CAA Amendment debates frequently referenced the Black Lung Fund as an example of a government program that was modest at first and then ballooned in costs (U.S. Congress, 1990a, p. 3952).

Challenges also emerged with the durability of funding. An excise tax on coal production paid by mine owners provided funds for the program

---

[13] The incidence of black lung is worsening in some places with the increased mining of coal seams with silica, which causes intense respiratory damage even among younger miners (Interview with coalfield activist, July 22, 2021).

created by the Black Lung Benefits Revenue Act of 1977. Since coal revenue has declined, the program has regularly been in debt, had to borrow funds, and go through debt restructuring.

The need to reauthorize funding complicates the politics of the program. The excise tax has to be frequently renewed by Congress, including modifications to the size of the tax. If not, these levels would expire and revert to 1970s levels. This happened as recently as 2019, which forced Congress to pass temporary extensions in 2020 and 2021 (Godfrey, 2022a). The Department of Labor apologized for the political whiplash, "[w]e recognized that the status of the excise tax and the Trust Fund may be causing miners stricken with black lung disease, and their families, to feel uncertain about their benefits" (Godfrey, 2022b).

At the insistence of Senator Manchin, the Inflation Reduction Act (IRA) included a provision that permanently extended the excise tax. The move was heralded as a huge breakthrough and echoes some insights about creating credibility from Chapter 2. However, this permanent extension does not solve an inherent structural problem. Lynda Glagola, the Director of a Southwest Pennsylvania group that works with black lung patients, explained, "[e]ven with a permanent extension of the tax, black lung benefits could face a long-term funding problem. The Black Lung Disability Trust Fund is already about $5 billion in debt. As more coal mines close, they will be paying less money into the fund" (Frazier, 2022).

Other local news reports flagged this issue, including how provisions in the IRA to expand renewables would come at the cost of coal and defeat the effectiveness of the tax extension (Hicks, 2022). Phil Smith from the UMW highlighted that while the benefits may continue to be paid, there is a political problem where the tax burden falls on the public, which is never popular. These tax burden concerns we developed in Chapter 2 can contribute to credibility challenges, of which coal country is acutely aware.

The legacy of black lung hung over the 1990 CAA Amendments not only in the arguments levied by opponents of compensation but also in the minds of workers, unions, and communities, where there was mistrust about the durability of federal programs. This skepticism was warranted in certain respects. The already pared-back training program expired, similar to how the black lung fund struggled to survive. This political whiplash contributes to uncertainty and a sense that the rest of the country has forgotten about or is not interested in helping coal communities.

Credibility at What Cost?

The thoughtful discussion in Patashnik (2014, Chapter 8) on the 1990 CAA Amendments conveys a success story. In many respects, it was a success. Pollution that caused acid rain declined, the market-based tradeable permit systems took hold, and interest groups eventually found common ground. One ingredient of the bargain that Patashnik argues helped to achieve this reform is that when it came to labor displacement, there was only a temporary accommodation with no commitments to future assistance.[14]

However, this bargain highlights a fundamental tension explored throughout our book. The front-ended and temporary compensation for the losers helped to close the deal by assuaging lawmakers concerned about future costs. It avoided a veto that the Bush administration threatened. It may well have also contributed to the durability of the overall set of laws. But the bargain did not create credibility for the communities and industries hallowed out by the law. Yet because of the divide-and-conquer tactics of the bill's proponents, their buy-in was not pivotal, so they were left behind. However, this may not work for future climate bargains. Moreover, analysts see the coal transition in Appalachia as an example of how *not* to do transitions from a social, economic, and moral perspective.

LESSONS FROM ABROAD? GERMANY'S COAL PHASE-OUT

Like Appalachia, Germany has historically been a massive producer and consumer of coal. Hard coal deposits drove the post–World War II industrial economy of West Germany.[15] Germany's industrial base, with steel at its core, was hungry for cheap energy. Domestic coal production satiated that appetite and played a significant role in West Germany's growth. Hard coal production employed over 600,000 people at its peak in 1957, but competition from cheap foreign oil quickly eroded the sector. After steep drops in the 1960s, hard coal employment gradually declined. In 2018, the last hard coal mine closed.

---

[14] Patashnik (2014, p. 144) writes of the concessions made to high-sulfur utilities and mine owners, "In sum, the main compensation payments for reform losers were not only front-ended (creating some immediate buy-in from economic interests), but they were relatively insulated from the political interventions of future Congresses."

[15] Hard coal has a high carbon content, so it can be used both for electricity production and industrial applications.

Germany also has lignite coal, sometimes called "brown coal," which has shaped the country's development. Lignite deposits are spread across the former West and East Germany. Lignite production grew until the reunification of Germany when it faced a sharp drop off, which was severe in East Germany such as in Lusatia due to the relative inefficiency of those mines. The decline of lignite hit communities doubly hard because the power plants that use lignite are often located near the mouth of the mine.[16]

Unlike hard coal, there is still active mining for lignite. In 2020, after pressure from the European Union and domestic groups, Germany announced plans for a phase-out, but this process has been challenging (Oei, Brauers, and Herpich, 2020). Despite recent success, the process has been slow and regularly impeded by deeply rooted coal sector opposition, industrial interests, and their political partners (Hermwille and Kiyar, 2022; Rentier, Lelieveldt, and Kramer, 2019). Unexpected events like the energy crisis sparked by the war in Ukraine prompted a lignite mining expansion, despite the phase-out plans (Reuters, 2023).

While the German experience contains instructive lessons, it, too, has faced challenges, even with the substantial resources brought to bear. Our contrast between Germany and the United States is for illustrative purposes. A slew of differences, including institutions, economics, and culture, implicate whether success stories travel to other countries. Some of these differences, such as institutions that provide broad social safety nets or a history of robust vocational training (e.g., Hall and Soskice, 2001; Thelen, 2004), may not appear realistic in other contexts, such as the United States with its aversion to social welfare programs (e.g., Gilens, 2000) and developing countries that lack resources. We revisit these issues in Chapter 9.

As early as 2007, the national and state governments decided to begin a phase-out of hard coal mining by 2018. In 2020, Germany enacted new programs to phase out all coal-powered electricity production and lignite mining. These reforms resulted from a multiyear process, including the establishment of a Coal Commission in 2018.[17] The first reform was a law that set timelines to decommission coal mines and power plants, provided generous payments to operations and supplied bridge funding for older workers before they could access their pensions. The second law made investments in coal regions to help them adjust.[18] Other countries

---

[16] This is to minimize shipping costs given the lower profitability of lignite coal, which burns less efficiently than hard coal due to its higher water content.

[17] The Commission for Growth, Structural Change and Employment.

[18] Coal Phase-Out Act and the Structural Support for Coal Regions Act.

Lessons from Abroad? Germany's Coal Phase-Out — 169

took note.[19] The structural support legislation established substantial funds for lignite coal mining regions, including resources for infrastructure investments. Total funding for the structural adjustment rang in at nearly 41 billion euros (Raitbaur, 2021).

Sources of (Relative) Success

Comparisons of the German experience with the United States highlight four factors that contributed to relatively positive transitions: stakeholder engagement, advance notice and planning, continuity for displaced workers, and diverse and robust investments. We unpack these factors, then turn to enduring challenges.

Just Listen to Us! Stakeholder Engagement

A crucial component of Germany's Coal Commission was its efforts to engage local stakeholders. Engagement happened on two fronts: the planning process that led to the policy reforms and the design and governance of investments. This local engagement echoes the suggestions from officials in the United States whom we surveyed in Chapter 3.

The composition of the Coal Commission reflects its emphasis on local stakeholder engagement. The commission includes representatives from unions, companies, civil society organizations, and regional policymakers. This group engaged in an eight-month deliberation to try to find a compromise from these societal interests. The history of industry, labor and government collaboration facilitated this process. Regional and local stakeholders could make their voices heard, which enabled them to advocate for their needs (Bang, Rosendahl, and Böhringer, 2022; Gürtler, Beer, and Herberg, 2021). The program helped regions to identify projects rather than having initiatives mandated from the top down (Heimann and Popp, 2020).

One reason for this broad stakeholder input is that Germany's electoral system, which uses proportional representation, creates a dynamic where parties need to form coalitions to govern. As a result, parties bring different interests to the bargaining table, which provides opportunities for diverse stakeholder engagement. That said, stakeholder input has emerged in other electoral contexts and, as we discuss below, the process has not always been inclusive (e.g., Bang, Rosendahl, and Böhringer, 2022).

---

[19] Spain, for example, adopted similar aspirations (Anzilotti, 2018).

Just Tell Us! Advance Notice and Planning

When workers and communities have ample advance notice of layoffs and economic disruption, they can plan with the active participation of companies, civil society, and the government. Germany's process surfaced the need for advance notice and planning to put transitions on the radar well ahead of time (Cunningham and Schmillen, 2021; Furnaro et al., 2021). Identifying who will be impacted, when, and their needs, such as training, social services, and income support, can help to smooth the transition.

Multiyear advance notice also allows participants to play an active role in the design of transition plans. If they feel part of the process to define their future, stakeholders are more likely to take those next steps, even if they are difficult and require substantial adjustments. In contrast, sudden unanticipated changes make it challenging to plan and garner buy-in from impacted workers, their families, and communities.

However, advance notice provisions need enforcement. The United States has struggled on this front, as we discuss in Chapter 8. Even Australia, which requires three years of notice for the closure of a power plant, has run into enforcement issues (Shields and Campbell, 2021, p. 5).

Nonetheless, advanced notice could give workers more time to prepare, which makes them more confident in their future. We conducted a survey experiment in the United States where we told participants that the government would fund a program for retraining. We told one group that the workers could participate before being laid off, while we informed the other group that they could only participate after being laid off. We find that advance notice led people to be modestly more confident in their economic future.[20] In practice, this "on-the-job" training will require that power plant or mine owners assume responsibility for these employees. It also requires sufficient funding (Sheldon, Junankar, and De Rosa Pontello, 2018, p. 57).

Keep It Smooth: Continuity for Displaced Workers

Unlike the experience of workers in Appalachia, Germany's coal phaseout takes place against the backdrop of an established welfare state. Both before and after a worker is laid off, Germany has a system of temporary income support, retraining, and social programs that workers and their families can access (Cunningham and Schmillen, 2021). This includes

---

[20] The effect size is a 4.4 percent increase. Linear regression model with controls ($p < 0.05$). Survey fielded in October 2022 with CAPS/Harris ($N = 2,006$).

health, counseling, and education services. Crucially, these programs are not limited to temporary income support. Workers need to be able to make ends meet while training. One often-cited reason Americans do not take advantage of workforce programs, a question we explore in Chapter 7, is that one cannot earn a living to support their families while training. This highlights the importance of retraining before economic dislocation, especially when there is not generous income support.

Much More than Jobs: Support for Community-Wide Development

Transitional support that includes community-wide investment is often seen as more effective than programs that solely target unemployed workers (e.g., Rosen, 2008). Place-based investments, including infrastructure, education, and even research and development, can catalyze a broad base of self-reinforcing economic activity. Germany's hard coal phase-out illustrates the value of place-based investments. During the initial years of the transition, entrenched coal interests limited the extent to which new, broad economic investments could be made. Over time, however, broader forward-looking policies were put in place that ushered in diversified investments that focused on community and regional level recovery (Oei, Brauers, and Herpich, 2020). The 2020 programs for lignite coal embraced this holistic approach to local investment as a cornerstone of the policy (Litz, Graichen, and Peter, 2019).

Enduring Challenges

Engaged Enough?

While Germany has attempted to adopt an inclusive process, this has not been without challenges. The Commission was not always transparent about the process and would often prioritize scientific "experts" or organized interest groups rather than citizens and communities, which resulted in political disagreement and delays (Gürtler, Beer, and Herberg, 2021; Heimann and Popp, 2020). The public participation period was only 24 hours, which calls into question how meaningful the process for input was and whose voices were heard (Raitbaur, 2021).

Weight of History

The memory of past transitions, like the reintegration of West and East Germany, casts a shadow over the politics of present coal phase-outs. In 1994, Eastern German unemployment was 14.8 percent compared to Western Germany at 8.1 percent. Despite further reintegration, in 2004, this gap expanded to 18 percent compared to the earlier 8.5 percent. This gap has shrunk in recent years but remains (Gramlich, 2019). These regional disparities color debates over coal phase-outs, which are also regional. The far-right AfD party has exploited these economic conditions to gain support by opposing the coal phase-out, which may account for its success in Eastern German lignite regions (Hermwille and Kiyar, 2022; MacGillis, 2022). Asked to characterize the mood about the phase-out in Lusatia, a region in Eastern Germany, Mayor Christine Herntier said, "I perceive a skepticism...even those who don't work directly in coal are unsettled. There was a de-industrialization of Lusatia after the fall of the Wall. Many people are now wondering how it was done this time if it failed before" (Zaremba, 2018).

This history also contributes to mistrust that exacerbates credibility challenges. "As a consequence of past experiences, there is a deeply rooted skepticism about well-sounding words and declarations of intent" (Mey et al., 2019, p. 50). These challenges lead Hermwille and Kiyar (2022) to characterize the Eastern German discourse as one of "transformation fatigue." This experience echoes the painful transformations undergone in the American Midwest, as well as the decline of steel and manufacturing.

Good Jobs and Wages, But for Whom?
It is not easy to find desirable new jobs. In Western Germany, a broad industrial base that includes automobile manufacturing facilitated its transition. In Eastern Germany, the economic opportunities are bleaker. While the Coal Commission recommended funds for retraining, these were left out of the final laws (Raitbaur, 2021). The consequences of this omission were less detrimental for Germany than for the United States' failure to fully fund training programs in the 1990 CAA Amendments; Germany already had more robust programs to support workers.

For example, in the hard-coal regions of Western Germany, the RAG Stiftung, a foundation established in 2007 for regional economic development, provides a range of support opportunities including for youths. The foundation was established when the giant mining company, RAG, exited the industry. Since it is part of a larger corporate conglomerate, it has a funding stream from its profits which enables the foundation to be well-resourced and less vulnerable to political oscillation.[21] However, no

---

[21] However, it relies on the economic vitality of the constituent companies (Brauers, Herpich, and Oei, 2018, p. 67).

Lessons from Abroad? Germany's Coal Phase-Out 173

comparable entity exists in the lignite regions of Eastern Germany (Wynn and Julve, 2016).

Green jobs are an option to help offset lost fossil fuel jobs. While that would appear promising in Germany, which pioneered solar energy equipment manufacturing, since 2011, their domestic industry collapsed due to China's entry into the market (O'Sullivan and Edler, 2020). Unanticipated economic change can upset even the best-made plans. Local economic opportunity challenges are also present in Germany. Mey et al. (2019) discuss studies conducted by unions that call attention to the currently lower wages of wind and solar compared to manufacturing. These issues have frustrated coal phase-out efforts and highlight the credibility challenge.

Bills Come Due

Germany's transition has also run into funding challenges. Some think that Germany allocated too much money, which could lead to future political frustration (e.g., Gürtler, Beer, and Herberg, 2021). A similar refrain was heard on the floor of Congress during the 1990 CAA Amendment debates, where legislators scoffed at setting up what might become a blank check that would be fiscally unsustainable.

While localities have experienced budget issues like in Appalachia, unlike the United States, regional tax-sharing programs have helped to smooth the transition (Furnaro et al., 2021). Renewable energy has also been proposed as a potential source for local tax revenue creation. Yet, Mayor Herntier, thinks, "In contrast to conventional energy generation, municipalities do not benefit from renewables" (Zaremba, 2018). There is a common problem, but the United States and Germany have taken different approaches.

Contrasts across Countries

How does the coal transition in Appalachia stack up against Germany, or other countries for that matter? One review of coal transitions in the Rhur Valley of Germany, the Limburg region of Netherlands, Northumberland and Durham in the United Kingdom, Appalachia in the United States, and Queensland in Australia reached the following conclusion:

The Appalachian region in the United States is a heartbreaking story of industry transition characterized by short-term, reactive and fragmented responses to closures of coal mines, resulting in entrenched, inter-generational poverty and social dysfunction. Compare this with the transition...in Germany's Ruhr region, where forward planning, investment in industry diversification, staggering of mine closures and a comprehensive package of just transition measures delivered a major reshaping of the regional economy with no forced job losses (Sheldon, Junankar, and De Rosa Pontello, 2018, pp. i–ii).[22]

Meckling et al. (2022b) and Mildenberger (2020) make a broader case for the role of institutional arrangements such as corporatism seen in several European countries, including Germany. Such a national, coordinated response has been long lacking in the United States and is not easy to change overnight. American transition policies have also focused on the immediate impacts of economic dislocation rather than longer-term investments that would make for more sustainable solutions (Roemer and Haggerty, 2021). Short-term grant cycles for economic development exacerbate these challenges, an issue local officials raised in our surveys and interviews. Examples of short-term fixes include career centers set up after displacement rather than as part of a "early warning strategy."

Unfortunately, other countries face similar challenges. For example, the Czech Republic appointed a Coal Commission in 2019. However, "in contrast to similar bodies in Germany, there are only two representatives from environmental movements and the affected communities have no representative at all" (Lehotský and Černík, 2019, p. 60). This underrepresentation persists, but unlike in Appalachia, many Czech communities and their politicians have opposed mining (Ocelík et al., 2022). Memories of past failed policies also constrain transition attempts in Poland (Brauers and Oei, 2020). Colombia's Guajira and Cesar regions also have substantial economic dependence on mining and face similar constraints.

CONCLUSION

Michael, our colleague, fortunately, did not get thrown out of the plane. Though he might well have if he had suggested "suitcase" solutions; policies that simply encourage people to pack up and leave their communities (Anderson, 2022). The episode exemplifies the long history and deep frustration surrounding environmental and climate policies and their impact on workers, their families, and communities. The political constraints we highlight in this chapter and throughout the book shape how compensation and investment efforts are seen by the very people and communities these policies hope to help. The experiences of the 1990 CAA Amendments and black lung fund, and even in the relatively more

---

[22] For similar perspectives on the European experience, see Green and Gambhir (2020).

Conclusion

175

successful German case, illustrate these frustrations and help to make sense of distrust of government promises that persists.

Much can be reduced to Ted Kennedy's expression, later borrowed by Ronald Reagan: "jobs, jobs, jobs." People want to work, they want it to be good, durable, decent work, and they would rather not be displaced from their communities. Commitments to help workers and communities to transition into new industries must be credible. Yet, the experiences of these communities, in regions historically home to steel, manufacturing, and fossil fuels create legitimate doubts about credibility, even if there have been places with relative success.

The following two chapters focus squarely on issues around jobs and investments. Chapter 7 explores what can be done to make workforce development more credible. Chapter 8 examines how transparency around investments in communities can make people think that these new opportunities will make them as well or better off than they were before.

7

Making Workforce Programs Work

Stephanie Frame was optimistic about her future. Despite the collapse of coal mining jobs in her West Virginian community, including her husband's, Stephanie had a new opportunity: coding.

In 2015, a nonprofit called Mined Mines entered Appalachian coal country with the tantalizing promise to train residents for high-paid computer programming careers. One of the organization's founders, Amanda Laucher, was no stranger to coal country. She came from Nemacolin, Pennsylvania, which the Youngstown Sheet and Tube Company founded as a company mining town in 1917, thought to be the largest mine in the country at one point. Although Amanda had moved away to Chicago, she returned to help her brother, Marvin, a coal miner who turned to coding to escape looming layoffs.

Amanda thought other miners could benefit from her brother's training, so she founded Mined Mines to create a coal-to-code pipeline. "The message from the community is, look, we aren't going to be hopeless. We aren't going to just accept the fact that things are changing and be left behind. Instead, we're going to seek new opportunities...," Amanda explained in a radio interview (WNYC, 2016).

Stephanie Frame bought into this vision. "I wholeheartedly believe, and will always that God has sent Mined Minds to us to save us from what could have been a very bleak future," Stephanie said in a self-recorded promotional video for the program (Robertson, 2019).

Participants like Stephanie would undergo 32 weeks of training, including an "intensive boot camp covering the fundamentals of software development," followed by 64 weeks of apprenticeship. At the end,

Making Workforce Programs Work

there was the promise of a local job to build websites and smartphone apps.

The concept was so captivating that a local job training agency received a $1.5 million grant from the ARC, a regional development organization run by the federal government, to work with Mined Minds. The grant provided funds to "teach high-demand skills in software engineering and development to displaced workers from the coal sector in Southwest Pennsylvania and West Virginia" (ARC, 2022, p. 69). The ARC's mission is to reduce poverty in Appalachia through economic development. It has also become the main vehicle for coal transition assistance.[1] This was serious money, but participants had to show up.

"We've had people thinking we were just a scam at the start," co-founder Jonathan Graham, and Amanda's partner, recalled in an interview (Gillespie, 2016). Yet, the Mined Mines program was an apparent success. When asked if graduates of the program found jobs, Amanda's answer was unequivocal: "Every single one of them. Yes" (CBS, 2017).

In reality, almost none of the participants found programming jobs. Instead, students felt they were sold a lie. Billyjack Buzzard, a former student and ex-coal miner, said, "they come to a poverty-stricken state, made a bunch of promises like a soapbox preacher, and they failed. They failed me multiple times" (D'Souza, 2019).

Why did such a promising training program collapse so spectacularly? In one word: dysfunction. A culture of heavy drinking and erratic management undermined the program from within (Robertson, 2019). The program went from the darling of the national media to a cautionary tale. The participants felt a fraud had been perpetrated upon them and filed a class action lawsuit. Although, a journalist who covered the issue assessed, "I suspect it was more of a mess than a crime."[2]

Some see the program's collapse as evidence that it is folly to teach coal miners to code. Former New York City Mayor Michael Bloomberg's remark, "[y]ou're not going to teach a coal miner to code," encapsulates this view (Smiley, 2015). This is the wrong lesson, and it can even be counterproductive. Residents of coal country view this kind of talk as patronizing. Payton May, a former coal industry employee and now a computer programmer in Pikeville, Kentucky, remembers Bloomberg's remark with dismay. "Bloomberg made this statement earlier on that 'I don't know what you're going to do with those coal miners, but

---

[1] Coal transitional assistance comes through the Partnerships for Opportunity and Workforce and Economic Revitalization (POWER) Initiative.

[2] Interview, September 27, 2022.

you're not going to teach them how to code.' That's the misconception that we're working against." Coal miners have some transferable skills with computer programming because "miners work with a high level of technology and sophisticated equipment."[3]

The right lesson is that workforce development is hard. "In theory, it should have been a good thing for the area ... If they would have done it right, it should have worked," said a Southwest Pennsylvania resident and business owner who grew up near where Mined Mines started.[4] Even Billyjack, who had not held anything back in his criticism, still thought coding could have worked. "If I had known then what I know now, I would have went and got a two-year degree in computer science ...The reason I was pushing myself to do this every day was to not go back to coal mining ...I still have to back underground because they abruptly fired me. I wish I would have got a degree" (Kronk, 2019).

When workforce programs get incentives right, the outcomes can be uplifting. In Kentucky, a company called Bit Source also trained coal miners to become coders. Unlike Mined Mines, which was only a training program, Bit Source was its own company. Rusty Justice, the founder, said, "we started this business not because we had some idea or a product, but because we wanted to create jobs that had earnings potential equivalent to mining jobs."[5] Rusty expressed how stereotypes held by people outside of Appalachia made it hard to do business at first, "I always say, hillbilly coal miners are the Jamaican bobsled team of tech." Yet Bit Source has succeeded. Rusty said, "fewer and fewer people we talk about this story to. We just want to be known as competent in our field."

Since the workers Bit Source trained would be the company's future employees, unlike Mined Mines, everyone had skin in the game. If the miners failed to learn, the business would fail and, with it, their jobs. If the miners succeeded, all would make money. The demand for employment at Bit Source speaks for itself. The region had undergone the loss of well-paid mining jobs, and people were desperate for work. Rusty remembers, "we had 950 applicants, and we interviewed 60 or so and selected 10...those were two of the hardest days in my life because we were only gonna hire ten of them ... heartbreaking stories." By aligning the incentives of the students and the company, Bit Source made the training program credible.

---

[3] Interview, November 16, 2022.
[4] Correspondence with Southwest Pennsylvania resident, September 26, 2022.
[5] Interview, November 16, 2022.

Why This Matters 179

Credibility is necessary because uncertainty hangs over workforce transitions. In Bit Source's headquarters, there is a striking mural of a miner staring through a seam of coal that opens into a fluorescent-lit room of sleek computers. "You get a bit of the depth there of the mystery of going from one type of work to another," Payton said. "I think it was like that for our folks. They were peering into a brand new world, and it was frightening, too, but they were ready to get into that. And where our mural is, on the other side of it is our development room where people work, which is symbolic."

WHY THIS MATTERS

This chapter is about this book's third puzzle: the green workforce shortage. Why have governments and the private sector struggled to build a green labor force despite the societal demand for clean energy? If there are not enough electricians, for instance, countries cannot move quickly enough to decarbonize our homes, buildings, and infrastructure. We also examine the flip side of this question, why have efforts to transition fossil fuel workers to new careers been so hard, and what be done?

Workforce programs will be central to building the green workforce and transitioning fossil fuel workers. These are programs that equip individuals with skills for new jobs. Training initiatives, sometimes called "active labor market policies," take several forms, such as classroom lessons for high school certificates, vocational training for an occupation, and on-the-job training with an employer (LaLonde, 2003). Governments, companies, unions, and nonprofits all play an active role independently and jointly. Workforce programs differ in their objectives. Some help workers adjust to economic disruption, while others are industry-led efforts to create a skilled workforce.

For workforce programs to succeed, they will have to inspire participation. Studies from labor economics focus on factors like the opportunity cost of lost time and income to explain the effectiveness of active labor market policies (e.g., Heckman et al., 1998), and emphasize interventions like nudges to encourage participation and completion (e.g., Babcock et al., 2012).

We argue that credibility is also crucial. First, perceptions of the local economic opportunities of industries should influence interest in career paths, with people preferring jobs in industries seen as stable sources of good livelihoods. Second, the credibility of the organization sponsoring training, be it the government or a company, impacts expectations about

180   *Making Workforce Programs Work*

the benefits of training for a new career. For instance, the prospect that a new political leader might come to power and cut a training program could chill participation.

Through surveys of the national public, youths, and middle schoolers in a fossil fuel community, we find that interest in career paths is highly related to the perceptions of whether an industry will grow in the future and provide well-paid, long-lasting, and local jobs. People are most eager to pursue careers in industries that provide for more certain employment. For middle schoolers in Southwest Pennsylvania, this translates into greater interest in occupations tied to the local oil, gas, and coal industries and less interest in energy efficiency careers.

Then, we evaluate whether the solutions we identify in Chapter 2 to create credibility make a difference. We find that when the government ties the hands of future leaders and sends a costly signal of its commitment to training program participants, people become more likely to enroll in green jobs programs and anticipate that the benefits from these jobs will go to the community. Making training programs credible could help unlock the clean energy workforce bottleneck.

Workforce development may seem obscure, but it is a crucial institution that shapes the economic prospects of nations (e.g., Thelen, 2004). Many policies that leaders pursue, including and beyond the clean energy transition, hinge on whether there is a talented labor pool. With the move to re-shore manufacturing back to the United States, such as computer chips, a key constraint will be whether there is a domestic labor force. Yet, this chapter shows how a shift into any new industry entails not only economic risks for individuals but also political uncertainties. How to make workforce development work is a task that companies, local leaders, and national policymakers urgently need to understand.

WORKFORCE AND THE ENERGY TRANSITION

Where Are the Electricians?

The world is far behind in its workforce needs for the clean energy transition. Markets might eventually adjust if a prolonged shortage increases wages. But the International Renewable Energy Agency (IRENA), an organization that collects information about renewable energy, declared in its annual assessment that the transition "...will require more vocational training, stronger curricula and greater training of trainers" (IRENA, 2021, p. 3). Training programs must recruit talented workers to

Workforce and the Energy Transition

prevent a labor bottleneck that could derail the potential progress from new climate investments like the Inflation Reduction Act (IRA) in the United States.

There are consequences of an insufficiently trained workforce. In Australia, a popular building insulation program imploded when inadequate training and poor management led to deficient projects (Bowen, 2012, p. 29). This uncertainty can dampen consumer appetite for energy efficiency upgrades. The more fundamental problem is that if there are not enough workers, renewable energy projects cannot be built with the speed that the climate crisis requires.

Despite the growth of clean energy, training programs for these jobs in the United States and elsewhere have struggled. For example, after the great recession, Congress funded a workforce program to the tune of half a billion dollars, much of it going to targeted grants for clean energy job training. However, a government audit interviewed 11 of the 103 green jobs training programs that received grants and found that "only 55 percent of program participants found jobs" (GAO, 2013, p. 27). The audit attributes part of the blame to "the lack of credible green jobs labor market information," which led to programs in places where there was little demand (GAO, 2013, p. 27).

More recently, a puzzling workforce gap has emerged in the wind industry. On the one hand, wind developers report not being able to find enough qualified workers. While on the other hand, wind training programs say that their graduates cannot find work. More than two-thirds of wind program graduates do not enter the wind industry after graduating (Keyser and Tegen, 2019, p. 22).

Why have workforce shortages persisted despite the societal demand for clean energy?

When the Pink Slip Arrives

Workforce programs will also play a part in helping fossil fuel workers transition into new careers. When the pink slip arrives, a notice of layoffs, people will need to look elsewhere for work. Workforce programs can help reduce the cost of this transition and ensure that communities benefit from the growing green economy. However, while green jobs represent one option, they are not – and should not be – the exclusive focus of training programs to help fossil fuel workers adjust.

An often overlooked consideration is that the fossil fuel workforce transition will look different across this wide-ranging and diverse sector.

182 *Making Workforce Programs Work*

The coal and oil industries are quite distinct, which implies different levels and types of workforce assistance for these populations (Ravikumar and Latimer, 2022). Even within coal-reliant industries, there are differences in approach. Contrast electric power and mining companies. Since electric utilities have clearly defined retirement schedules for their power plants, there is a more orderly transition process in place (e.g., Foster et al., 2022). A senior official at an electric power company described the importance of helping employees transition at a coal-fired power plant that had shut down. "One of the important things we did was around employees ... every employee, there was basically a guaranteed job if they wanted one."[6] Workforce training was also part of the utility's plan for the community. For example, the company paid for an aerospace internship program that "ended up being so successful that [the company] decided that they would just keep that program going and pay for it themselves." In contrast, coal mining companies have a worse reputation. Residents of Southwest Pennsylvania would recount stories of friends or family who arrived at work only to discover a pink slip in their locker since the mine had closed.[7] This type of abrupt disruption makes it harder for workers to plan to transition into new careers.

Even though notification can help, it does not remove the shock. For example, Tracy Bertram, recalls her surprise when Xcel alerted her that the coal-fired power plant in her community would be decommissioned, which will result in the layoffs of hundreds of workers. The utility promised to make investments in new community projects, including solar energy. However, even years later, you can hear the frustration in Tracy's voice.

Do you remember where you were on 9/11? Do you know exactly where you were, what you were probably wearing ...The day that Xcel called the meeting into the council chambers. I know exactly everything down to the smell of the room that day. It was, it was a shock.[8]

It's not just about coal, oil, and gas. The energy transition will impact workers across industries in unexpected ways. The United Auto Workers, the main auto worker union in the United States, acknowledged the need to begin planning for labor disruptions stemming from the growth of EVs (UAW, 2019, p. 4). In Chapter 2, we heard from autoworkers who know the risks to their jobs. Some worry that the jobs of the future will

---

[6] Interview, July 28, 2022.
[7] Interview with two Southwest Pennsylvania residents, August 12, 2022.
[8] Interview, August 30, 2022.

Credibility and Workforce Programs 183

require more than a high school degree: "I think a lot of people don't realize today that some of the jobs that only took a high school diploma to get a job are now taking someone that may have a bachelor's degree" (quoted in Foster et al., 2022, p. 14).

But as with the struggles to build a green workforce, efforts to transition fossil fuel workers confront a puzzle: getting people to sign up. For example, in Southwest Pennsylvania, where there have been layoffs in the coal industry, the participation rates for training programs were well below 20 percent after one notable mine closure (Volcovici, 2017). "[Four hundred] people were displaced from their work. We saw very few of them seeking help at the unemployment centers; very few of them went to the career centers and said, Hey, I need to retrain."[9]

There are many reasons why displaced workers might not try to retrain. For one, they might already have skills that align with jobs available in their community. Another common explanation in economic studies is that people fear that the lost time and wages of program participation outweigh any future gains in productivity or career advancement. People are often not paid during training, and when they receive stipends, the value often falls short of the cost of living. Potentially, for this reason, a large share of participants drop out of training programs (Heckman et al., 2000). Yet, attempts to encourage participation have been met with a tepid response. One large-scale randomized experiment found that only half of the job seekers targeted for enhanced counseling participated (Behaghel, Crépon, and Gurgand, 2014).

Why do these nudges fail? What could be done to encourage people to sign up for workforce programs?

CREDIBILITY AND WORKFORCE PROGRAMS

We argue that credibility is an important part of the answer to why green labor shortages persist and participation in workforce programs is low. Training for a new career is fraught with uncertainty. People care foremost about whether they will find a job on the other end and if they can afford the process. As one solar instructor from North Carolina said, participants "always ask, am I going to get a job after this...How much is it going to cost."[10] The lack of credibility increases uncertainty about finding a job, which leads people to either focus on different career paths or not enter a program in the first place.

---

[9] Interview with local politician in Southwest Pennsylvania, May 27, 2021.
[10] Interview, August 16, 2022.

184 *Making Workforce Programs Work*

When it comes to clean energy sector jobs, the government credibility and local economic concerns that we develop in the first half of the book explain why people might be uncertain about careers in green industries.

Political Uncertainty

When labor demand comes from targeted government investments in industries, as has been the case for green energy, employment prospects depend on sustained political support. One senior executive at a wind developer described how this political uncertainty undermines recruitment:

As a craft worker, you want steady employment. And when you see a ramp up, and then you know that at the end of the ramp up, there's going to be a slowdown, that's not what they need. And that's hard for them to take care of their families ... when there's the ebb and flow of projects, so long-term government policy will help that.[11]

A report from the National Renewable Energy Laboratory describes how shifting political winds undercut demand for the wind workforce. "[D]ue to stalling of wind projects from state policy several years ago...there are few companies actively recruiting students at our university" (Keyser and Tegen, 2019, p. 25). This uncertainty about sustained government support is not unique to green jobs but occurs in other industries, such as semiconductor manufacturing spurred on by industrial policy efforts (Clark and Swanson, 2023).

A tricky coordination problem also contributes to worries about the demand for new jobs. On the one hand, there must be a credible supply of employment. Otherwise, people may be reluctant to enter workforce programs for speculative career prospects on the other side. On the other hand, if there is not a ready supply of labor, companies may not want to make significant investments in a community since they fear not having an adequate workforce. There is no single solution to this coordination challenge, but at a minimum it will require stakeholders to come to the table to work together.

Local Jobs

Economic opportunity considerations like local jobs can also create reluctance to train for green jobs. A common reason cited for why training

---

[11] Interview with senior manager at wind energy developer, August 30, 2022.

Credibility and Workforce Programs

program participants abandon the wind industry is that they find better outside opportunities (Keyser and Tegen, 2019, p. 22). One wind turbine technician instructor in West Virginia emphasized the importance of local jobs as part of this decision.

The trainees, the overwhelming majority want to work locally ... I've had students offered jobs in Pennsylvania, but they turned them down because they eventually want to work in West Virginia. That's because family is here, and friends, and that's a priority ... if more jobs could stay local ... that might be something that would entice more students to go into the field.[12]

Other aspects of jobs like pay and temporariness should also shape expectations of the benefits of developing new skills. If a new career supports a good livelihood, people might entertain what is otherwise a costly and uncertain training program.

Not Listening

It also helps if potential participants trust the organization that facilitates the training program. For example, farmers in the peat transition in Ireland thought that workforce efforts were just a "political act" rather than a genuine attempt to help (Banerjee and Schuitema, 2022). Likewise, MacNeil and Beauman (2022, p. 122) interviewed individuals in Australian coal country, and uncovered a palpable distrust of the government's solutions.

Oh, right, that's where they're going to turn me into an [expletive] coder, yeah?... I do not actually even know what coding is, to be honest, but I doubt I'd be any good at it. I'm sure some of the guys here could do that sort of thing. But, look, even if they could, where exactly are they going to work? You reckon Google or Facebook are going to open a branch here in [rural Queensland]? Doubt it. And these guys do not want to move to the cities. We've lived here our whole lives, and most people here have no desire to leave, as far as I can tell.

The fact that the government did not recognize how unrealistic its proposed "solutions" were contributed to this coal miner's distrust.

Many discussions frame the workforce transitions in unhelpful ways, which may contribute to distrust. Emblematic of this is the label "retraining," which does not always acknowledge the skills that workers bring from previous occupations. The notion that one needs to be "retrained" can come across as patronizing from outsiders.

---

[12] Interview, September 12, 2022.

What I hear is we want to protect the environment, and it's gonna generate a lot of money. Well, what are we going to do with that money is my question. You gonna bring a manufacturing plant to my district, so when you put all my coal miners out of work, and everybody with a power plant out of work, they have somewhere to go? No, no, no, we're gonna, we're gonna educate and retrain them. *That's offensive to me because my coal miners and my union brothers and sisters are educated and trained.*

These remarks came from Democratic Pennsylvania State Representative Pam Snyder, voicing her opposition to RGGI, a regional program to limit emissions.[13] While this rhetoric might be strategic, it also reflects a genuine feeling of being left behind.[14] Coal, oil, and gas workers, as well as those tied to fossil fuels in less direct ways like gasoline engine builders, have serious skills that should be recognized and framed as advantages that enable the workforce transition. Pipefitters and boilermakers, for instance, have a skill set that can be applied to geothermal energy, which involves a sophisticated drilling process.

Narrow Focus on Green Jobs

For fossil fuel workers, there may be a reluctance to pivot into clean sector jobs. This reluctance often goes unrecognized despite the piles of optimistic analyses about the feasibility of reallocating fossil fuel workers to clean energy jobs (e.g., Curtis and Marinescu, 2022; Louie and Pearce, 2016; Pollin and Callaci, 2019; Sustainable Development Solutions Network, 2020). While these analyses may be valid in simple *economic* terms, they neglect the social and political context in which people make decisions about whether to prepare for a new career. For instance, Louie and Pearce (2016) contend that a small investment would be sufficient to train all coal workers for solar jobs. Yet there are practical questions like the geographic mismatches between where jobs are created and where people call home (e.g., Pai et al., 2020). Another issue is differential labor intensity, where fossil fuel jobs tend to require more workers per unit of energy produced than alternative energy sources.

Broken Promises

The history of promises to provide training for dislocated workers also injects uncertainty and mistrust that may make potential participants

---

[13] May 25, 2021 speech.

[14] Political leaders in the western United States have made similar criticisms (Woodruff, 2021).

Credibility and Workforce Programs

wary. Consider Trade Adjustment Assistance (TAA) to help workers hurt by trade. This program provides extended unemployment benefits and tuition reimbursement for training. One issue is low program responsiveness, where the areas hurt most by globalization do not receive aid (Autor, Dorn, and Hanson, 2013). Others disagree and show that adjustment assistance is slightly more responsive, but there is still an undersupply (Kim and Pelc, 2021). Even then, only about 25 percent of eligible workers in 2020 used their benefits and services (DOL, 2020). Of those workers using their benefits, less than half engaged in training.[15]

Studies evaluating the performance of TAA training outcomes reach mixed findings about the program's effect on long-run earnings. One analysis commissioned by the Department of Labor found that only 37 percent of training program participants found employment in occupations for which they received training. Moreover, participants had an average of $53,802 long-run lower earnings than the comparison group members (Dolfin and Schochet, 2012). In contrast, Hyman (2018) finds the opposite. Ten years after receiving training, participants have $50,000 higher cumulative earnings on average. Yet, what may be most relevant for dislocated workers are not long-term outcomes, which may be viewed as uncertain and even unhelpful, but one's short-term earnings. Given this uncertainty, it is more understandable why workers might be reluctant to enter training programs.[16]

Beyond TAA, studies of the effectiveness of workforce programs more broadly have reached mixed conclusions.[17] Whether a program worked is often evaluated using two criteria: employment rates and earnings. Crépon and van den Berg (2016) examine evaluations of active labor market policies and find little evidence for positive effects. Card, Kluve, and Weber (2010) conduct a meta-analysis of 97 studies and discover that training programs have positive, medium-term impacts but often appear ineffective in the short term. However, Heckman, Lalonde, and Smith (1999, p. 2080) investigate 75 studies and conclude that government-funded training has had little effect on the workforce's skills. Yet, there

---

[15] This is even with notification by an administrative law judge that one is eligible for benefits.

[16] There are also electoral consequences of (not) receiving assistance (e.g., Margalit, 2011; Ritchie and You, 2021).

[17] Previous studies focus on training programs designed to improve the earnings of unemployed and low-income workers, a population that differs from the individuals impacted by the energy transition.

are more optimistic assessments when it comes to particular programs. Barnow (1987) finds suggestive evidence that public service employment and on-the-job training were more effective at increasing earnings than classroom instruction and work experience.

Cross-national differences could influence the effectiveness of training programs. An issue raised in Chapter 6 is that in the United States, there is less robust continuity of income for dislocated workers than in European countries like Germany.[18] Workers often must rely on traditional "safety net" programs like unemployment insurance, which covers only 40 percent of lost wages. While employment and training services are available, the lack of income can make training hard, even when books, fees, rent, and childcare are sometimes subsidized (Spiker, 2020). The broader ecosystem of social programs influences the incentives and resources for entering workforce programs.

Sometimes workers receive assistance from their companies to help with training. However, the funds can be far from sufficient to support a family. One former worker at a "coke" plant (coal used in steel) in West Virginia described how when he was laid off, the company gave him an option to "retrain for HVAC," but that his income stipend felt like a joke. "You think $700 a week is enough to take care of them," he gestured to his two kids.[19] He eventually trained for a new career over one year and nine months, but the process was emotionally and financially scaring. It is hard to determine whether one could call this outcome a "success."

LOCAL ECONOMIC OPPORTUNITY REVISITED

Interest in different career paths should be related to expectations of local economic opportunity from an industry. There should be greater interest in industries seen as providing credible local benefits. These are the jobs for which there should be greater certainty about local demand.[20] To explore the relationship between credible local benefits and interest in green jobs, we revisit our results from Chapter 4, where we investigated beliefs about local economic opportunity.

---

[18] TAA is a partial exception.

[19] Interview, August 7, 2022.

[20] Uncertainty matters. Survey results in the online appendix show that most of the national public believes that changing industries would entail a moderate or large adjustment. Breaking the descriptive results down by youth and non-youth, youths are less likely to see industry changes as a large adjustment.

The Jobs People Want

What careers spark people's interest? Interest in an occupation is the first step to encouraging participation in a workforce program. If today's youths are uninspired by green jobs, that could spell trouble for the roll-out of clean energy.[21] Teenagers and people in their early 20s are making critical decisions about their career paths. A senior manager at a wind developer lamented the struggle of finding a skilled workforce and pointed to the next generation as a solution: "For the last 40 plus years ... parents have been encouraging their kids to go to college and not to pick up a trade ... our workforce is aging as a result of that...we really need to get on top of that, to start recruiting in middle school and high school...and push the trades to the younger generation."[22]

To answer this question, we asked adults and youths across the nation how interested they would be in careers across the same ten industries as before (e.g., solar energy, computer programming, etc.).[23] Figure 7.1 reports the percent of adults and youths who are very or moderately interested in a career for each industry. As before, healthcare garners the most interest, whereas coal mining invites little interest. Green jobs are somewhere in between. Environmental cleanup and solar energy are near the top of the list but still fall short of healthcare. Energy efficiency and wind energy are in the middle of the pack but are less intriguing than computer programming for youths. These patterns in career interest mirror beliefs about local economic opportunity uncovered in Chapter 4.

Career Day

It is already a challenge to reach youth across the nation. Even more daunting is accessing young people in fossil fuel communities. Yet the perspective of youths in areas that produce coal, oil, and gas is crucial. They are in the midst of consequential career choices that could help expand the clean energy economy in places that must transition.

Through interviews with senior staff at schools in the Southwest Pennsylvania area, we obtained internal surveys of middle school students conducted by the local career center. These surveys were fielded during

---

[21] Even elite higher education institutions have few resources and paths for pursuing clean energy and other energy transition careers (Holbrooke and Tingley, 2022).

[22] Interview, August 30, 2022.

[23] Fielded June/July 2022 with Qualtrics ($N = 1,136$).

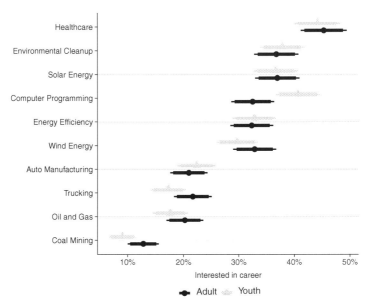

FIGURE 7.1 Percent of adults and youths who are very or moderately interested in industry careers.

2018 and used to inform the curriculum for the next school year, specifically what new career pathway program the center would develop. A total of 556 students took the survey.[24]

The survey is informative in two ways. First, the answers tell us about the preferences of middle schoolers. Second, the design of the questionnaire is also informative. Choices, such as what career pathways are included, reflect the beliefs of teachers and administrators about what industries and occupations are viable. Of the career pathways included, none were renewable energy jobs. There were four options for the students to choose from: heating, ventilating, and air-conditioning (HVAC); diesel mechanics; and construction and heavy equipment operation.[25] The closest to a "green" job was HVAC, which we refer to as energy efficiency.[26] Examples of career pathways listed for energy efficiency are

[24] Since the survey is of a vulnerable population, all personal identifying information is removed.
[25] Under each career option was a bullet-point list of common tasks performed in the career, such as installing and serving heating and air-conditioning units for energy efficiency, or maintenance and repair of trucks for diesel mechanics. The last page of the survey included a list of career pathways, such as an electrician for energy efficiency or a mine shuttle car operator for diesel mechanic.
[26] These are the key services provided for increasing energy efficiency as defined by DOE (2022, p. 130).

Local Economic Opportunity Revisited

electricians or air-conditioning technicians. Both will be needed for the energy transition.

When Alex asked about wind or solar jobs, the question was met with laughter. "It would take 16,000 wind turbines to replace [that coal plant]," said the vocational school director.[27] The same goes for solar. One superintendent said, "solar doesn't have the potential for jobs. Companies are starting to invest, but as far as adjusting the education process, you have issues – initially, you have jobs when you put a solar farm in, but how many people do you need afterward?" This is not dogmatic opposition to clean energy. As put by another local superintendent, "we're open to ideas, but we need an investment. We are willing to change. We are open to any industry or business that would promote jobs. We need help."

By contrast, the jobs most in demand by the local industries are in coal and gas. These occupations fall in the diesel mechanic, construction, and heavy equipment operation career pathways. The demand from these industries was part of the reason for the schools' interest in offering these specialized programs. There was a higher chance that students would find successful employment. As put by the head of the vocational school, "[we are] a catalyst of education in meeting the needs of business. We can't justify it unless we can make sure there are jobs for 25–30 kids."[28]

Each student ranked her top career pathways from most to least preferred. Figure 7.2 shows the percentage of people who ranked each career first, second, third, and fourth. Masonry receives the most first-place rankings, whereas energy efficiency receives the most last-place rankings. While the clean energy expansion is already creating considerable demand for energy efficiency type jobs, the middle schoolers do not perceive these economic opportunities.[29]

The middle schooler survey from Southwest Pennsylvania shows that students prefer career pathways for which there is local demand. Masonry, construction, and diesel mechanics are the top three occupations that excite students. This matches the business activity in the area,

---

[27] Interview, August 11, 2022.

[28] Interview, August 11, 2022.

[29] We also estimate the overall career pathway preference ordering. Since the data are ranked, we cannot simply average the ranks and must take special care in analyzing preferences. We conduct a rank aggregation analysis to find the optimal rank ordering. We employ machine learning techniques for this task. The results show that masonry comes in first, followed by construction, then diesel mechanics, and energy efficiency comes in last. This mirrors the patterns in the raw distribution of responses.

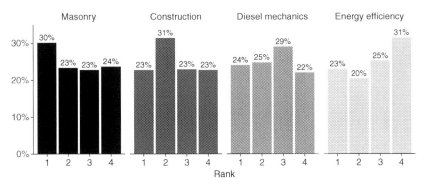

FIGURE 7.2 Rank ordering of career pathways by middle school students in a Southwest Pennsylvania fossil fuel community. Youths show greater interest in fossil fuel industry occupations compared to energy efficiency.

which engages in coal mining and gas extraction. Tangible job opportunities in the community matter for youth perceptions of the careers in which they might specialize.

THE DAY AFTER GRADUATION

The fear that political and economic changes could lead training programs and green investments to be cut, as well as doubts about whether the government acts in the interest of its citizens, creates credibility challenges that can undermine participation in workforce programs. However, the solutions developed in Chapter 2 offer a path forward to make workforce programs more credible. Specifically, we propose how the government could leverage debt to tie the hands of future leaders and send costly signals that the government is committed to creating green jobs.

Here's one way it could work. If the government made a considerable investment to prepare workers for green jobs, the fiscal burden would constrain a future administration that might otherwise prefer to roll back the investment and training program. This argument takes inspiration from the model by the political economists Alberto Alesina and Guido Tabellini (1990), who show how leaders could constrain the spending of future governments with current investment allocations. Imagine that a future government opposed renewable energy and sought to slash the investment and jobs programs. The politician would face a costly decision: cutting the investment would mean the government would not get its money back from workers. This budgetary trade-off would force the leader to compromise on other priorities, harming re-election prospects.

The Day after Graduation

The action to absorb the risk of the training program also sends a costly signal that the government represents the public's interests and can fulfill its promises, which further enhances credibility.

We use a survey experiment to see if these solutions to make workforce training more credible increase willingness to participate and expectation of local benefits from green jobs. We field the survey in a nationally representative sample.[30] The sample also includes youths between 16 and 24 years of age. These youths are just entering the workforce.

The survey vignette presented the respondent with a state government investment to expand renewable energy and a program to train workers for the new jobs. We focus on state governments because they often administer workforce development programs.

We translate the hand-tying and costly signaling solutions into our experiment with a conditional loan program. Here's how it works. The survey says the government will provide loans to help cover educational expenses during training for renewable energy jobs. We randomized a key detail of the loan program that determines whether it ties the hands of the government and sends a costly signal. In the control condition, repayment of the loan is unconditional. Whether an individual finds solar or wind energy work is irrelevant to their obligation to pay back the government. However, in the treatment condition, the student does not have to repay the loan if she does not find a green energy job within five years.[31]

The conditional loan treatment creates an incentive for the government to support the renewable energy industry to recoup its lending costs. This allows the current government to tie the hands of a future leader, which might face budget shortfalls if she repealed programs supporting green energy. The conditional loan treatment also has the government absorb more of the risk of the workforce program failing. Doing so sends a costly signal that the government truly represents the interests of its constituents.

Our primary outcome is an index of three survey questions that capture the perception of local benefits from the workforce program. The first outcome measure in the index asks how likely one would be to

---

[30] We fielded an earlier version of the survey, then added subsequent questions to validate our interpretation that credibility is responsible for the observed effects. We report results from the sample from June/July 2022 with Qualtrics that included the complete set of interpretation checks.

[31] We also randomized the loan size to control how respondents might understand the fiscal effects of the program.

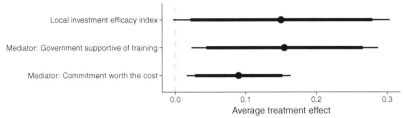

FIGURE 7.3 Effect of hand-tying and costly signals via conditional loans treatment on local economic opportunity index outcome and mediators.

recommend the training program to family or friends. Referrals through one's social network represent a meaningful way that people learn about workforce programs. The second question is how likely a respondent would be to consider entering the training program.[32] The final question captures expectations of how many people who train for green jobs successfully find them. Specifically, we ask what percentage of people who train would find solar or wind jobs in the next five years.

Figure 7.3 shows the effect of the conditional loan treatment – hand-tying and costly signaling – on the credibility of the workforce program.[33] Also in this figure are results from mediation analyses that we explain below. The first finding is that when the government ties its hands and sends costly signals, people anticipate that the workforce program delivers greater local benefits. The expectation that more people would find jobs after training drives much of this effect. These results show that solutions to create credibility lead to greater expectations that green jobs will be created in their community.

One might think these results are unrelated to credibility and simply reflect that people are less worried about their economic future when the government shoulders the risk. Theoretically, this is consistent with costly signaling. To explore how the conditional loan treatment influences credibility, we conduct two mediation analyses (Imai et al., 2011). Mediation

---

[32] To make this question apply to all respondents, some of whom may already have professions, we phrase the question in terms of if one were to pick a new career.

[33] Estimated with a linear regression model with controls. We present results from the treatment condition where the loans account for 1 percent of the government's budget, which is the most realistic of the scenarios and keeps the comparison fixed across respondents. We found some evidence that respondents are sensitive to the high budget treatment, a possibility we anticipated in our pre-analysis plan, which further motivates our analysis of the baseline budget condition. We validated this interpretation with a follow-on experiment described in the online appendix.

analysis allows us to unpack the process by which the treatment alters assessments of the workforce program. A mediation analysis examines a pathway connecting our experimental treatment to an intervening variable to our final outcome variable.

In the first mediation analysis, we assess whether hand-tying and costly signaling influence a respondent's expectations of policy reversal. We ask how supportive the respondent thinks a future government would be of the program to train workers for green jobs. Suppose the conditional loan treatment has the intended hand-tying and costly signaling effects. In that case, the public should believe that a future government would be more likely to support the workforce program. We find evidence that perceptions of reversibility mediate the effect of the conditional loans. Figure 7.3 shows that the treatment has a large and positive effect on expectations that the government would support the workforce program. Our mediation analysis uncovers evidence that this effect transmits through perceptions of government support.[34] The conditional loan treatment makes people believe the government would be more supportive of the workforce program – that is, enhances the government's credibility – which, in turn, improves expectations about local benefits from investments in green jobs.

Our second mediation analysis explores whether people become more willing to support government spending if it enhances credibility. This question is relevant because we find evidence in this experiment and our interviews that people worry about the costs of policy. We ask whether it is better to "not spend more money to protect the government's financial health" or "spend more money to show that the government is serious about jobs." If respondents think in terms of credibility, the treatment should increase willingness to spend money to show that the government is serious about jobs. Indeed, our analysis finds that willingness to pay to create credibility mediates the conditional loan treatment.[35] In other words, hand-tying and costly signals alter beliefs about the need

---

[34] The average causal mediation effect (ACME) is positive ($p < 0.05$). Sensitivity analysis of the sequential ignorability assumption suggests that for the ACME to go to zero, there would have to be an omitted confounder that jointly explains 30 percent of the variance of the outcome and mediator, which is unlikely.

[35] Figure 7.3 reveals that the treatment has a large and positive effect on willingness to incur costs to demonstrate commitment to jobs. The ACME is positive ($p < 0.05$), and sensitivity analysis suggests that for the ACME to go to zero, there would have to be an omitted confounder that jointly explains around 20 percent of the variance of the outcome and mediator, which is unlikely.

for credibility, which translates into greater perceptions of local benefits from green investments.

These additional analyses instill confidence that the conditional loan treatment exerts its effect through the proposed hand-tying and costly signaling credibility mechanisms.

OPEN THE DOOR FOR WOMEN AND PEOPLE OF COLOR

Credibility may be critical to make the clean energy workforce diverse and inclusive. Compared to all occupations nationally, the green workforce in the United States is more male and white dominated (E2, 2021; Muro et al., 2019). In 2017, racial and ethnic minorities comprised 31 percent of the wind workforce, while women made up only 25 percent, mainly in administration, accounting, and communications (Keyser and Tegen, 2019). Globally, only one in five workers in the wind industry are women (IRENA, 2021, p. 3). For renewable energy, more broadly, women account for only one in three jobs. However, participation by women varies across countries and industries (IRENA, 2021, p. 8).

When women and people of color enter green industries, they face attitudes, perceptions, and structural obstacles that can make it difficult to advance their careers. For example, there is a 26 percent gender wage gap in the solar industry, while the wage distribution across race and ethnicity is more equitable (Van Leuven and Gilliland, 2019, p. 9). In a survey of energy workers, Black respondents cited overcoming bias and prejudice in the workplace as their biggest challenge (Campbell et al., 2021, p. 9). The same survey found that women do not feel as supported in their career advancement and professional development as men.

These challenges are not unique to green industries. Other skilled trades confront gender and racial imbalances. Yet these barriers are essential to overcome, especially since the rapid expansion of clean energy represents an unprecedented opportunity to create a more equitable economy.

The lack of diversity in the industry erects barriers to making the clean energy workforce accessible and inclusive. One reason for the lack of diversity is social networks, which have a profound effect on job opportunities (e.g., Bayer, Ross, and Topa, 2008; Calvó-Armengol and Jackson, 2004). Networks provide information about job positions. Multiple studies show that most people find their jobs through personal contacts (e.g., Rees, 1966). Program participation can also lead one's peers to join (e.g., Dahl, Løken, and Mogstad, 2014). This may

Open the Door for Women and People of Color   197

inadvertently reinforce hiring of groups already well-networked in specific industries since, from the employer's perspective, referrals from current employees could be seen as more informative (Simon and Warner, 1992).

Our conversations with instructors in green energy training programs described a similar dynamic. Since informal ties serve as one of the primary mechanisms for finding jobs, the lack of diversity in the green workforce erects barriers to broader participation.

> I don't see anyone who looks like me. Yes, that's kind of a big thing again. When you think about families and dynasties of lawyers or doctors, it's because you have a familiarity. But if you don't know anyone who's working in that industry, it's harder for you to conceptualize or join. Most of the time, you find a job from someone you know. If you don't have a diverse group of people who know people, you end up with some of the same types of folks.[36]

This remark underscores not only the significance of informal networks as sources of information but also how peer contacts demonstrate the *viability* of a potential career path; that is, being able to visualize oneself as part of an industry. In surveys of the solar industry, over half of the top recruitment methods included reliance on networks, and about 25 percent of Latino and Black respondents strongly agreed that they lacked the right connections (Van Leuven and Gilliland, 2019, p. 10).

These studies speak to the supply side of the equation – whether people from underrepresented groups decide to enter green industries. However, demand-side problems, such as discrimination, could also keep people locked out of occupations. These issues go hand-in-hand since if one expects to not be welcome in an industry, she may not apply in the first place.

The lack of credible local benefits from green industries may also create barriers to fostering an inclusive workforce. If there is a perception that the new clean energy economy does not improve the lives of marginalized communities, members of these groups may not be interested in entering those careers. Consider EVs. One concern raised by people in Black, Brown, and Indigenous communities is the lack of access to financing (White-Newsome, Linn, and Rib, 2021, p. 26). There are racial disparities in auto financing and insurance that can further impede the uptake of EVs (Foster et al., 2022, p. 47), as well as in rooftop solar deployment (Sunter, Castellanos, and Kammen, 2019).

---

[36] Interview with solar energy instructor, August 16, 2022.

Taking steps so clean energy resources improve the lives of fenceline communities via employment and ownership provides one mechanism to address diversity in the green workforce (E2, 2021). As part of this effort, apprenticeship programs could target underserved communities. In St. Louis, Missouri, a nonprofit group called Employment Connection, started a program to encourage people of color and women to join the solar industry (Gray, 2021). Campbell, Ford, and Garcia (2021) recommend using project labor and workforce agreements to encourage hiring minority- and women-owned businesses.

As the clean energy transition unfolds, it will be crucial to focus on how to open doors for women and people of color. Communities on the fencelines of power plants that previously did not benefit from energy production despite bearing the costs also have a chance to be part of the new green economy. Building out the clean energy workforce will have to reflect on these inequities to avoid replicating them as the sector expands. Not only is this an issue of justice, but the lack of inclusivity could deter potential recruits needed to meet the demands of the green economy. We already see evidence of this in Chapter 4, where Black respondents had lower assessments of the local benefits of green industries. Efforts to address credibility concerns in a just transition will also make it a more effective transition.

CONCLUSION

Workforce programs will be essential for the clean energy transition. The massive roll-out of clean energy requires a dramatic workforce expansion, while labor market disruption to conventional fossil fuel jobs necessitates a coordinated transition plan for workers. The barriers and opportunities in workforce programs that we explore in this chapter speak to economic transformations more broadly. Technological and economic changes brought about by automation and globalization also create demands for programs to help dislocated workers find new opportunities. These opportunities can range from battery and computer chip manufacturing to computer programming and solar panel installation.

Our contribution in this chapter is to demonstrate the role that credibility plays. Training for a new career is fraught with uncertainty, best understood when one takes the ground-up perspective of the people and communities impacted by workforce programs and economic transitions. This uncertainty and the short-term costs of training help explain why workforce programs are often under-subscribed, despite their potential benefits. Moving beyond the standard answers that focus on economic factors (e.g., Heckman, Lalonde, and Smith, 1999), we show how *political* factors like the credibility of the government's commitment also influence the calculation to participate.

Our new surveys of the national public and youths, including middle schoolers on the front lines of the energy transition in Southwest Pennsylvania, reveal a preference for careers that provide more certain livelihoods. These patterns align with what we found in Chapter 4 with respect to the perceived local economic opportunity of industries. Healthcare, which the public sees as a stable and growing industry, attracts the most interest. Green industries like solar, wind, and energy efficiency receive more interest compared to coal, oil, and gas jobs, but overall interest is still relatively low. And in fossil fuel country, middle schoolers prefer jobs they know provide for more certain careers, those in coal and gas.

Despite credibility challenges, our survey experiment shows how hand-tying and costly signaling, as developed in Chapter 2, can increase expectations of local benefits from clean energy training programs and investments. Our experiment focused on one strategy to enhance credibility, but there are undoubtedly other approaches. Another tactic would be for potential employers to coordinate with workforce programs to signal to participants that a job will be waiting for them after training. Having the employer on board could indicate that the program is of high quality (Spaulding and Martin-Caughey, 2015). Relatedly, programs like on-the-job training could help with uncertainty; if one is concerned about whether a job would work out, training while earning a salary on the job can help build confidence that it is a viable career path.

There are also opportunities for public–private partnerships, which could help to alleviate mistrust that people might have of federal or state government promises. Payton May from Bit Source said the most successful approach would involve "the combination of private and public partnerships where you have someone with private capital, and they have the effort, not just a government-backed thing...Those weren't as successful." While one might interpret this as a reflection of a belief that the government should not intervene in the market, this is not an uncommon view, so it is a reality that must be confronted when it comes to workforce programs. These types of partnerships are common. For example, wind companies will often work with local technical schools to set up training programs, as seen with the Red Dirt wind farm in Oklahoma.

Another approach follows lessons from the Clean Energy Workforce Development study conducted in New Mexico. Embracing a ground-up approach, the study conducted interviews, focus groups, and surveys to engage community voices. They found that people would be more willing to participate in programs if they are located in the community the program aims to serve, which illustrates the importance of local economic opportunity.

Another example is Colorado's just transition initiatives, which pay attention to credibility. Recognizing that electric utilities aim to recover the costs of stranded coal assets when they are decommissioned, the state requires that electric generating facilities submit a workforce transition plan and authorizes "rate recovery" for the expenses. Consequently, it is in the utility's interest to attend to impacted communities and encourage workforce development to recoup the costs from closing down a coal plant early (Righetti, Stoellinger, and Godby, 2021).

Credibility is a crucial part of the workforce puzzle, but there are other challenges. Some programs are chronically underfunded. A wind turbine instructor in West Virginia recalled, "we're bootstrapping 24/7 for a while after I came on...Funding is too hard to come by. Equipment is too hard to come by." These are supply considerations that the top-down perspective usually emphasizes, but their everyday impact is clearly understood when one listens to people on the ground. There can also be unexpected regulatory hurdles (e.g., Aklin and Urpelainen, 2022). Infrastructure underinvestment can stand in the way. Some rural areas lack broadband, which presents a challenge for online classes, which is an essential way that people can receive training while still on the job (Beckfield et al., 2022, p. 50). A county librarian in Southwest Pennsylvania recounted to Alex how, during the pandemic, all of the library's WiFi hot spots were continually checked out since families did not have access to the internet for online school. If children cannot Zoom in for school, then there is little hope of adults training for a new career during their off hours.

Making workforce programs credible will also help to enhance perceptions of local economic opportunity. Take the local jobs issue. It may be more challenging for firms to hire from the community if there is not a local workforce. However, by encouraging participation in training programs, credible workforce development can help make sure that the benefits from green energy stay in the community. The existence of a trained local workforce also removes the excuse by companies that there are not enough qualified workers locally. In the next chapter, we explore how the government can implement transparency guardrails that further enhance the credibility of local benefits from green jobs.

8

Green Jobs under the Spotlight

It's not normal to spend hours counting license plates, but that is precisely what Lucas Franco found himself doing one September afternoon. Lucas parked at an intersection in Woodstock, Minnesota, to get the perfect view of the Stoneray Wind Farm Project construction site. For the next three hours and 30 minutes, according to his affidavit, Lucas recorded the number of license plates from the worker's vehicles, carefully cataloging their state of origin.

What Lucas found was striking. At a Minnesotan wind farm, most of the plates were from Texas and Utah. Only 15 percent were from Minnesota. Yet when the wind farm's developer pledged that the project would generate 150 temporary construction jobs, implicit in this promise was the expectation that benefits would go to Minnesotans, not Texans or Utahns.

Why would Lucas go through the trouble of meticulously documenting the share of Minnesotans at a wind project in Woodstock? Lucas worked for a regional labor organization called the Laborers International Union of North America (LIUNA), which represents over 12,000 skilled construction laborers that build energy infrastructure projects in the Great Lakes region. With the growth of wind energy in the area, these workers stood to benefit from the installation of new turbines, but only if the developers hired from the local labor force.

Despite the existence of a trained workforce that led the charge on wind development in the area, the new multinational developers entering the scene brought with them traveling crews from other states. When these companies promised to create jobs, they had no incentive to be forthright with any information that could reveal that benefits would go to workers from other states.

"[Y]ou look at the license plates: California, Oregon, Texas. To be honest, I can't think of a single person from our area working on the project. We've got skilled labor, and we need the jobs, so I don't understand why [the company] would shut us out," said Garritt Thomssen, a member of Operating Engineers Local 49 from Lake Benton, Minnesota (LIUNA, 2017).

Yet the group needed hard data to show that there was a problem, which is why Lucas found himself sitting at the intersection of 121st street and 180th avenue in Woodstock.

The concern about whether renewable energy jobs are "local jobs" is not unique to Minnesota or the wind industry. In Chapter 2, we developed the concept of local economic opportunity and provide examples from communities like Carbon County that worry about the local benefits from green energy. In Chapter 4, we showed that the public and especially residents of energy communities recognize these struggles, which leads to skepticism about the energy transition. Efforts to overcome this skepticism – making green jobs work – are essential to create new economic opportunities in the green economy and facilitate the energy transition.

Governments are in search of approaches to create local benefits from new investments. One tactic is a top-down mandate that new developments use a specified level of local employment. Such a requirement could be specified in a community benefits agreement (CBA) or a project labor agreement (PLA). However, no single approach will be a panacea. If mandates are too rigid, they could have the unintended consequence of stalling renewable development in places with nascent workforces. Local mandates may also be hard to pass due to opposition from developers.[1]

What other policy solutions might be on offer to make the clean energy transition inclusive and uplift workers and communities?

This chapter explores two tools that could make the government's promise to create local benefits from green investments more credible: transparency and clawbacks. Transparency is essential because one must understand who is hired and where investments go to hold developers accountable for promises of local benefits. The need to spotlight wind developers' labor practices is why Lucas found himself tallying license plates in rural Minnesota (Figure 8.1). Transparency can lay the groundwork for more ambitious policies such as CBAs and PLAs.

---

[1] Interview with senior Minnesota PUC official, August 17, 2022.

Green Jobs under the Spotlight

FIGURE 8.1 Photograph from Lucas Franco's license plate counting expedition. Source: LIUNA Minnesota and North Dakota

Clawbacks then build on transparency efforts. Local and national governments often provide generous tax incentives to encourage investments in green energy. As Chapter 2 argues, policies that make these tax benefits conditional on achieving targets, such as local hiring, *could* incentivize investments that serve workers and communities. Developers that fail to meet the requirement would have their tax credits "clawed back." We develop these ideas in the context of the energy transition, though the insights travel beyond renewable energy.

While we identify opportunities for transparency and clawback policies, we also highlight limitations. Accountability is not automatic. Unscrupulous companies can devise creative ways to keep their tax credits even if they break their promises. The erosion of institutions like the local media and the limited capacity of communities could short-circuit efforts to hold developers accountable.

Others question the political advisability of transparency. Politicians often oppose transparency because visible costs from policies can give rise to opposition (Arnold, 1990). In our context, transparency sheds light on benefits rather than costs. But a similar logic could apply. For example, one might worry if communities find out the benefits of green projects

204 *Green Jobs under the Spotlight*

are less than previously believed. This revelation would chill support for the energy transition.

This objection might make sense if there was widespread support for clean energy development, but we already see opposition to projects because they do not make communities better off. The political challenge is how to convince communities that the benefits are credible. Even if people held inaccurate beliefs about the benefits of projects, transparency would still be warranted. This is a long-term transition. While some communities might be willing to take the leap in the early stages, the next county or municipality will think twice if people learn that the benefits are not there. The green energy economy will not be built in a day.

Transparency initiatives, clawback policies, and the concerns they address are not hypothetical. American states have passed legislation with provisions to encourage firms to hire local workers for renewable energy projects. Examples include Virginia's 2020 *Clean Economy Act*, which requires that developers consider local employment. Recommendations from think tanks say that government spending programs should incorporate local labor provisions such as prevailing wage laws, PLAs, and community workforce agreements (e.g., Cliffton et al., 2021). Despite these proposals, it is unclear whether transparency and clawbacks could build public support for green investments.

This chapter tells the story of the fight for jobs between unions and multinational developers in Minnesota. Developers wanted to use cheaper teams of outside workers that would sidestep the local workforce. Unions fought back. We show how this process unfolded and evaluate why Minnesota's attempts to shed light on renewable energy development succeeded, but its neighbor North Dakota failed. We draw on interviews with firms, unions, local policymakers, as well as local news reports, public record documents, and hearings that we transcribe. We also leverage survey data from inside a regional union with members in renewable and fossil fuel industries. We find that transparency pressured developers to hire from the local workforce, which increased community and union members' support for wind jobs.

Then, we see if transparency makes a difference in the minds of the public, youths, and local officials. Would people expect more local benefits from green investments if there were transparency and clawback provisions? Using a survey experiment, we find that where there are transparency requirements, expectations of local jobs from green investments improve. However, there are mixed results for accountability. From an analysis of open-ended survey responses and geo-coded local news data, we find that accountability is not automatic but could

Windows Not Doors

depend on the strength of local institutions like the media. We also find a potential dark side of clawbacks, the fear that clawback provisions will discourage investments. These results are instructive for thinking about the trade-offs that communities face when deciding whether and how to enhance credibility.

WINDOWS NOT DOORS

Transparency in Theory and Practice

"Sunlight is the best disinfectant" is a mantra that policymakers and nongovernmental organizations apply to corporations and governments. Experts hail transparency as consequential for "democracy, good governance, economic efficiency, and social justice, at levels ranging from villages to global institutions" (Florini, 2007, p. 1). The literature on transparency is vast, spans multiple disciplines, and examines various outcomes (Heald, 2006). In our context, transparency denotes the availability of clear and accurate information for the public (Schnackenberg and Tomlinson, 2016).[2]

The incentives for leaders and companies to be opaque create a need for transparency. Information is costly. Politicians could lose reelection if the public learns of expensive blunders, and firms face boycotts if bad practices come to light. In local economic development projects, the stakes are high. Leaders dole out large tax credits to attract new industries and claim credit for job creation (Jensen and Malesky, 2018). Without transparency, it is often hard to determine if a company delivered on its commitments, so politicians and corporations are free from accountability.

This matters for the clean energy transition, where tax incentives are increasingly the tool of choice. Lawmakers and activists have increasingly turned away from policies like carbon pricing that can be politically unpopular (e.g., Cullenward and Victor, 2021; Jenkins, 2014), and toward supply-side policies that incentivize the deployment of clean energy (Meckling et al., 2015; Rodrik, 2014). The passage of the Inflation Reduction Act (IRA) in the United States reflects this political logic. The reliance on subsidies makes transparency provisions and accountability for when broken commitments come to light potentially crucial.

The logic of transparency is that by putting the processes of an organization out in the open, the threat of accountability can lead companies and governments to behave in the public's best interest. This assumes that

---

[2] On measuring transparency, see Hollyer, Rosendorff, and Vreeland (2014).

the preferences of the government and firms do not align with those of the people. One can represent this relationship with a principal-agent model. Think about the public as the principal that delegates to leaders the task of governing. Transparency serves as a check against moral hazard problems, where leaders seek to enrich themselves rather than represent their constituents. The economist Bengt Holmström (1979) shows how when there is transparency, the agent's actions are more observable to the principal, which reduces the cost of monitoring.

Transparency can also lead to accountability through bottom-up processes. Quality information can serve as a focal point that helps citizens engage in collective action and punish leaders who fail to keep their promises (e.g., Hollyer, Rosendorff, and Vreeland, 2018; Schelling, 1956). However, this is by no means guaranteed. Groups regularly face barriers to collective action, such as incentives to free ride (Olson, 1965).

Causes, Consequences, and Limits of Transparency

The political scientist James Alt (2019) reviewed 20 years of studies and documents an explosion in research following the publication of Bengt Holmström's article on moral hazard problems and observability. One series of studies focuses on the causes of transparency and asks why are some political institutions more transparent than others (e.g., Hollyer, Rosendorff, and Vreeland, 2011). Another line of research investigates the effects of transparency on outcomes such as political stability, electoral accountability, governance, economic development, and fiscal policy.[3] Some of this research raises questions about the efficacy of transparency (e.g., Dunning et al., 2019).

Core to our focus is the relationship between transparency and economic development. Unsurprisingly, there is widespread concern about the opacity surrounding the proliferation of local tax subsidies as state and local governments compete for investment (Bartik, 2019; Jensen and Malesky, 2018; Slattery and Zidar, 2020). One study finds that transparency created by the online publication of subsidy details and documentation of job commitments can enhance the effectiveness of tax incentives (De Simone, Lester, and Raghunandan, 2021).

However, there is mixed evidence about transparency's effectiveness (e.g., Hood and Heald, 2006; Thrall and Jensen, 2022). One reason is that companies often resist transparency initiatives. For example, one

---

[3] See, for example, Adserà, Boix, and Payne (2003), Alt and Lassen (2006), Alt, Lassen, and Rose (2006), Hollyer, Rosendorff, and Vreeland (2018), Jensen and Thrall (2021), and Snyder and Strömberg (2010).

Windows Not Doors

study of economic development programs in Texas found that companies that challenged public record requests about their tax incentives were more likely to have negotiated with local officials for a reduction in their job creation obligations (Jensen and Thrall, 2021).

Even with robust transparency provisions, the lack of enforcement may limit the power of sunlight. Scholars have begun to focus on how to combine transparency and enforcement. As Alt (2019, p. 11) notes, "[i]ncreasingly we see that transparency alone is often not the answer. The literature on corruption reminds us that enforcement power often has to be added..." Accountability may not be forthcoming for a variety of reasons (e.g., Bartik, 2019). Local governments may be unable to ensure that companies comply with transparency laws.[4] Rent-seeking bureaucrats might also become captured by businesses.[5]

Create Credibility with Transparency

Transparency is one tool to create credibility and bolster the local economic opportunities provided by green investments. Information and credibility go hand-in-hand. If the public cannot determine if a company or politicians are fulfilling their commitments, citizens cannot coordinate to sanction leaders or corporations with votes or protests. When there is greater transparency in the investment process, citizens should expect greater capacity to hold policymakers and companies accountable if they fail to deliver local benefits. Through this channel, transparency enhances the credibility of punishment for broken promises. Transparency could complement other commitment devices by helping to define what constitutes a broken promise and subsequently identify infractions.

Absent transparency, companies have incentives to use the most cost-effective practices, which do not necessarily provide the greatest benefits to the community. If the lowest-cost approach aligned with the interests of workers and the community, then transparency would not be needed. However, this is rare. There is often uncertainty about a company's promises of local benefits like job creation and tax revenue. Without any obligation to disclose this information and potentially facing disincentives if the company fails to generate tangible local benefits, information about the benefits of local investment is mired in opacity.

---

[4] When transparency is of government officials, their behavior might not improve if they do not face competitive electoral pressure (Grossman and Michelitch, 2018).

[5] Transparency could also lead politicians to do what is popular even when they know it is not the best policy (e.g., Canes-Wrone, Herron, and Shotts, 2001; Stasavage, 2004).

Green Jobs under the Spotlight

Transparency should be most effective when the information provided is salient and accessible while providing a clear set of actions that could change a company's activities (Fung, Graham, and Weil, 2007). Below we will further explore whether and how accountability might manifest if the public discovers that companies have failed to create local benefits.

SPOTLIGHT ON MINNESOTA

Local Jobs Wanted

We now return to Lucas, whom we met at the start of this chapter, and move from theory to practice to see how transparency works. To put Lucas' license plate counting expedition in context, over the last two decades, Minnesota has undergone rapid growth in wind energy development.

At first, these benefits largely went to Minnesotans. The first phase of development in the early 1990s, although conducted by a variety of companies, including local businesses and those based in California and Denmark, often employed construction contractors headquartered in Minnesota such as Mortenson (e.g., Inskip, 1993).[6] These hometown developers employed a largely local, unionized workforce.[7]

However, as the wind industry matured, many developers began to work with third-party companies that lacked historical ties to the state. Instead, they employed outside, nonunion contractors. "The existing workforce had pioneered wind development in the area, then multinational developers came in with their traveling crews," lamented a senior official of a regional labor union.[8] One notorious multinational company was RES, based in the United Kingdom. Local building trades that normally welcome new wind projects raised serious concerns about RES's promises of local job creation. Kevin Pranis, the campaign director of LIUNA Minnesota & North Dakota, testified before the Minnesota PUC that "RES is a company that...not only sidelined Minnesota workers but employed what we consider to be bait-and-switch tactics in promoting projects...around local jobs...less than 10 percent of jobs actually went to Minnesota residents."[9] These new companies came with big promises but had little incentive to be transparent.

---

[6] Interview with labor union staff, July 6, 2022; Interview with labor union staff, April 20, 2022; Interview with manager at wind developer, August 30, 2022.

[7] Public testimony from staff members of the Minnesota Department of Commerce suggests that contractors like Mortenson try to hire around "85 percent locally depending on qualifications" (Hartman, 2010, p. 42).

[8] Interview, July 6, 2022.

[9] December 6, 2018, testimony.

Spotlight on Minnesota 209

The cost of sidelining local jobs is high, especially for communities already undergoing energy transitions. The Sherco coal-fired power plant, in Becker, Minnesota, whose mayor you met at the start of Chapter 2, provides a case in point. Xcel Energy plans to close Sherco by 2030. This coal plant provides 300 jobs and 75 percent of the town's revenue. Joe Fowler, the manager of Laborers Local 563 in Minnesota, hopes that "when the jobs are coming down on the coal plants, we can train and transition those individuals to go work on the wind farms, on the solar farms" (Tomich, 2018). A key question is how many new, permanent, and well-paying jobs could be created for workers who must transition. The failure to get this right could mean real suffering for workers, their families, and communities.

The lack of local job creation could also undermine the support of labor unions in the clean energy transition. Unions with ties to fossil fuel industries often play a crucial role in climate policy-making (Mildenberger, 2020). However, many building trades are cross-pressured. They have workers employed on carbon-intensive projects like gas pipelines but also members working on green energy projects like wind turbines. These unions stand to benefit from the expansion of the green economy, as well as serve as a conduit for fossil fuel workers into clean sectors, but only if there are projects that employ their workers.

Kevin Pranis, when objecting to RES' wind project described the consequences of outside workers for the energy transition.

Minnesota is moving away from fossil fuels, and some would like the state to move even faster in that direction. That transition is going to result in a loss of hundreds and thousands of jobs for our members...And yet our unions have embraced this transition...because we've been told that there's a bright future for Minnesota workers in a clean energy economy, that there will be good, high-paying jobs that can support their families, at least as good as existed under the conventional economy...There is a risk that that promise is broken when speculative developers are allowed not only to build these projects but to do so with no scrutiny whatsoever in terms of the impacts...[10]

Local economic opportunity is crucial for the energy transition. Workers and their communities need to believe that the benefits from the green economy will reach them.

It takes a ground-up perspective to appreciate the importance of local jobs – that is, to view the issue from the vantage of the construction workers, electricians, and pipe-fitters employed in the building trades. However, it is hard to study the perspective of union members because of the challenges in recruiting them for surveys. To overcome these barriers,

[10] December 6, 2018, testimony.

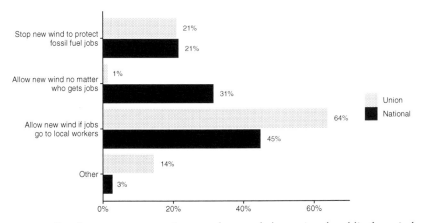

FIGURE 8.2 Support among union members and the national public for wind development depends on whether it creates local jobs.

we obtained and analyzed internal surveys conducted by a trade union in the Great Lakes region in 2020. Union organizers use these surveys to better understand the preferences of their members, which informs their political activities. These data provide an unfiltered look at the views of energy industry workers.

The main question on the survey assessed whether these workers would support wind energy if the new jobs went to locals. The survey reached 77 workers, which captures over one-quarter of the union's footprint in the area.[11] This union is of particular relevance to the energy transition because of the occupations of its workers. Around 84 percent have worked on coal- or gas-fired power plants, 68 percent in oil or gas pipelines and distribution, 65 percent in refineries or gas processing plants, and 26 percent on wind or solar farms. We also fielded this question in a nationally representative survey of Americans to provide a benchmark.[12]

Figure 8.2 shows what people in the national public and the union think about wind development. Sixty-four percent of the union members would support wind developments if the jobs went to local workers. This percentage is higher than the national public, which is more willing to develop wind no matter who gets the jobs. A similar share of union members and the national public would support stopping new wind farms to protect the jobs of fossil fuel workers. These results demonstrate the importance of making green jobs *local* jobs.

---

[11] We do not disclose the specific area to protect respondent confidentiality.
[12] Fielded August 2022 with CAPS/Harris ($N = 1,002$).

Spotlight on Minnesota

Brewing Backlash in Minnesota

Backlash began to grow in response to large developers' use of out-of-state labor. New projects such as the Red Pine Wind Farm that would construct 100 wind turbines raised concerns about the employment of local workers – or the lack thereof. Local news reported on how union members like Will Thomssen would travel to project sites "to scour the license plates of workers' cars and saw plenty of California, Texas, Oregon, and Nebraska, but not much Minnesota blue" (Evers-Hillstrom, 2017).

In response to the Red Pine Wind Farm project and others, the Minnesota Building Trades (2017) adopted a resolution that called "on renewable energy developers, project owners, and investors to commit to hire local skilled workers." The building trades, which represent 70,000 union construction workers, said that they would oppose any future projects that excluded local workers from employment.

Pushing Transparency

The resolution sent a statement, but the unions needed a way to hold developers accountable. Their solution? Transparency. If developers promised job creation, the community should have a way to find out if they actually benefited. So unions began to insist on a local labor reporting requirement. The idea was that by shedding light on the benefits of projects, developers would hire more locals or make more measured promises. If companies were creating local jobs, they should have nothing to hide.

In a series of reports entitled, *Catching the Wind*, about the economic consequences of local hiring practices, Lucas Franco (2019a, p. 5) said the reporting requirement aimed "to inform public policy and permitting decisions, and to encourage developers to close gaps between public job creation promises and realities."

The proposed policy had no compliance mechanism. "Our first big goal is just transparency – that we have reporting requirements so the public can know whether or not developers are following through," Lucas Franco told a local media outlet (Kuphal, 2018).

The major buildings trade group in the region, LIUNA, began pushing transparency in two arenas. LIUNA first started to negotiate directly with developers to request local labor reporting as a part of their projects. This process of securing commitments from developers did not involve the government and had fewer guardrails on agreements, save for reputational costs if a developer decided to back out.

The unions also began to participate in the permitting process, advocating for local job reporting. A senior member of the Minnesota PUC described how "the unions came in, mainly LIUNA, started showing up in our proceedings wearing orange shirts, saying you should really measure the amount of jobs created by this particular project."[13]

LIUNA's argument for including reports of local labor in the permit process appealed to Minnesota law. In Minnesota, the state must only site projects that are compatible with environmental preservation, sustainable development, and the efficient use of resources. The PUC conducts a balancing test to evaluate whether the project is net-beneficial. LIUNA argued, "it should be obvious that the employment of Minnesota and other local workers on the construction of energy projects is a key aspect of their socioeconomic impact" (Pranis, 2018, p. 2).[14] "It's kind of crazy that we know how many birds or bats could be killed by this project, but we have no idea how many people could be employed by it or help build it," a senior member of the Minnesota PUC exclaimed.[15]

Bitter Standoff

The local jobs fight reached a boiling point with the proposed Bitter Root Wind Farm project. On November 9, 2017, Flying Cow Wind submitted a permit to build 40 wind turbines in Yellow Medicine and Lincoln counties.[16] This playfully named company is a subsidiary of the multinational RES, which Kevin Pranis accused of engaging in "bait-and-switch tactics."

The site permit application totaled 115 pages, not counting 20 supplementary documents. These materials laid out in detail the steps that would be taken to mitigate environmental impacts for birds and bats, aesthetic impacts such as shadow flickers from spinning turbine blades, and even the potential impact of turbines on microwave bands used by telecommunication technology.

Buried within the application was a brief mention of the economic benefits of Bitter Root Wind: the project "will improve the local economy

---

[13] August 17, 2022 interview.

[14] They also claimed that since the demand for wind projects was so strong in Minnesota, projects that did not use local labor could crowd out projects that would have employed Minnesotans. However, there was less definitive evidence of this objection.

[15] August 17, 2022 interview.

[16] This project was proposed in 2008 and permitted in 2010, but no purchase power agreement was secured, so the project was not constructed and the Commission revoked the site permit in 2013. Flying Cow Wind acquired the project in 2016, which was when development resumed.

Spotlight on Minnesota   213

by providing revenue for landowners, *potential temporary jobs for local residents*, and local government tax benefits" (*emphasis added*, 21).

How many jobs? The permit application did not say. How long would they last? Most would be temporary. Would locals be employed? The developer equivocated, saying "[l]ocal contractors and suppliers will be used for portions of the construction" in one place (56), but later qualified the promise, saying "[t]he services of local contractors will be used, *where possible*, to assist in construction" (*emphasis added*, 99).

In an area with relatively high poverty, the local benefits of the Bitter Root project appeared ambiguous at best. The unions were not buying it. They conducted their own economic analysis through the North Star Policy Institute which concluded that the failure to hire Minnesotans would cause communities to lose out on $32 million of economic activity (Hatt and Franco, 2018). Part of the impetus for this report came from Lucas' license plate expedition that uncovered the lack of wind jobs going to Minnesotans.

Although the labor unions tried cooperating with RES to provide data on local job creation, RES resisted disclosure. This created a standoff between the building trades and the developer. RES planned to move full-steam ahead with the project. This left the unions, led primarily by LIUNA, with no choice. The project must be stopped. If not, union leaders feared it would green-light future projects to disregard Minnesotan workers.

It all came down to December 6, 2018. That is when the PUC held a public hearing to decide whether to proceed with permitting the Bitter Root wind farm. The day before this crucial hearing, Melissa Hortman, the incoming Democratic speaker of the Minnesota House of Representatives, put additional pressure on the PUC with a letter that stated, "[the unions] have made a persuasive case in the record that the proposed Bitter Root Wind project undervalues Minnesota's human capital based on the developer's track record and current refusal to make meaningful commitments to employ local workers..."

Proceedings were testy. "We had some developers who really pushed back strong, and we had this sort of crazy hearing about it. Normally our proceedings are pretty mellow," a senior PUC staff member recalled.[17]

RES, the developer, had concerns about what the reporting requirement would mean for the competitiveness of the project. However, the company indicated that it would hire local workers if qualified, but it would not make any firm commitments.

[17] August 17, 2022, interview.

214   *Green Jobs under the Spotlight*

One commissioner, John Tuma, although ultimately supportive of the union's labor reporting requirement, also voiced reservations:

be careful because Minnesota has two of the largest...most respected solar and wind developers in this state who hire and have our outside labor go to other states...I think it's a dangerous territory you could be walking in for Minnesota workers...I'm hoping this does not take off and become a regional thing.

As the hearing continued, it became clear from the questions that the PUC was skeptical of the socioeconomic effects of the project. However, the RES representative did not attempt to contradict the unions' economic claims.

The outcome was a 5-0 decision by the Commission to send the case to a contested hearing due to the concerns about nonlocal construction labor.[18] The decisive ruling demonstrated that local job creation was a valid consideration under the balancing tests used to assess wind energy siting in Minnesota.

The excitement of LIUNA's representative, Kevin Pranis, and the organization's orange-clad members in attendance was palpable. The workers fought the developers and won.

The local media covering the transparency fight reported on the outcome. Drab regulatory hearings do not usually receive much press. However, the media paid attention to the local reporting requirement and the Minnesotan workforce issue it sought to address.[19] Although the contested hearing process was intended to provide a space for the stakeholders to negotiate a compromise, the ruling took the wind out of RES' efforts. For its part, RES said it would "be searching for well-qualified workers in every way we can. That definitely will include local job postings and appearances at local job fairs" (Muchlinski, 2019).

However, in May 2019, RES sold the project to a developer that intended to employ a mostly Minnesotan workforce (Hughlett, 2019). Five days later, the PUC withdrew the project's certificate of need and site permit applications. To this date, the Bitter Root Wind Farm has not been built.

Here Comes Sunshine

The union's victory with Bitter Root paved the way for a transparency breakthrough. Fourteen days later, the PUC approved the Nobles II wind

---

[18] The contested hearing would provide parties with rights of discovery to evaluate the socioeconomic impacts of the project further.

[19] For coverage examples, see Hughlett (2018), Kuphal (2018), and Muchlinski (2019).

Spotlight on Minnesota

farm. The project included a local hire reporting requirement. Unlike the contentious process with RES, the reporting requirement was jointly proposed by LIUNA and the applicant, Tenaska. The motion to include the reporting language in the site permit passed 5-0.

Unsurprisingly, the unions that had fought for this requirement were pleased. "Mr. Pranis," the LIUNA representative, "is seeming to be showing up and smiling behind you back there right now," commented Commissioner Tuma as the hearing kicked off.

Under the requirement, Tenaska, an international energy company headquartered in Omaha, Nebraska, would file quarterly reports about the construction workers building Nobles II. These reports must include data about the number of hours worked by Minnesota residents, the number of hours worked by residents within 150 miles of the project, and the total number of hours worked. However, the requirement included no target of how many locals to employ or sanction for the failure to create local jobs. The union hoped transparency would generate enough pressure to hire local workers.

Since the Nobles II decision, the local reporting requirement has become standard practice before the commission. Even though the developer of the next wind project, NextEra, lacked enthusiasm and expressed a preference for a single report rather than quarterly reporting, that objection received no traction.[20] While the PUC has not formally created a transparency rule due to sensitivity about engaging in unpromulgated rule-making, union organizers attest that "it has become standard enough that we don't even bother to check."[21]

Did Transparency Work?

Did transparency make workers and their communities better off? While what constitutes success may be contested, a minimum criterion should be that the share of local jobs increased. The counterfactual necessary to uncover the true effect of transparency is a world where Minnesota had not required labor reporting, yet this hypothetical can never be observed.

We take two qualitative steps to investigate the effect of transparency on local jobs. First, we examine the variation of local wind jobs over time within Minnesota. Second, we compare local hiring in Minnesota with neighboring North Dakota, which lacks transparency. While we refrain

[20] Interviews with senior union organizers, July 6, 2022; Author correspondence with senior union organizers, August 24, 2022.
[21] Author correspondence with senior union organizers, August 24, 2022.

Change over Time

How did local hiring change in Minnesota after the labor reporting requirement? This analysis assumes that no simultaneous trend in the industry or workforce would have led to more local hiring, irrespective of the transparency provision. While it is impossible to rule out all potential objections, we evaluate candidate explanations for why this assumption might be violated. The primary one is that an out-of-state workforce's investment in wind projects would align incentives for the local workforce to invest in training for wind jobs. This would have led to the natural growth in the local, skilled workforce and, consequently, local employment on wind projects. However, this is not plausible because Minnesota already had a skilled local workforce. Further, the changes in local hiring described below indicate that the switch occurred rapidly following the new transparency initiative.

The *Catching the Wind* report by Franco (2019a, p. 1) claims that "the local share of Minnesota's wind energy construction workforce has shot up from under 20 percent in recent years to well over 50 percent in 2019." However, the report cautions that there is still work to be done, as some company disclosures showed that local workers accounted for only 32 percent of the hours worked on particular projects. Nevertheless, according to Mankato Building Trades President Stacy Karels, based in southern Minnesota where much of the state's wind development takes place, "it's been a big turnaround. In 2017 and 2018, you hardly saw Minnesota workers on wind energy projects. This summer, we might have a hundred local Building Trades members at Blazing Star alone, and we'll put even more to work shortly as Nobles II kicks off" (cited in Franco, 2019a, p. 7).

Our interviews with union members confirmed this trend.[22] A senior union member stated that from 2019 to 2020, local Minnesotans went from being a minority on wind farms to the majority.[23] The chair of the PUC, Katie Sieben (2021), also testified before the United States Senate that the transparency initiative had been a resounding success.

---

[22] Interview, July 6, 2022.

[23] The union's main objective is to create local jobs, so we have no reason to suspect misrepresentation when it comes to the effects of the labor reporting requirements.

Spotlight on Minnesota

Since we began requiring quarterly reporting on the use of local labor...we have seen a significant shift in the percentage of local workers hired. Recent wind project labor reports are showing a dramatic increase in the use of local labor; historic local labor use was estimated to be below twenty percent and is now showing local labor rates of 70 to 80 percent.

There are concrete examples of projects that committed to hiring more Minnesotan workers. For example, the new developer that took over the Bitter Root project promised to create local jobs. Xcel Energy is using local labor for the Blazing Star 1 and 2 wind farms. Both Xcel and the Great River Energy cooperative have incorporated explicit consideration of skilled local labor into their resource plans, "which has translated into hundreds of new jobs and growing local support for clean energy in Minnesota" (Ceres, 2020, p. 4). Lastly, Avangrid and EDF Renewables indicated they would support local labor at the Trimont and Fenton Wind Repower projects.

Wind developers are more reserved about the effects of the reporting requirement. "I'd say it has made some difference. I wouldn't say it's made a tremendous difference. I think there are more projects now being constructed union versus open shop in Minnesota, but there's still projects being constructed open shop."[24] A more structural issue the developer identified is the decline of union membership. "If they can't staff a project, they will have a national call. And they themselves will bring in folks from out of state." While transparency holds promise, it cannot address economic constraints such as the size or skills of the local workforce.

In all, local hiring practices at Minnesota wind projects have improved. The push for transparency by the local building trades and the positive response from the PUC is the most likely explanation for this improvement.

Change across Borders

North Dakota, which borders Minnesota, provides a useful comparison to see what difference transparency made. Both states have vast wind and solar energy potential. We do not claim that North Dakota is a perfect "control" case since the two states differ in meaningful ways. The comparison is simply illustrative of the potential for transparency.

One difference between the states that introduces bias against the hypothesis that transparency led to more local job creation is that North Dakota has experienced faster wind energy growth than Minnesota. The

---

[24] Interview, August 30, 2022.

rate of increase in electricity from wind in North Dakota began outpacing Minnesota in 2015. North Dakota has a higher share of renewable energy generation (42 percent) than Minnesota (32 percent) as of 2020 (Gigstad and Manzo, 2020). With this vast wind industry, one would expect that there are market signals to the local workforce to train for careers in wind energy, which would create a pool of skilled local workers for jobs at new wind projects.

There are three differences between the states that inhibited the emergence of transparency in North Dakota: fossil fuels, unions, and institutions. First, North Dakota has substantial fossil fuel resources, whereas Minnesota does not dig coal and imports most of its fossil fuels.[25] The fossil fuel industry's strength means there is little political constituency to lobby for transparency. When asked why North Dakota had not had similar success, a senior union official replied, "the industry had few friends in the state...so few blue-collar workers had made their living off of wind."[26] While the coal industry has politicized the threat of wind energy, there is an underlying frustration with the lack of local benefits from wind projects.[27]

The second difference between Minnesota and North Dakota is the strength of unions. North Dakota has a so-called "right-to-work law" that undermines union organizing, whereas Minnesota does not. Union organizers remarked how they have political capital in Minnesota that they lack in North Dakota since the Republican legislature that is more closely aligned with business is not friendly to labor.[28]

The final difference that has impeded the emergence of transparency in North Dakota is institutional. Minnesota's permitting process is more centralized, whereas North Dakota's allows counties to have more influence and even stop wind projects. We saw how LIUNA could use the centralized process to its advantage, lobbying for transparency without having to expend resources to oppose projects in dozens of jurisdictions. Another institutional contrast is that North Dakota's Public Service Commission (PSC) is elected, so "they do not want to antagonize too many people nor pick fights with counties," and they are worried about the possibility of burdening business, according to interviews with senior union

---

[25] North Dakota is the third largest crude oil producer in the nation, and hydraulic fracturing has opened up the Bakken Shale formation for a rush of development. North Dakota is also the fifth largest producer of coal (EIA, 2022).

[26] Interview, July 6, 2022.

[27] Interview, April 20, 2022.

[28] Interview, April 20, 2022.

officials.[29] Minnesota's commissioners are appointed by the governor to six-year staggered terms.

The result is that the building trades organizers have not brought transparency to North Dakota. The consequences for local benefits are stark. A report from Franco (2019b) puts the share of wind construction jobs available for North Dakotan workers at 14 percent. Other studies citing this work are critical of the lack of local job creation from the North Dakotan wind industry. "North Dakota's economy loses an estimated $62 million per year to out-of-state contractors on wind energy infrastructure projects alone. Non-local workers account for approximately 86 percent of the construction workforce on North Dakota's wind projects" (Gigstad and Manzo, 2020, p. 7). Jobs in the renewable sector pale in comparison to their potential (Kirk, 2021).

Of course, these differences cannot be attributed only to the lack of transparency. Some factors that prevent the emergence of transparency also contribute to these labor market outcomes. However, based on the trends in Minnesota after the introduction of the reporting requirements, it is plausible that the spotlight on local wind jobs altered the public's perceptions of these issues, a claim we evaluate in the next section.

Why Did It Happen?

Through our interviews, transcriptions of hearings, and review of regulatory submissions, we identified three mechanisms through which Minnesota's transparency requirement created economic opportunities for communities: credible demonstration of benefits, retraining incentives, and agenda-setting.

First, transparency helped to make promises of local benefits credible. For example, when residents had concerns about local jobs, the reporting requirement data helped inform the community about the actual benefits. One example is the Dodge County Commissioner, who worried that "projects wouldn't create jobs for local workers, but we have data that shows the local jobs work...with that project," whereas before "even non-labor people got misleading answers that there would be more local jobs."[30] Transparency clarified the benefits, opening the developer to reputational costs if they failed to deliver what they promised.

One might wonder if the distracted public even takes the time to read these reports. They probably do not. However, the local building trades pay attention to reports and choose to publicize them when they are

---

[29] Interview, April 20, 2022.
[30] Interview with senior union member, July 6, 2022.

bad.[31] This union channel helps to explain how information can reach an electorate that might otherwise be uninformed or not seek out the labor reports on their own.

The transparency provision also set off a virtuous cycle. By creating more local jobs, transparency has led to more training programs that further develop a skilled local workforce that can staff future projects. Katie Sieben, the PUC commissioner, testified that the labor reporting requirement has "resulted in a better-trained workforce in many areas of the state and has encouraged the development of worker training programs that lead to new job pathways" (Sieben, 2021).[32] This pattern aligns with our results in Chapter 7, which show how credibility is consequential for the decision to train for a career in a new industry.

Lastly, the transparency push by the PUC has led to an increase in local hiring due to agenda-setting and reputational concerns. Since the investor-owned utilities that build wind projects know they will have to deal with the PUC in the future, the developers care about their reputation for providing socioeconomic benefits, so their permits are more likely to gain approval in the future.[33]

These three mechanisms show how transparency holds the potential to enhance the local economic opportunities created by investments. The following section turns to public perception to understand whether transparency makes a difference in the public's perception of local benefits.

PROBING THE CONNECTION: EXPERIMENTAL EVIDENCE

In this section, we explore whether transparency initiatives more generally shape preferences, attitudes, and beliefs about the local benefits of green investments, willingness to train for wind and solar jobs, and support for politicians who back green energy. We leverage an experiment that we embedded in surveys of the national public, youths, and local officials. Here's how it works. The survey describes a government investment to create renewable energy jobs.[34] We randomize whether or not there is a transparency requirement that companies provide public

---

[31] Interview with senior union member, July 6, 2022.
[32] Our interviews corroborated these accounts (Interview with senior staff on the Minnesota PUC, August 17, 2022).
[33] August 17, 2022 interview with senior staff member of the PUC.
[34] We leave the policy instrument unspecified to focus on the survey-taker on transparency.

Probing the Connection: Experimental Evidence 221

reports on how many local jobs their investments create.[35] This treatment mirrors the debate over whether to require labor reporting in Minnesota and North Dakota.

We evaluate how transparency affects expectations about the share of jobs that would go to local workers, perceptions that one would find a job if they entered a local training program, and intention to vote for a local politician who supports green investments. Transparency should have a positive effect on these outcomes. To understand when and how transparency enhances credibility, we asked whether the failure to create local jobs would be detected and if companies would be held accountable. Transparency may not have a clear effect on perceptions of accountability, which depends on external factors like the presence of local journalism to publicize the broken promise. Finally, we synthesize the last five measures into a local benefits index to reduce measurement error and provide an overall sense of the transparency's impact.

Results

National Public

What difference did transparency make? Figure 8.3 shows the average effect of transparency on each outcome.[36] Look first at the primary outcome. When there is transparency, the public expects that investments in green jobs will generate greater local economic opportunities, as captured by the index.

In terms of jobs, transparency provisions lead the public to expect more jobs to go to local workers. The effect size is modest. People expect that about 2.5 percent more local workers would be hired. However, since the public likely does not have precise estimates of the share of local jobs, what matters most in interpreting this effect is the direction, which is positive.

---

[35] The control condition says the government will not provide transparency. An early version varied whether the control mentioned transparency. However, two concerns emerged: first, the contrast between transparency and no mention of transparency did not mirror the political debates where the choice was between transparency and none at all; second, the treatment could prime respondents to be worried about local benefits. We addressed these concerns by randomizing whether the prompt included the world "not," which matched debates over transparency and kept priming constant across conditions. We were only able to make this change on the national public survey since the local policymaker survey was already in the field. So the one outcome where we do not trim responses from the pretest is the jobs going to locals outcome, which is on both surveys. This should introduce bias against an effect.

[36] Linear regression model with controls.

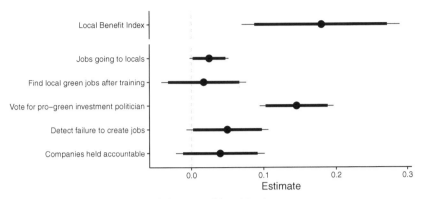

Notes: Thin and thick bars represent 95 and 90 percent confidence intervals.

FIGURE 8.3 Effect of transparency on the national public's expectations of local economic opportunities from green energy investments.

When it comes to whether people think they would find a green job in their area after training, there is no effect of transparency on average. However, youths are more likely than adults to think that they would find a green job after training where there is transparency.[37] The differences by age align with our expectation that older respondents with established career paths may be less sure about finding a job in a new industry, whereas younger respondents may be more optimistic.

When there is transparency, people indicate more support for politicians who back green investments. The strength of the finding suggests that there may be potential for bottom-up public coalitions for green investments accompanied by transparency provisions. However, future work should examine whether this effect could be neutralized by framing transparency as a costly regulation on companies, as developers and opponents in Minnesota and North Dakota attempted.

As we emphasize, transparency alone does not guarantee accountability, which our experiment shows. While there is suggestive evidence that when there is transparency, people expect that the public would find out if companies broke their promises to create local jobs, there is no evidence that there is an expectation of accountability. This skepticism demonstrates the limitations of relying solely on transparency to generate credibility. However, we will later show how the strength of local institutions like the press, when combined with transparency, can lead to expectations of accountability.

---

[37] Linear regression model with controls ($p < 0.05$).

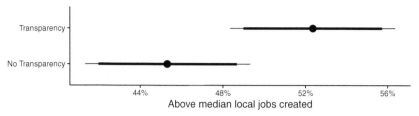

FIGURE 8.4 Percent of local policymakers with above-median expectations of the percent of jobs from green investments that would go to local workers.

Local Policymakers

What was the effect of transparency on how local officials thought about the benefits of green investments? When there is transparency, local policymakers are more likely to anticipate greater community benefits from green investments. Figure 8.4 plots the percentage of local officials in each treatment group who had above-median expectations of local job creation. The transparency condition caused an increase in expectations of local benefits by about seven percentage points.[38]

Read All about It: Local Media and Accountability

The results provide promising evidence that transparency can enhance perceptions of local economic opportunity. However, there is mixed evidence for whether companies would be held accountable if negative information came to light. This is unsurprising because accountability is necessary to make transparency meaningful, but requiring reporting does not guarantee a robust response to infractions.

To unpack beliefs about accountability, we use an open-ended question that asked the respondent to explain why or why not companies would be held accountable. Free-response questions are valuable because they provide the participant with the opportunity to explain her answer, which reveals the considerations that are top of mind. After our initial examination of the answers, we had research assistants comb through the text of each response and code them according to a list of themes. The coders were blinded to the treatment condition, so we could not prejudge them one way or another. This allows us to reanalyze our initial results to identify the conditions under which transparency facilitates accountability.

---

[38] The median expectation of the share of local jobs is 25 percent. We focus on the median since it is resistant to outliers. The results generally obtain with a continuous outcome.

Respondents frequently mention local media as a way they thought accountability would manifest.[39] One respondent said, "local media would likely be keeping tabs on the program to ensure that the program is working as intended to provide local jobs. While local media as a whole is in decline, my area has a reasonably strong network of local newspapers and local TV news." The role of local media is central to the study of government accountability (e.g., Hayes and Lawless, 2021; Snyder and Strömberg, 2010). For example, one study finds that local policymakers respond to pressure from the media; when city and county elected officials received news coverage about degraded infrastructure, the politicians became more likely to support investment in public goods (Mullin and Hansen, 2022).

We create two measures of local media presence to see if the effects of transparency differ when there is local journalism. The first measure is an indicator that we code from the open-ended responses. This is a *subjective* measure of whether an individual believes there is a strong news presence in her community. Since respondents do not always mention all of their considerations in a short open-ended question, and their perceptions of accountability may be influenced by their institutional context in ways they do not readily appreciate, for our second measure, we collect data on the *objective* presence of the local media.[40] We utilize data on daily print newspaper circulation, online media presence, and public broadcasting.[41] Lastly, we construct a binary variable for whether a respondent is subjectively conscious of the local news media and is in a county with more than one local news outlet, as defined by the objective indicator.

Next, we investigate whether the subjective (open-ended responses) or objective (newspaper data) measures influence the effect that transparency has on expectations of accountability. We expect the subjective measure should have a stronger effect because people are directly aware of local journalism as an instrument for accountability, whereas the objective measure should have a weaker but positive effect because

---

[39] Local media was the fourth most-mentioned topic behind community interest, word of mouth in a small town, and government mistrust.

[40] Data from the Center for Innovation and Sustainability in Local Media at the University of North Carolina (UNC) at Chapel Hill. These data are at the county level, with information on each publication cross-referenced with multiple sources.

[41] Examples of public broadcasting include the local affiliates of NPR, PBS, Pacifica, and APM.

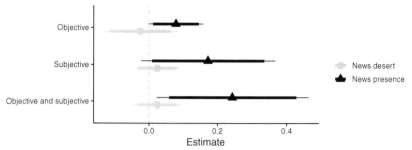

FIGURE 8.5 Effect of transparency on expectations that companies will be held accountable if they do not create local jobs broken down by whether there is a local news presence in the survey-taker's county, whether one subjectively believes there is a strong local news presence, or there is either an objective and/or subjective news presence.

the presence of newspapers is an underlying characteristic of one's community.[42]

What difference did local journalism make for expectations of accountability? Figure 8.5 presents the impact of the transparency treatment on the accountability outcome broken out by a respondent's objective, subjective, or combined local news presence.[43] These results suggest that local media presence enhances the impact of transparency on accountability. Respondents who live in locations with more than one daily print newspaper, local public radio station, or online news outlet believe that when there is a transparency requirement, companies will be held accountable if they failed to create local jobs. By contrast, individuals who live in news deserts do not think transparency is sufficient to hold companies accountable. Expectations of accountability are greatest when subjective belief in the strength of the local media overlaps with objective news presence, as indicated by the last row in Figure 8.5. While we interpret these results as consistent with the power of local journalism, they are only suggestive because there could be a hidden variable that we did not account for that explains the presence of local media and beliefs about accountability.

---

[42] We examine the moderating impact of the news presence variables on the accountability question, as our free response item is about this outcome variable.
[43] Linear regression model with controls. The model includes a measure of ruralness, which should dampen the strength of our news presence measures. We also add state fixed effects to account for state-specific features that influence the media presence.

CLAWBACK OR BLOWBACK?

Transparency is one tool in a vast box of policies that governments can use to make local investments credible. For example, local governments could structure business incentives by requiring companies that receive an investment to meet some observable metric like the number of local jobs created. If the business failed to meet the pledged threshold, the government would "clawback" its incentive (e.g., Jensen and Malesky, 2018).

Clawbacks are not theoretical. When asked how to make green jobs deliver local benefits, a Democratic policymaker from Wisconsin said, "clawback provisions with teeth." Examples of clawback provisions abound. In 2022, Georgia agreed to a plan to provide the electric car company, Rivian, with $1.5 billion in tax abatements, job tax credits, and workforce development assistance, but the state would maintain the right to recoup its investment if the number of jobs fell below the promised target during a 25-year period (Hurt, 2022). Organizations like *Good Jobs First* have long promoted both clawback and transparency provisions as tools for corporate accountability.

In theory, clawbacks should incentivize businesses to provide local benefits. However, there is a debate about whether clawbacks work (e.g., Jensen, 2017). Even less is known about what the public thinks of such incentives. Such perceptions matter for the energy transition, and economic development more broadly, because it might be possible to use clawbacks alongside transparency to create local economic opportunities from green jobs. Yet there is a risk that clawbacks could be controversial. For example, a Republican policymaker we surveyed from Arizona said, "do not tie these benefits [from green investments] to any other criteria, conditions or stipulations. Let the decision be free market-driven, not compensatory." Policymakers face trade-offs when it comes to how they structure investments to tie the hands of firms. We explore these trade-offs with survey experiments that evaluate what the public and local officials think about clawback provisions.

National Public Survey

Would the national public be more likely to support tax breaks to green companies, sometimes derided as "corporate welfare," if there were clawback provisions? To explore this question, we asked a nationally representative sample of Americans how likely they would be to support a local politician who provided substantial tax credits to attract renewable

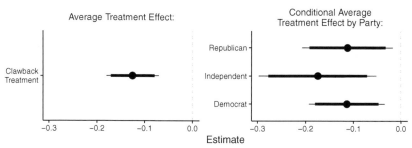

FIGURE 8.6 Effect of clawback provisions on the likelihood of voting for a politician who offers tax credits for green energy. The left panel shows the average effect. The right panel shows the effects broken out by party identification.

energy jobs.[44] Crucially, half of the respondents are randomly assigned to see that companies must pay back the tax credits if they failed to hire enough workers, while the other half sees the control condition where there are no clawbacks.

What difference did clawbacks have on support for politicians who provided tax credits? Contrary to expectations, the results in Figure 8.6 show that the national public penalizes politicians who attach clawback provisions to green investments.[45] This is true for people from all political parties. However, the effect size is modest compared to other covariates included in the model but not depicted in the figure.

The national opposition to clawbacks highlights one potentially significant limitation to conditioning investment: lack of public support. Voters may not want to punish firms, perhaps due to a concern that doing so would dissuade economic investment. One concern mentioned in open-ended questions on a related survey about clawbacks is unease about burdens on businesses.[46] One respondent wrote, "I would never blame the company for failing to hire enough workers because...it's a job that most people would [not] do." Another said, "I don't mind the tax credit. I do [mind if] companies fail to hire enough workers that they must pay back the tax. That's just the federal government trying to control businesses." This free market attitude could limit support for clawbacks, which might reduce the credibility of punishment if the public sides with the company.

---

[44] Fielded by in August 2022 with Qualtrics ($N = 2,019$).
[45] Linear regression model with controls. Heterogeneous effects from a linear regression model with controls that interacts the treatment indicator with partisan identification.
[46] National survey fielded August 2022 with CAPS/Harris ($N = 3,018$).

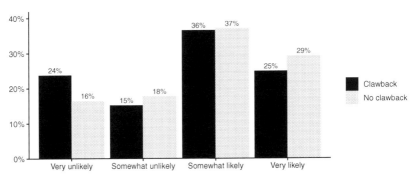

FIGURE 8.7 Effect of clawback provisions on local officials' likelihood of support for renewable energy tax incentives.

Local Policymaker Survey

The local policymaker sample provides a remarkable opportunity to study these officials' views of clawbacks. Local policymaker perceptions are significant because they are attuned to community public opinion and often have control over the design of tax incentives. Local officials also face trade-offs when deciding whether to grant special tax treatment to attract businesses. Politicians may find themselves responsible for the fallout of failed investments, which creates incentives to hold firms accountable. But push too much, and leaders might deter investment in the first place.

We asked local policymakers whether they would support providing substantial tax credits for renewable energy. The tax credits are "substantial" to make their provision appear costly and help avoid ceiling effects where everyone supports the policy. We randomized whether the credit includes a clawback provision.

Consistent with our national public results, clawback provisions may reduce local policymaker support for green tax credits. Figure 8.7 plots how likely local officials in the clawback treatment and the control group would be to support tax incentives for renewable energy. Overall, there is support for green tax credits. However, the addition of a clawback provision may lower support. This decrease in support is most detectable at the tail of the scale, where there is about an 8 percent increase in local officials who are very unlikely to support tax credits.[47]

While these results indicate that local policymakers are averse to clawbacks, some open-ended responses indicate a willingness to place

---

[47] Linear regression model with controls ($p < 0.1$).

Conclusion 229

conditions on investments. A Democrat from Kentucky said that green investment deals should "require hiring local [workers]." A Republican from California proposed a requirement "that 90 percent of the jobs created go to local residents." A Republican in Pennsylvanian fossil fuel community suggested that "jobs must have residence requirements." Another Republican from an oil county in Texas said that green investments should "include requirements in the contract provisions" to lock in local benefits. These answers indicate support for conditions on investment.

Given this support, why might clawbacks backfire in the survey experiment? For one, not all local policymakers believe requirements are good. Some have an ideological aversion to government intervention and prefer the free market to do its work. Another possibility is that the survey experiment presented respondents with too stark a contrast. For example, one Democrat from a municipality in Indiana said that local jobs should be made "a condition of funding, but allow it if it can be proven the [that] the local workforce isn't capable or available." There was no such flexibility in the clawback described in the vignette. Perhaps policymakers would have been more amenable to conditions that provide leeway if the local labor force lacked the requisite skills for green energy.

These results paint a more complicated portrait of investment conditions than policy debates commonly depict. While the open-ended responses indicate a willingness to place restrictions on investment among some policymakers, this does not guarantee public support. And for clawback conditions that offer little flexibility for companies, such provisions do not appear desirable to the average local elected leader nor the national public. Future work should explore what types of flexibility might win public support for conditions on businesses that could facilitate local benefits, not just from green energy but from all local investments.

CONCLUSION

Ensuring that green jobs create tangible local benefits for workers and their communities is crucial for the energy transition, which presents the dual challenge of offsetting job losses in fossil fuel communities while expanding the green workforce. Beyond the energy transition, green jobs also represent an unprecedented opportunity for local economic development, especially in stagnating areas, but only if the benefits accrue to communities.

However, in scores of interviews, media accounts, and our public opinion data, a repeated concern is that renewable energy jobs primarily benefit outside workers. While just one dimension of local economic opportunity, local job creation is salient. So much so that people like Lucas Franco would sit for hours at wind farm construction sites counting the number of local license plates.

This is not just the usual mantra of "American" jobs but reflects concern about state and even county job creation. While there is a vast literature on whether national or personal economic conditions influence political preferences, our interviews, and public opinion data indicate that *local* job opportunities are especially salient.[48] These community-level economic preferences may lead to support for place-based investments.

This chapter explored when and how putting green jobs under the spotlight could make the energy transition beneficial and inclusive for workers and their communities where new green jobs are located. Rather than mandates for local labor, which could confront strident political opposition, transparency provides an alternative institutional mechanism that could create credible local benefits while also laying the groundwork for more ambitious policies like PLAs and CBAs. Transparency provisions help shed light on where the benefits from the transition accrue, which creates opportunities to hold developers accountable if local workers and communities are left behind. Our surveys, experiments, interviews, and case study demonstrate the potential efficacy of transparency.

Transparency, however, is no silver bullet. Lacking clear mechanisms for implementation and enforcement, transparency provisions are unlikely to have a clear impact in many contexts (Alt, 2019). Our findings contribute to this literature by showing how local institutions like the news media can enhance transparency's effects. In news deserts, transparency may help to detect the failure to provide local benefits, but this information alone may not be sufficient to change firms' behavior without a robust media that pushes for accountability. Making transparency achieve its potential may also require investments in fundamental civic institutions like local journalism.

Implementation also matters. Local capacity may be necessary to enforce punishment when violations come to light. Senior staff members at the Minnesota PUC expressed concern that the Commission is

---

[48] For the importance of community economic circumstances, see Bisbee (2019) and Gazmararian (2022c).

Conclusion

short-staffed, which means they have not been able to scrutinize the labor reports from developers, "there's the question of what if they are not reporting, or reporting in not a great way. We don't hold them to account because we already issued a site permit. There's no real accountability or stick if they don't. It's problematic in terms of accountability."[49] However, despite the lack of formal accountability in Minnesota, our study provides cautious optimism that local hiring increased due to transparency.

It is also important to recognize that firms have choices about where to invest, and labor cost is a consideration that influences their calculi. Firms strike a balance between labor costs (which might, though need not be cheaper with nonlocal workers) and community support. Energy cooperatives we spoke with articulated the salience of community buy-in and the additional benefits that come from this. "Reporting the use of local labor, we don't have any problem with that. We have always committed. Part of what cooperatives do is that we commit to the local economies of our members...The energy transition that we're going to need to undergo is going to need to benefit local communities at the core."[50]

These considerations should be kept in mind when deploying transparency provisions, which have broad applicability. For example, advance notification of layoffs to employees, long-championed by unions like UMW, prepares workers to transition into other lines of work (Fung, Graham, and Weil, 2007). The WARN Act passed by Congress in 1988 represents an attempt to mandate this type of transparency, though its impact has been limited due to exemptions and noncompliance (Addison and Blackburn, 1994).

Another example is local economic development. The concern that green jobs go to outside workers applies in other industries. As local governments increasingly offer more generous and opaque tax incentives to attract businesses, the need for transparency over these investment deals grows (Bartik, 2019; Jensen and Thrall, 2021). One option to structure these investments to encourage the benefits to accrue to local workers and their community is to use transparency alongside clawback provisions that condition the receipt of special tax treatment on achieving a target for local jobs.

However, our findings reveal a potential dark side to attempts to structure investments to create credibility. Clawback provisions in tax

---

[49] August 17, 2022 interview.
[50] Interview, power company executive, November 8, 2022.

incentive programs may undermine public support for green energy projects, potentially out of fear of deterring investments. This challenge shows how investment conditions may not be credible if communities fear that firms would respond by taking their business elsewhere. With the industrial policy approach to the clean energy transition that is taking hold in the United States and abroad, learning how to enhance the credibility of tax credits and subsidies is crucial.

Even with transparency, concerns about reversibility remain. A Minnesota PUC senior staff member warned that transparency is "not set in stone. If the Commission turns over with the Republican who's running here...[wins]...I could see [transparency] changing pretty quickly if the new government gets control with conservative commissioners."[51] Such political swings reverberate through state-level bureaucracy and can create uncertainty and undermine credibility. As Chapter 2 discusses, enacting transparency provisions via legislation could provide more durable protections. Minnesota is now considering a law that would codify the transparency requirement, which shows how local changes can build up to binding legislation.

For transparency and investment structure to be most effective, incentives must be in place for accountability. A fundamental issue that constrains the ability of local governments to hold companies accountable and bargain for better community benefits is an asymmetry in leverage. Firms have the threat of exit, which has encouraged a race to the bottom. Research should turn to understanding the conditions when policies can push investors to compete for communities rather than the other way around. Encouraging a race to the top would enhance the bargaining position of communities, strengthening the credibility of not only green investments but investments more generally. Transparency provides a good place to start, as citizens must first understand the distribution of benefits and costs from investments to make informed political decisions that could constrain politicians and firms.

---

[51] August 17, 2022 interview. However, there are indications that transparency could be bipartisan. Local union organizers attributed their success to bipartisanship, with Democrats supporting green jobs and Republicans supporting local jobs (Interview with senior union members, July 6, 2022).

9

Conclusion

We began in Carbon County, then visited communities that have undergone economic transitions, like the Industrial Midwest and German coal country, and places on the front lines of climate transitions, such as Appalachia and the Gulf Coast. We heard from workers and their families, middle and high school students, fairgoers, renewable energy instructors, union officials, mayors, county economic planners, lawmakers, and electric power companies. Their stories revealed what the energy transition looks like from the ground up, why the problem is so vexing, and what might be done.

While the climate impasse in the United States puzzles experts who view the problem from the top down, we uncover deeper, less appreciated answers through our interviews, surveys, and case studies from the ground up. The policies that reformers hope will accelerate the energy transition are not always seen as credible by those they intend to help, and communities question whether new investments in unfamiliar industries will make them better off than they were before.

This ground-up perspective matters politically. If the energy transition is to succeed, we must convert opponents into advocates, doubters into believers, and the indifferent into participants. Companies, communities, and workers that produce fossil fuels must lessen their opposition. Countries, local governments, and neighborhoods throughout the world must welcome new clean energy projects into their backyards. Compensation and investments hold great potential to achieve these ends by building coalitions for the energy transition.

It also matters morally. Communities that produce fossil fuels have made sacrifices to power the industrial revolution which made the world

233

as we know it. But the costs of coal, oil, and gas for the planet and for the communities where they are located are clear. If the world is to have a shot at staving off the worst impacts of climate change, the future cannot be dominated by fossil fuels. But the history of economic transitions is littered with broken promises and failed initiatives. And people know this. There is an obligation to not leave workers, their families, and communities behind, especially when their dislocation is the direct result of government policy. We know in our hearts – and you know as well – that it is unacceptable to leave people behind.

Any attempt to solve the climate impasse must be clear-eyed about the source of the problem. We use our tools as social scientists to pinpoint where credibility challenges arise so that we could try to solve them. The underlying dilemma that confronts any long-term reform is that even well-intentioned leaders cannot control the future. Unforeseen changes in economic or political circumstances could spell the death of energy transition policies like compensation and investments.

We reveal how stakeholders, from workers to business leaders, recognize how credibility challenges give rise to uncertainty. When we listened, we repeatedly heard worries about the pendulum swing of political control from one party to the next and doubts about whether the government or companies have the best intentions or the ability to do what they promise. Our surveys, interviews, and case studies show that what might seem abstract is concrete in the minds of citizens, local officials, and business leaders who look into the future and consider whether promises will be kept – or not.

While experts wonder why communities oppose green energy projects and workers do not sign up for green jobs programs, when we listened to people in the communities that stand to benefit, we heard concerns about whether these investments would make them better off than before. One union organizer, whose group has members in both coal and renewable energy, scoffed at the idea of employment booms in renewable energy. He only half-jokingly said that one needs just "a lawn mower and glass cleaner" to maintain a solar farm. Compare that to the army that labors at a coal-fired power plant.[1]

Although green jobs are not always seen as a source of local economic opportunity, they could be with the right policies. As new legislation hopes to accelerate the energy transition, and with more efforts to come, it will be essential to figure out how to make green jobs work. This is crucial not only for the workers and communities where these projects

---

[1] Interview, April 19, 2022.

Solutions

will be built, but for the political logic that could unlock climate action. A potentially powerful argument that could create allies in the energy transition is that green industries will generate well-paid jobs that make communities healthier and better off. However, this message could be lost if reformers disregard real questions raised by potential recipients of green investments.

The credibility challenges our book identifies are relevant for any economic transition, but they are intense when it comes to the clean energy transition. This is because of the unprecedented scope and time scale of the challenge. Instead of falling equally on all citizens, the costs of the move away from fossil fuels and toward renewable energy concentrate in regions that produce coal, oil, and gas. There are also consequences that ripple beyond that for workers whose job exists because of demand for fossil fuels, such as the people who assemble engines for gasoline-powered cars or the attendants as gasoline stations. Climate policy must also be sustained long-term, given the significant emissions cuts required.

After our diagnosis of the problem, we proposed solutions that could help to break through the climate impasse with more credible policies and local economic opportunities. Our book lays the foundation to evaluate what strategies might generate credibility, and we proposed and tested an *initial* set of tools that hold promise. Our main finding is actions that enhance credibility help to garner support for the energy transition. The book contains many solutions, but we highlight four here and summarize what we found when we analyzed their political effectiveness.

SOLUTIONS

Make Policies Harder to Reverse

First, the public, local officials, and companies become more supportive of the energy transition when they see government policies as more durable. How can policies be made more durable? In our interviews, surveys, and messaging experiments, a consistent preference emerges for laws that require a majority to undo unlike executive actions that the next president could tear up or promises that might never be delivered. Tactics to insulate funding from the pendulum swing of party turnover also help. Long-term investment in communities, as opposed to funding that must be reauthorized every year, reduces worries about political reversal. Leaders could also tie the hands of their successors, such as with educational loans that the government can only get back if students find green jobs. These are just some of the solutions we propose to make policies more durable.

These less reversible policies unlock new opportunities. People become willing to train for green jobs. Citizens become more supportive of environmental protections for the climate, even when the reform is so costly that it would cause job losses at a major employer in one's community. What is the reason for this support despite the costs? Our solutions make credible the government's promise of investments in new industries and compensation to those impacted.

Consult Communities

Our next solution is to provide opportunities for community participation, control, and input. The local officials we surveyed and interviewed repeatedly raise the lack of local input as a barrier to energy transitions. One policymaker in a fossil fuel-dependent part of Colorado went so far as to say that solutions should begin with communities. "I support ground-up policymaking that is then supported by the federal government. When it is top-down policy, the loudest voices influence it the most, and rural areas suffer." In our messaging experiments, we find that when energy transition policies delegate control over implementation to communities and provide opportunities for public input, there is much greater support for costly environmental regulations. We also find that community involvement helps to build trust in the people who administer investment and compensation programs, which is essential because low trust can exacerbate credibility challenges.

Of course, a balance must be struck between local input and a fast transition. Communities can also oppose green energy projects. However, the knee-jerk reaction to write off community involvement because of the potential for NIMBY opposition misses a deeper point. Some residents, business leaders, and local officials believe that new green projects do not make their neighborhoods better off than they were before. Policies and investments that generate credible local opportunities could help counter these objections and reduce potential downsides of community participation. Residents would no longer be obstructionists but allies who ensure projects serve the community's needs.

Shine a Light

To create local economic opportunity, we uncover how greater transparency could improve perceptions of community benefits from green

Solutions 237

energy projects like solar and wind. Politicians and businesses often make grand promises about the jobs that they will create. Local governments roll out the red carpet and provide generous tax credits with the hopes that they will be the lucky recipients of a big, new investment. But it is hard to know if companies keep these promises because the actual economic impact of projects is complex and often hidden.

Yet, we show how transparency initiatives, such as a requirement that companies report on how many local jobs are created, can make a difference. These reforms have been tested in places like Minnesota, which subsequently saw an increase in local union laborers on wind projects. We also find that when there are transparency provisions for renewable energy investments, the national public, local officials, and youths become more likely to think that these projects will make their communities better off.

Build Bipartisan Coalitions

The last but not least finding is that efforts to build bipartisan coalitions can create credibility. When energy transition policies have bipartisan support, the public views them as less likely to be reversed. Because of that, support rises, even for costly environmental regulations.

In our highly polarized times, the idea of bipartisanship might seem fanciful. However, to discount efforts to build broad coalitions from the outset can create a self-fulfilling prophecy. The expectation that others will not cooperate can foreclose opportunities that could have emerged. To this point, we show that there is a hidden national consensus behind compensation and investment to help fossil fuel communities. Part of the problem is that this is not widely known or believed. But we show that revealing this consensus can shift expectations and leads to greater faith that energy transition policies will not be reversed. This suggests that efforts to build bipartisan consensus could be self-reinforcing and ultimately lead to a more effective and durable energy transition.

* * *

Policies to create credibility face their own challenges and might even appear politically infeasible. However, such expectations are, in part, a product of the view that the costs of the energy transition are an insurmountable political barrier. But how the public, companies, and elected officials understand costs is a direct function of credibility. If support for investments might not last in the future, one might not think they would benefit and could even anticipate being hurt. For this reason, some individuals and interest groups invest heavily in discrediting the government's ability to solve problems. However, our interviews and surveys show that people would pay the price of the transition if provided credible compensation and economic opportunities. The electric power and oil companies we spoke with were also not outright opposed to the energy transition. Instead, their business models are inherently conservative, so they need predictable and durable policy to bet on renewables in the long run. Of course, some opponents might never come along.

It would also be a mistake to write off fossil fuel communities as irredeemably beholden to the industry, confused by climate denial, or powerless to partisan polarization. While our research surfaces deep concerns about credibility, a remarkable spirit of resilience also emerges. People throughout the country express how through their faith, ingenuity, and perseverance, they see opportunities in the clean energy future. For example, Rusty Bell, the Commissioner of Campbell County, Wyoming, described his hope that coal ash could be repurposed for the clean economy:

rare earths is one thing that is a bright spot...not taking the rare earths out of the coal itself, but actually out of the ash...there's empty rail cars coming from every power plant across the country, back to here. So why are they not putting ash in that, bringing it back here for processing? ...there's some real opportunity there... I don't want to say they're gonna save the community, but certainly being part of what continues to keep this community valid and viable.[2]

One former coal miner in Southwest Pennsylvania who now works on a solar project expressed doubts about the cost of solar, but then in the next breath said, "I think once something's built and people see it, and it's working, then they would be more likely to be a part of it. Me working on this project myself makes me start looking at houses or buildings that we could put solar on, maybe looking into doing it on my own home."[3] Another resident and business owner in the same area said that if the solar panels are locally owned, "I see that as a very positive thing for the community. That puts us less dependent on [the power company]."[4]

---

[2] Interview, September 22, 2022.
[3] Interview, August 9, 2021.
[4] Interview, August 9, 2021.

GROUND-UP APPROACH

Policymakers have begun to awaken to the importance of ground-up engagement, at least in their messaging. For example, when Jennifer Granholm, the Secretary of Energy, visited a new solar company in West Virginia, she remarked, "this community is embracing new chances and opportunity in their own way. Nobody is coming here to tell West Virginia what it should do because West Virginia is figuring it out, and it's really exciting" (Coalfield Development, 2022). The clean energy transition is full of possibilities – but it needs durable policies.

Lessons from Listening

Our ground-up approach holds lessons for policymakers, nongovernmental organizations, and companies involved in the energy transition. First, listen to those impacted. When one hears skepticism about whether green projects will create local jobs, whether students will find new careers, and whether the government will keep its promises, the goal should be to understand why these concerns exist rather than carte blanche writing them off. Even when these concerns stem from disinformation disseminated by interest groups through public relations campaigns, political leaders, and the media, it remains crucial to understand why people are susceptible to these appeals, which may be in part due to the uncertain futures they face.

Second, think about the long-term. Focus on how to build lasting momentum through enduring partnerships. Press releases and campaign stops are not policy. Do not assume that good faith efforts and promises are sufficient, especially when these actions occur against the backdrop of broken promises to communities that already feel left behind.

Ground-up Research

Our book represents a pragmatic approach to scholarship that the climate crisis demands. While grand theories of politics have their place, the threat of global warming necessitates a new form of research: applied theoretical work. Scholars should test and experiment with the well-honed theories from across disciplines to understand how to unlock the climate impasse.[5] Even if these solutions fail, that information helps to understand when our theories might break down and what work remains to be

---

[5] See, for example, the call from McGuinness and Slaughter (2019).

240   *Conclusion*

done. And when solutions succeed, they put new political opportunities within arm's reach.

Our book deepens and advances an emerging research agenda on the energy transition. We take up the call to study the forms of compensation and investment that would be politically acceptable (e.g., Colgan, Green, and Hale, 2021; Gaikwad, Genovese, and Tingley, 2022b; Gazmararian, 2022a). The credibility concerns we identify help to make sense of when governments can fracture fossil fuel interest groups with compensation (e.g., Meckling and Nahm, 2022). Like Patashnik and Zelizer (2013) we show how the prospect of policy reversal can prevent the emergence of new constituencies that could drive decarbonization (e.g., Aklin and Urpelainen, 2013; Meckling et al., 2015; Stokes, 2020). Despite these profound challenges, we demonstrate how governments could create credibility to make reforms stick.

Our research suggests that the success of economic transitions is not simply a top-down technical task to supply and target compensation and investments but an endeavor that requires actions to foster trust and establish durable reforms through institutional constraints. Promises of compensation and investment must appear credible from the ground up. Our book brings credibility to the forefront, which enriches earlier work on how governments smooth the public's exposure to economic and technological change (e.g., Polanyi, 1944; Ruggie, 1982). Like these scholars, we explore the interplay of markets, society, and government. Whether transitions are the consequence of technological transformations like automation or policy-induced shifts like carbon pollution controls, governments have taken on the essential task of smoothing the costs of these changes.

A commitment to listening guides our research. To understand how to unlock the climate impasse required that we listen and learn from those most impacted. This meant extensive interviews with a range of stakeholders, archival expeditions into the depths of the *UMW Journal*, and innovation with our approach to survey research. Our surveys pivot from an earlier focus on consumer attitudes about energy and climate change (e.g., Ansolabehere and Konisky, 2014), to the public's views about the economic opportunities offered by these industries and the credibility of the government's energy transition policies. This meant reaching hard-to-access regions that are politically significant yet underrepresented in national surveys. It meant surveying local elected officials, union members, middle schoolers, high-schoolers, and county fairgoers. And it meant marrying evidence that provides a rich description of how people understand the energy transition with techniques from social science that help uncover cause-and-effect relationships

We hope the solutions we propose will go a long way to make political reforms stick and communities better off. However, we must be clear-eyed about the difficulties involved. There are interest groups with deep financial stakes in fossil fuels, which could lead them to oppose commitment devices that would unlock the climate impasse. Bipartisanship can enhance the durability of a policy, but polarization could impede efforts to build coalitions, and reformers reasonably do not want to leave opportunities on the table to pass legislation even if it means doing so unilaterally. Transparency can be effective, but the companies and individuals whose activities are illuminated may resist efforts to shine a light. And even when there is transparency, local institutions must be robust enough to punish promise breakers. Credibility challenges are hard. They are also ubiquitous in political and economic life.[6] Here are some of the problems that remain to be solved.

CHALLENGES THAT REMAIN

Trust

Questions of trust and whether governments are trustworthy permeate our book. However, there are further implications to unpack. First, climate transitions will impact society on a physical and temporal scale not seen before. Communities will feel the physical impacts from climate change, and will be asked to change their way of life and adapt. Fossil fuels are embedded in our infrastructure and societies in often unseen or underappreciated ways, which can give rise to unintended consequences. As the energy transition unfolds, citizens will regularly ask whether these changes are in their interest. The sheer level of uncertainty can create hesitancy, even for the potential benefactors (e.g., Fernandez and Rodrik, 1991). Political philosopher Michael Sandel (2020, p. 112) asks,

...what about those who oppose government action to reduce carbon emissions, not because they reject science, but because they do not trust the government to act in their interest, especially in a large-scale reconfiguration of the economy, and do not trust the technocratic elites who would design and implement this reconfiguration? These are not scientific questions to be answered by experts.

---

[6] This is the case both within countries (e.g., Persson and Tabellini, 2012; Shepsle, 1991) and between them (e.g., Fearon, 1995; Powell, 1990; Stone, 2012; Tomz, 2012; Walter, 2002).

They are questions about power, morality, authority, and trust, which is to say, they are questions for democratic citizens.

Given the complexity of modern government and climate transitions, bureaucracies with expertise will play a central role. An urgent task is to understand how bureaucrats can do so without being seen as biased, incompetent, or corrupt (Levi and Sherman, 1997). While political scientist Terry Moe (1985) reminds us that bureaucracies will never be neutral because politics is inescapable, there are some solutions like job tenure protections that could help (e.g., Gailmard and Patty, 2007). These issues will be essential to address since "[i]f citizens doubt the state's commitment to enforce the laws and if its information and guarantees are not credible, then the state's capacity to generate interpersonal trust will diminish" (Levi, 1998, p. 85). Put differently, if we lean into the climate transition and botch it, the result could be more distrust that makes the necessary reforms even further out of reach.

Finally, the physical impacts of climate change could also alter state-society relations. One estimate is that global warming will displace over 483 million people by global warming by 2200 (Cruz and Rossi-Hansberg, 2023). This mass migration could amplify issues of trust between migrant and native populations (Cook, Hardin, and Levi, 2005).[7] The damage from climate change could also make people unable to afford migration, which could create problems domestically (Benveniste, Oppenheimer, and Fleurbaey, 2022). How governments facilitate productive relations between different groups, especially when resources are scarce, will be important. Political control might also change in response to pressures from climate migration, and may even tilt toward extreme, anti-migrant parties that may worsen the climate crisis.

Low trust in government cannot be solved overnight. It is also unclear whether citizens should automatically trust their government if it does not respond to their needs. However, our book shows that even small changes to how policies are framed, such as more local input and community implementation, hold the potential to improve credibility and trust, even among individuals with the least faith in institutions.

Investments in Communities

Our ground-up approach also calls into question a common perspective in economics that policies should target people, not places. The concern

---

[7] But see Arias and Blair (2022) for evidence that publics may welcome climate migrants.

Challenges That Remain

is that investments in communities are a subsidy for people to live in unproductive areas (e.g., Kline and Moretti, 2014). Yet this top-down view sees people as atomized dots that can freely move from place to place in response to labor demand.[8] But that's not how people work. People have families, friends, and homes. These social ties are politically consequential but are often ignored by economic models because they are harder to quantify. If communities are left behind in transitions, it will reinforce the decay of already distressed regions (e.g., Anderson, 2017, 2022), which perversely could make it even harder for the people with the least resources to leave. Investments in communities recognize that people want policies that make their area better off, and they are unpersuaded by appeals to take a check and move elsewhere.

However, community-based investment is not without challenges. For example, local economic development directors would lament difficulties with the adequacy of basic infrastructure like housing supply and water treatment plants, which could deter a business from setting up shop. Moreover, investments in long-term projects like education to build a local workforce and attract new businesses take time for the benefits to manifest, time that short-sighted politicians might not have.

Our concept of local economic opportunity provides a helpful lens to understand how people perceive investments in their area. They focus on the growth prospects of industries, how well jobs pay, whether they will last, and if the benefits go to locals. Chapter 4 shows how taxes collected from new and old industries are also crucial since these fund public goods like roads, schools, and libraries. If new investments cannot make up for the shortfall as fossil fuel revenue evaporates, communities will see themselves as made worse off by the energy transition. Renewable energy could make up for the revenue gap, but this will depend on getting the policies and incentives right. The tools to encourage renewable energy deployment can sometimes undermine their ability to fill the local coffers. Tax incentives solve one problem but can undercut local benefits that could make communities accept new green projects.

---

[8] Newer research suggests that place-based investments should be effective in areas with high labor elasticity, the places where a small change in wages corresponds with a large shift in labor supplied. In other words, an employment subsidy in West Virginia will reduce more suffering than the same subsidy in San Francisco which has restricted housing supply (Austin, Glaeser, and Summers, 2018). Policymakers and scholars should pay close attention to these insights about place-based policies (Shambaugh and Nunn, 2018).

244 *Conclusion*

Even when there are policies to capture revenue from projects, the devil is in the details. For example, if localities tax the value of the equipment, then as wind turbines age and depreciate, there will be less money raised over time. Alternatively, governments could tax the energy produced to create a more stable revenue stream, as some communities already do. Like fossil fuels, how governments tax renewables differs both across and even within states. Learning can also occur as local officials realize they are deprived of benefits. Mayor Terry Weickum, whom you met at the start of the book, told us how he updated Carbon County's tax to be based on production instead of equipment, which helped to raise more money for the community.

Technological Futures

The technologies we have today to reduce emissions will change in the future, which could upend the political logic of creating allies with benefits. For example, heat pumps, heralded by advocates as an invention that dramatically cuts energy use and drives demand for electrician and installation jobs, are already being designed so homeowners can install them just as they would a window air conditioner. Battery manufacturing plants will face competitive pressures, which companies may respond to with automation. These innovations may be beneficial because they drive down the costs of the energy transition. Still, they could undercut the political argument of job creation and local benefits. The vast demand from the green economy might outweigh these challenges. For example, the labor required to build EVs will be dramatically less than gas-powered cars, but there may be such a large number of EVs to be built that there is still considerable job creation. But these are uncertain futures. It is important to be clear-eyed about the unintended consequences of technological changes we have not yet imagined.

Paying the Bills

As efforts to price carbon pollution fizzled, climate advocates have pivoted to policy tools like tax credits, grants, and subsidies that make green energy cheaper rather than fossil fuels more expensive. The scope of the investments needed is vast when considering how societies must adapt to climate change's effects, the incentives that must be expanded to accelerate green industries, and the investments that should be made to uplift communities harmed by their exposure to industrial activity.

Challenges That Remain

However, as climate scholars Dolšak and Prakash (2022b) point out, "[s]ubsidies are politically attractive but raise a different problem: who will pay for them? Given the rising budgetary problems across the world, how viable are the subsidy-based demand side interventions as a tool for climate policy?" Fiscal conservatives and those with low trust in government are less willing to support spending in general, let alone on climate and environmental issues (e.g., Rudolph and Evans, 2005). Our surveys in Chapter 7 also show that the public is sensitive to deficits. The public views expensive programs as more likely to be rolled back, which would undermine credibility. While countries like the United States can run large deficits, the public might not understand these economic nuances, and it is not clear that smaller countries have the same ability to subsidize their energy transitions.

While these subsidies create hurdles for green energy, they also represent a potential political weakness for fossil fuels. Countries already offer enormous subsidies for fossil fuels (e.g., Parry, Black, and Vernon, 2021). Some of these policies are popular because they lower energy costs for consumers, an appeal that subsidies for renewable energy might also make. However, it is harder for new green interest groups to create and maintain new subsidies than for established fossil fuel companies to defend what exists. Leaders have had a tough time when trying to reduce fossil fuel subsidies. When they do make reforms, they tend not to stick (Martinez-Alvarez et al., 2022). Weaning companies and consumers from these subsidies will be essential.

International Trade and Domestic Green Policies

The political strategy to create credible domestic benefits from the clean energy transition could also have unintended international consequences. Economic activity has ripple effects in a globalized world.[9] For example, Germany pioneered solar panel production, but now most photovoltaic panels are produced in China. Special incentives to use domestic products in solar panels or EV assembly could run afoul of international trade rules. Elements of the Inflation Reduction Act (IRA) in the United States succeeded partly due to its provisions to encourage domestic investment. However, these same provisions also sparked a dispute with American

---

[9] Beliefs about globalization may also be related to expectations of benefits from climate action (Bayer and Genovese, 2020).

trade partners (e.g., Davies, 2022; Rappeport, Swanson, and Kanno-Youngs, 2022).[10] Policymakers designed these same trade agreements so that countries could credibly commit to open trade despite domestic opposition (Maggi and Rodriguez-Clare, 2007). Unexpectedly, policies to enhance credibility at home run up against attempts to create credibility abroad.

Decarbonizing the Developing World

Decarbonization of developing countries will depend partly on access to resources from wealthy countries. However, credibility challenges impede this process. The United States and other wealthy signatories of the Paris Agreement, an international climate agreement where countries came together to coordinate their emissions reductions, promised to contribute to the climate efforts of developing nations.[11] On the surface, this approach holds great potential because emissions in the developing world will grow substantially, which will impact the globe since carbon dioxide inflicts the same damage no matter where it is emitted.

However, these promises of "climate finance" have fallen far short of stated goals, much to the displeasure of the developing world (Timperley, 2021; Yeo, 2019). For this reason, a coalition of developing countries made climate finance a top priority at the 2022 United Nations meeting on climate change (COP-27). These countries expressed frustration with the failure of wealthy countries to keep their commitments and how the money that came was in the form of loans that must be paid back rather than grants. Just what developing countries want, more debt. One reason climate finance promises have not been met is that the coalitions which support these flows in wealthy countries are weak. Like foreign aid, domestic politics in donor countries can impact whether the climate finance spigot opens or closes and where the flows go (Milner and Tingley, 2015). Public opinion about climate finance in the United States and other Global North countries reflects a reluctance to spend abroad when that money could be put to use at home (Buntaine and Prather, 2018; Gaikwad, Genovese, and Tingley, 2022a; Gampfer, Bernauer, and Kachi, 2014). When we asked the American public in a nationally representative survey whether they thought the United States would keep its

---

[10] Whether foreign countries and companies can credibly threaten the United States is another question. For example, foreign auto manufacturers have begun to announce plans to build EVs in the United States to benefit from the new subsidies.

[11] This built on earlier cross-border climate finance efforts (Barrett and Stavins, 2003).

Challenges That Remain

commitments to support climate efforts in developing countries, only 17 percent of respondents thought the government would be very likely to do so.[12]

Are there ways to create more support? Perhaps. For example, Gaikwad, Genovese, and Tingley (2022a) show how the structure of climate finance, such as whether it involves companies and organizations from the donor country, can increase domestic political support.[13] Creating domestic beneficiaries in donor countries could increase credibility. However, there are downsides of "tying" foreign assistance in this way, including that it can be less helpful to developing countries (e.g., Morrissey, 1993). As we saw with foreign trade, tools to lessen credibility challenges domestically can create new problems internationally. Finally, efforts to build bipartisan support for climate finance will be critical, as members of Congress note (e.g., Chemnick, 2022). As new large projects emerge in places like South Africa, Indonesia, and potentially India, credibility concerns around climate finance should be part of the discussion.

Beyond Credibility

Credibility is not the only challenge that confronts climate transitions. It can be tempting for social scientists such as ourselves to see the world in these terms, but there are also other meaningful issues at play. For one, technological advances have brought down the price of renewable energy and could further accelerate market-driven energy transitions. Nevertheless, more innovation remains to be done, like in areas of battery storage.[14] As Chapter 3 discusses, government policy and investments can help foster needed innovation, but such efforts face credibility challenges. Creative and scalable technological innovations will undoubtedly help climate transitions. Yet, there is evidence that many of the needed technologies already exist while others must be scaled up (e.g., Larson et al., 2021; Pacala and Socolow, 2004). Much of the remaining challenge is political.

Technological change alone is not sufficient to solve the problem. In his book, political scientist David Victor dispels the "engineer's myth"

---

[12] Fielded in 2022 ($N = 2{,}019$) with Qualtrics.

[13] In scholarship on foreign aid, this policy design is akin to "tied-aid," which is more popular in Congress because the aid must be spent on products and services from the donor country (Milner and Tingley, 2010).

[14] Interview with senior electric power company officials, July 28, 2022.

248   *Conclusion*

that once inventors have developed new technologies, these creations can rapidly be deployed. New technologies, especially those that are most useful, are radical transformations that involve risks. In this context, government policies are essential to managing financial risks, but "[e]ven when those policies are written in treaty registers and in national laws and regulations, firms that invest in new technology and practices must believe they are credible" (Victor, 2011, p. 11).[15] The other consideration is normative. Even if markets can send the right signals that lead to the optimal deployment of renewable energy (unlikely), workers and communities will face intense disruption to their livelihoods that should be managed.

Culture and social identity also weigh on economic transitions. In fossil fuel communities, these concerns emerge in the demand for recognition. Residents and workers in our interviews articulated a feeling that their community's sacrifices to power the country have not been recognized by "elites" from outside their area who benefit from their work but criticize them at the same time. Fossil fuel communities have formed distinct group-based attachments that are rooted in both place and industry (Bell and York, 2010). These attachments have a profound effect on their preferences and political behavior (e.g., Gaikwad, Genovese, and Tingley, 2022b; Gazmararian, 2022b). This makes sense in light of political theorists and scholars of identity who have long demonstrated how the need for recognition is a powerful force in politics (e.g., Taylor, 1995). Even places without fossil fuels might be concerned about the possibility their community would change if renewable energy comes, a concern raised in interviews but one that is more easily addressed. Any attempt at political reform must attend carefully to identity.

REAL HOPE

These enduring challenges are just that. Challenges. Challenges that, with sustained focus, ingenuity, and empathy, can be overcome. The political struggle will not be easy, but we have no choice. And the benefits of reduced and avoided harms from climate change make this struggle worthwhile. The clean energy transition also holds the prospect of improving the quality of life in unseen but consequential ways. For instance, the public health upside of reductions in fossil fuel pollution is staggering. One study estimates that around three million premature

---

[15] See Colgan and Hinthorn (2022) for more on this issue.

deaths occur worldwide each year because of air pollution, which could double by 2050 if there are no reductions in emissions (Lelieveld et al., 2015). Those who live near coal-fired power plants or busy roads traveled by gas-powered vehicles stand to live longer, healthier lives, as do the fenceline communities exposed to decades of industrial pollution that has poisoned them and the planet.

The green energy future also holds the possibility of new innovations, partnerships, and business models. For example, several oil majors are investing in geothermal energy, which is a natural glide path for workers because it requires similar skills as in oil and gas occupations. While we are clear-eyed that geothermal will not replace the primary activities of oil companies, it is encouraging that in our conversations with union leaders and members in pipe-fitting and boilermaker industries, there is enthusiasm about these careers. Another example of ingenuity mentioned above comes from Rusty Bell, who proposed how existing coal ash could serve as a source of rare earth metals needed for batteries or to reduce the carbon footprint of concrete production. These are just some of the innovations that could help reduce emissions and, at the same time, provide good jobs and resources for communities.

FUTURE RESEARCH

Beyond National Policies

While we spotlight the voices of local officials like commissioners and mayors, we spend less time on state and local policies that will play a role in climate transitions.[16] Different levels of governance will need to act independently and in coordination to reduce emissions and form transition policies, especially since global policies may struggle to generate trust among citizens and companies to enable collective action (Ostrom, 2009). Encouragingly, cities, municipalities, and states increasingly play a role in carbon mitigation and adaptation.

However, these subnational actors also grapple with the credibility challenges our book illuminates. For example, in 2016, Illinois passed the Future Energy Jobs Act which sought to dramatically expand renewable investments throughout the state. But the funds dried up and were not renewed, which led to a "bust" and widespread layoffs in the sector

---

[16] See, for example, Bulkeley (2010), Gazmararian and Milner (2022a), Hsu et al. (2019), Stokes (2020), and Stokes and Breetz (2018).

(Bristol, 2020). We are aware of less energy transition research on policy coordination that addresses credibility challenges between different levels of government. One example is how Illinois acted independently as it pursued its Clean Energy Jobs Act, in part, because of uncertainty about federal legislation as state lawmakers drafted the bill. The state's law also faced opposition from Southern Illinois districts home to coal-fired power plants (Olsen, 2021). With new federal investments in green energy, a crucial question will be how state-level policies could work alongside federal legislation in ways that could make climate transitions durable. Policymakers should pay attention to coordination, and scholars should study this nexus, including how it might work and who might champion it. Likewise, researchers should not limit themselves to governmental solutions, but should also explore decentralized policies that could complement top-down policies and independently accelerate the clean energy transition from the ground up (e.g., Gazmararian and Tingley 2023).

Don't Just Study the United States (Like What We Mostly Did)

Our book engages minimally with climate transitions in countries beyond the United States. While we focus on Germany in Chapter 6, and draw on examples and literature from other nations, including Australia, India, Indonesia, Ireland, and South Africa, our primary empirical evidence is from the United States. Based on our reading of media reports, academic literature, and discussions with country experts, the credibility problems we identify are salient worldwide. Some types of credibility problems might be more challenging in developing countries with fewer resources and less established institutions (e.g., Keefer and Vlaicu, 2008; Rodrik, 1989).

Much could be learned by exploring credibility in other national and subnational contexts. Countries have varied histories with redistribution, which could amplify or attenuate commitment concerns. For example, lack of faith in the apolitical execution of social policies in India might exacerbate worries about local benefits from investments (e.g., Gaikwad, Genovese, and Tingley, 2022b).

To name a few examples of fruitful research on climate transitions outside of the United States, Bayulgen (2022) examines Turkey and considers how the role of political elites in fossil fuel transitions may differ compared to other countries. Meckling and Nahm (2022) focus on institutions in parts of Europe, which Chapter 6 covers in detail. Shen, Cain, and Hui (2019) examine public receptiveness to wind energy investments

Future Research

in China. A significant challenge to a faster coal phase-out in China, which is arguably one of the single biggest political economy hurdles for the climate overall, is that millions of people work in the country's coal industry (e.g., Lee et al., 2021). Additional research in developing countries, including places like Indonesia with large coal reserves and power plants, will be important (Ordonez et al., 2021). For example, one study finds that complicated permitting processes undermine renewable energy investments in Indonesia (Yuliani, 2017).

While our book focuses on proximate institutional changes that could enhance credibility, cross-national comparisons could help understand the effects of macro-level differences in institutions. For example, Aklin (2021) shows how variation in the level of democracy can facilitate or impede the deployment of renewable energy. Mildenberger (2020) demonstrates how differences in government-business relations, whether a country has pluralist or corporatist institutions, can impact climate policy-making, an insight Meckling et al. (2022b) echo. While hard for policymakers to alter overnight, these macro-level differences provide contextual knowledge of the challenges reforms might face in a country with a given set of institutions.

Looking across countries also calls attention to trouble on the horizon due to economic interdependence, where fossil fuels represent a significant linkage between countries. Indonesia, Colombia, and Vietnam export considerable volumes of coal to developed countries. As rich nations phase out coal, these developing countries and their coal communities will face substantial challenges (Wehnert et al., 2019). Unless climate finance schemes pan out, fossil fuel export-reliant countries will not have the coffers of the EU, for example, to fall back on, unlike coal-intensive countries in Europe such as the Czech Republic (Keersmaecker and Dejon, 2022).

Timing Is Everything

The sequence on how climate policy ambition ratchets up may influence the success of energy transitions and the durability of political reforms (Meckling, Sterner, and Wagner, 2017; Pahle et al., 2018). Since political constraints can lead governments to pursue piecemeal and incremental measures with unknown efficacy, it will be important to understand the effects of partial policies. One question to explore is whether there are ways to use policy sequencing such that credibility can be enhanced rather than undermined. Politically expedient policies may not be the

252 *Conclusion*

most efficient. Still, if they accelerate action, in the long run, they could make future emissions cuts cheaper and increase the likelihood that subsequent policy is implemented sooner (Goulder, 2020).

Interest Groups, Media, and (Dis)Information

Firms with a financial stake in fossil fuels, especially those that cannot easily exit their position, have incentives to delay climate action. A classic idea from political economy helps to understand why. Political economist Albert Hirschman (1970) identifies two strategies for how one can respond when their group is in decline: exit or voice. Coal, oil, and gas companies have made large capital investments to extract fossil fuels, which makes it hard for them to exit their position, so voice – lobbying Congress and the public – is the natural option. Even if these firms were to sell their assets, unless they retire them from operation, the fundamental political situation does not change. There would still be a vested interest in fossil fuels but under a new name (Colgan, Green, and Hale, 2021).

It is crucial to understand the effects of these interest groups and the media environment within which their messages travel on how the public and lawmakers think about government credibility and local economic opportunity. The influence of interest groups and the media has long been studied and debated (e.g., Mutz, Sniderman, and Brody, 1996). Television, newspapers, and the internet are important channels through which people hear about climate change and energy transition topics (Boykoff and Roberts, 2007). Not only do fossil fuel interest groups spend considerable sums on lobbying lawmakers to block climate policy (Brulle, 2018), they also engage in a concerted effort to influence individual beliefs and the broader social discourse, including through disinformation strategies (e.g., Brulle and Roberts, 2017). Framing is also crucial. In the Czech Republic, media coverage on mining focused on the economic health of mining companies but not climate change (Lehotský et al., 2019).

The landscape of companies with a stake in the production and use of fossil fuels is vast and diverse. As such, companies differ in the content of their advocacy. A select group has engaged in a highly intentional and orchestrated campaign of climate denial (Oreskes and Conway, 2011), including through the use of foundations that shroud their motives (Brulle, 2014; Farrell, 2016). More recently, tactics have changed from outright denial to delay. Some interest groups work to manufacture uncertainty so they can continue to profit from fossil fuels.

Future Research

These deliberate efforts to shape the national conversation might explain some of the patterns we observe around government commitment and local economic opportunity. For example, fossil fuel interest groups often cast renewable energy in a negative light to obstruct climate policy (e.g., Sovacool et al., 2022; Stokes, 2020), and disinformation campaigns are ongoing (Simon, 2022). Lobbying can also distort how lawmakers understand their constituent's policy preferences, which leads to less responsive government (e.g., Hertel-Fernandez, Mildenberger, and Stokes, 2019). Deeper still, citizens underestimate the extent to which others think global warming is happening and support for climate action (e.g., Mildenberger and Tingley, 2019).

However, it would be erroneous to dismiss genuine worries, some of which interest groups amplify. Our book takes seriously that the people in places that the energy transition will impact have valid concerns about credibility and economic opportunity issues.[17] Our examples throughout show how stakeholders raise these concerns worldwide. And in the United States, both Democrats and Republicans in the national public and also local officials ask a similar set of questions. To dismiss these concerns as propaganda does little to persuade individuals about the benefits of the clean energy transition. Regardless, research on how malicious groups distort politics and undermine the future of the planet is essential. This includes both exaggeration and minimization of the challenges this book highlights.

Interest groups are not going away, so a key question will be how to work with them as stakeholders in climate transitions. One challenge is that some of the most devoted advocates for climate action are skeptical about the intentions of firms, especially those that have peddled climate denial. Earlier, we discussed the importance of trust. These lessons apply here, too. One productive step, perhaps, would be for firms to acknowledge this history as an olive branch to foster a cooperative relationship. For their part, advocates for the clean energy transition should also engage with firms that make good faith efforts.

Equity, Inclusivity, and Justice

Chapter 7 discussed how like other skilled trades, employment in renewable energy tends to be dominated by older, white, and male workers. These disparities extend beyond green employment. Sunter, Castellanos,

---

[17] Aitken (2010) makes a similar reflection.

and Kammen (2019) document inequities in rooftop solar installations in the United States, where Black and Hispanic census tracks are less likely to have solar, even when accounting for income differences. EV owners are also more likely to be wealthy and white. The disparities in the benefits of the green economy occur against a backdrop where Black, Brown, and Indigenous communities have borne the brunt of environmental harm from the fossil fuel economy. From the global perspective, climate transitions take place against the history where much of the Global North is directly responsible for pollution that will harm the Global South (e.g., Gazmararian and Milner, 2022a; Roberts and Parks, 2007). While our book does not focus on environmental justice, the credibility considerations we raise are salient in this context as well.[18] Trust may be especially low in fenceline communities that have had companies and government bureaucracies mislead them about the presence and effects of environmental toxins for decades. Interventions in the environmental justice space, such as those in the IRA, may begin to help, but much remains to be done for both research and policy. The credibility concerns we surface apply to promises of environmental remediation in these communities, as well as new green economic opportunities.

Adaptation and Remediation

Our exploration of climate transitions anchors the conversation on the energy transition. With the planet set to warm considerably even with substantial mitigation, adaptation to the impacts of an altered climate will also take center stage (e.g., Javeline, 2014). The framework we establish for credibility is also relevant when it comes to adaptation. Work has already begun to think about the politics of compensation and investment as part of both mitigation and adaptation (e.g., Gaikwad, Genovese, and Tingley, 2022b). The credibility problems around adaptation may be extremely challenging given the long-term investment nature of adaptation.

Similarly, environmental remediation is necessary given years of extractive industries polluting the soil and water, which can also be a source of employment. However, challenges abound, including issues around the predictability of funding by state and federal government (Hu and Tingley, 2022).

---

[18] For reviews of scholarly work on environmental justice, see Dolšak and Prakash (2022a) and Mohai, Pellow, and Roberts (2009).

MAKING GREEN INDUSTRIAL POLICY WORK

Countries worldwide have begun to tackle the climate crisis with what economists call "green industrial policy" (Rodrik, 2014). The idea behind industrial policy is that the government should actively support industries considered important, an idea that causes outcries in some circles. To say that industrial policy is "green" means that the policy aims to promote the development and deployment of technologies that address the climate crisis.

This book highlights how credibility challenges apply to green industrial policies, which are essentially government promises to support investments. For firms, the concern about the political pendulum swing is substantial. Another threat to the durability of these policies is that public support could sour. Think about high-profile failures of green investments in the United States like Solyndra, a company that received loans from a Department of Energy program. While this was not the only outcome of the initiative (they also funded a car company called Tesla), it led to cries to shut down the loans.[19] To the extent that the green energy expansion depends on industrial policy, uncertainty could emerge due to public backlash.

In the United States, the sweeping climate law passed in 2022, the IRA, as well as the infrastructure package, the IIJA, enacted in 2021, contain elements of green industrial policy. The laws will usher in a suite of incentives to deploy renewable energy, build EVs, and create domestic supply chains for green industries.

What does our diagnosis of the climate impasse tell us about the challenges that green industrial policies? It is always dangerous for social scientists to comment on current events. Time provides the benefit of more data and circumspection with which to judge one's hypotheses. With the recognition that the IRA has been freshly inked, we offer informed speculations about what we can learn about climate politics from this bill and what remains to be done. We are self-conscious that our assessment may reflect a snapshot in time. Still, we think our book's credibility challenges speak to a profound political and social reality that can shed light on the moment.

---

[19] It luckily survived, for now.

Bipartisanship Revisited

Unlike the infrastructure bill, the climate legislation passed with no Republican votes. Since Democrats held a narrow majority in the 50–50 Senate, no Republican support meant lawmakers had to use a special process called budget reconciliation. This process requires a lower vote threshold to pass and is not subject to filibuster, but it limits the content of what one could include in the law.[20] As this book discusses, the lack of a bipartisan coalition could implicate the durability of the legislation or parts of it. However, the fact that the provisions are in law and not an executive order could enhance its longevity. The ACA, also passed with no Republican support, has had some staying power. Yet, it was ultimately saved by an act of bipartisanship; the infamous thumbs down by Senator John McCain, a Republican from Arizona who spoiled his party's efforts to repeal the healthcare law. At the time of passage, scholars were cautious about the ACA's prospects, too (Jenkins and Patashnik, 2012, p. 5).

When it comes to the IRA, several senior officials in the energy sector that we interviewed expect that the provisions will stick so long as the benefits flow quickly. Even before the failure of Republicans to retake the Senate in the 2022 midterm election, Republicans acknowledged this reality. Senator Kevin Cramer from deep-red North Dakota said, "[o]nce these things are done, authorized and being built in Republican states and districts, the enthusiasm for repealing becomes very difficult" (quoted in Siegel and Tamborrino, 2022). Part of the perceived durability is because the climate law solved a credibility problem with long-term tax credits that provide a modicum of certainty.

However, there is good reason for caution. Federal tax credits have a way of disappearing. Between 1975 and 2001, lawmakers eliminated more than half of federal tax credit programs (Corder, 2004). And with tight partisan balances, the political scientist Morris Fiorina (2017) argues that parties have incentives to adopt extreme positions, which can lead to successful counter-mobilization against policy priorities of the other party (Patashnik, 2019, p. 51).

Policy reforms must also be implemented, which is one place where opponents can delay change, as political scientist Leah Stokes (2020) documents in her study of state electricity market reforms. House Republicans have indicated they plan to lead investigations and oversight efforts

---

[20] However, climate policy advocates did try creative efforts to convert a clean electricity standard into a form that could satisfy budget reconciliation rules.

of the IRA (Siegel and Tamborrino, 2022), including scrutiny of a consumer incentive program to replace fossil fuel heat pumps with electric alternatives (Lipton, 2022). The Biden administration has highlighted how Republicans could hold tax credits hostage through debt limit negotiations and the prospect of a government shutdown (White House, 2022). There are signs that Republicans will target the federal loan program for clean energy investment, which could freeze capital necessary for early stage technology to escape the valley of death (Thomas, 2023). With the surprise failure of Republicans to retake both branches of Congress, how this plays out remains to be seen.

Transmission

For the IRA to be effective, renewable energy needs to be sited and built. Otherwise, the power cannot reach its users. One estimate is that 80 percent of the emission reductions from the IRA will not happen without transmission build-out (Jenkins et al., 2022). Siting and transmission pose significant challenges. Officials at the electric power companies we interviewed consistently emphasized the need for permitting reform to facilitate new transmission.

Even with reform, community engagement remains essential. Less than one in five solar or wind projects in the queue to be added to the grid actually reach commercial operation, which is less than the rate for other projects added to the grid (Rand et al., 2021). One study that examines utility-grade renewable energy projects blocked in the United States between 2008 and 2021 finds that the lack of local dialogue contributed to community opposition (Susskind et al., 2022). Others document intense opposition to wind energy in wealthier parts of the Northeast United States and Ontario, Canada (Stokes, Lovering, and Miljanich, n.d.). There is an entire research program that studies the acceptance of wind energy (Bessette and Crawford, 2022). Land use issues will only intensify (Groom, 2022; Gross, 2020), and energy transmission challenges will continue to be more than just an engineering problem (Sovacool et al., 2022). As we write, the Biden administration and Congress have been unable to pass legislation to overhaul the permitting process to accelerate transmission projects.

Our book helps to make sense of how these challenges could be overcome. Local opposition might be placated if there were more community benefits from projects. This is necessary because the failure to alleviate opposition to renewable energy and transmission development could undermine the mechanisms in the IRA that were designed to make the legislation and its benefits durable. The slow roll-out of green energy projects would reduce or eliminate the sunk costs that the legislation hopes will lock in the shift to renewable energy. NIMBY opposition could make it easier to stay on or revert to fossil fuel energy sources.[21]

However, solutions like greater local control while enhancing community buy-in also have downsides. The individuals with the most time and resources to participate in local participatory institutions may be unrepresentative of the population.[22] For this reason, efforts to increase local participation should also be coupled with initiatives to improve access, so the entire community's views are genuinely considered (Few, Brown, and Tompkins, 2007). Further, there should be efforts to think through the precise rationale for forms of participation. Otherwise, as Bidwell (2016, p. 4) notes in a review on public participation in renewable energy transitions, "poorly designed processes, which do not meet the needs of the public and other stakeholders, may serve as an obstacle to reaching high-quality decisions."

Implementation: It's in the Way That You Do It

The IRA contains several "carrots" to incentivize renewable energy rather than the "sticks" that characterized earlier carbon pricing approaches. Research in political science and other disciplines indicates that an emphasis on "benefits" rather than "costs" is an effective strategy for passing national climate legislation. In our conversations with utility industry leaders, access to direct pay credits for renewable energy is an example of a substantial potential improvement.[23] Previously, nonprofit utilities like many cooperatives, which had no federal tax liability necessary to benefit from a tax credit, were left out and had to work through uncertain third parties to take advantage of green incentives (Storrow, 2022).

However, industrial policy is difficult to implement. Considerable lobbying is done during the implementation stage for any law (e.g., Stokes,

---

[21] Foster and Warren (2022) develop a bargaining model of NIMBYism and argue that it can result from when opposition groups erect onerous processes for developers that reduce surplus for the broader community.

[22] Einstein, Glick, and Palmer (2019) and Einstein, Palmer, and Glick (2019) find that people who are older, male, and own homes are much more likely to participate at zoning hearings.

[23] Interview, July 28, 2022.

Conclusion

2020; You, 2017), and the IRA is no different.[24] Firms might receive benefits in exchange for promises, but there are challenges with how to best monitor and enforce commitments (e.g., Jensen, 2017). Companies have the resources to execute complex corporate strategies to extract maximal economic benefits that may not be aligned with the goals of the clean energy transition. The politics of the IRA will not end with the tie-breaking vote cast by Vice President Harris.

CONCLUSION

Scholars have long explored the interplay of markets and society, with an emphasis on the politics that accompanies economic dislocation (e.g., Polanyi, 1944). Whether economic transitions result from technological transformations like automation or policy-induced shifts like emissions regulations, compensation to those harmed has been a central task of governments for political and moral reasons. And the provision of benefits from political reforms to potential allies has been a salient strategy for building enduring coalitions.

Our book shows how the success of economic transitions is not solely a top-down technical task to supply and target compensation and investments. Instead, it requires actions that foster trust and establish durable investments that are credible from the perspective of individuals, communities, and companies.

Our ground-up perspective elevates the voices and concerns of individuals confronted with substantial changes in their jobs, ways of life, and imagined futures. Rather than leading with "suitcase solutions" that neglect the profound social ties people have with their communities (Anderson, 2022), we engage with ways that governments, firms, nonprofits, communities, and local leaders can work together. In a moment where scholars and policymakers are debating new approaches to political economy and persistent maladies like economic inequality (e.g., Blanchard and Rodrik, 2021; Carugati and Levi, 2021), our contribution is to put climate transitions at the forefront. The move away from fossil fuels and toward cleaner energy is a vexing challenge that societies around the globe confront.

Climate transitions in the United States and elsewhere will not happen overnight. However, there is the exciting possibility that this transformation can be done in a way that is inclusive, credible, and effective. This

---

[24] Even seemingly mundane challenges like the staffing of federal agencies can be consequential (e.g., Brugger, 2022).

book presents a menu of credible policy design options that are grounded in not only the voice of communities but also powerful political economy theories. We hope that future work will further unpack how to implement these options, as well as how these solutions could best be combined to further enhance credibility. Our book's framework is crucial not only for making climate policy effective in places where broad political coalitions already exist for reform, but also to serve as the building blocks to bring leaders, civil society, and the public together for a collective purpose in places presently lacking consensus around the clean energy transition. Without a doubt, the best ideas on how to do this are not in this book, but we hope our insights about credibility propel others to find them. Failure to find a path forward is not a luxury we have left.

Bibliography

Acemoglu, Daron (2003). "Why Not a Political Coase Theorem? Social Conflict, Commitment, and Politics." *Journal of Comparative Economics* 31.4, 620–652.

Acemoglu, Daron and James A. Robinson (2006). *Economic Origins of Dictatorship and Democracy*. Cambridge University Press.

Acemoglu, Daron et al. (2016). "Transition to Clean Technology." *Journal of Political Economy* 124.1, 52–104.

Addison, John and McKinley Blackburn (1994). "The Worker Adjustment and Retraining Notification Act." *Journal of Economic Perspectives* 8.1, 181–190.

Adserà, Alícia, Carles Boix, and Mark Payne (2003). "Are You Being Served? Political Accountability and Quality of Government." *Journal of Law, Economics, and Organization* 19.2, 445–490.

Ahlquist, John and Margaret Levi (2013). *In the Interest of Others: Organizations and Social Activism*. Princeton University Press.

Aitken, Mhairi (2010). "Why We Still Don't Understand the Social Aspects of Wind Power: A Critique of Key Assumptions within the Literature." *Energy Policy* 38.4, 1834–1841.

Aklin, Michaël (2021). "The Off-Grid Catch-22: Effective Institutions as a Prerequisite for the Global Deployment of Distributed Renewable Power." *Energy Research & Social Science* 72, 101830.

Aklin, Michaël and Johannes Urpelainen (2013). "Political Competition, Path Dependence, and the Strategy of Sustainable Energy Transitions." *American Journal of Political Science* 57.3, 643–658.

(2022). *Enable a Just Transition for American Fossil Fuel Workers through Federal Action*. Brookings Institution. https://brook.gs/3MHGyoK.

Alabdulkareem, Ahmad et al. (2018). "Unpacking the Polarization of Workplace Skills." *Science Advances* 4.7, eaao6030.

Alden, Edward (2017). *Failure to Adjust: How Americans Got Left Behind in the Global Economy*. Rowman & Littlefield.

Bibliography

Aldy, Joseph (2019). "Promoting Environmental Quality through Fuels Regulations." In: *Lessons from the Clean Air Act*. Ed. by Ann Carlson and Dallas Burtraw. Cambridge University Press, 159–199.

Alesina, Alberto (1988). "Credibility and Policy Convergence in a Two-Party System with Rational Voters." *American Economic Review* 78.4, 796–805.

Alesina, Alberto and Guido Tabellini (1988). "Credibility and Politics." *European Economic Review* 32.2–3, 542–550.

— (1990). "A Positive Theory of Fiscal Deficits and Government Debt." *The Review of Economic Studies* 57.3, 403.

Alt, James (2019). "Twenty Years of Transparency Research." *Public Sector Economics* 43.1, 5–13.

Alt, James and David Dreyer Lassen (2006). "Transparency, Political Polarization, and Political Budget Cycles in OECD Countries." *American Journal of Political Science* 50.3, 530–550.

Alt, James, David Dreyer Lassen, and Shanna Rose (2006). "The Causes of Fiscal Transparency: Evidence from the U.S. States." *IMF Staff Papers* 53, 30–57.

Anderson, Michelle (2017). "Losing the War of Attrition: Mobility, Chronic Decline, and Infrastructure." *Yale Law Journal* 127, 522.

— (2022). *The Fight to Save the Town*. Simon & Schuster.

Ansolabehere, Stephen and David M. Konisky (2014). *Cheap and Clean: How Americans Think about Energy in the Age of Global Warming*. MIT Press.

Ansolabehere, Stephen et al. (2022). *The Roosevelt Project: A Low Carbon Energy Transition in Southwestern Pennsylvania*. Roosevelt Project Working Paper Series. MIT Center for Energy and Environmental Policy Research.

Anzilotti, Eillie (2018). "Spain Wants to Phase Out Coal Plants without Hurting Miners." *Fast Company*. bit.ly/3FnHEns.

AP (2022). "Rivian Electric Car Plant Blasted by Foes at Georgia Meeting." bit.ly/3jv8XDL.

ARC (2022). *POWER Award Summaries by State*. Appalachian Regional Commission. https://bit.ly/3VGiZk7.

Arel-Bundock, Vincent and Krzysztof Pelc (2023). "Buy-in for Buyouts: Attitudes toward Compensation for Reforms." Unpublished Manuscript.

Arias, Sabrina B. and Christopher W. Blair (2022). "Changing Tides: Public Attitudes on Climate Migration." *Journal of Politics* 84.1, 560–567.

Arnold, R. Douglas (1990). *The Logic of Congressional Action*. Yale University Press.

Austin, Benjamin, Edward Glaeser, and Lawrence Summers (2018). *Jobs for the Heartland: Place-Based Policies in 21st Century America*. w24548. NBER.

Autor, David, David Dorn, and Gordon Hanson (2013). "The China Syndrome: Local Labor Market Effects of Import Competition in the United States." *American Economic Review* 103.6, 2121–2168.

Autor, David et al. (2020). "Importing Political Polarization? The Electoral Consequences of Rising Trade Exposure." *American Economic Review* 110.10, 3139–3183.

Axelrod, Robert and Robert O. Keohane (1985). "Achieving Cooperation under Anarchy." *World Politics* 38.1, 226–254.

Bibliography

Ayres, Drummond (1990). "Ohio Valley of Tears Is Facing More." *New York Times*.

Babcock, Linda et al. (2012). "Notes on Behavioral Economics and Labor Market Policy." *IZA Journal of Labor Policy* 1.1, 2.

Baccini, Leonardo and Stephen Weymouth (2021). "Gone for Good: Deindustrialization, White Voter Backlash, and US Presidential Voting." *American Political Science Review* 115.2, 550–567.

Baker, Scott R. et al. (2014). "Why Has US Policy Uncertainty Risen Since 1960?" *American Economic Review* 104.5, 56–60.

Banerjee, Aparajita and Geertje Schuitema (2022). "How Just Are Just Transition Plans? Perceptions of Decarbonisation and Low-Carbon Energy Transitions among Peat Workers in Ireland." *Energy Research & Social Science* 88, 102616.

Bang, Guri, Knut Einar Rosendahl, and Christoph Böhringer (2022). "Balancing Cost and Justice Concerns in the Energy Transition: Comparing Coal Phase-Out Policies in Germany and the UK." *Climate Policy* 22.8, 1–16.

Barnow, Burt S. (1987). "The Impact of CETA Programs on Earnings: A Review of the Literature." *The Journal of Human Resources* 22.2, 157.

Barradale, Merrill Jones (2010). "Impact of Public Policy Uncertainty on Renewable Energy Investment." *Energy Policy* 38.12, 7698–7709.

Barrett, Scott and Robert Stavins (2003). "Increasing Participation and Compliance in International Climate Change Agreements." *International Environmental Agreements* 3.4, 349–376.

Bartik, Timothy (2003). *Local Economic Development Policies*. Upjohn Institute.

Bartik, Timothy J. (2019). *Making Sense of Incentives: Taming Business Incentives to Promote Prosperity*. Upjohn Institute.

Bayer, Patrick and Federica Genovese (2020). "Beliefs about Consequences from Climate Action under Weak Climate Institutions: Sectors, Home Bias, and International Embeddedness." *Global Environmental Politics* 20.4, 28–50.

Bayer, Patrick, Stephen L. Ross, and Giorgio Topa (2008). "Place of Work and Place of Residence: Informal Hiring Networks and Labor Market Outcomes." *Journal of Political Economy* 116.6, 1150–1196.

Bayulgen, Oksan (2022). *Twisting in the Wind: The Politics of Tepid Transitions to Renewable Energy*. University of Michigan Press.

Bayulgen, Oksan and Jeffrey W. Ladewig (2017). "Vetoing the Future: Political Constraints and Renewable Energy." *Environmental Politics* 26.1, 49–70.

Bechtel, Michael and Kenneth Scheve (2013). "Mass Support for Global Climate Agreements Depends on Institutional Design." *Proceedings of the National Academy of Sciences* 110.34, 13763–13768.

Beckfield, Jason et al. (2022). *The Roosevelt Project: How the Gulf Coast Can Lead the Energy Transition*. Roosevelt Project Working Paper Series. MIT Center for Energy and Environmental Policy Research.

Behaghel, Luc, Bruno Crépon, and Marc Gurgand (2014). "Private and Public Provision of Counseling to Job Seekers: Evidence from a Large Controlled Experiment." *American Economic Journal: Applied Economics* 6.4, 142–174.

Bell, Shannon Elizabeth (2009). "'There Ain't No Bond in Town Like There Used to Be': The Destruction of Social Capital in the West Virginia Coalfields." *Sociological Forum* 24.3, 631–657.

Bell, Shannon Elizabeth and Yvonne Braun (2010). "Coal, Identity, and the Gendering of Environmental Justice Activism in Central Appalachia." *Gender & Society* 24.6, 794–813.

Bell, Shannon Elizabeth and Richard York (2010). "Community Economic Identity: The Coal Industry and Ideology Construction in West Virginia." *Rural Sociology* 75.1, 111–143.

Benveniste, Hélène, Michael Oppenheimer, and Marc Fleurbaey (2022). "Climate Change Increases Resource-Constrained International Immobility." *Nature Climate Change* 12.7, 634–641.

Bergquist, Parrish, Matto Mildenberger, and Leah Stokes (2020). "Combining Climate, Economic, and Social Policy Builds Public Support for Climate Action in the US." *Environmental Research Letters* 15, 054019.

Bernanke, Ben (1983). "Irreversibility, Uncertainty, and Cyclical Investment." *Quarterly Journal of Economics* 98.1, 85–106.

Bernauer, Thomas (2013). "Climate Change Politics." *Annual Review of Political Science* 16.1, 421–448.

Berry, Christopher, Barry Burden, and William Howell (2010). "After Enactment: The Lives and Deaths of Federal Programs." *American Journal of Political Science* 54.1, 1–17.

Berthelsen, John (1979). "A Redwood Windfall." *Washington Post*.

Bessette, Douglas and Jessica Crawford (2022). "All's Fair in Love and WAR: The Conduct of Wind Acceptance Research (WAR) in the United States and Canada." *Energy Research & Social Science* 88, 102514.

Bidwell, David (2016). "Thinking through Participation in Renewable Energy Decisions." *Nature Energy* 1.5, 1–4.

Binder, Sarah A. (2003). *Stalemate: Causes and Consequences of Legislative Gridlock*. Brookings Institution Press.

Bisbee, James (2019). "What You See Out Your Back Door: How Political Beliefs Respond to Local Trade Shocks." Unpublished Manuscript.

Bisbee, James and B. Peter Rosendorff (2022). "Anti-Globalization Sentiment: Exposure and Specificity." Unpublished Manuscript.

Blackley, David et al. (2018). "Progressive Massive Fibrosis in Coal Miners from 3 Clinics in Virginia." *Journal of the American Medical Association* 319.5, 500–501.

Blanchard, Olivier and Dani Rodrik (2021). *Combating Inequality: Rethinking Government's Role*. MIT Press.

BLS (2021). *Occupational Employment and Wage Statistics*. U.S. Bureau of Labor Statistics. www.bls.gov/oes/.

Blyth, William et al. (2007). "Investment Risks Under Uncertain Climate Change Policy." *Energy Policy* 35.11, 5766–5773.

Botta, Enrico (2019). "An Experimental Approach to Climate Finance: The Impact of Auction Design and Policy Uncertainty on Renewable Energy Equity Costs in Europe." *Energy Policy* 133, 110839.

Bibliography

Bowen, Alex (2012). *"Green" Growth, "Green" Jobs and Labor Markets*. Policy Research Working Papers. The World Bank.

Boykoff, Maxwell T. and J. Timmons Roberts (2007). *Media Coverage of Climate Change: Current Trends, Strengths, Weaknesses*. Tech. rep. 3, 1–53.

Brauers, Hanna, Philipp Herpich, and Pao-Yu Oei (2018). "The Transformation of the German Coal Sector from 1950 to 2017: An Historical Overview." In: *Energiewende "Made in Germany."* Springer, 45–78.

Brauers, Hanna and Pao-Yu Oei (2020). "The Political Economy of Coal in Poland: Drivers and Barriers for a Shift Away from Fossil Fuels." *Energy Policy* 144, 111621.

Brewer, Paul and Barbara Ley (2013). "Whose Science Do You Believe? Explaining Trust in Sources of Scientific Information about the Environment." *Science Communication* 35.1, 115–137.

Bristol, Jen (2020). "Illinois Clean Energy Boom Goes Bust as State Program Runs Out of Funding, Forcing Layoffs at Solar and Wind Businesses." *Solar Energy Industries Association*. bit.ly/3Fs8ZFl.

Broadwater, Sarah (1990). "Boucher Predicts Coal Growth from Acid Rain Measure." *Office of Congressman Rick Boucher.*

Brown, Melissa and Frank Gluck (2022). "South Korean Firm to Spend \$3.2B in TN, Create 1,000 Jobs in What Governor Calls Historic Investment." Nashville Tennessean. bit.ly/3HdU16W.

Broz, J. Lawrence, Jeffry Frieden, and Stephen Weymouth (2021). "Populism in Place: The Economic Geography of the Globalization Backlash." *International Organization*, 1–31.

Brugger, Kelsey (2022). "How to Implement the Climate Law? Go on Hiring Spree." *PoliticoPro.*

Brulle, Robert J. (2014). "Institutionalizing Delay: Foundation Funding and the Creation of U.S. Climate Change Counter-Movement Organizations." *Climatic Change* 122.4, 681–694.

— (2018). "The Climate Lobby: A Sectoral Analysis of Lobbying Spending on Climate Change in the USA, 2000 to 2016." *Climatic Change* 149.3–4, 289–303.

Brulle, Robert J. and J. Timmons Roberts (2017). "Climate Misinformation Campaigns and Public Sociology." *Contexts* 16.1, 78–79.

Brunner, Eric J. and David J. Schwegman (2022). "Windfall Revenues from Windfarms: How Do County Governments Respond to Increases in the Local Tax Base Induced by Wind Energy Installations?" *Public Budgeting & Finance* 42.3, 93–113.

Brunner, Steffen, Christian Flachsland, and Robert Marschinski (2012). "Credible Commitment in Carbon Policy." *Climate Policy* 12.2, 255–271.

Buckley, Cara (2022). "Coming Soon to This Coal County: Solar, in a Big Way." *The New York Times*. https://tinyurl.com/2p8j7w2p.

Bulkeley, Harriet (2010). "Cities and the Governing of Climate Change." *Annual Review of Environment and Resources* 35.1, 229–253.

Buntaine, Mark and Lauren Prather (2018). "Preferences for Domestic Action over International Transfers in Global Climate Policy." *Journal of Experimental Political Science* 5.02, 73–87.

Bibliography

Busby, Joshua (2008). "Overcoming Political Barriers to Energy Reform." In: *A Strategy for American Power*. Ed. by Sharon Burke et al. Center for a New American Security.

Calvert, Randall (1985). "The Value of Biased Information: A Rational Choice Model of Political Advice." *Journal of Politics* 47.2, 530–555.

Calvó-Armengol, Antoni and Matthew O. Jackson (2004). "The Effects of Social Networks on Employment and Inequality." *American Economic Review* 94.3, 426–454.

Campbell, Natasha, J. Chris Ford, and Matthew Garcia (2021). *Energy Sector Workforce Diversity, Access, Inclusion, and the Policy Case for Investment*. National Association of State Energy Officials. https://bit.ly/3eArmgI.

Campbell, Natasha et al. (2021). *Diversity in the U.S. Energy Workforce*. National Association of State Energy Officials.

Canes-Wrone, Brandice, Michael C. Herron, and Kenneth W. Shotts (2001). "Leadership and Pandering: A Theory of Executive Policymaking." *American Journal of Political Science* 45.3, 532.

Canes-Wrone, Brandice and Jee-Kwang Park (2012). "Electoral Business Cycles in OECD Countries." *American Political Science Review* 106.1, 103–122.

Card, David, Jochen Kluve, and Andrea Weber (2010). "Active Labour Market Policy Evaluations: A Meta-Analysis." *The Economic Journal* 120.548, F452–F477.

Cardwell, Diane (2017). "What's Up in Coal Country: Alternative-Energy Jobs." *New York Times*. https://nyti.ms/3iIccnP.

Carley, Sanya, Tom Evans, and David Konisky (2018). "Adaptation, Culture, and the Energy Transition in American Coal Country." *Energy Research & Social Science* 37, 133–139.

Carley, Sanya et al. (2020). "Energy Infrastructure, NIMBYism, and Public Opinion: A Systematic Literature Review of Three Decades of Empirical Survey Literature." *Environmental Research Letters* 15.9, 093007.

Carugati, Federica and Margaret Levi (2021). *A Moral Political Economy: Present, Past, and Future*. Cambridge University Press.

Case, Anne and Angus Deaton (2020). *Deaths of Despair and the Future of Capitalism*. Princeton University Press.

CBS (2017). "KDKA Investigates: Program to Retrain Miners Over-Promises, Under-Delivers." https://cbsn.ws/3CIHMeN.

Ceres (2020). *Practices for Just, Equitable and Sustainable Development of Clean Energy*. https://bit.ly/3bRfANc.

Cha, J. Mijin (2020). "A Just Transition for Whom? Politics, Contestation, and Social Identity in the Disruption of Coal in the Powder River Basin." *Energy Research & Social Science* 69, 101657.

Cha, J. Mijin et al. (2021). *Workers and Communities in Transition: A Report of the Just Transition Listening Project*. Just Transition Listening Project. bit.ly/3CaKwlD.

Cha, J. Mijin et al. (2022). "A Green New Deal for All: The Centrality of a Worker and Community-Led Just Transition in the US." *Political Geography* 95, 102594.

Bibliography

Chan, Gabriel et al. (2012). "The SO2 Allowance Trading System and the Clean Air Act Amendments of 1990: Reflections on Twenty Years of Policy Innovation." *Harvard Environmental Economics Program.* bit.ly/3wohtxQ.

Chase, Brett and Dan Gearino (2022). "Illinois Clean Energy Law's Failed Promises: No New Jobs or Job-Training." *Inside Climate News.* bit.ly/3XbIY3r.

Chassot, Sylviane, Nina Hampl, and Rolf Wüstenhagen (2014). "When Energy Policy Meets Free-Market Capitalists: The Moderating Influence of World-views on Risk Perception and Renewable Energy Investment Decisions." *Energy Research & Social Science* 3, 143–151.

Chemnick, Jean (2022). "Facing Questions about Climate Aid, Democrats Blame the GOP." *PoliticoPro.* bit.ly/3BhJDaK.

Cheng, Ing-Haw and Alice Hsiaw (2022). "Reporting Sexual Misconduct in the# MeToo era." *American Economic Journal: Microeconomics* 14.4, 761–803.

Citrin, Jack and Laura Stoker (2018). "Political Trust in a Cynical Age." *Annual Review of Political Science* 21.1, 49–70.

Clark, Don and Ana Swanson (2023). "U.S. Pours Money into Chips, but Even Soaring Spending Has Limits." *New York Times.* bit.ly/3Hf4bEd.

Cliffton, Rita et al. (2021). *The Clean Economy Revolution Will Be Unionized.* Center for American Progress. https://ampr.gs/3KoPyUw.

Clinton, William (1994). *The Forest Plan for a Sustainable Economy and a Sustainable Environment. White House Press Office.*

Coal Week (1990). "Senate Set to Vote on Air Bill House Committee Nears Passage Also." *Coal Week* 16.14.

Coalfield Development (2022). "U.S. Secretary of Energy Tours West Edge, Participates in Coalfield Roundtable." http://bit.ly/3g0Yn6q.

Cohen, Richard (1992). *Washington at Work: Back Rooms and Clean Air.* MacMillan.

Cohen, Sharon (1990). "Soft Coal' Miners Fear Hard Times Lie Ahead Under Clean-Air Law Economics." *Los Angeles Times.* bit.ly/3ZDmFFu.

Colantone, Italo and Piero Stanig (2018). "The Trade Origins of Economic Nationalism: Import Competition and Voting Behavior in Western Europe." *American Journal of Political Science* 62.4, 936–953.

Colgan, Jeff, Jessica Green, and Thomas Hale (2021). "Asset Revaluation and the Existential Politics of Climate Change." *International Organization* 75.2, 586–610.

Colgan, Jeff D. and Miriam Hinthorn (2022). "International Energy Politics in an Age of Climate Change." *Annual Review of Political Science* 26.

Cook, Benjamin and Robert Godby (2019). *Estimating the Impact of State Taxation Policies on the Cost of Wind Development in the West.* University of Wyoming: Center for Energy Economics and Public Policy. bit.ly/3uQf9sv.

Cook, Karen, Russell Hardin, and Margaret Levi (2005). *Cooperation Without Trust?* Russell Sage Foundation.

Corder, J Kevin (2004). "Are Federal Programs Immortal? Estimating the Hazard of Program Termination." *American Politics Research* 32.1, 3–25.

Cramer, Katherine J. (2016). *The Politics of Resentment: Rural Consciousness in Wisconsin and the Rise of Scott Walker.* University of Chicago Press.

Crépon, Bruno and Gerard J. van den Berg (2016). "Active Labor Market Policies." *Annual Review of Economics* 8.1, 521–546.

Cruz, José-Luis and Esteban Rossi-Hansberg (2023). "The Economic Geography of Global Warming." *Review of Economic Studies* Forthcoming.

Cullenward, Danny and David G. Victor (2021). *Making Climate Policy Work.* Polity Press.

Cunningham, Wendy and Achim Schmillen (2021). "The Coal Transition." *World Bank.*

Currarini, Sergio and Carmen Marchiori (2022). "Issue Linkage." *Games and Economic Behavior* 135, 16–40.

Curtis, Mark and Ioana Marinescu (2022). *Green Energy Jobs in the US: What Are They, and Where Are They?* w30332. NBER.

Curtis, Sabrina et al. (2022). *The Roosevelt Project: Accelerating an Equitable Clean Energy Transition in New Mexico.* Roosevelt Project Working Paper Series. MIT Center for Energy and Environmental Policy Research.

D'Souza, Steven (2019). "'They Failed Me': How the Promise of Retraining U.S. Coal Miners Came up Empty." *CBC.* https://bit.ly/3ghlNEn.

Dahl, Gordon B., Katrine V. Løken, and Magne Mogstad (2014). "Peer Effects in Program Participation." *American Economic Review* 104.7, 2049–2074.

Dalby, Peder et al. (2018). "Green Investment Under Policy Uncertainty and Bayesian Learning." *Energy* 161, 1262–1281.

Davies, Christian (2022). "Hyundai Tackles Washington over Loss of Electric Vehicle Subsidies." *The Financial Times.* bit.ly/3uBaSJv.

Davis, Christina (2004). "International Institutions and Issue Linkage: Building Support for Agricultural Trade Liberalization." *American Political Science Review* 98.1, 153–169.

Davis, Jason S. (2019). "Protection as a Commitment Problem." Unpublished Manuscript. University of Pennsylvania. bit.ly/3CMKSPD.

De Simone, Lisa, Rebecca Lester, and Aneesh Raghunandan (2021). "Tax Subsidy Information and Local Economic Effects." Unpublished Manuscript. bit.ly/3ZEBl7l.

Dixit, Avinash and John Londregan (1995). "Redistributive Politics and Economic Efficiency." *American Political Science Review* 89.4, 856–866.

Dixit, Robert and Robert S. Pindyck (1994). *Investment under Uncertainty.* Princeton University Press.

DOE (2022). *United States Energy and Employment Report 2022.* Department of Energy. https://bit.ly/3CI11VR.

DOL (1993). *Trade Adjustment Assistance Program: Audit of Program Outcomes in Nine States.* Department of Labor.

— (2020). *Trade Adjustment Assistance for Workers Program: FY 2020 Annual Report.* Employment and Training Administration, Department of Labor. https://bit.ly/3D9Lb81.

— (2022). "Statement by Secretary Walsh on Termination of Trade Adjustment Assistance for Workers Program." bit.ly/3IS2pdn.

Dolfin, Sarah and Peter Schochet (2012). *The Benefits and Costs of the Trade Adjustment Assistance (TAA) Program Under the 2002 Amendments.* Mathematica Policy Research.

Bibliography

Dolšak, Nives and Aseem Prakash (2022a). "Three Faces of Climate Justice." *Annual Review of Political Science* 25, 283–301.

Dolšak and Aseem Prakash (2022b). "Climate Policy Lesson from Liz Truss's Resignation: Beware of Budget Deficits." *Forbes*. bit.ly/3VDWsnV.

Domonoske, Camila (2021). "Boom or Bubble? Skeptics Take Aim At Buzzy Electric Vehicle Market." *National Public Radio*. https://tinyurl.com/jt4fuphu.

Dorsey, Jackson (2019). "Waiting for the Courts: Effects of Policy Uncertainty on Pollution and Investment." *Environmental and Resource Economics* 74.4, 1453–1496.

Douglas, Stratford and Anne Walker (2017). "Coal Mining and the Resource Curse in the Eastern United States." *Journal of Regional Science* 57.4, 568–590.

Duke Energy (2022). *Advancing toward a Clean, Affordable and Reliable Energy Future*. 2022 Climate Report. bit.ly/3iBTuSx.

Dunning, Thad et al., eds. (2019). *Information, Accountability, and Cumulative Learning: Lessons from Metaketa I*. Cambridge University Press.

E2 (2021). *Help Wanted: Diversity in Clean Energy*. E2. https://bit.ly/3SnHXm2.

Eckhouse, Brian (2022). "Green Factories Are Changing Minds in Conservative US State." *Bloomberg*. bit.ly/3UwfoEY.

Economist (2009). "Greening the Rustbelt." *The Economist*. https://tinyurl.com/4xmbu5xu.

Egan, Patrick J. and Megan Mullin (2012). "Turning Personal Experience into Political Attitudes: The Effect of Local Weather on Americans' Perceptions about Global Warming." *Journal of Politics* 74.3, 796–809.

(2017). "Climate Change: US Public Opinion." *Annual Review of Political Science* 20.1, 209–227.

Egan, Timothy (1993). "Upheaval in the Forests; Clinton Plan Shifts Emphasis from Logging but Does Not Create Off-Limits Wilderness." *New York Times* A, 1.

EIA (2022). *North Dakota State Energy Profile*. Energy Information Administration. https://bit.ly/3pQdO2C.

Einstein, Katherine Levine, David Glick, and Maxwell Palmer (2019). *Neighborhood Defenders: Participatory Politics and America's Housing Crisis*. Cambridge University Press.

Einstein, Katherine Levine, Maxwell Palmer, and David Glick (2019). "Who Participates in Local Government? Evidence from Meeting Minutes." *Perspectives on Politics* 17.1, 28–46.

Ellerman, A. D. et al. (2000). *Markets for Clean Air: The US Acid Rain Program*. Cambridge University Press.

Ellison, Garret (2022). "In Michigan's Thumb, Wind Farm Tax Clawback Would Bankrupt Schools." *Mlive*. bit.ly/3XdEjOi.

Elster, Jon (1989). *The Cement of Society: A Study of Social Order*. Cambridge University Press.

EPA (2001). *Impacts of the Acid Rain Program on Coal Industry Employment*. 430-R-01-002. Environmental Protection Agency.

Evers-Hillstrom, Karl (2017). "Southwest Minnesota Construction Unions Push Back on Wind Farm Outsourcing." *The Globe*. https://bit.ly/3PJSRk4.

Fabrizio, Kira (2013). "The Effect of Regulatory Uncertainty on Investment: Evidence from Renewable Energy Generation." *Journal of Law, Economics, & Organization* 29.4, 765–798.

Fairbrother, Malcolm (2019). "When Will People Pay to Pollute? Environmental Taxes, Political Trust and Experimental Evidence from Britain." *British Journal of Political Science* 49.2, 661–682.

Farrell, Justin (2016). "Corporate Funding and Ideological Polarization about Climate Change." *Proceedings of the National Academy of Sciences* 113.1, 92–97. pmid: 26598653.

Fearon, James (1994). "Domestic Political Audiences and the Escalation of International Disputes." *American Political Science Review* 88.3, 577–592.

— (1995). "Rationalist Explanations for War." *International Organization* 49.3, 379–414.

— (1996). "Bargaining over Objects That Influence Future Bargaining Power." Unpublished Manuscript.

— (1997). "Signaling Foreign Policy Interests." *Journal of Conflict Resolution* 41.1, 68–90.

Fernandez, Raquel and Dani Rodrik (1991). "Resistance to Reform: Status Quo Bias in the Presence of Individual-Specific Uncertainty." *American Economic Review*, 1146–1155.

Ferry, Robert and Elizabeth Monoian (2023). "Build Back Solar Designing Solar Energy for a Just Transition." In: *Routledge Handbook of Energy Transitions*. Ed. by Kathleen Araújo. Routledge.

Few, Roger, Katrina Brown, and Emma Tompkins (2007). "Public Participation and Climate Change Adaptation: Avoiding the Illusion of Inclusion." *Climate Policy* 7.1, 46–59.

Finnegan, Jared J. (2022). "Institutions, Climate Change, and the Foundations of Long-Term Policymaking." *Comparative Political Studies* 55.7, 1198–1235.

Fiorina, Morris (2017). *Unstable Majorities: Polarization, Party Sorting, and Political Stalemate*. Hoover Institution Press.

Fiorino, Daniel J. (2018). *A Good Life on a Finite Earth: The Political Economy of Green Growth*. Oxford University Press.

Fishkin, James S. (2011). *When the People Speak: Deliberative Democracy and Public Consultation*. Oxford University Press.

Florini, Ann, ed. (2007). *The Right to Know: Transparency for an Open World*. Columbia University Press.

Foster, David and Joseph Warren (2022). "The NIMBY Problem." *Journal of Theoretical Politics* 34.1, 145–172.

Foster, David et al. (2022). *The Roosevelt Project: Electric Vehicles: The 21st-Century Challenge to Automotive Manufacturing Communities*. Roosevelt Project Working Paper Series. MIT Center for Energy and Environmental Policy Research.

Franco, Lucas (2019a). *Catching the Wind 2.0: An Update on Changing Employment Practices in Minnesota's Wind Energy Industry*. Local Jobs North Dakota & Minnesota. bit.ly/3iHpNzy.

Bibliography

(2019b). *Catching the Wind 3.0: The Impact of Local versus Non-Local Hiring Practices on Wind Farms in North Dakota*. Local Jobs North Dakota & Minnesota. https://bit.ly/3iIoixo.

Frazier, Reid (2022). "Climate Law has a Hidden Benefit for Coal Miners." *The Allegheny Front*. bit.ly/3Foaauc.

Fung, Archon, Mary Graham, and David Weil (2007). *Full Disclosure: The Perils and Promise of Transparency*. Cambridge University Press.

Furman, Jason et al. (2008). "Overcoming the Economic Barriers to Climate Change and Energy Security." In: *A Strategy for American Power*. Ed. by Sharon Burke et al.

Furnaro, Andrea et al. (2021). "German Just Transition: A Review of Public Policies to Assist German Coal Communities in Transition." *Resources for the Future*.

Gaikwad, Nikhar, Federica Genovese, and Dustin Tingley (2022a). "Climate Action from Abroad: Assessing Mass Support for Cross-Border Climate Compensation." Unpublished Manuscript.

(2022b). "Creating Climate Coalitions: Mass Preferences for Compensating Vulnerability in the World's Two Largest Democracies." *American Political Science Review* 116.4, 1165–1183.

Gailmard, Sean and John Patty (2007). "Slackers and Zealots: Civil Service, Policy Discretion, and Bureaucratic Expertise." *American Journal of Political Science* 51.4, 873–889.

(2012a). "Formal Models of Bureaucracy." *Annual Review of Political Science* 15.1, 353–377.

(2012b). *Learning While Governing: Expertise and Accountability in the Executive Branch*. University of Chicago Press.

Gampfer, Robert, Thomas Bernauer, and Aya Kachi (2014). "Obtaining Public Support for North-South Climate Funding: Evidence from Conjoint Experiments in Donor Countries." *Global Environmental Change* 29, 118–126.

GAO (1993a). *Dislocated Workers: A Look Back at the Redwood Employment Training Programs*. HRD-94-16BR. Government Accountability Office.

(1993b). *Dislocated Workers: Proposed Re-employment Assistance Program*. HRD-94-61. Government Accountability Office.

(1994a). *Multiple Employment Training Programs: Major Overhaul Is Needed*. T-HEHS-94-109. Government Accountability Office.

(1994b). *Multiple Employment Training Programs: Most Federal Agencies Do Not Know if Their Programs Are Working Effectively*. HEHS-94-88. Government Accountability Office.

(2013). *Employment and Training: Labor's Green Jobs Efforts Highlight Challenges of Targeted Training Programs for Emerging Industries*. GAO-13-555. Government Accountability Office. https://bit.ly/3CKgPaI.

García-Álvarez, María Teresa, Laura Cabeza-García, and Isabel Soares (2018). "Assessment of Energy Policies to Promote Photovoltaic Generation in the European Union." *Energy* 151, 864–874.

Gard-Murray, Alexander and Geoff Henderson (n.d.). "Producing Certainty: How Climate Coalitions Are Built and Broken." Unpublished Manuscript.

Bibliography

Gaventa, John (1982). *Power and Powerlessness*. University of Illinois Press.

Gazmararian, Alexander F. (2022a). "Building Climate Coalitions with Just Transition Assistance for Energy Communities." Unpublished Manuscript. bit.ly/3VKcSKM.

(2022b). "Geographic Mobility, Self-Interest, and Social Identity." Unpublished Manuscript.

(2022c). "Sources of Partisan Change: Evidence from Energy Transitions in American Coal Country." Unpublished Manuscript. bit.ly/3EjVffB.

Gazmararian, Alexander F. and Helen V. Milner (2022a). "Political Cleavages and Changing Exposure to Global Warming." Unpublished Manuscript. Princeton University. bit.ly/3EVzcdM.

(2022b). "Preference Updating Under Uncertainty: Evidence from Responses to Global Warming." Unpublished Manuscript. Princeton University.

Gazmararian, Alexander F. and Dustin Tingley (2023). "A New Polycentric Model to Expand Renewable Energy Access." Unpublished Manuscript.

Gearino, Dan (2022). "In the End, Solar Power Opponents Prevail in Williamsport, Ohio." *ABC*. bit.ly/3W9edLg.

Gielen, Dolf et al. (2019). "The Role of Renewable Energy in the Global Energy Transformation." *Energy Strategy Reviews* 24, 38–50.

Gigstad, Jill and Frank Manzo (2020). *Building Good Jobs in the Great Plains Through Clean Energy Investments: Impacts in Minnesota, North Dakota, and South Dakota*. Midwest Economic Policy Institute, Illinois Economic Policy Institute. bit.ly/3QGZshx.

Gilens, Martin (2000). *Why Americans Hate Welfare*. University of Chicago Press.

Gillespie, Patrick (2016). "Coal Miners Become Computer Coders." *CNN*. https://cnn.it/3VGjDym.

Godfrey, Christopher (2022a). "Black Lung Benefits for Miners not at Risk Despite Reduced Coal Excise Tax." *Department of Labor*. bit.ly/3Upy4Vy.

(2022b). "Funding for Miners with Black Lung Disease Permanently Extended by the Inflation Reduction Act." *Department of Labor*. bit.ly/3FrYGkD.

Goldstein, Judith and Robert Gulotty (2021). "America and the Trade Regime: What Went Wrong?" *International Organization* 75.2, 524–557.

Goulder, Lawrence (2020). "Timing Is Everything: How Economists Can Better Address the Urgency of Stronger Climate Policy." *Review of Environmental Economics and Policy* 14.1, 143–156.

Gramlich, John (2019). "East Germany Has Narrowed Economic Gap with West Germany since Fall of Communism, but Still Lags." *Pew Research Center*. bit.ly/3XTslu7.

Graves, Garret (2022). "U.S. Climate Change Policy in an Era of Political Polarization." *Harvard Project on Climate Agreements*.

Gray, Bryce (2021). "Solar Workforce Training Program in St. Louis Sees Success, Prepares for Second Round." *St. Louis Post-Dispatch*. https://bit.ly/3flNB9R.

Green, Fergus and Ajay Gambhir (2020). "Transitional Assistance Policies for Just, Equitable and Smooth Low-Carbon Transitions: Who, What and How?" *Climate Policy* 20.8, 902–921.

Bibliography

Green, Jessica F. (2021). "Does Carbon Pricing Reduce Emissions? A Review of Ex-Post Analyses." *Environmental Research Letters* 16.4, 043004.

Grimes, Marcia (2017). "Procedural Fairness and Political Trust." In: *Handbook on Political Trust*. Ed. by Sonja Zmerli and Tom WG Van der Meer. Edward Elgar Publishing, 256–269.

Groom, Nichola (2022). "U.S. Solar Expansion Stalled by Rural Land-use Protests." *Reuters*. bit.ly/3Hj7uKJ.

Gross, Samantha (2020). *Renewables, Land Use, and Local Opposition in the United States*. Brookings Institution. bit.ly/3w4nnxL.

Grossman, Guy and Kristin Michelitch (2018). "Information Dissemination, Competitive Pressure, and Politician Performance between Elections: A Field Experiment in Uganda." *American Political Science Review* 112.2, 280–301.

Gürtler, Konrad, David Löw Beer, and Jeremias Herberg (2021). "Scaling Just Transitions: Legitimation Strategies in Coal Phase-Out Commissions in Canada and Germany." *Political Geography* 88, 102406.

Hainmueller, Jens, Dominik Hangartner, and Teppei Yamamoto (2015). "Validating Vignette and Conjoint Survey Experiments against Real-World Behavior." *Proceedings of the National Academy of Sciences* 112.8, 2395–2400.

Hainmueller, Jens, Daniel J. Hopkins, and Teppei Yamamoto (2014). "Causal Inference in Conjoint Analysis." *Political Analysis* 22.1, 1–30.

Hale, Thomas et al. (2022). "Assessing the Rapidly-Emerging Landscape of Net Zero Targets." *Climate Policy* 22.1, 18–29.

Hall, Peter and David Soskice, eds. (2001). *Varieties of Capitalism: The Institutional Foundations of Comparative Advantage*. Oxford University Press.

Hartman, Larry (2010). *Public Comments*. PUC Docket Numbers: IP-6828/WS-09-1197, IP-6828/CN-09-937.

Hatt, Katie and Lucas Franco (2018). *Catching the Wind: The Impact of Local vs. Non-Local Hiring Practices on Construction of Minnesota Wind Farms*. North Star Policy Institute.

Hayes, Danny and Jennifer L. Lawless (2021). *News Hole: The Demise of Local Journalism and Political Engagement*. Cambridge University Press.

Heald, David (2006). "Varieties of Transparency." In: *Transparency: The Key to Better Governance?* Ed. by Christopher Hood and David Heald. Oxford University Press, 25–46.

Heckman, James J., Robert J. Lalonde, and Jeffrey Smith (1999). "The Economics and Econometrics of Active Labor Market Programs." In: *Handbook of Labor Economics*. Vol. 3. Elsevier, 1865–2097.

Heckman, James J. et al. (1998). "Characterizing Selection Bias Using Experimental Data." *Econometrica* 66.5, 1017–1098.

Heckman, James J. et al. (2000). "Substitution and Dropout Bias in Social Experiments: A Study of an Influential Social Experiment." *Quarterly Journal of Economics* 115.2, 651–694.

Heimann, Felix and Rebekka Popp (2020). "How (Not) to Phase-out Coal: Lessons from Germany for Just and Timely Coal Exits." *Carbon* 4, E3G.

Helm, Dieter, Cameron Hepburn, and Richard Mash (2003). "Credible Carbon Policy." *Oxford Review of Economic Policy* 19.3, 438–450.

Hermwille, Lukas and Dagmar Kiyar (2022). "Late and Expensive the Political Economy of Coal Phase-out in Germany." In: *The Political Economy of Coal: Obstacles to Clean Energy Transitions*. Ed. by Michael Jakob and Jan C. Steckel. Taylor & Francis.

Hernandez, Dan (2016). "Nevada Solar Industry Collapses after State Lets Power Company Raise Fees." *The Guardian*. https://tinyurl.com/2u627tva.

Hertel-Fernandez, Alexander, Matto Mildenberger, and Leah Stokes (2019). "Legislative Staff and Representation in Congress." *American Political Science Review* 113.1, 1–18.

Hetherington, Marc J. (1998). "The Political Relevance of Political Trust." *American Political Science Review* 92.4, 791–808.

— (2006). *Why Trust Matters*. Princeton University Press.

Hicks, Justin (2022). "A Tax to Provide Benefits to Black Lung Victims Is Permanent, but It Might Not Fix the Fund." *Louisville Public Media*. bit.ly/3UuZ463.

Hirschman, Albert O. (1970). *Exit, Voice, and Loyalty: Responses to Decline in Firms, Organizations, and States*. Harvard University Press.

Hochschild, Arlie Russell (2016). *Strangers in Their Own Land*. The New Press.

Hoffmann, Roman et al. (2022). "Climate Change Experiences Raise Environmental Concerns and Promote Green Voting." *Nature Climate Change* 12, 148–155.

Holbrooke, Missy and Dustin Tingley (2022). "The Future of Climate Education at Harvard University." bit.ly/3VUFxx3.

Hollyer, James R., B. Peter Rosendorff, and James Raymond Vreeland (2011). "Democracy and Transparency." *Journal of Politics* 73.4, 1191–1205.

— (2014). "Measuring Transparency." *Political Analysis* 22.4, 413–434.

— (2018). *Information, Democracy, and Autocracy: Economic Transparency and Political (In)Stability*. Cambridge University Press.

Holmström, Bengt (1979). "Moral Hazard and Observability." *The Bell Journal of Economics* 10.1, 74–91.

Hood, Christopher and David Heald (2006). *Transparency: The Key to Better Governance?* British Academy.

Hovi, Jon, Detlef F. Sprinz, and Arild Underdal (2009). "Implementing Long-Term Climate Policy: Time Inconsistency, Domestic Politics, International Anarchy." *Global Environmental Politics* 9.3, 20–39.

Hsu, Angel et al. (2019). "A Research Roadmap for Quantifying Non-State and Subnational Climate Mitigation Action." *Nature Climate Change* 9.1, 11–17.

Hu, Alison and Dustin Tingley (2022). "Regional Remediation Opportunities for a Job-Driven Cleaner Environment." In: *The Roosevelt Project: A Low Carbon Energy Transition in Southwestern Pennsylvania*. Ed. by Stephen Ansolabehere et al. Roosevelt Project Working Paper Series. MIT Center for Energy and Environmental Policy Research, 25–37.

Hu, Jane (2021). "New Wind Projects Power Local Budgets in Wyoming." *High Country News*. https://tinyurl.com/2p8mcsfm.

Hughlett, Mike (2018). "Regulators Table Canby Area Wind Farm over Labor Concerns." *StarTribune*. https://bit.ly/3nDwJMO.

Bibliography

(2019). "New Developer Will Take on Minnesota Wind-Farm Project after Hiring Flap." *Star Tribune*. https://bit.ly/3KeQlkZ.

Hull, Jonathan Watts (2002). *Tobacco in Transition*. Southern Legislative Conference.

Hurt, Emma (2022). "Rivian's Georgia Incentive Package under the Microscope." *Axios*. https://bit.ly/3PVhDOv.

Hyman, Benjamin (2018). "Can Displaced Labor Be Retrained? Evidence from Quasi-Random Assignment to Trade Adjustment Assistance." *Proceedings. Annual Conference on Taxation and Minutes of the Annual Meeting of the National Tax Association* 111, 1–70. https://bit.ly/3eJsMp5.

Imai, Kosuke et al. (2011). "Unpacking the Black Box of Causality: Learning about Causal Mechanisms from Experimental and Observational Studies." *American Political Science Review* 105.4, 765–789.

Inskip, Leonard (1993). "Wind Farm for Minnesota Generating Debate." *Star Tribune*, 11A.

International Energy Agency (2022a). *Coal 2022: Analysis and Forecast to 2025*. bit.ly/3YYYoux.

(2022b). *Coal in Net Zero Transitions*. bit.ly/3C9vFYP.

IPCC (2022). "Summary for Policymakers." In: *Climate Change 2022: Impacts, Adaptation, and Vulnerability*. Ed. by H.-O. Pörtner et al. Contribution of Working Group II to the Sixth Assessment Report of the Intergovernmental Panel on Climate Change. Cambridge University Press.

IPPP (2021). "Independent Power Producers Procurement Programme: An Overview." *Journal of Industrial Relations*, 00221856211051794. bit.ly/3Wda7BR.

IRENA (2021). *Renewable Energy and Jobs: Annual Review 2021*. International Renewable Energy Agency.

Iversen, Torben and David Soskice (2001). "An Asset Theory of Social Policy Preferences." *American Political Science Review* 95.4, 875–893.

(2006). "Electoral Institutions and the Politics of Coalitions: Why Some Democracies Redistribute More than Others." *American Political Science Review* 100.2, 165–181.

Jacobs, Alan (2011). *Governing for the Long Term: Democracy and the Politics of Investment*. Cambridge University Press.

(2016). "Policy Making for the Long Term in Advanced Democracies." *Annual Review of Political Science* 19, 433–454.

Javeline, Debra (2014). "The Most Important Topic Political Scientists Are Not Studying: Adapting to Climate Change." *Perspectives on Politics* 12.2, 420–434.

Jenkins, Jeffery and Eric Patashnik (2012). "Living Legislation and American Politics." In: *Living Legislation: Durability, Change, and the Politics of American Lawmaking*. Ed. by Jeffery Jenkins and Eric Patashnik. University of Chicago Press, 3–19.

Jenkins, Jesse (2014). "Political Economy Constraints on Carbon Pricing Policies: What Are the Implications for Economic Efficiency, Environmental Efficacy, and Climate Policy Design?" *Energy Policy* 69, 467–477.

Jenkins, Jesse et al. (2012). *Beyond Boom and Bust*. Brookings. https://tinyurl.com/2p9ebe5e.

Jenkins, Jesse et al. (2022). "Electricity Transmission Is Key to Unlock the Full Potential of the Inflation Reduction Act." *REPEAT Project*. bit.ly/3Y2DOYi.

Jennings, Kent (1998). "Political Trust and the Roots of Devolution." In: *Trust and Governance*. Ed. by Valerie Braithwaite and Margaret Levi. Russell Sage Foundation, 218–244.

Jensen, Nathan M. (2017). "The Effect of Economic Development Incentives and Clawback Provisions on Job Creation: A Pre-Registered Evaluation of Maryland and Virginia Programs." *Research & Politics* 4.2, 1–8.

Jensen, Nathan M. and Edmund Malesky (2018). *Incentives to Pander: How Politicians Use Corporate Welfare for Political Gain*. Cambridge University Press.

Jensen, Nathan M. and Calvin Thrall (2021). "Who's Afraid of Sunlight? Explaining Opposition to Transparency in Economic Development." *Business and Politics* 23.4, 474–491.

Jerolmack, Colin (2021). *Up to Heaven and Down to Hell*. Princeton University Press.

Kahneman, Daniel and Amos Tversky (1979). "Prospect Theory: An Analysis of Decision Under Risk." *Econometrica* 47.2, 263.

Kalt, Tobias (2022). "Agents of Transition or Defenders of the Status Quo? Trade Union Strategies in Green Transitions." *Journal of Industrial Relations* 64.4, 499–521.

Karneyeva, Yuliya and Rolf Wüstenhagen (2017). "Solar Feed-In Tariffs in a Post-Grid Parity World: The Role of Risk, Investor Diversity and Business Models." *Energy Policy* 106, 445–456.

Katz, L. F., J. R. Kling, and J. B. Liebman (2001). "Moving to Opportunity in Boston: Early Results of a Randomized Mobility Experiment." *Quarterly Journal of Economics* 116.2, 607–654.

Keefer, Philip and Razvan Vlaicu (2008). "Democracy, Credibility, and Clientelism." *Journal of Law, Economics, & Organization* 24.2, 371–406.

Keersmaecker, Stefan De and Célia Dejon (2022). "EU Cohesion Policy: €1.64 Billion for a Just Climate Transition in Czechia." *European Union Press Release*. bit.ly/3HiYCEU.

Kennan, John and James R. Walker (2011). "The Effect of Expected Income on Individual Migration Decisions." *Econometrica* 79.1, 211–251.

Keohane, Robert O. (1984). *After Hegemony*. Princeton University Press.

(2015). "The Global Politics of Climate Change: Challenge for Political Science." *PS: Political Science & Politics* 48.01, 19–26.

Keyser, David and Suzanne Tegen (2019). *The Wind Energy Workforce in the United States: Training, Hiring, and Future Needs*. NREL/TP-6A20-73908. National Renewable Energy Laboratory. https://bit.ly/3CHhmKo.

Kim, Sung Eun and Krzysztof Pelc (2020). "The Politics of Trade Adjustment Versus Trade Protection." *Comparative Political Studies*, 001041402095768.

(2021). "How Responsive Is Trade Adjustment Assistance?" *Political Science Research and Methods* 9.4, 889–898.

Bibliography

Kirk, Karin (2021). "Wind and Solar Energy Are Job Creators. Which States Are Taking Advantage?" *Yale Climate Connections*. https://bit.ly/3cqlFAO.

Kline, Patrick and Enrico Moretti (2014). "People, Places, and Public Policy: Some Simple Welfare Economics of Local Economic Development Programs." *Annual Review of Economics* 6.1, 629–662.

Kono, Daniel Yuichi (2020). "Compensating for the Climate: Unemployment Insurance and Climate Change Votes." *Political Studies* 68.1, 167–186.

Krehbiel, Keith (1998). *Pivotal Politics*. Chicago University Press.

Kronk, Henry (2019). "*I Wish I Got A Degree*" Billyjack Buzzard Reflects on His Time at Mined Mines. E-learning Inside. http://bit.ly/3QC25RC.

Kuntz, Phil and George Hager (1990). "Showdown on Clean-Air Bill: Senate Says 'No' to Byrd." *Congressional Quarterly Weekly*, 983–987.

Kuphal, Kyle (2018). "Wind Workers: One Union's Push to Keep Them Local." *Pipestone County Star*. https://bit.ly/3ARWm45.

Kuran, Timur (1991). "Now Out of Never: The Element of Surprise in the East European Revolution of 1989." *World Politics* 44.1, 7–48.

Kydland, Finn and Edward Prescott (1977). "Rules Rather than Discretion: The Inconsistency of Optimal Plans." *Journal of Political Economy* 85.3, 473–491.

Laffont, Jean-Jacques and Jean Tirole (1996). "Pollution Permits and Environmental Innovation." *Journal of Public Economics* 62.1–2, 127–140.

Laird, Frank and Christoph Stefes (2009). "The Diverging Paths of German and United States Policies for Renewable Energy." *Energy Policy* 37.7, 2619–2629.

Lakhanpal, Shikha (2019). "Contesting Renewable Energy in the Global South: A Case-Study of Local Opposition to a Wind Power Project in the Western Ghats of India." *Environmental Development* 30, 51–60.

LaLonde, Robert (2003). "Employment and Training Programs." In: *Means-Tested Transfer Programs in the United States*. Ed. by Robert Moffitt. University of Chicago Press.

Lamont, Michèle (2000). *The Dignity of Working Men: Morality and the Boundaries of Race, Class, and Immigration*. Russell Sage Foundation.

Larson, Eric et al. (2021). *Net-Zero America: Potential Pathways, Infrastructure, and Impacts*. Interim Report. Princeton University. https://bit.ly/3uzlQ2y.

Lazarus, Richard J. (2009). "Super Wicked Problems and Climate Change: Restraining the Present to Liberate the Future." *Cornell Law Review* 94.5, 1153–1234.

Lee, Henry et al. (2021). *Foundations for a Low-Carbon Energy System in China*. Cambridge University Press.

Lehotský, Lukáš and Mikuláš Černík (2019). "Brown Coal Mining in the Czech Republic–Lessons on the Coal Phase-Out." *International Issues & Slovak Foreign Policy Affairs* 28.3/4, 45–63.

Lehotský, Lukáš et al. (2019). "When Climate Change Is Missing: Media Discourse on Coal Mining in the Czech Republic." *Energy Policy* 129, 774–786.

Leiserowitz, Anthony et al. (2021). *Politics & Global Warming, December 2020.* Yale Program on Climate Change Communication: Yale University and George Mason University. bit.ly/3I5WrF8.

Lelieveld, J. et al. (2015). "The Contribution of Outdoor Air Pollution Sources to Premature Mortality on a Global Scale." *Nature* 525.7569, 367–371.

Levi, Margaret (1998). "A State of Trust." In: *Trust and Governance.* Ed. by Valerie Braithwaite and Margaret Levi. Russell Sage Foundation, 77–101.

Levi, Margaret and Richard Sherman (1997). "Rationalized Bureaucracies and Rational Compliance." In: *Institutions and Economic Development: Growth and Governance in Less Developed and Post-Socialist Countries.* Ed. by C. Clague. Johns Hopkins University Press.

Levi, Margaret and Laura Stoker (2000). "Political Trust and Trustworthiness." *Annual Review of Political Science* 3.1, 475–507.

Lewin, Philip (2019). "'Coal Is Not Just a Job, It's a Way of Life': The Cultural Politics of Coal Production in Central Appalachia." *Social Problems* 66.1, 51–68.

Lewis, David E. (2004). "The Adverse Consequences of the Politics of Agency Design for Presidential Management in the United States: The Relative Durability of Insulated Agencies." *British Journal of Political Science* 34.3, 377–404.

Liang, Chao et al. (2022). "Climate Policy Uncertainty and World Renewable Energy Index Volatility Forecasting." *Technological Forecasting and Social Change* 182, 121810.

Lipton, Eric (2022). "Ahead of the Midterms, Energy Lobbyists Plan for a Republican House." *The New York Times.* bit.ly/3h9aw9U.

Litz, Philipp, Patrick Graichen, and Frank Peter (2019). *The German Coal Commission: A Roadmap for a Just Transition from Coal to Renewables.* Tech. rep. Agora Energiewende und Aurora Energy Research.

LIUNA (2017). "Unions Say Local Workers Should Build Renewable Energy Projects." https://bit.ly/3SScNV2.

Lockwood, Matthew (2021). "Routes to Credible Climate Commitment: The UK and Denmark Compared." *Climate Policy* 21.9, 1234–1247.

Looney, Bernard (2022). "Just Transition: Investor and Company Perspectives." *CERES.* www.youtube.com/watch?v=Jt3iJQoersA.

Louie, Edward P. and Joshua M. Pearce (2016). "Retraining Investment for U.S. Transition from Coal to Solar Photovoltaic Employment." *Energy Economics* 57, 295–302.

Lynch, John E. (1987). *Economic Adjustment and Conversion of Defense Industries.* Westview Press.

MacGillis, Alec (2022). "What Germany's Effort to Leave Coal Behind Can Teach the U.S." *ProPublica.* https://bit.ly/3OZGQqR.

MacNeil, Robert and Madeleine Beauman (2022). "Understanding Resistance to Just Transition Ideas in Australian Coal Communities." *Environmental Innovation and Societal Transitions* 43, 118–126.

Maggi, Giovanni and Andres Rodriguez-Clare (2007). "A Political-Economy Theory of Trade Agreements." *American Economic Review* 97.4, 1374–1406.

Maltzman, Forrest and Charles Shipan (2008). "Change, Continuity, and the Evolution of the Law." *American Journal of Political Science* 52.2, 252–267.

Mansfield, Edward D. and Nita Rudra (2021). "Embedded Liberalism in the Digital Era." *International Organization* 75.2, 1–28.

Mares, Isabela, Kenneth Scheve, and Christina Toenshoff (2022). "Compensation, Beliefs in State Effectiveness, and Support for the Energy Transition." In: American Political Science Association. Montreal.

Margalit, Yotam (2011). "Costly Jobs: Trade-related Layoffs, Government Compensation, and Voting in U.S. Elections." *American Political Science Review* 105.1, 166–188.

Marlon, Jennifer et al. (2021). "Hot Dry Days Increase Perceived Experience with Global Warming." *Global Environmental Change* 68, 102247.

Martinez-Alvarez, Cesar B. et al. (2022). "Political Leadership Has Limited Impact on Fossil Fuel Taxes and Subsidies." *Proceedings of the National Academy of Sciences* 119.47, e2208024119.

Maxmin, Chloe and Canyon Woodward (2022). *Dirt Road Revival: How to Rebuild Rural Politics and Why Our Future Depends On It*. Beacon Press.

Mayer, Adam (2018). "A Just Transition for Coal Miners? Community Identity and Support from Local Policy Actors." *Environmental Innovation and Societal Transitions* 28, 1–13.

Mayhew, David R. (2005). *Divided We Govern*. 2nd ed. Yale University Press.

McCarty, Nolan, Keith T. Poole, and Howard Rosenthal (2006). *Polarized America: The Dance of Ideology and Unequal Riches*. MIT Press.

McGuinness, Tara and Anne-Marie Slaughter (2019). "The New Practice of Public Problem Solving." *Stanford Social Innovation Review* 17.2, 26–33.

McKibben, Bill and Ezra Klein (2022). "Bill McKibben on the Power That Could Save the Planet." *The Ezra Klein Show*. bit.ly/3FzWA2d.

McKinsey & Company (2022). *The Energy Transition: A Region-by-Region Agenda for Near-Term Action*. bit.ly/3Xa5YzT.

Meckling, Jonas and Jonas Nahm (2022). "Strategic State Capacity: How States Counter Opposition to Climate Policy." *Comparative Political Studies* 55.3, 493–523.

Meckling, Jonas, Thomas Sterner, and Gernot Wagner (2017). "Policy Sequencing toward Decarbonization." *Nature Energy* 2.12, 918–922.

Meckling, Jonas et al. (2015). "Winning Coalitions for Climate Policy." *Science* 349.6253, 1170–1171.

Meckling, Jonas et al. (2022a). "Busting the Myths around Public Investment in Clean Energy." *Nature Energy* 7.7, 563–565.

Meckling, Jonas et al. (2022b). "Why Nations Lead or Lag in Energy Transitions." *Science* 378.6615, 31–33.

Meinshausen, Malte et al. (2022). "Realization of Paris Agreement Pledges May Limit Warming Just below 2°C." *Nature* 604.7905, 304–309.

Metcalf, Elizabeth Covelli et al. (2015). "The Role of Trust in Restoration Success: Public Engagement and Temporal and Spatial Scale in a Complex Social-Ecological System." *Restoration Ecology* 23.3, 315–324.

Mettler, Suzanne (2011). *The Submerged State: How Invisible Government Policies Undermine American Democracy*. University of Chicago Press.

Mey, Franziska et al. (2019). "Case Studies from Transition Processes in Coal Dependent Communities." *Greenpeace*. bit.ly/3VxeoQY.

Mildenberger, Matto (2020). *Carbon Captured: How Business and Labor Control Climate Politics*. MIT Press.

Mildenberger, Matto and Dustin Tingley (2019). "Beliefs about Climate Beliefs." *British Journal of Political Science* 49.4, 1279–307.

Mildenberger, Matto et al. (2022). "Limited Impacts of Carbon Tax Rebate Programmes on Public Support for Carbon Pricing." *Nature Climate Change* 12.2, 141–147.

Milgrom, Paul, Douglass North, and Barry Weingast (1990). "The Role of Institutions in the Revival of Trade: The Law Merchant, Private Judges, and the Champagne Fairs." *Economics and Politics* 2.1, 1–23.

Miller, Gary and Andrew Whitford (2016). *Above Politics: Bureaucratic Discretion and Credible Commitment*. Cambridge University Press.

Mills, Mike (1990). "Aiding Displaced Workers." *Congressional Quarterly Weekly Report* 48.43, 3589.

Mills, Sarah Banas, Douglas Bessette, and Hannah Smith (2019). "Exploring Landowners' Post-Construction Changes in Perceptions of Wind Energy in Michigan." *Land Use Policy* 82, 754–762.

Milner, Helen V. (2021). "Voting for Populism in Europe: Globalization, Technological Change, and the Extreme Right." *Comparative Political Studies* 54.13, 2286–2320.

Milner, Helen V. and Dustin Tingley (2010). "The Political Economy of US Foreign Aid: American Legislators and the Domestic Politics of Aid." *Economics & Politics* 22.2, 200–232.

(2015). *Sailing the Water's Edge*. Princeton University Press.

Mitchell, George (2015). *The Negotiator: A Memoir*. Simon and Schuster.

MN Building Trades (2017). *Renewable Energy Resolution Adopted by MN Building Trades 71st. Convention*. https://bit.ly/3upTDuZ.

Moe, Terry (1985). "The Politicized Presidency." In: *The New Direction in American Politics*. Ed. by John Chubb and Paul Peterson. Brookings Institution Press.

Moe, Terry M. (1990). "The Politics of Structural Choice: Toward a Theory of Public Bureaucracy." In: *Organization Theory*. Ed. by Oliver Williamson. Oxford University Press.

Mohai, Paul, David Pellow, and J. Timmons Roberts (2009). "Environmental Justice." *Annual Review of Environment and Resources* 34, 405–430.

Moniz, Ernest and Michael Kearney (2020). *The Roosevelt Project: A New Deal for Employment, Energy and Environment*. Roosevelt Project Working Paper Series. MIT Center for Energy and Environmental Policy Research.

(2022). *The Roosevelt Project Phase 2: Case Studies Overview*. Roosevelt Project Working Paper Series. MIT Center for Energy and Environmental Policy Research.

Moravcsik, Andrew (1998). *The Choice for Europe: Social Purpose and State Power from Messina to Maastricht*. Cornell University Press.

Morrissey, Oliver (1993). "The Mixing of Aid and Trade Policies." *World Economy* 16.1, 69–84.

Bibliography

Muchlinski, Jim (2019). "Bitter Root Project Targets the High Ground in YMC." *Marshall Independent*. https://bit.ly/3AmS2Z3.

Mullin, Megan and Katy Hansen (2022). "Local News and the Electoral Incentive to Invest in Infrastructure." *American Political Science Review*, 1–6.

Muro, Mark et al. (2019). *Advancing Inclusion through Clean Energy Jobs*. Brookings Institution.

Mutz, Diana Carole, Paul Sniderman, and Richard Brody (1996). *Political Persuasion and Attitude Change*. University of Michigan Press.

National Academy of Sciences, National Academy of Engineering, and National Research Council (2010). *Electricity from Renewable Resources: Status, Prospects, and Impediments*. National Academies Press.

National Research Council (2009). *Informing Decisions in a Changing Climate*. National Academies Press.

Navarro, Mireya (2011). "Christie Pulls New Jersey From 10-State Climate Initiative." *New York Times*. http://bit.ly/3hDDm1K.

New York Times (1988). "A Break in the Acid Rain Impasse." bit.ly/3h2so6f.
— (2010). "Acid Rain 30 Years On." https://nyti.ms/3iBq6vk.

Niskanen, William A. (2003). *A Case for Divided Government*. CATO Institute. bit.ly/3CPDbIK.

Noailly, Joelle, Laura Nowzohour, and Matthias van den Heuvel (2022). *Does Environmental Policy Uncertainty Hinder Investments towards a Low-Carbon Economy?* w30361. NBER.

North, Douglass (1990). *Institutions, Institutional Change and Economic Performance*. Cambridge University Press.

North, Douglass and Barry Weingast (1989). "Constitutions and Commitment: The Evolution of Institutions Governing Public Choice in Seventeenth-Century England." *The Journal of Economic History* 49.4, 803–832.

O'Sullivan, Marlene and Dietmar Edler (2020). "Gross Employment Effects in the Renewable Energy Industry in Germany: An Input-Output Analysis from 2000 to 2018." *Sustainability* 12.15, 6163.

Obama, Barack (2020). *A Promised Land*. Crown.

Ocelík, Petr et al. (2022). "Facilitating the Czech Coal Phase-Out: What Drives Inter-Organizational Collaboration?" *Society & Natural Resources* 35.7, 705–724.

Oei, Pao-Yu, Hanna Brauers, and Philipp Herpich (2020). "Lessons from Germany's Hard Coal Mining Phase-Out: Policies and Transition from 1950 to 2018." *Climate Policy* 20.8, 963–979.

Olsen, Dean (2021). "Landmark Clean Energy Legislation Passes Senate; Pritzker Pledges to Sign Bill into Law." *State Journal-Register*. bit.ly/3h8YDk9.

Olson, Mancur (1965). *The Logic of Collective Action*. Harvard University Press.

Olson-Hazboun, Shawn (2018). "'Why Are We Being Punished and They Are Being Rewarded?' Views on Renewable Energy in Fossil Fuels-based Communities of the U.S. West." *The Extractive Industries and Society* 5.3, 366–374.

Olson-Hazboun, Shawn, Peter Howe, and Anthony Leiserowitz (2018). "The Influence of Extractive Activities on Public Support for Renewable Energy Policy." *Energy Policy* 123, 117–126.

Ordonez, Jose Antonio et al. (2021). "Coal, Power and Coal-Powered Politics in Indonesia." *Environmental Science & Policy* 123, 44–57.

Oreskes, Naomi and Erik M. Conway (2011). *Merchants of Doubt: How a Handful of Scientists Obscured the Truth on Issues from Tobacco Smoke to Global Warming.* Bloomsbury Press.

Ostrom, Elinor (1990). *Governing the Commons.* Cambridge University Press.

(1998). "A Behavioral Approach to the Rational Choice Theory of Collective Action: Presidential Address, American Political Science Association, 1997." *American Political Science Review* 92.1, 1–22.

(2009). *A Polycentric Approach for Coping with Climate Change.* The World Bank.

Pacala, S. and R. Socolow (2004). "Stabilization Wedges: Solving the Climate Problem for the Next 50 Years with Current Technologies." *Science* 305.5686, 968–972.

Page, Benjamin and Robert Shapiro (1983). "Effects of Public Opinion on Policy." *American Political Science Review* 77.1, 175–190.

Pahle, Michael et al. (2018). "Sequencing to Ratchet up Climate Policy Stringency." *Nature Climate Change* 8.10, 861–867.

Pai, Sandeep et al. (2020). "Solar Has Greater Techno-Economic Resource Suitability than Wind for Replacing Coal Mining Jobs." *Environmental Research Letters* 15.3, 034065.

Parry, Ian, Simon Black, and Nate Vernon (2021). *Still Not Getting Energy Prices Right: A Global and Country Update of Fossil Fuel Subsidies.* International Monetary Fund. bit.ly/3Z6CDYk.

Patashnik, Eric (2000). *Putting Trust in the US budget: Federal Trust Funds and the Politics of Commitment.* Cambridge University Press.

(2014). *Reforms at Risk.* Princeton University Press.

(2019). "Limiting Policy Backlash: Strategies for Taming Countercoalitions in an Era of Polarization." *The ANNALS of the American Academy of Political and Social Science* 685.1, 47–63.

Patashnik, Eric and Julian Zelizer (2013). "The Struggle to Remake Politics: Liberal Reform and the Limits of Policy Feedback in the Contemporary American State." *Perspectives on Politics* 11.4, 1071–1087.

Peel, Mark (1998). "Trusting Disadvantaged Citizens." In: *Trust and Governance.* Ed. by Valerie Braithwaite and Margaret Levi. Russell Sage Foundation, 315–342.

Persson, Torsten and Guido Tabellini (1994). "Representative Democracy and Capital Taxation." *Journal of Public Economics* 55.1, 53–70.

(2012). *Macroeconomic Policy, Credibility and Politics.* Routledge.

Pew Research Center (2022). *Public Trust in Government: 1958–2022.* http://bit.ly/3WWTHPC.

PG&E (2022). *PG&E Climate Strategy Report.* bit.ly/3VMICz2.

Pierson, Paul (2000). "Increasing Returns, Path Dependence, and the Study of Politics." *American Political Science Review* 94.2, 251–267.

Bibliography

Pindyck, Robert (1988). "Irreversible Investment, Capacity Choice, and the Value of the Firm." *American Economic Review* 78.5, 969–985.

Plumer, Brad (2022). "Quitting Oil Income Is Hard, Even for States That Want Climate Action." *New York Times*. bit.ly/3HDeEJT.

Polanyi, Karl (1944). *The Great Transformation*. Farrar & Rinehart.

Pollin, Robert and Brian Callaci (2019). "The Economics of Just Transition: A Framework for Supporting Fossil Fuel–Dependent Workers and Communities in the United States." *Labor Studies Journal* 44.2, 93–138.

Popp, David et al. (2020). *The Employment Impact of Green Fiscal Push*. w27321. NBER.

Posner, Richard (2014). *Economic Analysis of Law*. Wolters Kluwer.

Powell, Robert (1990). *Nuclear Deterrence Theory: The Search for Credibility*. Cambridge University Press.

(2006). "War as a Commitment Problem." *International Organization* 60.1, 169–203.

Pranis, Kevin (2018). *Laborers District Council of Minnesota and North Dakota Exception to Administrative Law Judge's Report*.

Rabe, Barry George (2004). *Statehouse and Greenhouse: The Emerging Politics of American Climate Change Policy*. Brookings Institution Press.

Raimi, Daniel (2020). *Environmental Remediation and Infrastructure Policies Supporting Workers and Communities in Transition*. Resources for the Future and Environmental Defense Fund. https://tinyurl.com/yck6smhv.

Raimi, Daniel and Sophie Pesek (2022). *What Is an "Energy Community"?* Resources for the Future. bit.ly/3F8XPnA.

Raimi, Daniel et al. (2022). *The Fiscal Implications of the US Transition Away from Fossil Fuels*. Resources for the Future.

Raitbaur, Louisa (2021). "The New German Coal Laws: A Difficult Balancing Act." *Climate Law* 11.2, 176–194.

Rand, Joseph et al. (2021). *Queued Up: Characteristics of Power Plants Seeking Transmission Interconnection As of the End of 2020*. Lawrence Berkeley National Laboratory. bit.ly/3C8XPTO.

Rappeport, Alan, Ana Swanson, and Zolan Kanno-Youngs (2022). "Biden's 'Made in America' Policies Anger Key Allies." *The New York Times*. bit.ly/3uyMWq8.

Ravikumar, Arvind and Timothy Latimer (2022). "Notes from the Oil Patch: Planning for a Worker-Focused Transition in the Oil and Gas Industry." preprint.

Rees, Albert (1966). "Information Networks in Labor Markets." *American Economic Review* 56.1/2, 559–566.

Rentier, Gerrit, Herman Lelieveldt, and Gert Jan Kramer (2019). "Varieties of Coal-Fired Power Phase-out Across Europe." *Energy Policy* 132, 620–632.

Reuters (2023). "German Police Clash with Activists in Showdown over Coal Mine Expansion." bit.ly/3Xjik8i.

Rickard, Stephanie (2020). "Economic Geography, Politics, and Policy." *Annual Review of Political Science* 23.1, 187–202.

(2023). "The Electoral Consequences of Compensation for Globalization." *European Union Politics* 24.3.

Righetti, Tara, Temple Stoellinger, and Robert Godby (2021). "Adapting to Coal Plant Closures." *Environmental Law* 51.4, 957–990.

Ritchie, Melinda N. and Hye Young You (2021). "Trump and Trade: Protectionist Politics and Redistributive Policy." *Journal of Politics* 83.2, 800–805.

Roberts, J. Timmons and Bradley C. Parks (2007). *A Climate of Injustice: Global Inequality, North-South Politics, and Climate Policy*. MIT Press.

Roberts, Margaret E, Brandon M Stewart, and Dustin Tingley (2019). "Stm: An R package for structural topic models." *Journal of Statistical Software* 91, 1–40.

Roberts, Margaret E. et al. (2014). "Structural Topic Models for Open-Ended Survey Responses." *American Journal of Political Science* 58.4, 1064–1082.

Robertson, Campbell (2019). "They Were Promised Coding Jobs in Appalachia. Now They Say It Was a Fraud." *New York Times*. https://nyti.ms/3uQ8SfY.

Rochet, Jean-Charles (2004). "Macroeconomic Shocks and Banking Supervision." *Journal of Financial Stability* 1.1, 93–110.

Rodrik, Dani (1989). "Promises, Promises: Credible Policy Reform Via Signalling." *The Economic Journal* 99.397, 756–772.

– (2014). "Green Industrial Policy." *Oxford Review of Economic Policy* 30.3, 469–491.

Rodrik, Dani and Richard Zeckhauser (1988). "The Dilemma of Government Responsiveness." *Journal of Policy Analysis and Management* 7.4, 601–620.

Roemer, Kelli and Julia Haggerty (2021). "Coal Communities and the US Energy Transition: A Policy Corridors Assessment." *Energy Policy* 151, 112112.

– (2022). "The Energy Transition as Fiscal Rupture: Public Services and Resilience Pathways in a Coal Company Town." *Energy Research & Social Science* 91, 102752.

Rogge, Karoline and Elisabeth Dütschke (2018). "What Makes Them Believe in the Low-Carbon Energy Transition? Exploring Corporate Perceptions of the Credibility of Climate Policy Mixes." *Environmental Science & Policy* 87, 74–84.

Rogoff, Kenneth (1985). "The Optimal Degree of Commitment to an Intermediate Monetary Target." *Quarterly Journal of Economics* 100.4, 1169.

Rosen, Howard (2006). "Trade Adjustment Assistance." In: *C. Fred Bergsten and the World Economy*. Ed. by Michael Mussa. Peterson Institute for International Economics, 79–113.

– (2008). *Designing a National Strategy for Responding to Economic Dislocation*. bit.ly/3IdwDqF.

Ross, Michael L. (1999). "The Political Economy of the Resource Curse." *World Politics* 51.2, 297–322.

Rudolph, Thomas and Jillian Evans (2005). "Political Trust, Ideology, and Public Support for Government Spending." *American Journal of Political Science* 49.3, 660–671.

Ruggie, John Gerard (1982). "International Regimes, Transactions, and Change." *International Organization* 36.2, 379–415.

Sabel, Charles F. and David G. Victor (2022). *Fixing the Climate: Strategies for an Uncertain World*. Princeton University Press.

Bibliography

Sandel, Michael (2020). *The Tyranny of Merit: What's Become of the Common Good?* Penguin.

Scheiber, Noam (2021a). "Building Solar Farms May Not Build the Middle Class." *The New York Times.* https://tinyurl.com/2p8atxvd.

— (2021b). "Can a Green-Economy Boom Town Be Built to Last?" *The New York Times.* https://tinyurl.com/22hzk3mp.

Schelling, Thomas C. (1956). "An Essay on Bargaining." *American Economic Review* 46.3, 281–306.

— (1966). *Arms and Influence.* New Haven, CT: Yale University Press.

Scheve, Kenneth and Theo Serlin (2023). "The German Trade Shock and the Rise of the Neo-Welfare State in Early Twentieth-Century Britain." *American Political Science Review* 117.2, 557–574.

Schnackenberg, Andrew and Edward Tomlinson (2016). "Organizational Transparency: A New Perspective on Managing Trust in Organization-Stakeholder Relationships." *Journal of Management* 42.7, 1784–1810.

Schumpeter, Joseph (1942). *Capitalism, Socialism, and Democracy.* Harper & Brothers.

Searcey, Dionne (2021). "Wyoming Coal Country Pivots, Reluctantly, to Wind Farms." *New York Times.* https://nyti.ms/3Nuikhw.

SEIA (2020). *Illinois Clean Energy Boom Goes Bust as State Program Runs Out of Funding, Forcing Layoffs at Solar and Wind Businesses.* Solar Energy Industries Association. https://tinyurl.com/yckr738f.

Sendstad, Lars et al. (2022). "The Impact of Subsidy Retraction on European Renewable Energy Investments." *Energy Policy* 160, 112675.

Shambaugh, Jay and Ryan Nunn, eds. (2018). *Place-Based Policies for Shared Economic Growth.* Brookings Institution.

Sheldon, Peter, Raja Junankar, and Anthony De Rosa Pontello (2018). "The Ruhr or Appalachia? Deciding the Future of Australia's Coal Power Workers and Communities." *University of New South Wales.* Industrial Relations Research Centre.

Shen, Shiran Victoria, Bruce E. Cain, and Iris Hui (2019). "Public Receptivity in China towards Wind Energy Generators: A Survey Experimental Approach." *Energy Policy* 129, 619–627.

Shepsle, Kenneth (1991). "Discretion, Institutions, and the Problem of Government Commitment." In: *Social Theory for a Changing Society.* Ed. by Pierre Bourdieu and James Coleman. Westview Press.

— (2006). "Rational Choice Institutionalism." In: *The Oxford Handbook of Political Institutions.* Ed. by Robert Goodin. Oxford University Press.

Shields, Tony and Rod Campbell (2021). *We Can Work It Out: Could Germany's Multi-Stakeholder Approach Help Move Australia Out of Coal-Fired Power?* The Australia Institute. bit.ly/3QF3oke.

Shuler, Liz (2021). *Shuler at COP26: We Cannot Leave Workers Behind.* https://bit.ly/3tPnzAR.

Sieben, Katie (2021). *Renewable Energy – Growth and Opportunities for Our Rural Economies.* Senate Agriculture, Nutrition and Forestry Subcommittee on Rural Development and Energy Hearing. https://bit.ly/3yI3EGn.

Siegel, Josh and Kelsey Tamborrino (2022). "Republicans Plan an Energy Agenda Designed to Keep Democrats on Their Heels." *Politico*. bit.ly/3Fe50e7.

Simon, Curtis J. and John T. Warner (1992). "Matchmaker, Matchmaker: The Effect of Old Boy Networks on Job Match Quality, Earnings, and Tenure." *Journal of Labor Economics* 10.3, 306–330.

Simon, Julia (2022). "In the Misinformation Wars, Renewable Energy Is the Latest to Be Attacked." *National Public Radio*. n.pr/3FbXbFH.

Skocpol, Theda and Alexander Hertel-Fernandez (2016). "The Koch Network and Republican Party Extremism." *Perspectives on Politics* 14.3, 681–699.

Slattery, Cailin and Owen Zidar (2020). "Evaluating State and Local Business Incentives." *Journal of Economic Perspectives* 34.2, 90–118.

Smiley, Lauren (2015). "Can You Teach a Coal Miner to Code?" *Wired*. https://bit.ly/3CAiSoU.

Smith, Barbara Ellen (2020). *Digging Our Own Graves: Coal Miners & the Struggle over Black Lung Disease*. In collab. with Earl Dotter. Updated edition. Haymarket Books.

Smith, Kristin, Mark Haggerty, and Jackson Rose (2021). *Federal Fossil Fuel Disbursements to States State Policy and Practice in Allocating Federal Revenue*. Headwaters Economics. bit.ly/3H7gmTs.

Snyder, James M. and David Strömberg (2010). "Press Coverage and Political Accountability." *Journal of Political Economy* 118.2, 355–408.

Sobel, Joel (1985). "A Theory of Credibility." *The Review of Economic Studies* 52.4, 557–573.

Sovacool, Benjamin et al. (2022). "Conflicted Transitions: Exploring the Actors, Tactics, and Outcomes of Social Opposition Against Energy Infrastructure." *Global Environmental Change* 73, 102473.

Spaulding, Shayne and Ananda Martin-Caughey (2015). *The Goals and Dimensions of Employer Engagement in Workforce Development Programs*. Urban Institute. https://urbn.is/3s6rXJU.

Spence, Michael (1973). "Job Market Signaling." *Quarterly Journal of Economics* 87.3, 355.

— (1976). "Informational Aspects of Market Structure: An Introduction." *Quarterly Journal of Economics* 90.4, 591.

Spiker, Katie (2020). *A 21st Century Reemployment Accord*. National Skills Coalition. https://bit.ly/3VCYXqL.

Stasavage, David (2002). "Credible Commitment in Early Modern Europe: North and Weingast Revisited." *Journal of Law, Economics, and Organization* 18.1, 155–186.

— (2004). "Open-Door or Closed-Door? Transparency in Domestic and International Bargaining." *International Organization* 58.4, 667–703.

Stefek, Jeremy et al. (2019). *Economic Impacts from Wind Energy in Colorado Case Study: Rush Creek Wind Farm*. National Renewable Energy Laboratory. https://bit.ly/3tRgWha.

Stern, Nicholas (2022). "New Approaches to the Economics of Climate Change: Urgency, Scale, Opportunity." Presentation at Princeton University.

Stokes, Donald E. and Warren E. Miller (1962). "Party Government and the Saliency of Congress." *Public Opinion Quarterly* 26.4, 531.

Bibliography

Stokes, Leah (2020). *Short Circuiting Policy: Interest Groups and the Battle Over Clean Energy and Climate Policy in the American States*. Oxford University Press.

Stokes, Leah and Hanna Breetz (2018). "Politics in the U.S. Energy Transition: Case Studies of Solar, Wind, Biofuels and Electric Vehicles Policy." *Energy Policy* 113, 76–86.

Stokes, Leah, Jessica Lovering, and Chris Miljanich (n.d.). "Prevalence and Predictors of Wind Energy Opposition in the US and Canada." Unpublished Manuscript.

Stokes, Leah and Christopher Warshaw (2017). "Renewable Energy Policy Design and Framing Influence Public Support in the United States." *Nature Energy* 2.8, 17107.

Stone, Randall (2012). *Lending Credibility: The International Monetary Fund and the Post-Communist Transition*. Princeton University Press.

Storrow, Benjamin (2022). "Why Utilities Are Lining Up behind the Climate Bill." *E&E News*. bit.ly/3VxSltn.

Storrow, Benjamin and Heather Richards (2022). "Inflation's next Victim: U.S. Offshore Wind Projects." *PoliticoPro*. bit.ly/3kc3Fot.

Sunter, Deborah, Sergio Castellanos, and Daniel Kammen (2019). "Disparities in Rooftop Photovoltaics Deployment in the United States by Race and Ethnicity." *Nature Sustainability* 2.1, 71–76.

Susskind, Lawrence et al. (2022). "Sources of Opposition to Renewable Energy Projects in the United States." *Energy Policy* 165, 112922.

Sustainable Development Solutions Network (2020). *America's Zero Carbon Action Plan*. https://bit.ly/36hLujq.

Szymendera, Scott and Molly Sherlock (2019). *The Black Lung Program, the Black Lung Disability Trust Fund, and the Excise Tax on Coal: Background and Policy Options*. R45261. Congressional Research Service.

Taylor, Charles (1995). "The Politics of Recognition." In: *Multiculturalism*. Ed. by Amy Gutmann. Princeton University Press, 25–74.

Thelen, Kathleen Ann (2004). *How Institutions Evolve: The Political Economy of Skills in Germany, Britain, the United States, and Japan*. Cambridge University Press.

Thomas, Michael (2023). "How Republicans Plan To Use Their House Majority To Delay Climate Action." *Distilled*. bit.ly/3QanfGr.

Thrall, Calvin and Nathan M. Jensen (2022). "Does Transparency Improve Public Policy? Evidence from a Tax Incentive Transparency Initiative." Unpublished Manuscript.

Times Union (2022). "Editorial: Is N.Y.'s Green Too Lean?" *Times Union*. bit.ly/3UwIog2.

Timperley, Jocelyn (2021). "The Broken $100-Billion Promise of Climate Finance – and How to Fix It." *Nature* 598.7881, 400–402.

Tingley, Dustin and Michael Tomz (2014). "Conditional Cooperation and Climate Change." *Comparative Political Studies* 47.3, 344–368.

(2021). "The Effects of Naming and Shaming on Public Support for Compliance with International Agreements: An Experimental Analysis of the Paris Agreement." *International Organization* 76.2, 1–24.

288 *Bibliography*

Tomer, Adie, Joseph Kane, and Caroline George (2021). *How Renewable Energy Jobs Can Uplift Fossil Fuel Communities and Remake Climate Politics.* Brookings. https://tinyurl.com/bdcnztrm.

Tomich, Jeffrey (2018). "PUC Punts on Wind Project to Weigh Labor Issue." *E&E News.*

Tomz, Michael (2012). *Reputation and International Cooperation.* Princeton University Press.

Tongia, Rahul, Anurag Sehgal, and Puneet Kamboj (2020). *Future of Coal in India.* Notion Press.

U.S. Congress (1989a). "Clean Air Act Amendments of 1989: S.816, the Toxics Release Prevention Act of 1989." *Hearing before the Subcommittee on Environmental Protection of the Committee on Environment and Public Works, Senate.* 101st Congress (1st session).

(1989b). "Clean Air Act Amendments of 1989. National Acid Precipitation Assessment Program." *Hearings before the Subcommittee on Environmental Protection of the Committee on Environment and Public Works, Senate.* 101st Congress (1st session).

(1989c). "Effects of Proposed Acid Rain Legislation on Workers and Small Business in the High Sulfur Coal Industry." *Hearing before the Subcommittee on Environment and Labor of the Committee on Small Business, House of Representatives.* 101st Congress (1st session).

(1990a). "House of Representatives – Thursday, March 8." *Congressional Record* 136.3, 3836–4053.

(1990b). "Senate – Thursday, March 29." *Congressional Record* 136.4, 5811–6094.

(1990c). "Senate – Wednesday, May 23." *Congressional Record* 136.8, 11724–12108.

(1991). "Unemployment Compensation." *Hearing before the Committee on Finance, Senate.* 102nd Congress (1st session).

(1994). "The Reemployment Act of 1994." *Hearing before the Committee On Education and Labor, House of Representatives.* 103rd Congress (2nd session).

(2013). "EPA's Regulatory Threat to Affordable, Reliable Energy: The Perspective of Coal Communities." *Hearing before the Subcommittee on Oversight and Investigations of the Committee on Energy and Commerce, House of Representatives.* 113th Congress.

UAW (2019). *Taking the High Road: Strategies for a Fair EV Future.* UAW Research Department. https://bit.ly/3CLHMdY.

Ulph, Alistair and David Ulph (2013). "Optimal Climate Change Policies when Governments Cannot Commit." *Environmental and Resource Economics* 56.2, 161–176.

UMW Journal (1988a). *United Mine Workers Journal* February.

(1988b). *United Mine Workers Journal* June.

(1988c). *United Mine Workers Journal* December.

(1989). *United Mine Workers Journal* March.

(1990a). *United Mine Workers Journal* February.

(1990b). "The Rank and File." *United Mine Workers Journal* April/May.

Bibliography

(1991a). "Acid Rain Breakthrough in Indiana." *United Mine Workers Journal* June.

(1991b). "Illinois Miners Win Legislation to Save Thousands of Jobs." *United Mine Workers Journal* October.

(1991c). "Rank and File." *United Mine Workers Journal* July.

(1993). "Scrub, Don't Switch: A Fight to Save Jobs." *United Mine Workers Journal* May.

Unruh, Gregory C (2000). "Understanding Carbon Lock-In." *Energy Policy* 28.12, 817–830.

Van Leuven, Mary and Ed Gilliland (2019). *U.S. Solar Industry Diversity Study 2019: New Resources on Diversity and Inclusion in the Solar Workforce.* The Solar Foundation, Solar Energy Industries Association. https://bit.ly/3SbVZqc.

Victor, David and Kassia Yanosek (2011). "The Crisis in Clean Energy: Stark Realities of the Renewables Craze." *Foreign Affairs* July/August, 112–120.

Victor, David G. (2011). *Global Warming Gridlock: Creating More Effective Strategies for Protecting the Planet.* Cambridge University Press.

Vogel, David (1993). "Representing Diffuse Interests in Environmental Policymaking." In: *Do Institutions Matter?* Ed. by R. Kent Weaver and Bert Rockman. Brookings Institution Press, 237–271.

Volcovici, Valerie (2017). "Awaiting Trump's Coal Comeback, Miners Reject Retraining." *Reuters.* https://reut.rs/3SqYgOJ.

Walker, Reed (2013). "The Transitional Costs of Sectoral Reallocation: Evidence from the Clean Air Act and the Workforce." *Quarterly Journal of Economics* 128.4, 1787–1835.

Wallace-Wells, Benjamin (2019). "A Louisiana Republican Reckons with Climate Change." *The New Yorker.* bit.ly/3QIHcnY.

Walls, WD, Frank Rusco, and Jon Ludwigson (2007). "Power Plant Investment in Restructured Markets." *Energy* 32.8, 1403–1413.

Walter, Barbara (2002). *Committing to Peace: The Successful Settlement of Civil Wars.* Princeton University Press.

Walter, Stefanie (2010). "Globalization and the Welfare State." *International Studies Quarterly* 54.2, 403–426.

(2021). "The Backlash Against Globalization." *Annual Review of Political Science* 24.1.

Walton, Robert (2018). "Advocates Warn New Jersey Solar Market Could Collapse Again." *Utility Dive.* https://tinyurl.com/mry2ydxk.

Wehnert, Timon et al. (2019). *Challenges of Coal Transitions: A Comparative Study on the Status Quo and Future Prospects of Coal Mining and Coal Use in Indonesia, Colombia and Viet Nam.* Wuppertal Institute for Climate, Environment and Energy. bit.ly/3uwtjPp.

Weingast, Barry and William Marshall (1988). "The Industrial Organization of Congress; or, Why Legislatures, Like Firms, Are Not Organized as Markets." *Journal of Political Economy* 96.1, 132–163.

Westwood, Sean J. (2022). "The Partisanship of Bipartisanship: How Representatives Use Bipartisan Assertions to Cultivate Support." *Political Behavior* 44.3, 1411–1435.

White House (2022). "Congressional Republicans' Five-Part Plan to Increase Inflation and Costs for American Families." *White House Press Release.* bit.ly/3uBbij3.

White-Newsome, Jalonne L., Colleen Linn, and Kira Rib (2021). *Driving toward Environmental Justice and Health.* WP-2021-RP-IH-2. https://bit.ly/3D6sXnz.

Wike, Richard and Bruce Stokes (2018). "In Advanced and Emerging Economies Alike: Worries About Job Automation." *Pew Research Center.* bit.ly/3UpnHkw.

Williamson, Oliver (1983). "Credible Commitments: Using Hostages to Support Exchange." *American Economic Review* 73.4, 519–540.

– (1989). "Transaction Cost Economics." *Handbook of Industrial Organization* 1, 135–182.

– (1991). "Comparative Economic Organization: The Analysis of Discrete Structural Alternatives." *Administrative Science Quarterly* 36.2, 269–296.

WNYC (2016). "As Coal Country Struggles, Miners Find New Hope in Coding." bit.ly/3CMQCcp.

Woodruff, Chase (2021). "Republicans Called Colorado's Just-Transition Office for Coal Workers 'Orwellian.' Now They Want to Boost Its Funding." *Colorado Newsline.* https://bit.ly/3ySLdyy.

Wuthnow, Robert (2018). *The Left Behind: Decline and Rage in Rural America.* Princeton University Press.

Wynn, Gerard and Javier Julve (2016). "A Foundation Based Approach for Phasing Out German lignite in Lausitz." *Institute for Energy Economics and Financial Analysis.* bit.ly/3UzNCWG.

Yeo, Sophie (2019). "Where Climate Cash Is Flowing and Why It's Not Enough." *Nature* 573.7774, 328–332.

You, Hye Young (2017). "Ex Post Lobbying." *Journal of Politics* 79.4, 1162–1176.

Yuliani, Dewi (2017). "Is Feed-in-Tariff Policy Effective for Increasing Deployment of Renewable Energy in Indonesia?" In: *The Political Economy of Clean Energy Transitions.* Ed. by Douglas Arent et al. Oxford University Press.

Zaller, John (1992). *The Nature and Origins of Mass Public Opinion.* Cambridge University Press.

Zaremba, Nora (2018). "Brandenburg: 'Then the Frustration Will Be Even Greater.'" *Tagesspiegel PNN.* bit.ly/3Bb36tk.

Index

1990 CAA Amendments, 31, 40, 60, 143, 147–175
  acid rain, 31, 148, 151–153, 167
  Byrd Amendment, 147–149, 155–161, 165
  Clean Air Employment Transition Assistance Program, 163
  group of nine, 153
  Wise Amendment, 161–163, 165

accountability, 27, 32, 64, 203, 205–208, 221–226, 230–232
adaptation, 9, 33, 65, 244, 254
advance notice, 169–170
  WARN Act, 231
Affordable Care Act, 54, 256
Affordable Clean Energy rule, 71, 143
agriculture, 6, 11
air pollution, 45, 92, 151, 249
Alesina, Alberto, 25, 32, 36, 37, 57, 192
Alt, James, 206, 207, 230
Anderson, Michelle, 14, 19, 20, 32, 151, 174, 243, 259
Ansolabehere, Stephen, xi, 8, 23, 32, 74, 75, 97, 99, 240
Appalachia, 10, 75, 85, 94, 97, 154, 156, 167, 170, 173–174, 176–178, 199, 233
Appalachian Regional Commission, 23, 177
Arizona, 84, 226, 256
Arkansas, 87
Arnold, R. Douglas, 59, 203

asset specificity, 26, 40, 62, 126–127, 143
Australia, 43, 98, 170, 185, 250
  Home Insulation Program, 181
  Queensland, 173
automation, 10, 17, 23, 198, 240, 244, 259
automobile manufacturing, 10, 75, 85, 99, 100, 103
Axelrod, Robert, 25, 58

Barna, Rebecca, 165
Baucus, Max, 158
Bell, Rusty, 18, 87, 238, 249
Bertram, Tracy, 34, 40, 182
Bethlehem Steel Corporation, 154
Biden, Joe, 28, 116, 160, 257
Bit Source, 178–179, 199
black lung, 165–166, 174
  Black Lung Benefits Revenue Act of 1977, 166
  Black Lung Disability Trust Fund, 56, 166
  Inflation Reduction Act, 166
Bloomberg, Michael, 177–178
Boucher, Rick, 152
British Petroleum
  Looney, Bernard, 17, 144
broken promises, 42, 83–84, 89–90, 93, 165, 186–187, 207, 221, 234, 239
budget reconciliation, 16, 256
bureaucracy, 56, 242
Bush, George H.W., 153, 155, 158, 160, 162, 163, 167

Buzzard, Billyjack, 177, 178
Byrd, Robert, 148, 154–162

California, 18, 50, 63, 65, 136, 144, 202, 208, 211, 229
    Kern County, 112
    San Francisco, 243
Canada, 64, 94
    Ontario, 257
CAPS/Harris, 73, 81, 83, 85, 86, 90, 110, 113, 170, 210, 227
carbon pricing, 12–13, 62, 94, 205, 258
Carter, Jimmy, 21
Case, Anne, 14, 75, 154
Ceres, 6, 17, 49, 144, 217
Chafee, John, 157, 158
Chatterjee, Neil, 116
China, 8, 173, 245, 251
Christie, Chris, 37
Citrin, Jack, 41, 42
CivicPulse, 29, 77, 80
clawbacks, 32, 67, 137–138, 202–203, 225–229, 231
    Good Jobs First, 226
clean electricity standard, 256
Clean Power Plan, 70, 143
climate change, 2–3, 14, 26, 44, 45, 65, 74, 83, 147, 234, 240, 242, 244, 246, 248
climate denial, 6, 22, 252
climate finance, 33, 246–247, 251
climate migration, 242
Clinton, William, 19
coalition building, 58–61
    bipartisanship, 25, 29, 59–60, 86, 120, 122–124, 131, 133, 142, 163, 232, 237, 241, 247, 255–257
    shift expectations, 25, 60–61, 133–134, 237
Coats, Dan, 154
Colombia, 251
    Cesar, 174
    Guajira, 174
Colorado, 88, 155, 200, 236
    Rush Creek Wind Farm, 49
commercial driver's license, 96
community benefits agreements, 202, 204, 230
computer programming, 100, 103, 176–179, 189, 198
Connecticut, 138
Cooper, Jim, 162

COP-27, 246
costly signals, 26, 66–67, 120–121, 124–125, 180, 194
    absorb risk, 66, 192–196
    unexpected investments, 66–67
county fair, 28, 76–77, 81, 106–109, 240
Cramer, Katherine, 8, 42, 89, 94
Cramer, Kevin, 256
Czech Republic, 37, 174, 251, 252

Dalton, Jody, 152
deaths of despair, 14, 75, 154
Deaton, Angus, 14, 75, 154
deindustrialization, 17, 41, 75, 85
Democratic Party, 20, 60, 86, 116, 256
Denmark, 23, 208
developing countries, 168, 246–247
Dole, Bob, 157, 158

Electoral College, 16
electric power companies, 7, 26, 30, 46, 59, 62, 93, 108, 141–146, 149, 152, 163, 182, 233, 238, 247, 257, 258
    Avangrid, 214, 217
    Consumer Energy, 112
    cooperatives, 258
    DTE, 112
    Duke Energy, 144
    Great River Energy, 217
    Northern States Power Company, 155
    PG&E, 144
    Xcel Energy, 34, 182, 209, 217
electric vehicles, 10, 39, 48, 50, 75, 99, 115, 125–129, 197, 244–246, 254, 255
    General Motors, 48
    Lordstown Motors, 48
    Rivian, 48, 226
electricians, 11, 50, 74, 99, 138, 179, 180, 191, 209, 244
Elster, Jon, 43
embedded liberalism, 5, 20, 240
Environmental Defense Fund, 147
Environmental Protection Agency, 41, 70, 71, 164
environmental remediation, 99, 104, 189, 254
ethane cracker plant, 75
European Union, 91, 168, 251

Federal Energy Regulatory Commission, 116
Fernandez, Raquel, 44, 241

Index

Ferri, Dominic, 157
Fiorina, Morris, 256
firm investment, 89–93
fisheries, 6, 65
Ford, Wendell, 156
fossil fuel subsidies, 12, 245
Fowler, Joe, 209
Frame, Stephanie, 176–177
Franco, Lucas, 201–203, 208, 211, 213,
 216, 219, 230
Freeman, John, 112

Gaventa, John, 14
gender, 53, 61, 106, 196–198,
 253–254
Georgia, 138, 226
geothermal energy, 186, 249
Germany, 31, 44, 46, 60, 64, 150–151,
 167–174, 188, 233, 245, 250
 AfD, 172
 Coal Commission, 168, 169, 171
 Coal Phase-Out Act, 168
 East Germany, 168, 171
 energiewende, 92, 171
 Lignite coal, 167–168
 Lusatia, 168
 RAG Stiftung, 172
 Rhur, 173
 Structural Support for Coal Regions Act,
 168
 West Germany, 168, 171
Glagola, Lynda, 166
Glenn, John, 154
globalization, 10, 17, 18, 20–21, 159, 198,
 245
Goldstein, Judith, 20
government preferences and ability, 22, 36,
 193
government trustworthiness, 8, 22, 23, 26,
 31, 41–43, 72, 82–83, 88, 93, 94,
 139, 141, 172, 175, 185–186, 199,
 224, 241–242
Graham, Jonathan, 177
Granholm, Jennifer, 239
Graves, Garrett, 38, 65
Gray, William, 162
green industrial policy, 4, 33, 205, 232,
 254–259
Gulf Coast, 10, 17, 28, 46, 74–75, 92, 97,
 103, 104, 106,
 114, 233
Gulotty, Robert, 20

hand-tying, 25, 56–58, 180, 192–196, 236
 constrain with costs, 57–58
 decision rules, 57
 issue linkage, 58
Harris, Kamala, 116, 259
Hawaii, 87
Hawkins, Gerald, 153
healthcare, 30, 51, 96, 97, 100–103, 106,
 110, 199
Heinz, John, 154, 159
Herntier, Christine, 172, 173
high-sulfur coal, 31, 148, 149, 151–152
Hirschman, Albert, 252
Hochschild, Arlie, 17, 94
hold-up problems, 15, 39–40, 126
Holmström, Bengt, 26, 67, 206
Hortman, Melissa, 213
House Select Committee on the Climate
 Crisis, 38

Illinois, 39, 49, 88, 89, 135, 136, 154, 159,
 164, 250
 Clean Energy Jobs Act, 250
 Future Energy Jobs Act, 249
 Southern Illinois, 153, 250
implementation, 16, 55, 61, 91, 138, 149,
 163, 258–259
India, 8, 11, 47, 94, 247, 250
Indiana, 75, 88, 138, 154, 161, 163, 229
Indonesia, 8, 247, 250, 251
Industrial Midwest, 10, 28, 75, 85, 103,
 104, 233
Inflation Reduction Act, 4, 16, 31–34, 49,
 58, 62, 67, 80, 86–88, 116–117,
 126, 141–143, 181, 205, 245,
 254–259
 direct pay tax credits, 258
informational uncertainty, 44–45
Infrastructure Investment and Jobs Act,
 116–117, 254–259
institutions, 43–44
 constraints, 24–25, 54–56, 121,
 131–133
 delegation, 55–56, 138–141,
 236, 258
 electoral systems, 44, 169
 insulate funding, 25, 56, 124, 138–141,
 167, 235
 laws, 54–55, 129–131, 142,
 232, 235
 state-business relations, 44
 veto points, 44

294 Index

Intergovernmental Panel on Climate Change, 2
International Renewable Energy Agency, 180
international trade, 33, 173, 245–246
Iowa, 60
Ireland, 43, 185, 250
issue indivisibility, 45

James, Danny, 161
Japan, 147
Job Training Partnership Act, 163
Johnston, Bennett, 160
just transition, 13–14, 43, 144, 145, 159, 174, 198, 200
Just Transition Fund, 23
Justice, Rusty, 14, 178

Kansas, 6, 157
Karels, Stacy, 216
Kennedy, Edward, 175
Kennedy, John F., 20
Kentucky, 89, 116, 135, 152, 156, 178, 229
  Pikeville, 14, 177
Keohane, Robert, xi, 4, 25, 58, 63
Kerry, John, 158
Korologos, Tom, 160
Kuran, Timur, 60, 134
Kyoto Protocol, 147, 148, 160

land use, 11, 24, 107, 137, 257
Laucher, Amanda, 176
Lee, Payton, 179
Lent, Norman, 161
Lerud, Greg, 34, 40, 51
Levi, Margaret, 23, 26, 28, 42, 43, 64, 161, 242
LIUNA, 201–203, 208, 211–215, 218
  Catching the Wind, 211
lobbying, 6, 15, 22, 71, 114, 241, 252, 253, 258
local economic opportunity, 23–24, 45–53, 96–115, 134–138, 173, 188–192, 194, 200
  future jobs, 47–49
  local jobs, 49–50, 201–232
  pay, 50–51, 173
  temporariness, 51–52
local energy ownership, 137
local journalism, 32, 148, 223–225, 230

local policymakers, 29, 72, 81, 87–90, 93, 97, 107, 109–111, 118, 129, 134–138, 146, 204, 220, 222–224, 227–229, 237, 240
lock-in effects, 25–26, 61–63, 87, 125–129, 143
  benefits, 62–63
  place-based investments, 61–62
Louisiana, 6, 65, 74, 160

Maine, 152
Manchin, Joe, 16, 34, 116
Mankato Building Trades, 216
Mansfield, Edward, 21, 37
Maryland, 135, 136
Massachusetts, 137
Mass. vs. EPA, 70
May, Payton, 177, 199
McCain, John, 256
McCarthy, Gina, 70
McConnell, Mitch, 116
McKibben, Bill, 73
media, 47, 223–225, 252–253
mediation analysis, 194–196
Mettler, Suzanne, 17, 72, 93
Michigan, 75, 112, 137
middle schoolers, 28, 31, 189–192, 240
Mildenberger, Matto, 16, 26, 32, 44, 45, 129, 134, 174, 209, 251, 253
Milner, Helen V., xi, 21, 247, 254
Mined Mines, 176–178
Minnesota, 32, 50, 135, 136, 201–202, 204, 208–221, 232, 237
  Bitter Root Wind Farm, 212–214
  Blazing Star 1 wind farm, 217
  Blazing Star 2 wind farm, 217
  Building Trades, 211
  City of Becker, 34–35, 40, 51, 209
  Department of Commerce, 208
  Dodge County, 219
  Fenton Repower project, 217
  Lincoln County, 212
  Nobles II, 214–215
  North Star Policy Institute, 213
  Public Utilities Commission, 32, 208, 212–214, 216, 220, 230
  Red Pine Wind Farm, 211
  Sherco, 34, 209
  Trimont Wind Repower project, 217
  Woodstock, 201
  Yellow Medicine County, 212

Index

Missouri
St. Louis, 198
Mitchell, George, 152, 156, 158, 160, 162
Mitchell, Kris, 27, 42, 136
Moe, Terry, 37, 56, 242
Moniz, Ernest, xi, 8, 28, 74–76
Moniz, Ernie, 92
Montana, 107, 158
Montreal Protocol, 151
Mortenson, 208
Moving to Opportunity experiment, 15
Murphy, Phil, 37

National Clean Air Coalition, 157
National Renewable Energy Laboratory, 184
Nebraska, 211, 215
Nelson, Colleen R., 79
Net-Zero America, 3, 6, 247
Netherlands
Limburg, 173
Nevada, 49
New Jersey, 37, 49
New Mexico, 10, 28, 75, 103, 104, 106, 111
Clean Energy Workforce Development study, 199
New York, 41, 161, 177
NIMBY, 56, 236, 258
North Carolina, 53, 155, 156, 183, 224
North Dakota, 32, 50, 154, 204, 215, 217–221, 256
Public Service Commission, 218
North, Douglass, 22, 25, 43, 55

Obama, Barack, 70–71, 143
offshore wind, 6, 37, 39, 65, 144
Ohio, 50, 75, 136, 154, 157, 163
Lordstown, 48
Williamsport, 6
oil major, 30, 93, 141–146, 238
Oklahoma, 50, 199
Red Dirt wind farm, 199
Olson, Mancur, 15, 206
on-the-job training, 179, 188, 199
Oppenheimer, Michael, 147–148, 174, 242
Oregon, 18, 52, 202, 211
Ostrom, Elinor, 26, 63, 249

Pacific Northwest logging, 18–20, 85, 151, 159

Northwest Forest Plan, 19
Redwood Employee Protection Program, 19
Redwood National Park, 19
spotted owl, 19
Paris Agreement, 3, 58, 246
Patashnik, Eric, 24, 25, 32, 40, 43, 54, 56, 61, 167, 240, 256
path dependence, 12, 61
peat farming, 43, 185
pendulum swing, 7, 22, 37, 38, 48, 54, 87–88, 93, 117, 118, 142, 234, 235, 255
Pennsylvania, 16, 50, 51, 135, 138, 154, 185, 229
Beaver County, 75
Fayette County, 96
Greene County, 11
Nemacolin, 176
permitting reform, 87, 143, 257
Phares, Ron, 159
place-based, 61–62
place-based policies, 5, 25, 33, 81, 121, 171, 230, 242–244
Poland, 174
polarization, 6, 38, 59, 88, 238, 241
policy sequencing, 251
POWER initiative, 177
Pranis, Kevin, 208, 209, 212, 214, 215
principal-agent problem, 26, 55, 206
project labor agreements, 202, 204, 230
Pruitt, Scott, 71

Qualtrics, 73, 76, 83, 86, 98, 107, 126, 129, 131, 139, 189, 227, 247
Quayle, Dan, 160

Rabe, Barry, 29
race, 53, 61, 105, 106, 136, 196–198, 253–254
rare earth minerals, 238, 249
Reagan, Ronald, 21, 37, 175
Regional Greenhouse Gas Initiative, 37, 186
relocation, 14–15
renewable energy developers, 30, 32, 49, 93, 141–146, 211
EDF Renewables, 217
NextEra, 215
RES, 208, 209
Flying Cow Wind, 212–214
Tenaska, 215

Index

Republican Party, 60, 65, 70, 86, 116, 256
reputation, 26, 63–66
  local input, 26
  provide information, 65–66,
    169–170
  public input, 63–65, 135, 138–141, 169,
    236, 258
Resources for the Future, 11, 79,
  111, 112
Rhode Island, 157
Rickard, Stephanie, 10, 21, 32
Rodrik, Dani, 4, 22, 36, 44, 45, 57, 205,
  241, 250, 255
Romer, Roy, 155
Roosevelt Project, 8, 28, 46, 50, 74–76, 92,
  99, 103, 114, 182, 197, 200, 254
Rudra, Nita, 21, 37
Ruggie, John, 5, 20, 240
rural, 10, 11, 16, 18–20, 27, 42, 76, 79,
  84, 88, 89, 94, 96, 97, 103, 104,
  106, 135, 136, 138, 200, 225, 236

sample
  county fairs, 76–77
  local policymakers, 77–80
  national, 73
  transition communities, 74–76
  youth, 73–74
Sandel, Michael, 241
Sanford, Terry, 156
Scheuer, James, 161
Schumpeter, Joseph, 13
Scotland
  Aberdeen, 144
scrubbers, 152, 163
second-order beliefs, 60, 134
semiconductors, 96, 184, 198
shale gas boom, 50
Shuler, Liz, 39
Shumard, Lloyd, 19
Sieben, Katie, 216, 220
Simon, Paul, 154
Simpson, Alan, 157
Sinner, George, 154
skills transferability, 11–12, 186,
  249
Smith, Phil, 166
Snyder, Pam, 186
social identity, 52, 72, 248
social networks, 196–197
Social Security, 57
Solyndra, 255

South Africa, 8, 46, 247, 250
South Dakota, 51
Southwest Pennsylvania area, 7, 28, 45,
  48, 50, 51, 75–77, 89, 96, 97, 99,
  103, 104, 106, 108, 111, 166, 177,
  178, 180, 182, 183, 189, 191, 192,
  199, 200, 238
Spain, 169
Spence, Michael, 25, 26, 32, 36, 56, 63, 66
Springsteen, Bruce, 36
status quo bias, 44
Stern, Nicholas, 38
Stoker, Laura, 41, 42
Stokes, Leah, 16, 26, 32, 49, 59, 60, 91,
  129, 163, 240, 249, 253, 256, 257
Stoneray Wind Farm Project, 201
structural topic model, 127, 128, 140
submerged state, 17, 72, 93
Sununu, John, 160, 162
Superfund program, 54
Supreme Court, 70, 71
survey experiment, 29
Swift, Al, 153
Switzerland, 94

Tabellini, Guido, 25, 32, 57, 192
tax burden, 40–41, 173, 244–245
tax credits, 38, 67, 127, 128, 143, 256
  wind production, 49, 142
tax incentives, 231
tax revenue, 1, 11, 14, 19, 62–63,
  111–113, 154, 243–244
technological change, 244
Tenaska, 214–215
Tennessee, 162
Texas, 50, 60, 88, 98, 157, 201, 202, 211,
  229
  Harris County, 79
  Schleicher County, 11
textile manufacturing, 85
Thomssen, Garrit, 202
tied-aid, 247
time inconsistency, 22, 25, 32, 35–41, 57
tobacco, 85, 151
Trade Adjustment Assistance, 20–21, 37,
  159, 186–188
transmission, 33, 63, 65, 257
transparency, 171, 205–208
  accountability, 67
  of benefits, 26–27, 32, 67, 136–137,
    201–232, 236–237, 241
trucking, 99, 100

Index

Trumka, Richard, 147–148, 152, 153, 160, 163
Trump, Donald, 58, 71, 88, 143
Tuma, John, 214, 215
Turkey, 250

U.S. Department of Labor, 164, 166, 187
U.S. Treasury Department, 143
Ulysses, 56
unions, 6, 16, 20, 27–29, 32, 46, 49–51, 67, 94, 153, 157, 161, 166, 169, 173, 179, 204, 208–220, 231, 234, 240
  AFL-CIO, 39, 157
  right-to-work laws, 218
  United Auto Workers, 182
  United Mine Workers, 31, 147, 153, 163, 166
    journal, 31, 148, 150, 152, 153, 157, 161, 163, 165
United Kingdom, 208
  Durham, 173
  Northumberland, 173
United Mine Workers, 231
United Mine Workers Journal, 240
Utah, 50, 85, 201
utility-scale solar, 137

Victor, David, 37, 247
Vietnam, 251
Virginia
  Clean Economy Act, 204

Ward, Keith, 153
Washington, 18, 52, 67, 94, 135, 153
  Initiative 732, 94
Waxman-Markey cap-and-trade bill, 70
Weickum, Terry, 1–2, 24, 49, 107, 244
Weingast, Barry, 22, 25, 43, 55
West Virginia, 16, 27, 52, 75, 85, 116, 137, 148, 155, 156, 161, 164, 176, 177, 185, 188, 200, 239, 243
  Boone County, 11, 27, 42, 136
  Boone County Development Authority, 27
West Virginia vs. EPA, 71
William, Gramm, 157
Williams, Walter, 154
Williamson, Oliver, 15, 39, 62, 92, 126
Wisconsin, 42, 50, 88, 137, 226
Wise, Bob, 161
workforce programs, 6, 19, 31, 40, 58, 62, 77, 138, 159, 171, 176–200
Wuthnow, Robert, 14, 18
Wyoming, 51, 103, 112, 135, 157
  Campbell County, 2, 18, 87, 238
  Carbon County, 1–2, 4, 7, 11, 24, 49, 79, 107, 112, 202, 233, 244
  Rawlins, 2

Youngstown Sheet and Tube Company, 176
youths, 27, 28, 73–74, 85, 180, 188–193, 199, 204, 220, 222, 237, 240

Printed in the United States
by Baker & Taylor Publisher Services